LONG
VOYAGE
BACK

LONG VOYAGE BACK

LUKE RHINEHART

DELACORTE PRESS / NEW YORK

For Ann,
who made me aware

Published by
Delacorte Press
1 Dag Hammarskjold Plaza
New York, N.Y. 10017

Manufactured in the United States of America

First printing

Library of Congress Cataloging in Publication Data

Rhinehart, Luke.
Long voyage back.

I. Title.
PS3568.H5L6   1983   813'.54   82-23586
ISBN 0-440-04617-3

Behold, the day of the Lord comes,
cruel, with wrath and fierce anger,
to make the earth a desolation and
to destroy the sinners from it.
For the stars of the heavens and
their constellations
will not give their light;
the sun will be dark at its rising
and the moon will not shed its light. . . .
Therefore will I make the heavens
tremble,
and the earth will be shaken out
of its place. . . .

—ISAIAH 13:9–10, 13

PREFACE

This is not a ship's log nor an official report. Although notes we have all taken over the last year have certainly helped, it's also not our collective diaries and journals. What we've tried to do, for ourselves primarily, for some future readers if there are any, is to recreate what it was like for those we knew and for us, for this small family of people who are still survivors.

We make no effort to take a global view, nor have we any pretensions to being historians. We have no thesis. We are interested in people, in those who survived the initial holocaust, whom we met, knew, tried to save, in some cases failed to save; how all of us, the remnants, coped with the aftermath; how we were dragged down by it, so often failing.

Yet some of us survive. At this point that alone gives our story significance.

CONTENTS

PART ONE

FIRE

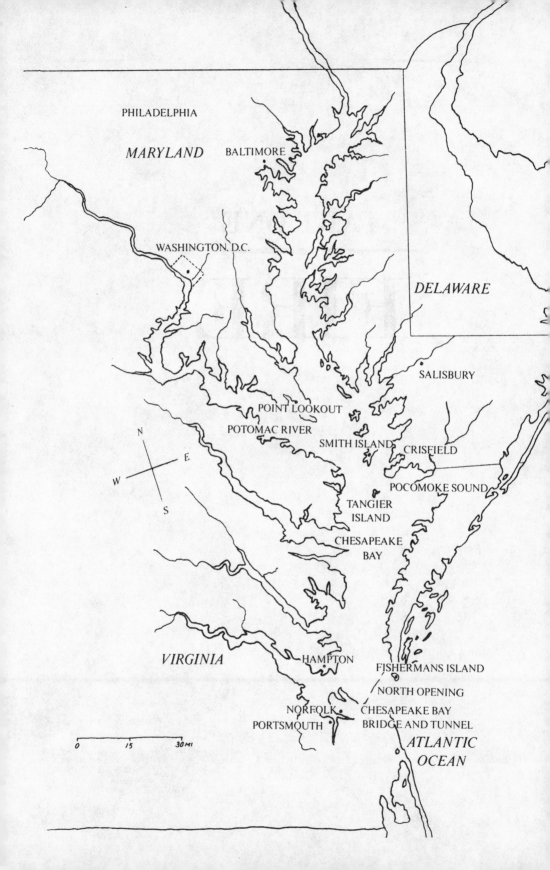

PHILADELPHIA

MARYLAND   BALTIMORE

WASHINGTON, D.C.

DELAWARE

SALISBURY

POINT LOOKOUT

POTOMAC RIVER

SMITH ISLAND   CRISFIELD

N

E

W

POCOMOKE SOUND

S

TANGIER
ISLAND

CHESAPEAKE
BAY

VIRGINIA   HAMPTON

FISHERMANS ISLAND

NORTH OPENING

NORFOLK   CHESAPEAKE BAY
PORTSMOUTH   BRIDGE AND TUNNEL

ATLANTIC
OCEAN

0   15   30 MI

THE room was crowded. Many of its occupants were scurrying from place to place in organized chaos. A gigantic video screen filled the north wall, showing a map of the earth with lighted and blinking symbols indicating the deployment of weapons, forces, counterforces. A second, smaller screen high on the east wall spewed forth printed messages with an inventory of warheads, explosive power, probable targets, and predicted casualties. Along the south wall were ten desk-size computers, each with a uniformed man watching it, just as ancient priests watched moiling entrails. Along the western wall was a long table at which thirteen men were sitting, all but one of them in uniform, listening to a man at the head of the table who was speaking to them in a sullen, lugubrious tone of the intentions of the enemy, the probability of surviving various war scenarios.

There was no joy or humor in the room. The seriousness had a disjointed, alienated quality, as of men working hard at a job they didn't quite understand, discussing alternatives they didn't quite believe in. The sullenness that marked many of their faces was the expression of men who were doing the job expected of them, but found themselves doing things they hadn't expected to be doing. Their voices were sometimes high-pitched, close to cracking. The eyes of a few of them seemed wild. When one general burst out passionately in favor of one course of action, a few looked at him as if he were mad; others looked at him gloomily, nodding. When an admiral spoke for the opposite course of action, a few looked at him as if he were mad; others looked at him gloomily, shaking their heads.

The words spoken, whether coolly or in anger, sadness, or nervous panic, all had about them a scientific detachment as consistent and codified as the uniforms most of them wore. They were eminently reasonable words, and they poured out across the table with the sporadic urgency of a teletype machine rolling out its messages: nullify evasive evacuation . . . no more than eighty million . . . reduce counterstrike potential by forty-two percent . . . state of belligerency inherent in . . . dilute the economic infrastructure . . . diversification of missile response . . . the reduced military options necessitated by the higher kill ratio . . . the incidental effects of maximizing radiation . . . nullifying recuperative capacity . . .

Behind the ten desks the ten uniformed men stared at the ten computers. On the north wall the giant screen blinked out its kaleidoscope of pulsating lights like a pinball machine; a few uniformed men stared up at it as if waiting for it to tally the final score.

Eventually the men at the table seemed to have reached some sort of decision. A telephone was brought to one of them. With the receiver at his ear he waited patiently for the connection. The others watched, some smoking, others staring at the table. No one spoke. No one bothered to look at either of the video screens. No one smiled.

The man with the phone began speaking respectfully into the receiver, paused, listened, then spoke again. After less than two minutes he hung up. The others looked at him. Two orderlies began placing cups and saucers in front of the officers and poured out a hot, steaming liquid. He cleared his throat and uttered a simple declarative sentence indicating that the man he had spoken to had decided to adopt the course of action they had just recommended. No one spoke. No one leapt into action. No one smiled. One man sipped at the hot, steaming liquid; then another man followed suit. At the end of the table opposite the presiding officer a man began to cry. The officer opposite glared angrily; two other men looked away, tight-lipped.

The presiding officer began to speak again in a tense, gloomy voice, addressing first one man and then another down the table. One by one they rose to depart. Most hurried. No one spoke. No one smiled.

Finally there were only two of them left at the table—the presiding officer and the man who was crying. The first, sullen and gloomy, rose and left. Only one man was left.

———————————————

Her three white hulls slicing quietly through the water, her giant genoa bellying out to starboard, *Vagabond* sailed into the bay. Neil Loken sat in the port cockpit of the large trimaran, watching the causeway of the Chesapeake Bay Bridge-Tunnel, through which they had just passed, recede behind them. At the wheel Jim Stoor was peering ahead and shifting his weight excitedly from one foot to the other. Although his father owned *Vagabond,* this was the first time Jim had made landfall after a long ocean passage, and his boyish face, haloed by the rays of the early morning sun, showed it. He looked to Neil at that moment—his slender, broad-shouldered body bronzed by their five days at sea—like a seagoing Pan.

But Neil didn't share Jim's excitement and joy. Sailing up into the wide mouth and throat of the bay depressed him. He was an ocean sailor, and he rarely enjoyed leaving the clear, deep waters of the open sea for the mud and shallows of inshore bays and inlets.

And it didn't help that the Chesapeake was a sort of home. He'd attended the U.S. Naval Academy at Annapolis for four years and, after serving in Vietnam for three, captained a forty-six-foot sloop based in Norfolk for several summers. Sailing *down* the bay out to sea had often meant adventure, freedom, escape. Sailing into it meant land, civilization, the complications of returning home.

As he looked forward to examine the set of the mainsail and genoa and to check Jim's course toward the next buoy, he was also troubled by the quite mundane fact that *Vagabond's* propeller shaft had been struck and bent by a submerged log off Cape Hatteras, which had left the big trimaran with no auxiliary power. How long it would take to sail her the next seventy-five miles up to Point Lookout to pick up

Frank Stoor and his guests would depend on the wind, a notoriously unreliable friend, especially in the Chesapeake.

"Hey, look!" Jim suddenly said, pointing past Neil toward Norfolk. "Warships. Three of them."

Turning, Neil sighted along the horizon and saw three long, gray vessels moving out of Hampton Roads, heading out the southern channel toward the bridge and the ocean. Two were destroyers, the third a ship the Navy must have designed since he'd resigned his commission. A supply ship maybe—but since when was a supply ship accompanied by two destroyers?

"I wonder where they're going," Jim went on, looking past Neil now through binoculars, holding the large stainless steel wheel in place by the pressure of his bare chest. Like Neil he was wearing only a pair of blue jean cutoffs.

"There are always a few ships from the Norfolk naval base either coming or going," Neil said quietly, but even as he said this he recognized still another reason he was depressed: the slow, awkward, terrifying way the U.S. and Russia seemed to be trying to frighten each other into war. For the last three days the radio news reports had been increasingly disturbing. Wednesday an American reconnaissance plane was downed by an Iraqi missile, probably fired from a launcher manned by Russians; yesterday the U.S. had rejected the Soviets' bilateral troop-withdrawal proposal, denouncing it as extortionate; today the U.S. government had reinforced its Marine units in Saudi Arabia. Neil had listened to these radio reports alone.

"You ever serve in ships like those?" Jim asked, lowering his binoculars and smiling, still excited about the recent landfall.

"No, I was lucky," Neil replied, turning back toward Jim. "They put me in the smallest combat vessels the Navy had—coastal patrol boats."

"You ever get sunk?" Jim asked next.

Neil smiled, his stern face suddenly lit up, his blue eyes crinkling. Jim's boyish curiosity about things compensated for some otherwise annoying habits: his penchants for listening to loud rock music at every opportunity and for leaving food, towels, dishes, and clothing strewn around the boat as if they were precious jewels he was magnanimously bestowing upon the poverty-ridden ship. But Jim's enthusiasm redeemed him in Neil's eyes—that, and the important fact that he'd turned out to be an excellent sailor.

"No, I can't say I did," Neil replied, standing up and watching the distant warships. "In fact, most of the war I and some of my men were thoroughly depressed that no one ever fired at us."

"But dad said you were wounded," Jim said.

"Oh, yes," Neil agreed. "Occasionally we got lucky."

"And you sunk a lot of ships."

"So they say," said Neil, feeling himself getting tense about the direction the conversation was taking. He walked toward Jim and began doing chin-ups from the edge of the wheelhouse roof. He had a muscular gymnast's body, browned by the sun like Jim's, but thicker, more mature, that of a well-conditioned athlete in his thirties. Like Jim he held his six-foot frame with military erectness. But his face, unlike Jim's, was weathered and lined, a light scar running into his hairline at his right temple. His blue eyes often pinned people with distracting coldness but could suddenly light up and crinkle with the warmth of his smile. His shock of thick brown hair was uncombed and stiffly awry from the salt water and wind.

"Well?" insisted Jim.

Neil lowered himself from the last chin-up and moved into the wheelhouse and stood beside the eighteen-year-old. Two empty glasses sat on the wheelhouse shelf, reminders of the whiskey they'd drunk at dawn when they'd sighted land for the first time since northern Florida. Neil picked up one and drained it.

"It was a push-button war, even for the smallest ships," he said slowly. "We killed at long range. If we ever happened to see what havoc we had wrought, it was always a little disconcerting to find that the 'enemy gunboat' or 'Cong supply ship' looked suspiciously like a fishing boat, and the dead and dying like bony fishermen."

Neil paused, staring through the windows of the wheelhouse, forward past *Vagabond*'s wide white deck and mainmast to the gray waves stretching out ahead.

"Some of them must have been . . . Cong," said Jim.

"Oh, sure," said Neil.

"Is that why you resigned your commission?"

"That and a dozen other reasons."

He didn't go on. He walked back out of the wheelhouse to end the conversation. He knew he'd been the wrong man for the job. When he'd graduated from Annapolis, he'd been fully prepared to stand on the quarterdeck and fight to the last man. But he wasn't prepared to stand and blast away, not knowing whether he was killing good guys or bad guys, rarely being fired at in return, and forbidden by standing orders to pick up the wounded survivors.

Resigning his commission had been both a protest against a specific war, and an acknowledgment that for him, even if the war could be "justified," the technological and impersonal means of fighting it could not. For years after resigning he'd been a loner, unsuited to either the unregimented chaos of civilian life or the companionship with his old Navy friends. A woman had brought him back to life, but after a year and a half, with the abrupt arbitrariness of battle, she had been killed in an auto accident. Since then he'd found a healthier solitude as professional captain of wealthy men's yachts, reestablishing some of the order that he'd liked in military life, and finding a closeness with the sea and sky that seemed to heal.

Staring up at the set of the mainsail he noticed two trails of jet vapor inching across the sky, the thin cotton lines tinged with pink and seeming to emerge from nowhere in the west and to be disappearing into nowhere in the east. The planes themselves were invisible. When a loud sonic boom broke the stillness of the early morning, Jim turned quickly toward Neil.

"What was *that*?!" he exclaimed.

Neil pointed to the vapor trails in the sky.

Jim seemed momentarily frightened, but then grinned.

"I thought the destroyers had opened fire on us," he said.

Neil watched the cotton trails disappear into the brightness to the east.

"Welcome back to civilization."

Throughout the morning *Vagabond* sailed up the bay at a little over seven knots, and Neil went over the boat, making sure it would be ready for its owner's inspection that night. *Vagabond* was a fast, roomy trimaran that moved through the water like a strange three-legged insect skipping from wave to wave. You entered the cabins in the side hull from the two side cockpits and went down steps to the long narrow floor area. The berths were up in the "wing" area over the water, separated from the main cabin by a plywood and veneer partition. *Vagabond* was steered from the enclosed wheelhouse that was a little aft of the center of the boat, between the main cabin with its galley and dinette area and Neil's aft cabin. On either side of the wheelhouse were the open cockpits with settee seats and the sliding hatchway leading down into the side cabins. All this space meant that people could get away from each other at sea, and Neil, being a private man, found that important, almost as important as *Vagabond*'s ability to go fast, without heeling, in almost any kind of weather.

At noon he relinquished the helm to Jim in order to put through a call to Frank at his office in New York City. Jim turned on the transistor radio to catch the news, which was unusual, since he usually preferred to listen to music on his cassette tapes.

Neil's aft cabin contained only twelve square feet of standing room between his double berth dead aft and the bulkhead that separated his cabin from the ship's engine compartment. Although it was not as spacious as the cabins in the two side hulls, Neil preferred it to anyplace else aboard. The radiotelephone, a shortwave radio, and a chart table had all been installed here; his books were crammed onto two long shelves. With the large gray radio, the navigational equipment, and the sparse furnishings, it was a very masculine room, "about as pretty as the inside of a tank," as one woman had described it.

When the marine operator put the call through to New York, Neil was glad to hear Frank's husky voice.

"This stupid war stuff is screwing up everything," Frank announced loudly. "I can't get a flight to Washington; they're booked solid. You think you could meet me today in Crisfield? I can get a flight to Salisbury, Maryland, and then rent a car." Crisfield was a small fishing town about twenty-five miles across the bay from Point Lookout.

"Sure," he replied. "That's as easy as Point Lookout. What about the Foresters?"

"We'll sail *Vagabond* across the bay and pick them up as soon as you get me. What time you figure you'll make it to Crisfield?"

"If the wind holds or improves, we'll be there by six tonight. But if it drops or we're headed—"

"Well, do your best," Frank said into the pause. "I know you must be beat. *Vagabond*'s a lot of boat for just two men, especially when one of them's a goof-off."

"Your son's a good sailor," Neil commented quickly.

"Yeah?" Frank replied, surprised by the news.

"In that blow off St. Augustine," Neil went on, "Jim went up the mast when the mainsail jammed. He also took the helm for almost four hours and let me sleep through half my watch."

"Neil!" Jim's voice broke into the conversation from the deck just outside the cabin hatchway. "I've got to talk to dad. There's going to be a war."

"What are you talking about?" Neil asked, looking up at Jim.

"I just heard the news," Jim went on. "We rejected the Russian offer. Let me speak to dad."

"Uh, Frank, Jim wants to talk to you," Neil said. "We'll meet you tonight in Crisfield unless we're becalmed. If we are, I'll try to get a message through to Carter's Bluewater Marina. Got it?"

"What? Sure. Good."

Neil hopped up the cabin steps and hurried to the wheel as Jim took over the mike.

"Holy Jesus, dad," Jim said. "We're going to be fighting the Russians. There's going to be a war!"

For a moment there was silence on the other end, then Frank's voice replied slowly and huskily.

"Don't worry about it, Jimmy," he said. "This is just another war *scare*. Just like three months ago. Just like two years ago. This is international poker, and the secret is never to call, just keep raising."

"The radio said we rejected their offer of bilateral troop withdrawals," Jim went on. "Why!?"

"If we withdraw any troops now," said Frank, his husky voice again coming in only after a pause, "we'd be seen as giving in. Our President may be a jerk, but he's a macho jerk, so we can be sure that now that our troops are in Arabia, they're going to stay, even if no one's around to kill."

"Dad, we ought to take the boat back south," said Jim, gripping the mike in both hands. "When the war starts—"

"Now cut that crap," Frank interrupted with abrupt annoyance.

"This is just another game of international brinkmanship, and neither their assholes nor our assholes are stupid enough to go to war. The Russians don't really care about Saudi Arabian nomads, and we don't really care about Asian democracy."

"But we care about oil!"

"Not enough to blow up the world," said Frank. "Now give me Neil. No, don't bother. Just hang up and get your ass up to Crisfield." The line went dead.

Jim stood alone in the aft cabin. He was angry. He hated the way his father treated him. Since he'd been only an average student and had never held a job, his father had always made him feel he was some kind of good-for-nothing. He enjoyed rock music, playing his guitar, getting high with his friends and partying, and making it with Celia or occasionally some other girl. None of these qualified in Frank's eyes as anything but a waste of time. On the three or four occasions he'd sailed with Frank on *Vagabond* there'd been a lot of older people aboard who'd helped Frank handle the boat. Jim had ended up retreating to his cabin to get stoned and listen to music. His father had inevitably come to shout at him to turn it down and to criticize him for not helping more with the sailing. It had been a downer. He didn't even think he liked sailing much until this trip up from Florida alone with Neil.

He climbed slowly up the ladder from the aft cabin and went back into the wheelhouse. Neil, who'd heard Jim's end of the conversation and its abrupt termination, stared forward.

"There's going to be a war," Jim stated angrily. "And Frank doesn't care."

Neil glanced at Jim and then back forward.

"I don't know," Neil replied. "I suppose it's possible our troops and theirs may be killing each other in a month or two. But maybe the world will pretend everyone's a guerrilla and we won't have to call it a war."

"But there's that retired general who says we ought to hit Russia before they hit us," said Jim. "And those TV evangelists say the same. If the Russians read that, then *they'll* have to strike first. Don't you see!?"

"No, Jim . . ."

"They're going to do it," Jim insisted, his long hair falling down his forehead so that it obscured his left eye; he tossed it back angrily. "I know they are. I can feel it!"

Neil looked forward, reminded of a young sailor on his last patrol who had panicked while watching B-52's bomb the coast two miles away. He knew from Frank that when Jim was fifteen he'd had a bad acid trip, hallucinated an imminent nuclear holocaust, and kept insisting that his family leave the country and fly to Australia. He'd had to be sedated for most of three weeks, and since then, according to Frank, Jim tended to become upset whenever there was an accident at a nuclear power plant or a nuclear test explosion or a threat of war. There'd been a lot to be upset about in the last three years.

"The Russians aren't going to start a nuclear war," Neil said softly.

"Then *we* are!" he shot back. "There's no way the two sides can go on this way. It's going to happen!"

"Take it easy, Jim," Neil rejoined sharply, putting his hand on Jim's shoulder. "Shouting isn't going to stop anything."

"Damn it! You don't care either." Jim stood facing Neil defiantly, but Neil didn't look at him.

"Look," Neil persisted softly. "It's no more appropriate to get into a panic now than it would be if we were heading into a storm at sea. You just do what has to be done when it has to be done."

"We should find a fallout shelter, stock up food. We—"

"Right now," Neil interrupted firmly, "our job is to sail *Vagabond* to your father."

"Oh, Neil," Jim responded. "It's so sad. It's so—"

"Drop it," said Neil. He was still staring forward. "Here, take the helm," he went on. "It's still your watch." He walked away into the port cockpit and stood with his back to Jim. The shore was far away and only dimly visible now.

He was feeling distinctly uneasy. Jim's fears struck a responsive chord; he could feel it vibrating in his own gut. A part of him also wanted to return and run back out the mouth that he felt closing now behind them. His instinct was to get out to sea, away from the mess that men might make on land. He turned back to Jim.

"We're meeting Frank in Crisfield instead of Point Lookout," he said quietly. "Our course is changed to zero one zero. You got it?"

fuss as most men went to the corner drugstore. He loses his engine to a freak accident and will still probably make it on schedule.

Oh-oh. He hadn't gotten through to Jeannie Forester yet about the change in plan.

He returned to his big chair, buzzed Rosie, and waited for her to place the call. He felt a warm glow of anticipation for that throaty, sexy voice of hers, sexy especially because she didn't really *mean* to be sexy. For two years now Jeannie had become the only thing that ever took his mind off business, and he was aware that whenever he thought of her he fell victim to an almost adolescent melancholy and longing. They'd been friends for five or six years and he knew she must be aware that he'd developed feelings for her beyond friendship. But she wasn't so much rejecting his feelings as kind of ducking and letting them slide past her.

"Frank, hi," he heard her say. "Everything still on for the sailing?"

"Hi, Jeannie. Sure," he replied, smiling at nothing. "Only I've had to change my plans for getting to the boat."

"Are you still coming here this evening?"

"No, that's just it. I can't get a flight into Washington, but I got one to the Eastern Shore—Salisbury—and I'm meeting the boat at Crisfield—that's just across the bay on the eastern side."

"I know. You want us all to meet you there?"

"No, no. We'll sail over to Point Lookout and pick you up. Unless something goes wrong, we should still get there late this evening."

"That's great. I'm sorry you're not going to be here though."

Frank felt himself flush slightly with pleasure. "We'll see so much of each other in the next ten days, you'll probably remember with great fondness your last evening without me."

Jeanne laughed. "I like *you*, Frank," she countered, "but I confess I'm a little nervous about spending that much time on the bay. I prefer water to be in a glass or a bathtub."

"Baloney."

"No, it's true. Now that you've finally got me to sail with you I'm going to be the worst kind of landlubber."

"You're a terrific swimmer," said Frank.

"Only when I can see both the bottom and other end of the pool," she replied. "Hold it a sec," she added, and her next words were spoken to someone in the room with her. "What's that, Rita? No. In the second drawer, I think. With the clippings from the *Post*. . . . Sorry, Frank, where were we?"

"What was that all about?"

"My antinuke group is meeting here today," she answered. "Emergency meeting because of the Arabian mess."

"Oh, yeah, right," said Frank, made uncomfortable by the subject. Jeannie became too emotional about any kind of war scare. He thought of making a joke about her group's being sure to stop the war for at least ten more days so they could finish their cruise, but stopped himself. "It's a tough situation," he finally said lamely.

"I've lost heart," she replied with unexpected weariness. "We haven't accomplished anything in these four years. And now it's really hopeless. I feel like a fool for even trying."

"Well, maybe that's good," Frank said. "Shows you need a vacation."

"I suppose so," she replied after a pause. "Some of my friends think I'm going off to fiddle while Rome burns."

"No, you don't," he said firmly. "You've promised me. Let Rome burn."

"I know, Frank, I'll be there. Tonight, I hope, or tomorrow morning at the latest."

"At Point Lookout."

"Fine. What, Rita? . . . Okay. Frank, look, I guess I've got to go. I'm looking forward to the sail and . . . I've got to go."

"Sure, Jeannie. See you soon."

"Bye, Frank."

Frank lowered the receiver slowly back onto its cradle and sighed, feeling that ridiculous tingling she somehow created in him. Then he shook his head and grunted. Why did she bother with that anti-war stuff? Peace groups had been marching and protesting for five years, but peace demonstrations never stopped a war and never would. They only weakened the unlucky country that let them get too influential.

Sighing again, he leaned back in his chair, rocking slightly, looking out at the sky above the harbor past the twin Trade towers. He had finally gotten her to go sailing with him though. In the past he'd invited her and her husband, Bob, and always ended up getting stuck with just Bob. It was strange. An outdoorsy woman like Jeannie, good swimmer, tennis player, hiker—why the aversion to water? Or was it her way of resisting him? He knew that he liked her a lot more than was good for either of them, but he hadn't done much about it so far. But now for ten days they'd be together on *Vagabond*.

His intercom buzzed, and Rosie's crisp voice informed him that his wife was on the line. He remembered he'd promised to call her.

"Hi, sweetheart," he boomed out when he heard her soft, musical voice through the phone. "Yep. Everything's go for this afternoon. I . . . What? . . . Oh, don't be silly, it's just a war scare. Like the last time. A lot of sound and fury signifying—" Frank frowned and grimaced as he listened.

"No, no, no," he finally interrupted. "It's going to be all right. Bob Forester says it's all just a big bluff, the Pentagon and the Russians know exactly what they're doing. . . ." Again he listened for a while, and then broke in.

"Hey, more good news. You should be proud of me. I made over eight thousand dollars on my shorts today. . . . No . . . no, not that kind of shorts . . . stocks, selling stocks short, you know. . . . He's *fine*. Captain Loken just told me he was a great sailor. Brought the ship single-handed through a terrific storm. When the sail . . . What? . . . No, no, no, there wasn't any storm . . . I was just exaggera— He's fine, I tell you. I bet he looks like a bronze Greek god. He's so good-looking, it's obscene. Girls'll be coming into heat all over the Chesapeake. . . . Damn it, no. If there was going to be a war, they would have mentioned it in *The Wall Street Journal*. . . . Yeah, yeah, right, sweetheart. Look, I got to get going to the airport. . . . Ten days. . . . Oh, sure, don't worry. . . . Good-bye, honey. . . . Right. . . . You too. . . . So long."

Frowning, Frank hung up. In the last year or two Norah seemed to be all anxiety, mostly about Jimmy, her "baby," but sometimes about everything. Maybe that's where Jimmy got *his* panic from. He was glad Susan was home from college while he and Jimmy were off cruising. Norah needed company these days, but couldn't join them in the Chesapeake until the last weekend of the cruise.

Rosie buzzed again.

"Mr. Tyler on the line."

"Put him on," said Frank, reaching for the phone to speak to George Tyler, a partner in several real estate ventures.

"Well, Frank, it was no go," Tyler's voice announced loudly, as if all important news had to be shouted. "I'm afraid Mulweather called and gave me some cock-and-bull story that boils down to the fact that his clients are considering backing out of the West Eightieth Street deal."

"What the hell. Why?"

"My guess is that his clients decided that an apartment house, no matter how attractive, tends to lose its cash flow when reduced to rubble."

Frank didn't reply, stunned by the sardonic comment.

"Well," he said after a pause. "I don't think cash or stocks sitting at Chase are going to retain much of their value either when they're fluttering down over the Atlantic in a million pieces."

"I know," said Tyler with incongruous cheerfulness, "but what are we going to do? Mulweather found a clause in our preliminary agreement, and he can back out. In this climate I think everyone's more interested in vacationing in Tierra del Fuego than in negotiating any new business deals."

Frank could feel himself becoming unreasonably angry at Mulweather and his clients for being panicked out of a deal that would make good money for all parties concerned. He stared gloomily at his desk.

"Okay, George, keep after it," he finally said with a sigh. "Make them feel like they're chicken or something. Maybe they'll change their minds next week."

After Tyler had hung up, Frank felt depressed. Worse, it was getting late. What time was it? Almost four. Jesus, he had to be at La Guardia by five for his flight to Salisbury, so he'd have to hurry it.

He made one last call to his broker and learned that the Dow Jones Industrial Average was down something like fifty-one points, the high-speed printer still almost twenty minutes behind. When he hung up, even though he'd made money on his shorting, he was even more depressed. As he rose and began to gather up his things for the boat he remembered his own favorite axiom with a strange sense of irritation. *The stock market never lies.* . . .

By late afternoon the Chesapeake was as still as a pond. Only the tiniest breaths of wind occasionally hinted at movement, and Captain Olly and his son, Chris, worked steadily in the clear sunshine, enjoying the luxury of the calm water. They were harvesting their last oyster bed, using the long wooden shafts of their rakelike metal tongs with practiced ease. Both Captain Olly, a small, wizened old man, wrinkled and bald, and his twenty-year-old son, a thickset, husky youth, had huge forearms and biceps from their years of working the oyster beds. Their twenty-seven-foot fishing smack, *Lucy Mae,* with only a small deckhouse forward and a huge well aft for depositing the oysters, was old and paint-chipped and heeled over groggily as both men leaned out over the same side.

The two men had been working the beds since one o'clock that afternoon, starting a couple of hours before the three-P.M. low tide. They planned to quit a couple of hours after the tide turned. In all that time their work proceeded in a casual, persistent rhythm, Olly talking away occasionally in what seemed like stream-of-consciousness monologues, Chris, quiet, steady, always puffing on a cigarette, now and then grunting a comment or asking a question. When Olly would lapse into silence or lean on his rake, Chris would continue raking, wielding the heavy tongs until he could feel that he had a full load, then raising them to the surface and depositing their contents on the afterdeck. Most of the sorting would come later. The monologues and silences succeeded each other in a mood as relaxed as the becalmed bay. Chris would occasionally down a bottle of beer, his father a glass of water, sometimes "colored" with a dash of whiskey. They never had to talk about their work; they knew their routine so thoroughly they could have oystered efficiently from dawn to dusk and not uttered a word. Smith Island, their home, lay to the east of them, Tangier Island to the south, and Point Lookout and the wide mouth of the Potomac to the west.

As Captain Olly neared the end of his working day he was feeling depressed by how tired he felt. After less than four hours work his back ached, and if he didn't stop and lean on his rake handle every five minutes or so, he got winded. This embarrassed him, and he knew that even if he tried to pretend to be so absorbed in his own monologues that he couldn't work, Chris would be able to tell he was shirking.

Ever since Jill had run off to Florida two years ago with Cap'n Smithers, his life had gone downhill. It was the first time since he was fourteen he hadn't had a woman reg'lar, and he felt his health was deteriorating fast as a result. The main reason he went oystering with Chris most every day was so he wouldn't get stuck alone in his house watching the TV. A man could go nuts watching those game shows and soaps.

"I don't know, son," he found himself saying in an effort to cheer himself up, "seems to me some of these oysters must have meningitis or something. Seem sorta stunted. We may have to sell them to the circus as midgets." He had deposited a load of oysters and muck onto the deck and was staring at it with exaggerated gloom. "Though I s'pose midgets ain't in fashion anymore, even in the circus. People these days want things big: big money, big boats, big tits." As he wiped the sweat from his bald head he squinted southward at a couple of sailboats sitting like marble monuments in the bay. That'll teach 'em, he thought vaguely, the rich playboy good-for-nothings.

"They even seem to want their wars bigger these days," he went on, turning back to his work, "settin' up there in Moscow and Washington calculatin' how they can build a real big elephantlike war that'll flatten the earth like a pancake so the gods can use it for a Frisbee. . . ."

As Olly lowered his tongs back into the water Chris allowed himself an unaccustomed pause in his work.

"There ain't gonna be a war, is there, pop?" he asked.

"Well, now, you know I never predict what the rake'll bring up," he snapped back automatically, "but I got to say that imagination ain't created the stupid terrible thing which man ain't fool enough to up and do."

"They ain't fighting yet," Chris commented, pausing to light a fresh cigarette.

"The way I figure it is the only reason they ain't made a Frisbee of earth before this is that they got a lot of *smaller* terrible things they want to do first." Olly spat over the side of the boat into the bay. That's my great hope for mankind, he thought. Man's got so many little sins he's got the hots for, he'll never get around to the big one.

"You think so?" his son asked after a pause.

"Course I don't think so," Captain Olly snapped back irritably, again wiping his sweaty forehead with his thick-veined right arm. "You know I don't like to do any thinking." He chuckled. "Whenever I think—get a really deep thought, you know?—I always have to take a crap." He paused and glared at his son, his eyes twinkling. "Standing at the helm alone in a blow, I got to watch my mind like a cat, be sure no deep thoughts come, cause taking a crap on a bouncy ship when you're alone at the helm and it's all you can do just standing, much less squatting, over a pail on a roller coaster while you're watching the compass and sail and handling the wheel is a trick I done once but don't hanker to do again."

He paused and frowned in concentration.

"The deep thought I had that time was 'Time will tell.' See? Deep thoughts just ain't worth the fuss and bother."

As he looked with mock severity at his son, who grinned back at him, Olly remembered that sail: in the old Chesapeake Bay skipjack that he'd owned and captained, dragging for oysters in those days instead of fiddling around with these tiny rakes. But he couldn't afford a skipjack now and couldn't pull his weight as crew, so he'd settled for *Lucy Mae*. It kept him alive, but barely.

Shit, he thought, as he had to pause again, I wish to hell I'd just get it over with and croak. Not much sense in living if you can't work and can't fuck. Nowadays, when he'd go into restaurants or bars and flirt with the cute little taut-butted waitresses, they'd either be shocked at him or treat him like a harmless child. When a man couldn't turn on a woman, it was time to cash in his chips. Women used to always be pestering him, first for his cock and then for his deep thoughts; he wished one was pestering him now.

"Women are always asking what I'm thinking." He spoke aloud, watching three seagulls fly noisily around the stern of *Lucy Mae* and then plop expectantly into the bay. "But after four wives I finally figured how to handle 'em. I always say I'm thinking about the wind and weather and repairing my dinghy and how much I love her ass. Well, every woman I've known will frown and frown and frown until I get to my deep thoughts about her ass, and then everything's jolly. A man who limits his deep thoughts to his woman's ass is a sober man, trustworthy and true, and likely to stay out of trouble."

Chris was smiling as he worked, but Olly's face was as stern as a Baptist preacher's. He paused and took a long drink of water from the glass on the deckhouse shelf. He damn well wished he had a lady these days whose ass he could praise, even if her ass was flatter than an ironing board.

"Gettin' late, pop," Chris said, making him suddenly aware he was leaning on his rake again.

"Late!" Olly snapped back. "We just begun." But he began to clean out his rake with a sense of relief. "I been talkin' so much today I'm pooped," he added.

I do love talking, he thought as he emptied his last load into the boat. Especially my own talking. As Chris's mother once said, I think it was his mother, could've been someone else's, "Olly, I never know'd a man who listened to hisself as good as you do." He smiled.

"Cal Markham said this morning the radio makes it sound like war," Chris suddenly said as if it had been on his mind much of the day. Olly looked at him in surprise.

"Son, you got to stop listening to people who babble," he said firmly. "Course there's gonna be a war. They ain't keepin' all those jets dancing across the sky just for skywriting forever, you know. A gov'ment is a business, and sooner or later the gov'ment is gonna want its money's worth."

His son looked at him with youthful seriousness.

"What you gonna do, pop, when that happens?" he asked.

Captain Olly tossed his empty tongs into the forward cabin with a sense of relief and then stared out across the water.

"I'm gonna run, son," he said with a sigh. "That's why I'm gonna take up jogging. I would have taken it up years ago, but I ain't learned how to do it on water yet. Christ knows the Chesapeake's got enough mud in it to support a man three times my weight, but somehow I just can't get the hang of it.''

He wouldn't run though. He would almost welcome it if it came, especially if the war would just take him and let Chris live to enjoy asses for another forty years as he had done. He'd always hated seeing old geezers sitting around in front of the general store, useless and unneeded, and although he was probably now a geezer, he wasn't gonna be a sitter.

No, he wouldn't run—unless he figured there was a live lady up the road a ways, or a solid bit of honest work he could do. Then maybe he'd stick around. Take up jogging.

Lethargically Jeanne gathered up and packed her clothes and sleeping bags for the cruise aboard *Vagabond*. She had no heart for the trip, no heart, really, for anything these days. She was packing only for herself, Lisa, and Skip, since Bob had telephoned at three that afternoon to tell her that the Defense Department had asked everyone over the level of G-2 to work over the weekend. He couldn't sail with them in the Chesapeake. He would be coming home only to eat and get a change of clothes.

As she moved around Skippy's bedroom and then her own, Jeanne was close to tears. It was anger and frustration at the insane way the Americans and Russians were stumbling toward war, frustration at her own incapacity to do anything, anger at Bob's failure even to *see* what was happening, anger that she was married to him. Normally lithe, catlike, and intense, she moved dully, her long dark hair hanging limply down her back instead of bouncing as it usually did when she moved. She felt she had married the wrong man and was living only half a life. As she carefully closed her suitcase she imagined Bob's superior, ironic smile at such a cliché. He would assure her that, of course, she had married the wrong man, everybody did, but that was no reason to be miserable.

Lisa came into her bedroom to ask if she could go visit her girl friend Nancy before dinner, and Jeanne had to focus her eyes for a moment to see her daughter clearly. Framed in the doorway, Lisa held her tall, budding fifteen-year-old body with that strange, stiff dignity she'd adopted over the last two years to show she was no longer a child. It irritated Jeanne, reminding her of the worst of the Forester family stuffiness. Compared to Lisa, round, energetic, happy-faced Skippy still seemed, at five, spontaneous and free.

"Have you finished your packing?" she asked.

"I did it last night," Lisa replied. "But don't forget to pack the lotions and towels you promised."

"I will, I will. But look, honey. I need your help here. We'll be eating as soon as your father gets home, and I'd like you to go downstairs and start heating up the leftover stew. I'll be down soon."

"Oh, Mother," Lisa replied. "Can't you do that?"

"Go!" said Jeanne.

And she went, with a promptness that never ceased to amaze Jeanne—was that Bob's doing?—and in another moment she was alone again with her two suitcases and her sleeping bags.

Living with Bob wasn't working anymore, and she knew why: the war thing had gotten too big, and was too important to both of them. The whole world was divided into two groups, those desperately trying to avoid a war and those desperately trying to make sure that their side won it. She and Bob were on opposite sides, and the tension between them was becoming too strong.

The tension often tempted her just to give up. The cause she was working for seemed so hopeless. For close to three years she'd been active in a Washington-based group called SMN, Stop the Madness Now, an eclectic collection of feminists, political radicals, pacifists, scientists, doctors, and even a few former high-ranking military officers, all of whom agreed on only one issue: the necessity of taking drastic action to reverse the momentum toward nuclear war. She'd begun as a volunteer, in effect an unpaid secretary, but a year ago had been put on part-time staff as fund-raiser and occasional speech writer and editor for one of the retired admirals.

But her promotion had, over the last six months, only made her increasingly depressed. The admiral spoke to the same audiences; the fund-raising events raised the same piddling amounts of money—

their yearly total budget would barely finance the cost of a single jet fighter; the letters got published in *The Washington Post* and *The New York Times* and sank out of sight like pebbles in the sea; the marches got marched—and forgotten; and the great masses of Americans, vaguely worried about war, remained quite precisely and seriously worried about how they were going to meet their mortgage payments or feed their children. The prolonged worldwide economic crisis, which was so critically exacerbating global political tensions, also made the tasks of reducing nuclear armaments and creating a United Nations superforce very low priorities on most people's agendas. The United States and the Soviet Union argued and maneuvered for power; she and Bob argued and maneuvered for . . . for what she didn't know, and all four sides became increasingly alienated from one another.

Bob came home at six, gave a big hug to Skippy, a dignified kiss to Lisa, several words and caresses to their terrier, Banjo, and a cheerful "Hi, honey" to her. He went straight upstairs to change his clothes and pack an overnight bag. Ten minutes later they all had dinner together.

Jeanne's scruffy jeans, open-necked cotton blouse, and her long dark hair falling wildly about her face and shoulders contrasted sharply with her husband's neat three-piece suit, neatly combed dark hair, and chiseled good looks, but she sensed that their moods were aligned: they were both subdued and anxious, hoping to control their conflict. They sat at opposite ends of the table with Lisa on Jeanne's left and Skip, propped up on two pillows, on her right. Lisa looked to Jeanne that evening, with her erect posture and precise, adult-sounding speech patterns, like a young governess in some Victorian melodrama. Her husband was the villain. And she . . . ?

She certainly no longer felt like a heroine. Now that her sporadic idealistic efforts to promote disarmament and peace had proved to be so clearly ineffective, she felt as weak and foolish as Bob had always accused her of being. Yet as she watched him eating his dinner so meticulously and talking with such total seriousness with Lisa about the clothing she planned to take with her, she could feel herself getting angry. It was her anxiety being transmuted into anger, anger at those who were causing her to be afraid: the Russians and the Pentagon and people like Bob, who could so coolly calculate and contemplate the probabilities of various world catastrophes.

"And what are you going to be doing, daddy?" Jeanne heard Lisa say, and saw Bob start in surprise that the forbidden subject had been broached.

"Just playing with Mars," he replied with a soft smile. He poured himself more wine and awkwardly signaled with the bottle to ask her if she wanted some more. She shook her head.

"Is that all you ever do?" Lisa asked, a little impatiently.

"I suppose so," he replied. "But the situation these days has been changing so fast we have to feed our monster fresh food five times a day instead of once or twice a week." She noticed his eyes flash as he said this.

"It still sounds boring," said Lisa.

"Calculating the probability of various war scenarios is many things, some of which your mother has strong feelings about," Bob replied, "but one thing it never is, is boring."

"You're enjoying this crisis, aren't you?" Jeanne said quietly as she leaned forward to wipe some spilled gravy from Skip's shirt. "I suppose for you it's like playing in the Superbowl."

Bob put down his fork and took a sip of wine.

"People are rather interested in our calculations these days," he said, smiling nervously. "I'm human enough to enjoy using my capabilities to the fullest and knowing I'm needed."

"That's fine," Jeanne said slowly. "But are you also human enough to be scared?"

He looked startled, then laughed.

"As a matter of fact, yes," he replied. "The world is in a critically dangerous situation. I'm rather proud that our department, probably more than any other, is responsible for determining just *how* dangerous."

"Why proud?" she asked quietly. Whenever they began to argue, their voices would get softer and softer, a trait that she realized she had adopted from him. Their civility went with the French Provincial furniture, but she had once told him that if he ever really got mad at her, his voice would get so low no one could hear it.

"Because we're the ones who can warn the President which of his policy decisions are *most* dangerous," Bob answered. "Without us he might do something that would provoke the Soviets into attacking us."

Jeanne took a last spoonful of stew and wiped her mouth.

"And does your computer tell you what happens if they do attack?" she asked next.

"No, Jupiter does," Bob replied, absently pushing Skippy's hand away from the plate of chocolate chip cookies. "Jupiter calculates who will probably win once a war starts. We on Mars just calculate the chances of a war's starting."

"And what are the chances?" she asked with a coolness she didn't feel. "Pretty high, aren't they?"

He looked at her somberly and shook his head.

"You know better than that," he replied. "Obviously no one really knows, not even Mars, and if it did, I wouldn't tell you."

"Thanks," she said.

"But if I thought I knew, I'd bundle you and the kids off to the South Pacific. I certainly wouldn't be chatting with you ten miles from the White House with a glass of wine in my hand."

"Instead you send me off to the Chesapeake," she countered, feeling even as she spoke that it was a childish remark.

"I *do* want you to go, Jeanne," he said to her with unusual seriousness.

"Why?" she answered, frowning. "You know I'm not fond of being on the water, and it's no safer there than anyplace else."

"Because I want you and the children to get away and have a good time," he replied. "Lisa's always had a crush on Jimmy," he went on, smiling at his daughter, "and Neil Loken's a hunk, if you like the type."

"Give me back my cookie!" Skippy said abruptly.

"What's the type?" Jeanne asked, remembering that the previous summer Bob had found the captain officious and remote.

"You've had enough," announced Lisa.

"Horatio Hornblower," Bob replied. "The quiet he-man always standing tall on the poopdeck squinting into the salt spray, letting everyone know he's in command."

"I have not," Skippy whispered in his squeaky voice. "I've had six, same as you."

"Well, we've had enough."

"You make him sound like a pain in the neck," said Jeanne.

"I have not," Skippy said firmly. "Give me—"

"Let go!" Lisa hissed as Skippy's little body sprawled across the tablecloth, lunging for the plate of cookies.

"Ouch! You shit!" said Skippy.

"Skip!" Bob Forester exclaimed. "Don't swear like that, and sit down!"

"She pinched me."

"Lisa, leave Skip's punishment to us," Jeanne said wearily.

"He was stealing a cookie," Lisa insisted with dignity.

"I was not!" Skippy exclaimed.

Bob erupted finally from his chair and pulled his son firmly back into his seat, twice striking him sharply on the hand, Jeanne wincing with each slap. As the boy pouted and fought back tears Bob resumed his seat and looked self-consciously back at Lisa and Jeanne.

"Yes, now, where were we?" he said.

"At sea," said Jeanne ironically.

"Oh, yes, Neil," Bob went on, adjusting his cloth napkin in his lap, his narrow eyes scowling. "He's too quiet to be a pain in the neck." His eyes crinkled into a smile. "You have to be *aware* of his loud quietness in order to be annoyed. Some people like him. Women, I imagine, would find him attractive."

"Not if he never leaves the poopdeck," Jeanne commented.

Bob glanced at his watch and stood up, smiling awkwardly.

"Oh, Frank tells me he's perfectly willing to come down to . . . shall we say, ride frailer vessels?"

Jeanne glanced over at Lisa.

"Daddy means he can be a makeout artist," she explained to her mother.

Jeanne laughed for the first time that day.

"Thank you, sweetheart," she said.

"Mommy?" said Skippy.

"Yes, dear?"

"If there's going to be a war, I think we should eat *all* the cookies now."

And this time they all laughed.

But when Bob prepared to return to Washington twenty minutes later, she didn't laugh.

He called her over to him and took her in his arms and said simply, "I love you." For years he hadn't said the words; their separations were marked by such parting comments as "Where did you leave the keys to the Rabbit?" or "I hope you left the refrigerator well stocked." But that evening, just when she felt herself most alienated from him and their life together, he said, "I love you."

She looked across at him, her large dark eyes widening with both surprise and attention.

"All right" was all she could say.

"Go down to Point Lookout tonight," he went on. "Get on the boat. Forget the mess the world's in."

Again at first she could only stare at him.

"You come too," she said impulsively, feeling a sudden fear.

"I've got my job," he said.

"Leave it," she countered desperately.

He smiled softly, a tinge of sadness in it.

"I like my job," he replied.

And she felt the wall fall between them again. As he started to turn, though, she grasped his arm and held it.

"You're a good man," she said.

"Really?" he said, with that same half-sad smile.

They looked at each other, and for the first time she saw that he was afraid too. Then she saw the emotion click off and the computer come back on. He frowned.

"Did you remember to get some frozen dinners in the freezer?" he asked.

"Yes," she answered.

"Good," he said, pecked her cheek, and was gone.

With *Vagabond* becalmed Neil finally had Jim put the seven-horse-power outboard on the inflatable dinghy to tow the trimaran into the docks of Tangier Island. Earlier, even after the wind had fallen to mere puffs in the late afternoon, they'd been able to ride the incoming tide northward toward Crisfield. But as the sun set and the tide was about to turn against them they were still almost fifteen miles short of their goal. Finding himself only a mile off the little village of Tangier and needing to let Frank know what had happened to them, Neil had *Vagabond* towed in with the dinghy.

He moored her at the end of the gas dock, which was closed for the night. With her three white hulls gleaming under the glow of the dock lights, the fifty-foot trimaran lay among the old fishing boats and conventional stinkpots like a futuristic fighter plane among World War II relics. But towing her in was a joke: like pulling a space satellite with a tricycle.

While he had Jim secure and adjust the spring lines and fenders he went into his cabin to change for going ashore. He was tired now, the dull fatigue of trying for six hours to nurse a sailing vessel toward her goal with winds that sometimes wouldn't ruffle a feather on a flea. He poured himself a shot of brandy and switched on the short-wave radio. After he had pulled off his blue jean cutoffs, he stood naked for a moment trying to tune in the BBC frequency. He finally located it and, after pulling on a pair of pants, sat back on his bunk with the brandy and listened. The cultured English announcer reported with the usual stylized indifference that a flotilla of thirty private boats had left England for Ireland or the Azores, that international flights out of the country were booked solid, with near hysteria reigning at Heathrow. The exodus was stirring up a national outcry, and one M.P. categorized the fugitives as "no better than rats deserting a sinking ship," an analogy that made Neil smile sardonically: "sinking ship'' was a devastatingly apt metaphor for Great Britain on the eve of a possible nuclear war.

When the BBC announcer began to discuss more parochial events, Neil turned the set off.

He was tired and depressed, a combination he knew from experience often went together. He felt a restless need for a woman, a feeling he knew was often associated with low-level anxiety. It was the Mideast crisis, of course, but also the fact that in a few hours Frank would be joining them and Neil would lose his freedom. He always resented it when an owner first rejoined a boat he'd been living aboard as captain and king. The owner inevitably liked to run things differently, and he hated to relinquish the control that was his when he was sailing with just a crew. Frank was about the only owner he'd sailed with who consistently shared Neil's exhilaration at the grueling joys of an ocean passage; Frank genuinely loved sailing, loved being out on the water, and wasn't aboard simply to impress clients or make a few women, but Neil was still a little depressed at the prospect of his return.

Jim interrupted his gloom by shouting down the hatchway that he was going to change and spruce up. Neil stood up and searched for a clean sport shirt. Jim might be a sailor like his father, but this trip north had been too easy a passage to be a true test. In the last four hours of their crawling with the tide Jim had given up on sailing and spent his time with his guitar and cassette player. Well, that was cool. He himself had read half a novel.

Glancing at his watch he saw that it was nine ten. He quickly switched on the shortwave radio again and tried tuning it to a ham radio operator he'd discovered on the trip north who broadcast sometimes at nine. After the news from the BBC, listening to a farmer from East Tennessee might be a welcome relief. Soon he had located the farmer's gruff voice, speaking as usual in a casual folksy monologue as if he were chatting with neighbors around a hot wood stove in mid-winter.

''. . . not everyone so happy. Mel Hutchins says the rain we got last night was too much for his spring rye and not enough for his tomatoes. Course Mel wouldn't be satisfied unless God rearranged the whole upper atmosphere every day to reroute the right weather patterns over ever' one of Mel's seventy acres. Last time I known

Mel to praise the weather was when the remains of a hurricane struck here one October after he'd harvested everything, but Jack Pillitson had half his crops still in the ground. Mel and Jack don't get along too well, and Mel said the hurricane showed good timing.

"It's getting towards sign-off time. I sure hope the Russians stop their messing around over there in Arabia. Izzy Klein says people thinking there may be a war cleaned out half his A&P this morning— and that was *before* he opened. Just joking, friends. He did say it appeared that everyone in town seemed to be expecting guests this weekend and had to stock up on three times the normal amount of food. Well, as for me, if *I* thought there was going to be a war, you wouldn't catch me buying canned baked beans, and you wouldn't catch me sitting in a fallout shelter next to anyone who had. That's sure enough not the way *I* want to go. But I don't expect to die for a while yet, so I'll be talking to you again on Sunday. This is Charlie Wittner signing off."

When Wittner's voice died away, Neil smiled and stood up. At least there was *one* man who was showing no panic.

Up on deck, under the star-studded sky, Jim was waiting for him, dressed like Neil in jeans, sport shirt, and deck shoes. Jim hadn't shaved since they'd left Fort Lauderdale, and his slight beard, longish hair—salt and sun-streaked—and bronzed skin tone gave him precisely the salty air he probably was trying to achieve. He looked as pleasantly excited as he had when they'd entered the Chesapeake sixteen hours earlier.

The only bar in Tangier was a fisherman's hangout rather than a tourist trap, so there were no fishing nets on the walls or stuffed fish, but instead dart boards, video games, pool tables, and a television set. There were half a dozen men sitting at the bar and two old men playing chess at a table. Neil led Jim to a booth next to the bar; through the window they could see *Vagabond*'s masts and cabin top above the docks and pilings.

"Where you fellas in from?" a large bearded man with a pot belly asked them from his seat at the bar.

"Fort Lauderdale, Florida," Jim answered proudly. "We made it in five and a half days."

"That's pretty good," the bearded man replied promptly. "That must be one hell of a powerful dinghy engine."

While Jim looked startled and uncertain, Neil and the men along the bar all burst out laughing. Jim, realizing they'd seen *Vagabond*'s entrance, soon joined them.

"Once or twice we cheated and used sails," Neil said, and remembered he had to phone to get a message to Frank.

"Don't blame you," said the man.

Neil stood up, went to the bar to order two beers, and then went over to the pay phone. The wife of the marina owner answered, and Neil explained the situation to her and asked her to tell Frank to take the ferry to Tangier. When he returned to his table, he was glad the television set wasn't on to remind Jim of the outside world.

"Well, mate," he said to Jim after he'd taken a long swallow of beer, "I'd say we'd made a damn good passage, even if we did fall a little short."

"*Vagabond*'s a great boat, isn't she?" Jim said.

"She even tows well," Neil replied with a smile.

"I like crewing for you," Jim went on. "It's a lot better when there are only two of us. With Dad and his friends I feel like a passenger. I never get to *do* anything. But being alone at the helm, especially at night, or when she's surfing down a big swell . . ." He stopped, smiling, flushed with the pleasure of the memory. "Anyway, I really enjoyed your putting me to work."

"I wish all my crew would say that," Neil commented, smiling.

"Blast 'em, I say. Hit 'em first," came a voice from the bar.

"You tell 'em, Charlie," another voice countered. "And don't forget to duck."

"Hey, my friend," Neil said to the large man at the end of the bar, hoping to change the subject. "Are there any women on this island?"

"Oh, yes, there's women all right."

"You keep them locked up?"

"Don't have to," the bearded man replied. "We keep 'em so tired from screwin' they ain't got no energy to go out."

Laughter tumbled along the length of the bar.

"Must be all the oysters you fellas eat," Neil suggested.

"Eat oysters!?" the bearded man exclaimed, grinning. "Shit, us baymen can't afford to eat oysters. Too expensive."

A few men laughed.

"Still," said Neil. "It's too bad you don't have a few women in especially good shape to greet tired sailors returning to land after a long stint at sea."

"We got two or three ladies like that," a little man next to the bearded man said. "But they always get themselves laid by tourists in speedboats from the Eastern Shore—men who tell 'em they're all pooped from motoring 'cross the bay."

The quick burst of laughter at this remark made Neil think it was an allusion to some actual women they all knew. He finished his beer and went to the bar to order two more. As he was standing there a pudgy woman came in and complained to the bartender, "The TV don't work." Could he fix it? After handing Neil two bottles of beer and making change, he followed her through a doorway into what were probably living quarters.

"See what we mean?" the little man at the bar said, turning to grin at Neil. "Ol' Jake's going back there now to give her a quick one. That TV business is all a front."

But Jake returned almost immediately with a frown on his face. He went up to the television set above the bar and turned it on. Neil and the others were all watching him. The screen remained dark for a few seconds, but the voice of the talking head that appeared on the screen immediately began in a tense, hurried voice:

". . . I repeat, this is not a test, this is not a test. The Emergency Broadcasting System announces a national war alert. All precautionary measures should be taken immediately to prepare for the possibility of an enemy attack. This is not a test. Civil Defense workers are to report immediately to their assigned posts. Police, fire, and emergency medical personnel on standby for national war alert should also report to their assigned posts. I repeat, this is not a test, this is not a test. The Emergency Broadcasting System is announcing a national war alert. All precautionary . . ."

It was only when he realized that the announcer was not going to say anything else that Neil became aware of himself standing next to his table, still holding his beer bottle, his mouth open in stunned bewilderment. As the bartender lowered the volume and began switching channels—and Neil could see the same announcer flash by on all the operating channels—he also became aware of the total silence in the room.

Finally someone at the bar spoke.

"Oh, good Jesus," a tired voice said. *"Now* what the fuck are the silly bastards trying to prove?"

Then the television picture disappeared, the lights in the bar went out, and the whole room was in total darkness.

Frank flung his lanky body back and forth across the end of the ferry dock at Crisfield with an impatience unusual even for him. Everything was running late. Traffic had been so bad going out to La Guardia that afternoon that the twenty-five-minute drive had taken over an hour, and he'd arrived ten minutes after his plane was supposed to have taken off. But La Guardia was a madhouse, and his plane was delayed forty minutes, so he'd made it. Then it was delayed another half-hour on the runway awaiting takeoff, the long line of taxiing planes reminding him of sailors outside a Bangkok whorehouse.

So he'd arrived in Salisbury almost an hour late, taken an agonizing thirty minutes to rent a car (so much for O.J. Simpson flying through the airport), and finally made it to Crisfield after nine o'clock in the evening.

And no *Vagabond.* When he'd inquired at the marina, it had taken him so long to find someone with a message from Neil that he figured he'd missed the last ferry to Tangier Island. The damn woman said only that Neil was becalmed at Tangier and to take the ferry. But there was now a light breeze blowing. Would Neil try to sail on to Crisfield?

Then it turned out he hadn't missed the last ferry, because the last ferry hadn't even gotten back *in* from Tangier. So he was pacing back and forth across the dock, a half-dozen locals sitting on the waiting benches staring at him as if he were a performing acrobat. He didn't care. He had the new propeller shaft, he had his fishing gear and swimsuits and scuba equipment, and he was eager to be out on the bay. The smell of salt water and dead fish had even eased his annoyance at first, since he felt such a sudden stab of joy after nothing but the smells of Manhattan for three months.

Finally the lights of the tiny ferry appeared in the distance. Frank placed himself at the edge of the dock, leaning out toward it, as if he were a magnet capable of drawing the stupid thing in faster. The local fishermen and their families simply sat there smoking and joking and generally behaving with that air of calm self-sufficiency that drove Frank crazy—until he'd been aboard *Vagabond* for a few days and began to recreate it for himself.

The ferry was a big launch with a long deckhouse roof and six or seven benches that would probably seat forty people during the height of the tourist season. There were only four people coming off the island.

Some of the locals came up as the boat approached the dock and took the two mooring lines. A skinny little man was at the wheel and a young kid put out the fenders. When the launch was secured, the little man came out of the wheelhouse, puffing on a pipe. After Frank had walked back to where he had left his duffel bags and then got himself and his stuff onto the ferry, the captain helped a woman he apparently knew to climb on board.

"You folks heah about the woah?" he asked her and the two men with her.

"What war is that, Cap?" one of the men asked in return.

"I don't know as whether they've named it yet," he answered, a quizzical frown on his round face. "But it's another one of *our* woahs."

"What do you mean?" the woman asked nervously, sitting down next to Frank on a middle bench.

"My radio says theah's going to be a woah. With the Russians."

"Oh, that," said Frank, feeling the tension that the captain's vague statements had created beginning to lessen.

"When'd you hear this?" another man asked.

"Five minutes ago, I'd guess," the captain said. "Made it seem pretty impohtant. National emergency or something. Like an air-raid wahning."

"Air-raid warning for where?" Frank asked irritably.

"Well, I guess for just about the whole country," the little man replied.

"What are you going to do about it, Cap?" the first man asked.

"Not much I can do till I finish this last ferry trip," he said, motioning to the kid to free the mooring lines.

"Has anyone been killed yet?" the woman asked.

"Not that they mentioned," the captain replied as he went through to the wheelhouse. He turned back to them when he got halfway to the wheel. "They just kep' saying emergency," he concluded.

The forty-five-foot ferry swung out of the dock area and began its hour-and-a-half-long trip through the darkness to Tangier. Frank leaned back on the bench, hugging his right knee for balance, and sensed the anxiety rising within him. It was one thing to have a war scare but another to declare some sort of national emergency that made people start telling their neighbors there was a war.

He stared unseeingly off to his right and began to consider the effect an escalation of the panic might have on his business fortunes when a glow caught his attention. He concentrated his attention to his right.

There *was* a strange, steadily increasing glow across the bay, like the lights of a huge city being slowly turned on. It didn't seem like fire; the light was too diffuse, too much just a glow. Unless it was a long way off.

"What's that?" the woman next to him asked the man beside her. Along with the seven or eight other passengers Frank watched fascinated as the light, like the spreading hood of a cobra, slowly loomed up to fill the sky. Feeling a stab of horror he stood up.

"Looks like a fire," someone said.

Frank pushed past the knees of the two people next to him and strode forward to the wheelhouse.

"What's our heading?" he asked the little captain in the dimly lit wheelhouse.

"Heading?" the little man asked, squinting up at him.

Frank could read the compass bearing for himself by the soft reddish light over the binnacle. Their course was southwest. The glow then was to the northwest, perhaps a little north of northwest. He tried to visualize the map of the Chesapeake that he'd been studying the day before, then looked back at the spreading and intensifying glow.

Washington. There were no cities along the Chesapeake northwest of Crisfield. The first city northwest of Crisfield was way inland, was Washington. A hundred miles away.

A hundred miles away. Holy sweet Jesus. The light glowed more brightly. Frank staggered out of the wheelhouse.

Captain Olly was dozing in his faded and worn overstuffed chair, the television set gleaming in front of him, the sound turned down low, though still audible. Hours before his son had gone out to a Smith Island bar, but Olly had decided to stay home, bushed as usual.

The face of a newscaster was on the screen murmuring in tense, anxious tones, but Olly didn't hear. Then, with a gentle popping sound, the screen went dark, and the lights Olly had left on behind the set and in the kitchen went out also.

Olly stirred and, awakened by the change, opened his eyes.

"Chris?" he said into the darkness.

He began feeling with his hands for the thin blanket Chris sometimes put over him when he'd fallen asleep in his chair and Chris didn't want him to wake up. But his lap was bare. It didn't *feel* like he'd been sleeping that long, but if Chris was home and had turned out all the lights it must be damn late.

He shuffled slowly to the bathroom and without bothering to turn on the light, pissed into the sink—no problem with aiming at such close range. Then he shuffled off to his small bedroom at the rear of the house. He hesitated for a moment at his bedroom door, a vague feeling of uneasiness nagging at him. In years at sea and in the bay he'd learned to be responsive to such intuitive hints of trouble, but he was in his own little house, anchored solidly to Smith Island, which was anchored less solidly in Chesapeake mud. It was the moonlight streaming in the bedroom window that bothered him, but he couldn't tell why.

He was old, and he was tired. He fell onto his bed fully clothed and closed his eyes. Something was wrong, but damned if he could think of anything that wouldn't wait till morning. Soon he was asleep in the empty house, the half-moon not yet risen in the east, but light streaming in his window from the northwest.

Jeanne was driving the station wagon through the darkness on Route 5 south toward Point Lookout, having already traveled more than forty of the seventy miles from Washington. Lisa was sitting silently beside her, Skippy sprawled asleep in the rear with the dog, when a brilliant flash of light filled the car, as if some enormous vehicle with its brights on had suddenly come up fast behind them. When Jeanne glanced in her rearview mirror, the brightness was more like a gigantic, diffuse searchlight on the horizon, aimed at her. Lisa turned to stare back out the rear window, and then, her face glimmering in the light, looked fearfully at Jeanne.

"What *is* it, Mother?" she asked.

Jeanne, following fifty yards behind a blue pickup truck, didn't reply. The inexplicable and terrifying brightness had numbed her mind.

Then her car suddenly went out of control, picked up by an invisible hand and flung forward at ten or fifteen miles faster than she'd been going, the rear end swinging sickeningly to the left, then gliding back as if they'd hit a patch of ice. The pickup truck had swerved into the ditch on the right, then careened back across the highway into the other lane. Finally, wobbling as if all four tires had gone flat, it steadied in the center of the highway, with Jeanne following it, almost oblivious of what was happening to her own car. When the pickup's brake lights glowed, she began to slow her wagon, both vehicles quickly reducing speed.

When Jeanne glanced at Lisa, she saw her daughter staring speechlessly at her in wide-eyed horror. Still not thinking, she slowed down, letting the pickup disappear ahead of her into the eerily lit night. When she saw a turnaround in front of a fruit stand, she pulled the car off the road and stopped.

"I'm trembling" was the first thought she had, and she gripped the steering wheel tighter, trying to control the incredible vibrations of her arms. Yes, trembling was what it was called, she thought stupidly.

"Oh, Mommy, Mommy, what's happening?" Lisa cried, and Jeanne felt her daughter pressing against her, gripping her arm, her face against Jeanne's shoulder. Jeanne raised her head to look back into the rearview mirror, which was still filled with light. She glanced to her left and watched two cars speed by, lit by the yellow glow from behind. Then she turned to look back: a light was ballooning outward and upward, the central brightness growing dimmer as more and more of the sky was lit up. Lisa's fingers dug into her still-trembling arm, and Jeanne thought simply, "A nuclear bomb has hit Washington." There was no conscious terror or fear, only the simple fact. "And this is what it's like forty miles away."

Two more cars sped past toward Point Lookout. No one was now heading back toward Washington. She closed her eyes and lowered her head to the wheel.

"Mommy . . . Mommy . . ." Lisa pleaded beside her, but Jeanne couldn't seem to function, couldn't seem to *think* anything. She had a sudden image of the house in Alexandria being shattered into tiny pieces by the blast, but she felt nothing. The wheel was cold against her forehead. From the backseat the dog barked twice nervously, apparently disturbed by the light.

Jeanne raised her head and sat up straight, staring forward. She turned the engine back on. She shifted into forward, swung the car in a U, and began to drive back toward Washington.

Beside her Lisa began to whimper.

"Where are we going, Mommy?" she gasped out between low moans.

Ahead of them a bell-shaped clump of light expanded into the sky, its upper rim rising but growing dimmer, the lower part spreading out horizontally and retaining its brightness. When the car headed straight toward it, Jeanne had trouble seeing the road. When an oncoming car honked its horn at her and she swerved to the right, her right wheels slid off the shoulder, skidded, then climbed back onto the road.

"Oh, Mommy, Mommy."

How long it's been since Lisa has called me Mommy, she thought, driving unthinkingly onward.

And then she saw a fire. Two cars tangled by the other side of the road, one of them engulfed in flames. She slowed down as she passed them and then after a minute stopped the car at the side of the road. From the slight rise, she could see ahead for miles, where several other small fires were burning in the half-darkness, whether cars or houses she couldn't tell. Off to the right a whole village seemed to be burning. The landscape was otherwise obscure.

"You're in shock. Get the children to safety. You're in shock, get the children to safety, you're in shock . . ." She was experiencing her mind as some alien machine functioning mechanically and improperly, while she herself was dumb, helpless.

"Mommy, let's go the other way," Lisa whispered against her shoulder.

"Yes, sweetheart," she found herself saying calmly, her arm still trembling. "We'd better get down to Point Lookout."

She swung the car a second time in a U, almost colliding with a van that was already speeding southward, which she had seen and yet not seen. Then she was in line with the other vehicles, speeding through the night away from Washington.

Neil ran down the dock and began casting off *Vagabond*, feeling vulnerable, naked. Leaving the Tangier bar, he'd seen the glow to the northwest and known what it meant, but had not broken stride toward the boat. As Jim leapt onto *Vagabond* and ran aft to descend into the inflatable dinghy that was tied off between the hulls Neil sensed that now that Jim's nightmare had come true he was acting with unpanicked calm. With the wind still light out of the east Jim would have to tow them out to the bay before they could pick up a breeze. But even as Neil was making active preparations to get them to their rendezvous with Frank at Crisfield, a part of his mind was still focused on the problem of heading the boat *south,* out of the Chesapeake and onto the open sea.

When Jim came sliding between the hulls in the dinghy, Neil dropped him the towline. The glow to the northwest was brighter now, and a surge of panic forced Neil to steady himself, holding on to the forestay and staring at the glow on the horizon.

"Get going," he said sharply to Jim and ran aft to raise the sails.

Five minutes later *Vagabond* was out of the cove and sailing northward behind her dinghy at almost four knots. Neil knew Frank might be on some late ferry to Tangier, so he was keeping his boat in the marked channel. As they moved forward he realized that there was not a single light showing on Tangier and Smith islands or the entire Eastern Shore. The battery-operated buoy lights were working, but the rest of the world was in darkness.

Some twenty minutes out into the bay he spotted the ferry closing on them fast and bearing away. He put the spreader lights on, so that Frank, if he was aboard, would be certain to recognize his trimaran. When he trained his glasses on the passengers, some of whom were visible in the ferry's lights, he saw Frank standing on the stern waving his arms at them like a drowning man.

Neil signaled Jim to drop the towline and get over to the ferry. When he looked back through the binoculars he saw Frank standing on the ship's side, a duffel bag in each hand; after staring dubiously at the widening gap between the ferry and *Vagabond* and then at the water, the tall gangly figure stepped awkwardly off the boat and disappeared into the blackness, the ferry speeding on to Tangier. While Neil watched—feeling both fear and admiration for Frank—it took Jim only a half-minute to reach Frank and another two to bring them both back to the trimaran. As Neil let *Vagabond* come up into the wind and rushed over to the port cockpit Frank tossed his two wet bags on deck and prepared to swing himself up.

"Thank God we found you," Neil said, grabbing Frank's hand to pull him aboard.

"There's a war on, did you know?" Frank shot back.

"Yes," Neil answered.

"You got a towel for me? I'm freezing to death."

Neil carried the two duffel bags into the wheelhouse and found a towel Jim had left on a settee. As Frank began undressing and vigorously drying his body Neil went back to speak to Jim.

"Come back aboard," Neil shouted to him. "We'll tow the dinghy and sail." As Jim began to obey, Neil went back to the wheel to get *Vagabond* turned around and headed down the bay toward the Atlantic Ocean.

"Where the hell are you going?" Frank asked, pausing in drying his legs to look up at Neil as he was winching in the mainsail.

"We've got to escape this madness," Neil said, taking *Vagabond* off the wind on a starboard tack. "The Chesapeake will soon be nothing but a saltwater burial ground. The whole East Coast is probably doomed."

Frank stared at him.

"We've been at war less than an hour," he snapped back. "Are you surrendering already?"

The question startled Neil. He *was* ready to surrender in some sense, not to an invading army—that he'd be willing to fight—but to the invisible, anonymous destruction that he knew had been unleashed.

Jim had made the dinghy fast and now appeared in the wheelhouse, watching their confrontation uncertainly.

"*You* may want to run immediately," Frank went on angrily, "but

I've got a wife and daughter thirty miles outside of New York City who may still be alive. I've got Jeannie and Bob to pick up.''

"The Foresters can't have survived what happened to Washington," Neil said.

"They may have come down to Point Lookout earlier this evening," Frank explained. "In any case it's damn certain it's our job to go over and see."

"All right," said Neil. "But then we've got to get out into the Atlantic—before we're blown up or buried in radioactive ash."

"Don't give me any more crap about an ocean voyage," Frank shot back. "We're at war! We have to stay here!"

"There may not *be* a here much longer," Neil insisted.

"Neil's right, dad," Jim broke in. "We've got to get out of the Chesapeake."

"Shut up! Both of you!" Frank shouted. He paced past Jim out into a side cockpit and then, after staring at the eery ballooning glow on the horizon, returned.

"Even if New York's already been hit, no one can be certain how wide the radius of destruction is around the cities." He paused. "I'm going to try to fly north. I've got to get to Norah and Susan."

Neil stared at him in disbelief.

"I figure there's a chance they're still alive," Frank continued huskily. "I can charter a plane in Salisbury to fly to Oyster Bay and bring her back."

Neil searched Frank's anguished face.

"It's madness, Frank," he said softly. "That whole area has probably been hit. If your wife did survive, she's already fled farther out the island. There's no way—"

"I'm going," Frank interrupted sharply. "If there's only one chance in ten, I've still got to try."

"And what are Jim and I supposed to do?" Neil asked, brushing roughly past Frank to adjust the mainsheet. "Sit here for two or three days waiting for the fallout or the next explosion?"

"You try to get the Foresters over at Point Lookout."

"All right, we'll do that," Neil said. "But then what?"

"You pick me up in Crisfield tomorrow night."

Neil grimaced and turned away, shaking his head.

"We'll sail to Crisfield now," Frank went on, "and I can get to

Salisbury by eight or nine in the morning.'' Both he and Neil watched
Vagabond sail past a red buoy, both instinctively noting the ship's
speed. "I should be able to get a plane by ten or eleven. New York
by noon. If I give myself six hours to find her and Susan, that'll get
me back at Crisfield by . . . nine tomorrow.''

Neil stared at him for a moment.

"Look, Frank,'' he began, glancing at Jim, who was listening with
grim attentiveness. "Not many people are going to survive what's
happening. The ones who do are going to have to act fast and . . .
ruthlessly. They'll have to know enough to cut their losses and run.
Don't go. We can go over to Point Lookout to check for the Foresters
now and then ride the tide down out the bay later tomorrow morning.''

Frank flushed.

"I'm going,'' he said. "And you're not using my boat to escape
your responsibilities.''

"*What* responsibilities!'' Neil exploded. "Tell me what in God's
name you think any of us can do now against incoming missiles except try to survive. Every second you delay us you're risking my life
and your son's and the Foresters'.''

"I have to try to save my family,'' Frank went on. "We can't just
run.''

"We can't help anyone dead,'' Jim blurted out.

"Jim's right,'' Neil said.

Frank leaned against the wheelhouse shelf, put his face in his hands,
and rubbed his forehead. When he looked up, much of his color
seemed to have drained away.

"I'm going to try,'' he said softly. "Get *Vagabond* turned around.
If I'm not back by nine tomorrow night . . . by ten . . . that's when
the tide's high . . . you can leave without me.''

As Neil stared forward past the mainmast and across the water he
felt resentment at the way Frank had cast him in the villain's role.
During the last crisis, three months before, he'd considered what he
would do if a nuclear war broke out and had decided he'd probably
have it easy, because he'd be on a boat at sea or on the coast and
thus could flee the explosions and fallout. But the holocaust had actually found him becalmed without an engine seventy-five miles up a
bay in the middle of dozens of prime targets, with his passengers

scattered to the winds. Frank's insane scheme of searching for his family up north had complicated things further. Every moment they remained in the Chesapeake decreased their chances of survival.

"Don't go, dad," Jim said after a long silence. "Please don't go. We can't help mom now."

"I've got to go," Frank replied, turning to walk out into the port cockpit. "I could never forgive myself if . . . I didn't try . . ."

Neil turned the wheel over to Jim, told him to bring *Vagabond* about, and walked after Frank.

"All right," he said when he had caught up to him, looking into Frank's frightened, determined face. "If you've got to go, so be it. We'll take you to Crisfield and then go to Point Lookout to try to help the Foresters, then back into Crisfield tomorrow."

"And you can leave without me at ten," Frank concluded.

"I plan to sail south at no later than ten tomorrow night," Neil agreed impassively.

Frank nodded gloomily. As *Vagabond* swung about to take Frank back to Crisfield they all stared forward at the terrifying glow on the horizon. On every other side the world was dark.

"Be back on time, you fool," Neil said softly to Frank. "We need you."

"Yeah," said Frank huskily. "I can't let you steal my boat."

By the time Jeanne was within a few miles of Point Lookout she was out of her state of shock. Point Lookout, she knew, was a dead end: a small town at the end of the huge V-shaped peninsula bordered on one side by the wide Potomac River and on the other by the Chesapeake. The nearest bridges were almost fifty miles away and might have been destroyed by the airburst over Washington. She would meet *Vagabond* in Point Lookout or have to get herself and the children onto another boat. Hundreds, thousands of survivors from the destruction to the north would be funneled south to this tiny town, and everyone would be looking for a boat.

She knew that *Vagabond* might not come for her, that Frank might have concluded that she and her family had been killed. She could only hope the trimaran was already *in* Point Lookout and would wait a few hours at least.

Lisa too had regained control. She seemed to need to talk, so Jeanne nodded and grunted while her own mind worked along in its own channels. Mostly Lisa recited what she could remember from reading their pamphlets about radioactive fallout, a subject Jeanne already knew well. Neither of them mentioned her father, dead, Jeanne assumed dully, in Washington. Her strongest emotion when she emerged from shock was anger: anger at the Russians and Americans who had created this war that had killed Bob and was threatening to kill Lisa and Skip.

As they neared Point Lookout it struck Jeanne as strange that she could see other drivers, like herself reacting to the largest crisis of their lives, yet say nothing to them. Each vehicle was its own separate island, its occupants shipwrecked alone.

And something else was strange: there didn't seem to be anyone at home along the road. The area was deserted. Then she realized: there was no electric power. The lights were out. Forever.

The word *forever* chilled her even as she recognized it as melodrama; she shook her head to get rid of it. But she felt her anger rising again at the sight of the dark houses on either side of the road, as if already everyone inside them were dead. The stupid, thoughtless life-haters were doing it: they were blowing up the world.

When she entered the village of Point Lookout, it too was dark. By the time she arrived at the waterfront, it was a little after eleven. The only light came from the cars and the glow to the northwest.

She drove past a place called Kelly's Marina, but turned in when she saw a sign saying Municipal Marina.

The parking lot was not crowded, and she chose a spot off at the end next to a small saltwater creek and parked. For a moment she sat there staring down at the barely visible black waters of the creek and ignoring Lisa's question—"What are we going to do now?" Then, after watching someone running through the yard carrying a kerosene lantern, she turned to her daughter.

"I want you to stay here with Skippy," she said quietly. "Lock the car doors. Don't let anyone in. I'm going to see if Frank is here yet."

"Yes, Mother."

"If he's not here," she went on, "we'll have to wait. Maybe we'll go to the motel or perhaps we'll stay here. But *you* stay here no matter how long it takes me to get back."

"I will, Mother," Lisa answered. "You be careful."

When Jeanne leaned over to give Lisa a kiss, she found herself being hugged by Lisa's long arms.

"It's going to be all right, honey," she said softly as she loosened herself from the embrace. "The bastards haven't killed us yet."

After she got out of the car, Jeanne waited until Lisa had locked the doors and then hurried through the parking lot toward the docks. In the darkness she noticed clusters of people gathered quietly in the lot and along the dock. She felt alone and vulnerable, then frightened whenever a car's headlights swept over her like a memory of the nuclear blast. She knew what a trimaran looked like—thank God Frank had such a strange-looking boat—but in the darkness it was difficult to tell if three hulls together belonged to three separate boats or one large trimaran. Several boats were lit up, and most people hurrying along the waterfront had flashlights.

How she wished she could talk to someone. There was a war, a war, and everyone just hurried past, ignoring her.

The dock was a giant T, but after searching along both its arms, she had not found *Vagabond*. Finally she stopped someone hurrying toward the shore.

"Excuse me, do you know if there's a trimaran—"

"Can't help you, lady," the man replied, not even slowing his pace.

Closing her eyes, Jeanne moved over to a piling and held on to it to steady herself. She noticed several boats riding at anchor that were barely visible from the dock, and she wondered if *Vagabond* was among them. She could feel her arms trembling again and thought of Skippy and Lisa in the car, depending on her.

Okay. Eleven twenty and the trimaran's not at the municipal dock. It might not get here until dawn. She'd check with the dockmaster and the motel desk for messages; she'd take a look at any other marinas here in the heart of town; and then all she could do was wait.

There was no dockmaster on duty, and when she finally got someone to listen to her, he said he didn't know anything about any trimaran. She returned wearily to her car.

Lisa, wide-eyed, lowered the window on the passenger's side.

"Frank's not here yet," Jeanne said with exaggerated nonchalance. "He may not arrive until dawn. I'm going to check the motel down the street to see if maybe he got a message through to us before . . . I'll be gone another half-hour," she concluded. "Why don't you climb in back beside Skippy and try to get some sleep."

"I'm not sleepy."

"You need some rest."

"I've been keeping an eye out for Frank."

Jeanne examined her frightened, eager-eyed daughter.

"I'll be back," she said, and walked away.

In the darkness the motel was difficult to locate. Lit only by the glow from the northwest, the place seemed like a deserted set for some horror film, the main street like a path through a dark canyon.

There was no message at the motel, and they had no room reserved for her, having given it to some "personal friends." Sorry.

She searched Porter's and Kelly's and then the municipal docks again, but there was no trimaran. As she returned to her car she realized that in an hour and a half she hadn't heard a friendly word.

Lisa was still in the front seat, slumped to one side, asleep. When Jeanne unlocked the driver's door, she stirred but slept on. Jeanne decided that she herself should sleep. If Frank arrived now, he'd certainly wait until morning before leaving again. She relocked the driver's door and climbed over the seat to settle down on the sleeping bag beside Skippy and Banjo. After pulling the light blanket up over herself and Skip, she stared up at the dark ceiling of her station wagon. A strong sense of unreality flowed through her. Was she really lying in her car three hours after the start of a nuclear war? The warm softness of Skippy's body beside her seemed so human, so nice, so reassuring. She lifted her head to look out the window: figures with lanterns and flashlights were moving in the darkness along the dock. Someone shouted. The war was real.

After a while she slept. She was awakened once in the night by a scream, but when she sat up saw nothing. There was only one light moving in the darkness. Near dawn she was awakened again by someone shaking her foot and then pulling her bodily out the back of the station wagon. When she sat up, she banged her head on the car roof and, wide awake now, saw two men, one of whom had hold of her feet and was dragging her out the back of her own car. Banjo was growling.

"Stop it!" she shouted, but the man dragged her up to the rear door and then took hold of her arm and pulled her roughly out.

"Give us the car keys," he said, his fingers digging into her upper arm, his face, tensely expressionless in the early predawn light, only a foot away from hers. Fully alert, but still groping for reality, she looked speechlessly back at him.

"Yes . . . yes, of course," she finally said. "But let us get our stuff out."

When she tried to turn back to the car, the man held her fast.

"I found them," she heard the other man say, and saw he had her handbag and now the keys.

The first man flung her off to the side, sending her stumbling over the small embankment, and down onto her face, rolling toward the shallow creek. The cold water struck her legs like a slap.

"Let's go," she heard a voice say.

———————————————

Vagabond was moving toward Point Lookout with agonizing slowness. The nightmare of the war was compounded for Neil by the more personal and immediate nightmare of running in place, being unable to move forward no matter how hard he tried. It had seemed like an endless crawl toward Crisfield with Frank in the wee hours of the morning, and since they had put him ashore just before dawn an endless crawl in light winds across the bay.

And as they struggled the horror of the unfolding nuclear destruction was becoming more real. At the dock in Crisfield Frank had tried to telephone his wife and reported back dully to Neil and Jim:

"The operator didn't even try. She said—the operator said . . . 'I'm sorry, sir, New York State has been disconnected.' " He laughed joylessly.

They had all listened in the darkness to the transistor radio, and on the entire AM dial they were able to bring in only five stations where normally there would have been forty or so. Dribs and drabs of hurried, sometimes barely coherent news drifted out. It often took the reporters several repetitions of each frightening report before a piece of grim news could be accepted as confirmed and indisputable. The idea that Washington and New York and apparently fifty to a hundred other places had been destroyed and that twenty to eighty million people had already been killed, that almost all major radio and television stations were not operating, and that the war was continuing: all this was almost beyond their ability to cope. It seemed to be beyond some of the announcers' abilities to cope as well. A few read the news items as if they were reading a weather report and made it seem so absurd that at one point Frank giggled. Others would become emotional and eventually be replaced by a more controlled voice.

One commentator pointed out that there was no way of knowing how many nuclear warheads had hit a given target, whether the target had been struck directly or peripherally, and whether the explosion had occurred on the ground or in the air. Knowledge that a place had been hit at all usually could only be deduced from its total silence. There were few eyewitness reports.

All United States military personnel had been ordered to report for duty. If it was "no longer feasible" for reservists to make contact with their units, they were ordered to report to the nearest "base of the appropriate service."

The President issued a statement at four thirty A.M. indicating that he and all cabinet members were safe, but that dozens, perhaps hundreds of U.S. Congressmen had been killed by the blasts over Washington and other major cities. Offensive action had been commenced against the Soviet Union; nuclear war was being waged in Europe and Asia too. Although at least twenty major American cities had already been reported hit and twice that many missile installations and other military targets, the implication was that for some unstated reason the Russians hadn't unleashed as devastating an attack as might have been expected. To Neil it meant only that worse might be yet to come. One exchange between two announcers on the Norfolk radio station particularly depressed and frightened him.

"Is there anything new from the national news wire, Herb?" a man's voice asked shakily.

"There's still no contact with NBC news in New York, John. All we've got, actually, are the items we're picking up from WTUV in Richmond, but they seem to have a direct connection with the federal government."

"What about WBZE here in Norfolk? Do they have access to the ABC news wire?"

"No. All three network news services are out."

"What about the West Coast centers?"

"Los Angeles and San Francisco were both hit, John. There's just no contact—"

"What about military targets here in the Norfolk area?"

"The mayor has ordered the evacuation of all nonessential personnel," the other voice replied. "I'm afraid that with the U.S. naval base here and the shipyards in Portsmouth, this would appear to be a prime target area. . . ."

Neil knew that if Norfolk, at the mouth of the Chesapeake, were hit, they might never escape to the open sea.

By the time they were away from Crisfield and on their way to Point Lookout the net effect on Neil of listening to the frenzied preliminary reports of destruction had been to produce a strange and unexpected emotion that, he realized after a moment, was shame. He felt like a child whose classmates had run amok: although he wasn't personally involved, the destruction was somehow his responsibility.

Yet the dawn and early morning hours apparently belied the reports they were hearing. A third of the way across the bay the day was clear; the sun shone brightly on the still water. A mile away Smith and Tangier islands lay lush and green and silent like some bucolic utopia. Land and houses on the now receding Eastern Shore lay gleaming with postcard clarity. There even seemed to be an oysterman up and working the beds to the southeast. It was as if the radio reports had been an Orson Welles prank.

But to the northwest the nightmare was very much in evidence: a huge gray cloud had spread over half the horizon, a shapeless mass whose lower reaches were quite dark, its upper borders, high overhead now, diffuse and ill defined. A second area of cloudiness to the northeast was merging with it. Philadelphia? Only from the east through south to due west was the sky still clear. Norfolk still lived.

By eight A.M. the breeze began to pick up, and Neil felt that if it held or freshened further, they would make Point Lookout by ten thirty.

As their progress became routine and they stopped listening to the radio Neil was saddened that he felt no desire to try to rush northward to anyone's rescue. When he imagined his parents struggling to survive after an explosion over Boston and the devastation of their home town of Ocean Bluff, he felt depressed and vaguely ashamed, but the idea that he could get there and become a rescuer simply had no reality. Frank's plan seemed insane. For Neil it was as if the war had created a new world, one that ended all previous relationships. Your family would now be defined as whoever you found yourself with. And the new world, for Neil, would survive only if they could make it out to sea.

"What do you know about nuclear fallout?" Jim asked from beside him, interrupting his thoughts.

"Enough," Neil replied.

"That stuff we see ahead of us is radioactive fallout," Jim said. He looked at Neil as if searching to see how horrible this fact really was. The gray cloud cover to the northwest was more pronounced now that the sun was higher in the sky. It also seemed to be spreading slightly toward them.

"Yes," said Neil. "I expect it is."

"It's going to spread," Jim said.

"Yes," Neil replied quietly. "But we're almost a hundred miles away."

"We won't be at Point Lookout," Jim replied. "And even so, I think it's gotten closer since the sun came up."

Neil squinted at it, as if noting this fact for the first time.

"Maybe," he said. "But this northeast wind is helping us. It's moving the stuff away at right angles."

"You told me earlier you thought the wind will be shifting to the north," Jim persisted.

Neil went out into the port cockpit to adjust the genny sheet and then returned to the wheel.

"We do what we must do, Jim," he said. "Right now we're sailing *Vagabond* to Point Lookout."

"And when that stuff starts falling on deck?" Jim asked, still searching Neil's face for any sign of fear.

Neil looked back at him neutrally.

"Then we sweep it off," he replied.

Jeanne and Lisa, with Skippy and the dog huddled around them, blinked in bewilderment at the chaos that was now the waterfront of Point Lookout. Two hours after they'd been thrown out of the station wagon, there were several hundred people where the night before there had been perhaps two dozen. In places along the docks and on the wooden picnic tables a thin layer of ash had been discovered at dawn, a discovery that had increased the panic. Jeanne had already seen people siphoning gasoline from parked cars for boat engines or their own cars, seen men rush past with guns stuffed in their belts, rifles in their hands. People milled along the dock, pleading with anyone on board a boat to take them along, the women sometimes weeping, the children silent. She had seen five or six people with burned faces and arms and two people being carried on makeshift stretchers. One of the cars that had driven into the parking lot had most of its red paint blistered.

One by one over the two hours since she'd been up searching for *Vagabond*, vessels had motored away from the dock area, a few completely packed and low in the water, others with only two or three people aboard. Some were motor yachts, some sailboats; most were open boats with inboard and outboard engines. All wanted to get away from Washington and the fallout.

Although many boats had already left, the waterfront was still crowded. Several of those that had been at anchor were now coming in to get fuel or to pick up passengers. Others were arriving from down the Potomac.

Jeanne had recovered from the shock of being thrown out of her car. The men had let Lisa and Skippy leave and had tossed out the children's duffel bags, her larger suitcase, and a sleeping bag, but had driven off with her smaller suitcase, her handbag, and a lot of little stuff in the car, including snack food she'd tossed together. She had no money or credit cards, and they hadn't eaten breakfast. When she'd rolled into the creek, she'd wet her jeans through, so had changed into white shorts and blouse; her wet boat shoes she'd had to leave on, since her other shoes were in the missing smaller suitcase.

As she stood with one arm around Lisa's waist and the other holding Skippy's hand, she was tremblingly considering other options. With every minute that passed the chances of the trimaran's arriving at Point Lookout grew smaller. She could conceive of no reason for Frank not to have arrived by now. He'd said he hoped to come at ten last night, early morning at the latest. What could possibly stop him from motoring across the bay? Her only conclusion was that Frank had decided that she and her family were dead. He wasn't coming.

So what could she do? She had no husband, no home, no car, no money, no friends, and no place to stay. Her isolation and powerlessness saddened and angered her. The burned faces, sightless eyes, and the shuffling, numb way so many people moved frightened her. She had to focus on her alternatives, but when she did she could see only one: she should try to get across the bay to Crisfield. Frank would probably not be there, but it seemed like her only hope. At least they would keep moving. She should try to hitch a ride on some other boat.

Even as she decided, she could feel herself absorbing the alternating numbness and hysteria she saw all around her. The people on shore were becoming more numerous and the remaining boats fewer. Two fistfights had broken out at the gas dock, and just after ten a man had been shot. The absence of electric power had forced the marina to develop some sort of mechanical siphoning system and the dockmaster's efforts to ration the amount of fuel he pumped seemed to have provoked the shooting. Within two minutes of the gunshot everyone seemed to have forgotten about it. The wounded man had staggered off alone. There were no policemen.

When she went in search of a boat owner who might be willing to take her and her family across the bay, she left Lisa by the marina office to take care of Skippy and their two bags and went out on the docks alone. The stretch of dock next to each remaining boat was thronged with men and women either dully or passionately begging for a chance to get on board. Clustered around the first boat were two families, two stony-faced mothers, their children cowering big-eyed around their legs, the husbands, angry, holding out money. She didn't see any sense in competing, so she moved on.

The second boat was a twenty-five-foot motor yacht with two men working on its engine. One of them looked up at the group accosting him from the dock. She saw the man stare appraisingly at an attractive blond woman who was pleading with him to take her and her child, and then his gaze shifted to Jeanne herself, first her bare legs, and then her breasts, and finally her eyes. She felt a sensual shock: from fifteen feet away and without uttering a word the man seemed to have propositioned her.

She hurried on. The third boat was filled to overflowing, but as she passed it she had the feeling that these people had boarded an empty boat and that no one really knew what was going on. She was walking back from the end of one of the arms of the T, when a slender young man about thirty came up and stopped her.

"Are you looking for a boat?" he asked.

"Yes," she replied eagerly. "I want to get across the bay to Cris-field."

"I might be able to help you."

"Thank God. I've got two children too. Where's your boat?"

"Two children?" the man said, frowning. "We've only got room for one more person."

"They're only children . . . ." Jeanne pleaded. "They won't take up much . . . ."

"I'm sorry, ma'am, we're just too full."

When he brushed nervously past her and hurried away, she stared after him in shock.

"You *bastard*!" she shouted at his retreating back.

As she headed back down the docks toward the marina office she realized how vulnerable she was, especially with two children. No one wanted that additional responsibility. Lisa and Skippy were still where she'd left them, hot and hungry. Lisa had fished a half-eaten banana out of a trash can, and Skippy, after first accusing it of being dirty, had finally eaten it. She grabbed Skippy's hand, and they traipsed like the war refugees they were down the fifty feet of road to the entrance to Kelly's, but seeing that Porter's Boatyard seemed much less crowded, she decided to try there first.

At the gate two men with shotguns greeted her.

"Can we help you, ma'am?" one of them asked.

"Yes, I hope so," Jeanne replied, thankful for the first sign of politeness she'd encountered all day. "I . . . I need to get a boat ride across the bay."

"Do you know anyone in here?" the man asked.

"No."

"Our orders are that no one is permitted to enter the yard unless they're friends or guests of owners of one of the boats here. I'm sorry."

"Oh."

She hurried back to Kelly's Marina, which was slightly less crowded than the town docks, but the situation was the same: boat owners nervously preparing their boats, refugees looking for rides. She paused in the yard before going out. She had nothing to offer that the others didn't have, but she had to try.

"Lisa," she said to her daughter at her side. "I want you to keep yourself and Skippy thirty or forty feet behind me and out of sight. Follow me, watch me, don't lose me, but stay away until I call you. Do you understand?"

"Yes, Mother," Lisa replied. "What are you going to do?"

"I'm trying to get us a ride across the bay, where I hope to find Frank."

Jeanne had noticed a sailboat tied a little way off a small dock between the municipal marina and Kelly's, and now that a family of four was leaving, there was only one man on the nearby dock.

"Do you have a hairbrush?" she asked her daughter. "Mine was in my handbag."

"I think so."

Lisa dug out her hairbrush from the duffel bag, and Jeanne let down her hair, which she had tied back earlier, and brushed it out. She had no fresh makeup on, but hoped she didn't need it.

"How do I look?" she asked Lisa.

Lisa stared at her uncertainly.

"You . . . you look fine," she answered.

"I mean my mascara's not running . . ."

"No . . . Mother, what are you going to do? Let me come with you."

"No, honey, stay here," she replied and walked away.

She moved without haste and without the sense of desperation that, she realized now, had been with her all that morning. It was still with her, of course, but since she was playing a part, her desperation was under control. She was trying to walk like a beautiful woman out for a stroll on a lovely summer morning. A wave of horror at the image surged through her. She felt ridiculous. She kept walking.

She saw that the man on the dock was adjusting a line that ran out to the sailboat, twenty feet off the dock, where two other men were working hurriedly. They looked like they were about to leave port.

"Hi," she said as the man watched her approach down the gentle embankment that led to the dock.

"Hello," he said, glancing at her nervously. He was a muscular-looking man in his mid-twenties, dressed in khakis and a polo shirt.

"I could use a boat ride," she said.

"You and half the rest of the world," the man answered, his eyes flicking quickly over her, his expression neutral.

She tried to smile.

"There *are* a lot of us," she agreed.

"What's *she* want?" an older man called from the boat.

"Says she wants a boat ride," the first man answered.

When she turned to the sailboat, she saw that the two men had stopped whatever they were doing and were staring at her. There was no friendliness in their faces, only appraisal.

"I'd like to get a ride over to Crisfield," she said, still smiling.

The older man, in his forties she guessed, gray-haired, wearing glasses, looked her up and down. "Can you cook?" he asked.

"Cook?" Jeanne echoed, then nodded. On a twenty-mile voyage?

"Come aboard then," he said.

Jeanne hesitated.

"Are you going to Crisfield?"

"We haven't decided," the man answered, still staring at her without smiling. "If you want to come, come. We're leaving."

She slowly let her eyes drift to her left and then attentively off to her right. Lisa was sitting on the grass fifty feet away, feeding Skippy something while watching Jeanne.

"I hope to find a friend on a big trimaran in Crisfield," she explained to the man on the boat.

The two men in the cockpit whispered together urgently. The other was a round, heavyset man in his twenties with a full black beard.

"We've got work to do. Come aboard, and let's talk about it," the older man repeated. "Pull us up to the dock, Gary."

The man next to her pulled on a line, and the stern of the sailboat eased toward the dock. The bearded man came around to the transom of the sailboat to help her down.

She hesitated, half of her wanting to run, the other half knowing that this was probably her last chance to get a ride across the bay to find Frank. Then she felt the hands of the man on the dock take hold of her waist from behind.

"Ready?" he said.

"What?" she replied.

But he lifted her up and held her out toward the big man in the stern, who grabbed her under the armpits and slowly lowered her onto the deck, grinning in her face.

"Welcome aboard," he said, "I'm Carl."

"Thank you," she said, smiling at him uncertainly. She turned to the older man.

"I . . . I need a ride to Crisfield," she said again, feeling stupid.

"Come down below and have a drink," he said. "Carl, warm the engine up."

Again she wanted to run, but the children were safe and . . . she had to get them to Frank. After a five-second hesitation, she smiled again.

"Thank you," she said. She moved past him to the hatchway and then down the steps. The two men followed her.

Inside was a pleasant galley and dinette area on one side and a long settee on the other. She sat down on the settee. The older man stopped to pour out three glasses of bourbon while Carl got the key and went back up on deck to start the engine. The older man handed her a small glass.

"Here's to survival," he said.

"To survival," she replied, and they clinked glasses.

"You can come," he said to her. "We can use a female aboard the boat."

"I just want to go across the bay," she said.

"What if you don't find your friend?" the man countered. "Then what are your plans?"

"Then I guess I'm open to . . . suggestions," she replied slowly. "My husband's dead and my chil—"

"If you sail with us," the man said, "you'd be expected to cook for us, clean up, and perform . . . all the duties a woman usually . . . performs."

"If . . . if I don't find Frank . . . then that . . . will be fine."

"She'll cook for all of us," Carl said to the older man as he returned to the cabin. "And perform all her duties for all of us. Agreed?"

The man looked at Carl coldly but nodded.

"You understand?" he asked Jeanne.

"Yes," she said after a pause. "But if . . . if my friend is in Crisfield?"

"We'll leave you with your friend."

"Oh," she said, relief flooding through her. "It sounds fair enough."

"Good," the man said. "Let's see how good a cook you're going to be."

"I beg pardon?"

The man put his glass down on the dinette table and came up close to her, still not smiling. He reached down with large hands and cupped her breasts, squeezed them, then ran each thumb and index finger along until he was first squeezing and then rolling her nipples through her T-shirt and bra.

"You should be an incredible cook," he said, flushed and grinning awkwardly.

Jeanne suppressed the desire to try to free herself and simply leaned back against the cushion of the settee, her arms folded in front of her.

"Yes, I can be," she said steadily as the man let his hands fall away but kept standing in front of her and grinning. "But there's one other clause in the agreement," she went on.

"What's that?"

"You also have to bring my two children."

The older man frowned. "Children?" he said. "Who said anything about children?"

"I just did," Jeanne answered. "If they don't go, I don't go."

"We can't take *kids,*" Carl said sharply.

"Survival, my dear young woman," the older man said, stepping back and finishing his drink. "We're low on food as it is."

"Take it or leave it," Jeanne answered firmly, now hoping just to get off the boat. "Three of us or none. And a dog."

"Your kids will be safer on shore," the man said. "If they come with us, we might end up having to throw them overboard."

"Or we might have to eat them," Carl said. "We only want to eat you."

Carl laughed, and the older man again smiled awkwardly.

"Just take us to Crisfield then," Jeanne persisted.

"No, honey," the older man said. "A cook like you—"

"Then I'm leaving," said Jeanne, and she stood up and began walking toward the steps, but Carl grabbed her by the arm.

"How about it, Ned?" he said to his friend. "Shall we cast off?"

The older man looked at Jeanne, swallowed, then looked away.

"Yes," he said. "Tell Gary to untie the mooring lines, come aboard, and haul in the anchor."

"Let me go," said Jeanne, struggling.

"Take it easy, honey," Carl said. "We're not going to hurt you."

She hit him in the face with her right hand and pulled away, but he simply grabbed her with both arms in a bear hug and held her close. He grinned down at her.

With all her strength Jeanne screamed for help.

It was ten twenty when Neil and Jim brought *Vagabond* in close to the municipal dock at Point Lookout. Earlier they'd noticed many boats on the water, especially coming down the Potomac. Two vessels had been close to foundering because of the masses of people aboard, but these sights hadn't prepared them for the hysteria and chaos they now encountered at the docks.

"Bring her around into the wind, Jim," Neil ordered from the port cockpit. He'd already lowered the mizzen and genoa and was sailing now with just the main. "We're going to anchor off. Swing her! Swing her!"

As Jim finally brought the boat around into the wind thirty yards from the dock Neil rushed forward and threw out the thirty-five-pound CQR anchor.

"Drop the mainsail!" he shouted back, and Jim rushed out of the wheelhouse.

When they had the sail secured and the anchor well hooked, *Vagabond*'s stern lay only about twenty-five feet from one end of the T formed by the main dock.

"What do we do now?" Jim asked, looking with amazement at the scene before them. Already a dozen people had rushed down to their end of the dock and were shouting at them.

"Go get your .22," Neil replied coldly. While Jim went below to get his rifle Neil considered the situation. He'd already decided during the sail over that if the Foresters didn't appear immediately—*Vagabond* would be easy to spot, even in this chaos—then he would make one quick sweep around the docks and after thirty minutes get the hell back to Crisfield. Seeing the anarchy ashore made him question whether he should risk even a brief sortie off the boat. Certainly he would wait half an hour, but was there any sense in going ashore?

Jim emerged beside him with the .22.

"Is it loaded?" Neil asked.

"No."

"Load it."

While Jim loaded the .22—in full view of the crowd on the dock, Neil noted with satisfaction—Neil wondered whether he could risk sending Jim ashore. It was important to him to get more food aboard, and that he couldn't expect Jim to handle. Whether there would be any chance to buy, barter, or steal any food he didn't know, but it was worth a trip into town to find out.

"I'm going ashore," he said to Jim.

"But do you know what the Foresters all look like?" Jim asked.

"Frank showed me photographs," Neil replied quickly. "I want you to . . . I want you to shorten the anchor line twenty feet so we'll be farther away from the dock. Don't let anyone aboard."

"Aren't we going to help some of these people?" Jim asked.

"Yes," Neil answered, still staring at the crowd, whose numbers were still growing. "But not until we know how many of our own people we'll be sailing with."

"Okay," said Jim. "But what do I do if someone tries to board us? I can't shoot them."

"No, I guess not," he said after a pause. "Try to keep them off with bluff. If you can't, I'll be back and we'll take it from there."

Neil climbed down into the dinghy and had Jim pay out the line so he would be blown slowly down onto the dock by the wind. When he was less than ten feet away, he stood up in the dinghy and shouted for silence from the crowd.

"I'm coming ashore," he announced loudly. "In half an hour we're sailing across the bay to Crisfield. At that time we'll take passengers who want to get to Crisfield. Until then you all wait on the dock. Do you understand?"

A few nodded eagerly as if they were anxious to please; others started shouting. Neil ignored them all, signaled to Jim to pay out ten more feet of line, and soon pulled himself up onto the dock. Steadfastly ignoring the people pressing in around him, he watched Jim pull the empty dinghy back toward *Vagabond*. Then he began pushing his way through the crowd to get to land. He looked closely at the clusters of refugees along the docks, searching for the Foresters, hoping that they had seen *Vagabond* sail in and would be here

on the dock. But they weren't. If they were alive and in Point Lookout, they would have to be at another marina or else somewhere away
from the waterfront for some reason. He couldn't imagine what such
a reason might be.

When he reached the marina office, he went in and questioned a
harried and frightened teenager, the only one there, who knew nothing about anyone looking for a trimaran. Outside, Neil looked toward
the two marinas to the north but decided he'd go into town first to
check there and see if he could buy some supplies.

He had started toward the street, automatically looking at everyone
in sight, when he saw a figure running along the street shouting for
help, a girl, a young girl. Trying to catch what she was screaming,
Neil abruptly realized that she looked something like the picture he'd
seen of Lisa. She ran past him and turned into the entrance of the
municipal marina, still running and now moving away from him.

"Lisa!" he shouted.

The girl stopped and looked around. It *must* be her.

"Lisa Forester!" he shouted and ran over to her.

"Who . . . who are you?" she asked.

"Neil Loken, Frank Stoor's captain," he answered quickly. "I've
come—"

"Come quick!" Lisa cried. "I think they're kidnaping my mother!"

"What!?"

"Some men took my mother on their boat, and I heard her scream
and they're leaving!"

"Show me," said Neil.

Lisa began running back along the street with Neil running beside
her.

"There!" she shouted, without slowing her pace, and she pointed
at a long, low yawl that was slipping away from a nearby dock.
"She's on that boat."

"You're sure?" Neil asked, looking into the young stranger's eyes.

"Yes! Yes! Please save her!"

Neil ran down the embankment and out onto the dock, and in one
motion dove into the water. A part of him felt uncertain and ridiculous, but it was no time for second thoughts. Where was Lisa's father?

As he surfaced after his first six strokes he realized that the yawl was easing up over its anchor and he was gaining on it quickly. There was one man in the cockpit and another handling the anchor line. They didn't seem to notice him.

In another twenty strokes he was even with the vessel's raked stern and, grabbing a cleat, he hauled himself up over the transom and onto the afterdeck. When he stood up, the man in the cockpit, a man in his forties, caught sight of him.

"Who the hell are you?" he asked.

Neil walked forward, stepped down into the cockpit, smiled at the man, and walked down into the cabin. A big bearded man was standing in the galleyway with his back to Neil, and beyond him was a woman, barely visible past the man's bulk. Carl swung around when he heard Neil, and the two men confronted each other.

"Excuse me," Neil said and walked past Carl. The woman, crouching at the far end of the cabin, had a butcher knife in her hand. It was Jeanne Forester. He was startled by the sudden impact of her tensed animal beauty, accentuated by her gleaming wide dark eyes and the long black hair falling wildly across one side of her face.

"Hey, Ned!" Carl shouted up to the cockpit. "Who is this guy?"

"Hand me up the gun!" Ned shouted back.

Neil had stopped three feet from Jeanne. What a beautiful woman, he was still thinking irrelevantly.

"Can you swim?" he asked her softly.

"What?" she said back. "Who are you?"

As Neil started forward again she raised the knife, but he picked her up in his arms. She brought the knife down and held its point against his chest and stared at him. With her eyes only inches from his and the knifepoint pricking his skin, Neil felt a strong sexual surge pass through him.

"Can you swim?" he asked her softly.

"Yes," she answered, still holding the knife tight against his chest, her eyes searching his.

Neil swung around and began to leave just as Carl handed a gun up to Ned in the cockpit. Neil again brushed past Carl, climbed the stairs, went out into the cockpit, walked up to and past the man with the gun, and in one unbroken motion threw Jeanne out into the water. She landed with an undignified splash, but began immediately swimming for shore.

"What the hell?" the older man said, rushing up beside Neil and looking down at Jeanne.

Neil hit him a crushing blow to the side of the head that sent him sprawling against the cockpit seat, the gun clattering to the deck. Neil picked it up and glanced back. The big bearded man had been about to spring forward but stood frozen now in a crouch. Neil stuffed the gun firmly into his belt and dove overboard.

He swam the first thirty feet underwater, and when he surfaced, he looked back to see if the men on the yawl had any other weapons, but they had already resumed their preparations to put to sea. Neil began swimming after Jeanne.

He came up to her where she was resting with her two slender hands grasping the edge of a small boat dock at Kelly's, her head bowed, her wet black hair clinging in strands down her back. When she turned to him, she looked puzzled.

"Are you Neil Loken?" she asked.

"Yes, I—"

"Are you really Neil?" she persisted, suddenly smiling and crying all at once. "Thank God. Is Frank here? The boat? I couldn't find it. We waited and waited. I was trying to get—"

"It's okay," he interrupted, reaching out with his free hand and touching her shoulder. "Let me help you up onto the dock."

"At first I thought you were another member of their crew," she went on, still crying and laughing at the same time. "When you asked, 'Can you swim?' I thought . . ." She shook her head. "How did you find me?" she asked next, pulling her head back and smiling up at him, tears mingling with the salt water on her face.

"Lisa found me," Neil answered.

"Oh, my God, where are Lisa and Skip?"

When Neil pointed to Lisa, who was standing on the dock watching them, she began trying to pull herself up onto the edge of the dock. Neil spread his right hand across her buttocks and lifted her up; she sprawled forward onto the dock. With a quick surge he pulled himself up beside her.

"Let's get to *Vagabond*," he said, helping her up. They ran up the gangway to the main dock, where Lisa and her mother hugged each other.

"Where's Skippy?" Jeanne asked as they all rushed on.

"Still on the grass," Lisa said happily, pointing.

While Neil picked Skippy up into his arms, Lisa and Jeanne grabbed their bags. Together they hurried back along the street to the town dock, Neil already beginning to worry about *Vagabond*.

As he surveyed the end of the dock Neil was surprised to see that the crowd had evaporated, but just as he was feeling reassured he saw trouble: seven or eight people had gotten aboard *Vagabond*, which had somehow drifted back to the dock. The stern of its starboard hull was banging periodically against a piling.

Neil felt a flush of anger at Jim. When he went to board *Vagabond*, he saw a man in a bright pink shirt and green pants standing on the hull and brandishing a pistol.

"No more on board," the young man said to Neil.

Feeling an incongruous rush of bitter mirth, Neil laughed. The man frowned, made uneasy both by the laughter and by the gun in Neil's belt.

"If you plan to try to sail this boat," Neil said, "you'd better let me aboard."

"Neil!" he heard Jim shout and saw him standing in the side cockpit behind the man with the pistol.

"Okay," the man said. "You can come aboard. But you'll have to give me that gun."

"Like hell I will," Neil replied.

"He's the captain," Jim said. "No one can sail us out of here except him."

The man stared at Neil and then shrugged.

Neil stepped down and then helped Jeanne, Lisa, and Skip down after him. He could feel his body tense at the invasion of his boat and remained on deck for the moment to steady himself. Lisa had rushed up to Jim and buried her head against his chest, clinging to him. Neil noticed a woman breast-feeding her child in the side cockpit, three suitcases scattered around her feet. As he went past Jim and Lisa into the wheelhouse he saw two men and a woman standing on one side looking nervously at a thickset man sitting opposite them. In the farther cockpit someone was sprawled on the deck with a woman bent over him weeping. Neil turned to Jim, who had followed him into the wheelhouse.

"How many people have guns?" he asked.

"Just that young guy guarding the starboard hull and *him*," Jim replied, nodding toward the man who was sitting on the settee at the rear of the wheelhouse, one leg crossed over the other, dressed in a brown business suit, a large .45 and Jim's .22 cradled in his lap. The man met Neil's gaze with alert coldness.

"What happened?" Neil asked.

"The wind shifted a little," said Jim earnestly. "And *Vagabond* swung around closer to the docks. When I went forward to shorten up the anchor, a whole mass of people got aboard. The two guys with guns herded half the crowd back up onto the docks and . . . shot the man in the side cockpit when he refused to get off."

Jeanne had passed them and was kneeling now beside the weeping woman. Lisa stayed with Skippy, listening. Neil turned to the man with the .45. In his mid-thirties, thickset, with dark, receding hair, he stared back at Neil with quiet confidence.

"We're sailing over to Crisfield to pick up a friend," he announced. The man simply nodded. "I don't appreciate people forcing themselves onto my boat at gunpoint," Neil added coldly.

"These are tough times, buddy," the man said softly. "And I didn't notice you or your friend selling tickets."

"You had to shoot someone?" Neil asked.

"There were thirty people on board," the man replied quietly. "Your young friend said this boat couldn't sail out of here with that much weight. Jerry and I kicked twenty of them off. A guy pulled a knife on Jerry, and Jerry shot him. It's only a shoulder wound, and I already patched it up. Nothing serious."

"I'd like our .22 back," Neil said quietly.

The man looked down at his lap, as if surprised to find Jim's rifle lying there.

"Sure," he said after a pause. "Just borrowed it for a minute." He handed it to Neil.

"Lisa," said Neil, turning to the young girl, "get Skippy and your mother down into the port cabin. Jim, get the sails back up."

He turned back to the man with the .45.

"Do you know much about sailing?" he asked him.

"Not much," he said.

"How about your friend, Jerry?"

"He thinks he's standing on the front of the boat."

Neil glanced at the pink-shirted Jerry, who stood nervously at the stern of the port hull, watching the dock.

"All right," said Neil. "The motor's out, so I'll trust you're not stupid enough to get rid of Jim and me, since we're the only ones who can sail it. I'd appreciate it, however, if you'd both put your guns away."

"Sure," said the man with a slight smile. "You're the captain."

Jim had raised the two forward sails, and as Neil headed there to help him with the anchor Jeanne appeared from below.

"Where's Frank?" she asked.

"We're meeting him in Crisfield."

"And then?"

"Out to sea," he replied, and as he moved forward he frowned at how simple those three words made it sound. He doubted they'd ever see Frank again, and their chances of getting past Norfolk to the ocean in one piece were probably small. He'd be happy if they made it to Crisfield without the wind dying or one of the outlaws shooting someone. But one step at a time. Jim came aft after making fast the main halyard.

"Take the wheel, Jim," he said, "and put her on the port tack. I'll handle the anchor."

"I couldn't stop them," Jim burst out unexpectedly. "The guy in the wheelhouse said he'd shoot me."

Neil nodded and thought of the man in the wheelhouse.

"He would have," Neil said. "Now go."

In five minutes *Vagabond* was laboring across the bay at six knots in a nice breeze. Neil found himself looking for Jeanne, but the wheelhouse remained empty except for Jim and the cold-eyed Buddha with the gun. With *Vagabond* moving again Neil felt almost content, even strangely happy. Then, looking aft, he saw that the cloud mass from Washington was still spreading; the sky directly above them was no longer blue. He watched it for a moment, feeling both angry and afraid, then went back to work.

Although the traffic between Crisfield and Salisbury had been thin, at the airport the parking lot was overflowing. There were three Maryland State Police cars and eight or nine policemen, but they seemed unclear about what they were supposed to be doing.

Inside the drab terminal, people were strangely quiet. The room was crowded, but what little movement there was, was slowed down, as if everyone were moving through molasses.

As Frank walked directly toward the door marked Manager's Office he had to push his way through two long lines that stretched far out into the room from the ticket counter.

"I want to buy or charter a plane," he said to the small, spare man seated at a desk who had invited him in when he knocked.

After looking at Frank for a moment, the man frowned down at the papers he'd been going through.

"All the regular charter planes are filled," he said. "There are also twenty or thirty private planes operating out of this airport, and a few are unofficially selling seats to passengers. The going rate is five thousand dollars a seat."

"Any of them going to New York?" Frank asked eagerly.

"None going north," the manager replied. "Most are going to the Bahamas or the West Indies. One or two of the bigger ones to South America."

"Then I want to buy a plane and hire a pilot."

"No one will fly you to New York."

"Money talks," said Frank.

"Not very loud as far as heading north is concerned." The manager squinted up at Frank. "May I ask why you're so hot to get to what's left of New York?" he asked.

"Family."

"Ahhh," the manager said and shook his head. "Well, I can't help you. The private planes are housed in C and D Hangars at the west end of the field. If someone wants to sell a plane, that's where they'd be."

When Frank got to Hangar C, he came upon a flurry of activity: two small planes being worked on, one being pushed out of the hangar, and three or four clusters of people talking. Frank began asking people who might sell him a plane to fly north.

"There's only one guy here I know of who said he'd let his plane go north if the money was right," one man told him, "and that's Tommy Trainer over in Hangar D."

"How'll I find him?" Frank asked.

"Little guy. Wears a natty white suit," the man answered. "He owns the two-engine Beechcraft over in the back corner. But, buddy, you don't think you're going to make it north and back through what's happening up there, do you?"

Frank wheeled and headed off toward Hangar D. Tommy Trainer was a flashily dressed little man with dark, slicked-down hair and an absurdly large cigar. He was checking his Beechcraft with a mechanic when Frank found him. After listening to Frank explain what he wanted to do, the little man just continued to stare at him and chewed lightly on his unlit cigar.

"Well, suh," he said with the dignified drawl of a southern gentleman, completely at variance with his bookmaker's appearance. "Ah'd like to help you, I really would. But I believe the general opinion is that it's dangerous traveling north these days. I believe there's just a bit of risk involved. Wouldn't you agree, suh?"

"A lot of risk," Frank said. "I'll pay accordingly."

"That's right generous of you, suh, and I appreciate it. I'll tell you what," he continued in his southern drawl, "I can't charter you my plane 'cause the *in*surance doesn't cover it, you know, but I'll sell you the plane. Let's see. One hundred thousand dollars. How does that sound, suh?"

"What about a pilot?"

"I believe I might be able to obtain you a pilot for . . . yes, for another twenty."

Frank, who sometimes quibbled over the price of a twenty-five cent sinker, felt a flash of anger. The beat-up plane couldn't be worth more than twenty-five thousand dollars, and the pilot would be doing at most a half-day's work.

"It's a deal," he said.

"In cash, gold, or silver," said Tommy Trainer.

Frank frowned, his forward momentum checked. He looked at Tommy Trainer. Where the hell could he get the money?

"Where's the nearest bank?" Frank finally asked.

"Bank!" Tommy Trainer exclaimed. "It's a little late for banks, I'm afraid."

Frank stared at him uncertainly.

"I'll be back," he said.

On the short drive from the airport into Salisbury, Frank realized that it wasn't going to work. He needed a plane this instant, and the banking system, even at the best of times, was not used to producing a hundred and twenty thousand dollars in an instant. In these times . . .

The situation turned out to be worse than he had imagined. Most banks hadn't even opened. The two that had were mobbed, with long lines outside their doors. And he realized, of course, that there was no phone or teletype contact with either of his New York City banks nor his bank in Oyster Bay.

"They're not doing any banking business with anybody except their regular customers," a man told Frank. "I doubt that there's a single 'bank in the country today that doesn't have the same policy."

Defeated, Frank returned to his car and sat slumped in shock. He might be able to steal the plane, he thought, pay for it later. But he couldn't fly it.

He supposed he could kidnap a pilot. . . . But gradually he realized that there was no way. He couldn't get there by car. He couldn't fly. He was stuck.

As he slowly drove back to Crisfield he felt disoriented by the succeeding shocks of the day. All his life he had been a doer, a man who faced problems squarely and set about solving them. His success in the world of New York City real estate was based partly on this ability to deal with problems as soon as they arose, to make fast decisions, and to get the job done. It also helped that he wasn't afraid of risks. He enjoyed taking risks.

He had wanted to treat the unthinkable catastrophe of nuclear war as he would an emergency cash-flow problem, for the *challenge* of the war stimulated him, the logistical challenge of rescuing his wife, retrieving his financial position, surviving—all these got his adrenaline flowing, had him acting decisively, rationally, quickly.

But the experiences he'd had in his three hours in Salisbury represented for him the psychological equivalent of being bombed. He had begun to realize that all of his paper wealth—his stocks, bonds, mutual funds, Treasury certificates—were probably worthless. And the tangible assets he owned—the apartment houses in New York City, his home in Oyster Bay, the shopping center in Englewood—had all, with the hopeful exception of his house in Oyster Bay, been destroyed. But worse, he realized that the "problems" and "challenges" presented by the holocaust were not something that could be dealt with. He couldn't buy a plane, or a car, or even, maybe, a tank of gasoline. He couldn't even *telephone* anyone. He was almost helpless. Suddenly, overnight, he was an unemployed pauper.

But a live pauper. As he drove back toward Crisfield with the car radio tuned to the appalling news—cities with which all communication had been lost, *countries* with which all communication had been lost—a large part of him began to fear for his life and wanted to scurry for the nearest hole. The numbing, incomprehensible, dreamlike list of American cities and defense installations that had been struck by nuclear missiles or bombs dazed him. He heard the Secretary of Defense urging people to stick to their jobs if their jobs were important, to report for service if they weren't. In one sentence the secretary warned against needless panic and in another advised people to evacuate "contaminated" areas. (He didn't mention any by name.) Frank learned that the United States had bombed Cuba, that Europe was being devastated, London wiped out, Moscow, Leningrad, numerous other unpronounceable Russian cities, Russian forces in Iraq had been attacked. China and Japan had been hit. Several countries in South America and Africa had loudly proclaimed their neutrality.

His fear for himself began to grow. He knew that part of his frantic activity to get up north to his wife was based on the simple fact that it was the expected thing to do. It was a man's job to protect his wife. The thought of her there in their house, helpless, confused, worried about Jimmy, worried about him, too, huddled together with Susan—that thought made him sad, made him feel needed, made him want to find a way north. But the only thing left now was *Vagabond*. He was frightened: he pressed his foot down on the accelerator. All hope of salvation lay with *Vagabond*.

With the wind shifting further to the north, *Vagabond* had one long tack across the bay to Crisfield. Despite the extra ton of weight from the new passengers and their luggage, she plugged along at six or seven knots until she had gotten within two miles of the town and the wind fell. Then her speed dropped to two knots and she began to wallow and crawl. Neil hailed a small cruiser and bribed its owner to tow them the last two miles to the dock.

The trip was uneventful. Although thin wisps of the dark cloud mass over Washington seemed to have floated almost directly overhead, there was no obvious sign of radioactive fallout. The ten passengers displayed a kind of stunned obedience that made the boat handling easy. Jeanne had spent the first hour and a half below, but with Skippy napping and Lisa helping Jim at the helm, she came up and stood beside Neil in the port cockpit.

He was again aware of her as a woman, her bare brown legs and arms set off by the white shorts and shirt. Her long hair was brushed now and tied up on top of her head. She stared forward for a while without speaking.

"Do you think Frank will be there?" she finally asked.

"There's no way of knowing," he answered. "We'll just have to see."

"And then what?"

"I suppose that will be mostly up to Frank," he said after a pause.

"We should leave," she said with unexpected force. "Get out of the country."

He glanced at her. She seemed more angry than fearful.

"I agree," he said, "but I'm afraid Frank doesn't."

"I just listened to a radio down in the cabin," she went on. "The whole world is collapsing."

Neil felt a tremor of fear, partly because of what she said and partly because of her intensity.

"I imagine it is."

"And we've done it," she continued, staring forward again. "Our country and Russia are destroying the world."

Neil was aware that two of the women sitting in the wheelhouse were looking at her uneasily.

"If we live through this madness, we'll have to create a new world," she said, her eyes seeming to make a personal appeal to Neil. "We'll have to create a family, support each other, put an end to the selfish distinctions that led us to this horror." She looked at him for confirmation.

Neil felt an unaccountable heaviness. He supposed it was because he didn't think the species that had killed a hundred million of its own kind in one day was likely to be too great on its next go-round. If there was a next go-round.

"First we have to survive," he replied.

"Yes," she said, seeming to relent somewhat. "But, my God, how coldhearted this war is making us survivors. I think you're the only friendly face I've seen all day."

"Cornered and fleeing animals aren't nice," Neil said. She nodded and frowned.

"Back before you rescued me, I could have killed someone with that butcher knife," she said softly, looking quite puzzled and a little saddened by the knowledge. "How depressing that is."

Neil didn't comment. Two passengers were leaning out over the combing in the port cockpit, and he wondered why until he saw that one of them was being seasick.

"And that way madness lies," Jeanne went on, then paused and looked up at him. "I'm glad I spared you," she said. Suddenly and unexpectedly she was smiling up at him.

"I am too," he replied, smiling back.

"My personal Captain Luck," she said.

"How so?" he asked, puzzled.

"You said that before we can create a new world we have to find the luck to survive," she said, strangely gay all of a sudden. "I guess I found you." She paused. "Although I hope your style isn't always to throw me overboard."

After the horror of Point Lookout, Crisfield was as quiet and relaxed as a picturesque fishing village should be. There were no mobs and few boats. Neil supposed that survivors from the Philadelphia area had more escape routes open to them than those who were south and east of Washington and Baltimore.

After *Vagabond* was tied up at the dock in front of a large green fishing trawler named the *Lucky Emerald*, he helped his passengers ashore. Most were bewildered; it seemed to Neil that if someone had offered them a boat ride back to Point Lookout many of them would have crowded aboard. As they were leaving, Jeanne came up beside him where he stood overseeing the exodus.

"Can't we invite some of them to stay with us?" she asked him.

"That's Frank's decision," he replied, feeling like something of a liar. "When he comes, we can reconsider it."

"They have no place to go."

"And we have nothing to feed them with," Neil explained.

"I was in their place four hours ago," she said, looking away.

"I know," he said gently, frowning. "But we can't save everybody. We'll be lucky if we can save ourselves."

"We should try to save as many as we can," she said.

"We haven't even enough food to last ourselves more than two or three days," he went on. "That's our job now: to try to get some supplies aboard."

"I'd like to invite that woman with the baby," Jeanne persisted.

Neil looked at the retreating passengers.

"All right, Jeanne," he answered. "But explain to her about the food situation."

While Jeanne hurried forward to overtake the nursing mother Neil turned to speak to Jim; as he did he saw that the man with the .45 was still sitting on the settee and beside him the much younger man with the pink shirt and green pants. Neil went over to them.

"What are your plans?" he asked the older man.

"What are yours?"

"We wait here until ten to pick up the owner, then we're probably heading out the bay into the Atlantic."

"All right."

"All right what?"

"We'd like to come along."

Neil studied the man. His business suit seemed somehow inappropriate, fraudulent. His round unshaven face never seemed to lose its placid expression. The young man beside him looked morose.

"Who are you?" Neil asked.

"Conrad Macklin," he replied. "This is my friend Jerry."

"What do you do?"

The man shrugged. "I used to be a Marine," he said. "Paramedic.. After Vietnam, I flew planes, freelancing. Now . . . I sail a trimaran."

"We don't have much food," Neil said.

Macklin shrugged again.

"We're going shopping," Neil said, starting to feel irritated. "Could you two contribute some cash to the cause?"

Macklin took out his billfold, removed two bills, and handed them to Neil. They were hundreds.

"Jim," said Neil, turning away. "I want you and Jeanne to go into town to the nearest supermarket and buy everything you can carry. I'll give you three hundred dollars and don't hesitate to pay double for anything you can get. Triple if you have to."

Jeanne reappeared in the wheelhouse alone.

"What happened?" Neil asked.

"She'd hooked up with a man and he had a car," she answered, apparently disappointed that her offer had been rejected.

Neil wrote out a brief list of basics for Jeanne and Jim and sent them off. Skippy had fallen asleep during the crossing, so Neil had

Lisa begin making an inventory of the supplies already on hand. Although uneasy about the presence of Macklin and his friend, he decided Macklin already had what he wanted—namely a boat to escape in—so now there should be nothing to worry about.

He took a few minutes to get Lisa started on the inventory and was impressed by how quickly she worked; then he went back up into the wheelhouse.

"I've got an important job I'd like you to do for us," he said to Macklin.

"Yes?"

"The boat's got a bent propeller shaft and we can't get it out," Neil explained. "We need a slide-hammer puller—it's a tool. I want you to try the boatyard over there and see if you can rent, buy, or borrow one. How about it?"

"Why don't you go?" Macklin asked.

Neil met the man's cold gaze with equal coldness.

"You'll help when I ask you to help or you're not sailing with us," he said, feeling absurdly for an instant as if he were in some western and both he and Macklin were about to go for their guns.

Macklin in fact looked down at the pistol in his lap and caressed the barrel with his left hand.

"That sounds reasonable," Macklin said and, standing up, put the gun into a shoulder holster beneath his suit jacket. He smiled for the first time. "Relax, captain," he went on. "I'm just out to save my ass like the rest of you."

"A slide-hammer puller," Neil repeated coldly.

"Got it," Macklin said and ambled off the boat.

"And I want you," Neil said to the man named Jerry, "to go along the docks and see if there's an outlet we can get water from." The man—he seemed to be only a couple of years older than Jim— nodded and went off.

The other thing is fishing gear, Neil thought, and his mind immediately returned to the task of preparing the boat for a long survival voyage. It would help if they had extra nylon line and metal lures, another rod maybe too. Those might actually be easier to pick up than food. He looked restlessly ashore: Jeanne and Jim were already returning, empty-handed. The two of them jumped down onto the side deck and came over to him.

"There was a line forty yards long outside the supermarket," Jeanne explained. "And then the manager came out, counted off about twenty people, and told the rest of us to go home."

"Every other grocery store was closed," Jim added. "Half of them were boarded up and the others had an armed guard."

Neil simply nodded.

"Give me the money, Jeanne," he said. As Jeanne fished in her pocket he said to Jim, "We need to get water aboard. All we can get. I sent that guy Jerry to locate an open tap. Fill the tank and all the plastic jugs."

"How about that leaky ten-gallon container?" Jim asked.

"That too," Neil replied. "I sent Macklin—that's the one with the .45—after the puller. I'm going to take a shot at getting us some supplies. Stay here, get your .22 out again, and don't let anyone aboard except Macklin. When he's back, have him stand guard."

"You trust him?" Jim asked.

"I trust him to keep unnecessary people off the boat," Neil explained.

"Okay."

Neil hesitated, gauging Jim's character.

"This time . . ." he began, as Jim looked at him attentively, "if you feel you have to shoot . . . shoot."

"Macklin?" asked Jim.

"Anybody," Neil replied.

The situation in Crisfield was just as Jeanne and Jim had described it. Fortunately the local hardware store was open.

"Cash only," a clerk announced as he entered. "All prices triple what's marked."

Neil went to the fishing gear section and quickly picked out three lures, two wire leaders, and 500 feet of 30-pound test line. As he walked over to the cashier he grabbed two kerosene lanterns. The manager said he didn't sell kerosene, but Neil bought the lamps anyway.

Back out on the main street he considered his tactics. He'd hidden his gun under a loose-fitting jacket and the bag of supplies he was carrying. He'd become aware throughout the day of a feeling he hadn't had for a long time: that he was ready and able to kill, that he had killed in the past, and that this readiness gave him a power and confidence in this situation that was essential for survival. He felt he could sense when others lacked that readiness—as with the gray-haired man on the yawl who had kidnaped Jeanne—and when they *did* have it, as Macklin did.

This feeling of power had always bothered him, ever since he'd first sensed it in Vietnam more than a decade ago, but he knew that now it was one of his chief assets.

Neil passed a closed grocery store, behind the door of which sat a fat man with a shotgun across his knees. Neil felt it would be easy enough to take such a store, but it didn't feel right, and he walked on. Ahead he saw a line of about twelve people outside a large Foodtown store. He went around to the back. The first door he came to was locked but at the other end of the building he saw another. A man in a white apron was leaving with an armload of boxes. When Neil followed him back to the door, he turned around.

"You can't come in this way," the young man said.

Neil pulled out a hundred-dollar bill and held it out to him.

"I'd like to go in and do a little shopping for my family," he said casually.

The boy squinted at the bill, grimaced, and shook his head. "I just can't do it," he said. "The manager would know."

Neil let the bill flutter to the ground and pulled out his gun.

"Tell the manager I pulled a gun on you but that I promised to pay double for all my food."

Neil pushed past him, slipped the gun back under his belt, and went in the back of the supermarket.

Inside was frenzied order: it was like a normal supermarket, except that everyone was moving twice as fast as usual and their carts were twice as full. The shelves were three-quarters empty. The room was unlit: the usual harsh glitter of a supermarket was lacking. Neil looked back at the aproned clerk—whom he noticed pocketing something, presumably the hundred—and patted his waist where the gun was. The boy smirked uneasily.

Neil took an empty metal cart, put in the bag of fishing gear, and entered the fray. He knew he'd have to take what he could get, which wasn't much. He found six cans of pears in syrup and eight cans of mixed fruit: that was all that was left in the canned fruit section.

In the dried fruit section he was luckier. Since dried fruit was ridiculously expensive and not all that essential except to a starving man,
there was a lot left. Neil took it all. There were still a few boxes of
dried noodles and spaghetti, and he threw those in, followed by a
large bag of potatoes. Frozen and refrigerated foods were mostly gone,
which reminded him that Crisfield had no electricity. He wondered
whether the lights were out in the rest of the world as well. There
were some tinned crackers left and he grabbed them, but all the canned
meats were gone.

Forty minutes later, his cart overflowing, Neil headed again for the
back door. There was a man standing beside it with a rifle, its butt
resting awkwardly on the floor. Neil took out all of the rest of his
money, a hundred and sixty dollars, and held it out to him.

"To save time I'd like to leave by the back way," he said. "Here's
what I owe, plus tip."

"What's the trouble, Calvin?" a voice called out behind him.

"He wants to leave by the back way," said Calvin.

"Here's more than enough money to cover my purchases," said
Neil.

"How much money you got?"

"A hundred and sixty dollars," Neil said, handing it to him.

"Shit, mister," the manager said, taking the money. "This don't
cover much more than half what you've got there. Our prices are
triple."

"Then I'll go to my boat and bring back more money."

"You do that."

Neil pulled out his gun and pointed it at the belly of the man with
the rifle.

"I'll take my food with me now though," Neil said. *"Won't I?"*
he asked the manager sharply.

"Let him go," the manager said, backing away.

And Neil left.

As he pushed the cart across the bumpy back lot of the supermarket he felt tremendous relief. The food situation had been his greatest
worry. Now, although what he'd bought normally wouldn't last six
people more than a week at the most, rationed it might go a month.
He'd even bought a large container of dog food as a compact, non-
perishable source of protein.

He picked up the pace when he hit the smoother sidewalk of the main street. It was almost five o'clock, and if Macklin had located the puller, he could start work on the propeller shaft before Frank got back. If Frank got back.

When he came around the corner and made for the dock, Neil stopped. He couldn't believe what he was seeing. Ahead of him was the fishing trawler *Lucky Emerald*, and in front of it was nothing. *Vagabond* was gone.

Abandoning the shopping cart in the marina parking lot, Neil ran to the dock, his eyes searching the water for the trimaran. It wasn't in sight. Even while the dread in his stomach told him the boat had been pirated he tried to think of why else it might have been moved. Frank had returned and taken it to a boatyard . . . But they would have left somone to tell him, and as he let his eyes search up and down the docks, he saw no sign of either *Vagabond* or any of its passengers.

He needed a boat he could use to give chase. But chase where?

"Ahoy, *Lucky Emerald*!" he shouted at the trawler. A big red-faced man came to the door of the deckhouse and looked down.

"What happened to the trimaran?" he shouted up to him.

The man looked at the spot where *Vagabond* had been, then out into the bay.

"Sailed out of here close to an hour ago," he said.

"Was there any trouble aboard?"

"Not that I saw."

"Where was she heading?"

The man stroked his chin and scowled.

"Southwest," he said. "Out the main channel."

"Have you got a small boat I can borrow to give chase?" Neil asked. "My boat's been stolen."

The man shook his head.

Neil went back to his food cart and wheeled it up to the dock next to the *Lucky Emerald*.

"Keep an eye on this for me," he shouted and went to find a boat. Macklin had hijacked *Vagabond*, and Neil raged at his own stupidity. He'd assumed Macklin wasn't a sailor and wouldn't try anything with a crippled sailboat, but if he had gotten hold of a puller, he may have felt he should take *Vagabond* while the taking was good. Poor Jim.

Over the next forty minutes Neil went down the docks and around to two marinas trying to buy, borrow, or steal a small boat. No one would help him. Twice he was turned away at gunpoint. After he'd tried the last dock in the village, he turned back in a fury. He stopped a young man who was walking along carrying a fuel tank and asked him for help but got another "Sorry, fellow." On the street again, a police car came toward him with its siren wailing, and Neil tried to wave it down. It whizzed past.

At the dock where *Vagabond* had been tied up he found Frank standing with his hands in his pockets staring dull-eyed out at the water.

"Frank!" he called.

"Where are you hiding my boat?" Frank asked with a puzzled frown as Neil came up to him.

"She's gone, Frank," he answered. "Stolen. Close to two hours ago."

Frank's already tired face looked stunned.

"Wh-what?"

"Two men, I think," he went on. "And as far as I know Jim and Jeanne Forester and her children are still aboard."

"Stolen?" Frank repeated, looking even more bewildered. He walked past Neil to the edge of the dock to look out the channel toward the bay. Several gulls were circling behind a small runabout, but there was no sign of *Vagabond*.

"We've got to get a fast boat and catch *Vagabond* before she gets too far down the bay," Neil said to him.

Frank looked at Neil with glazed eyes and didn't reply. He hadn't shaved, and he looked haggard. He turned back toward the water.

"If *Vagabond* gets too far away, there's no hope for any of us," Neil persisted. "I can't get through to the Coast Guard by phone.

We've probably got to get her back ourselves. In another few hours everything will be lost.''

Neil saw that Frank was in shock, and he felt a similar sense of helplessness beginning to flood through his own body. A small fishing smack putted by along the channel, and the little old man standing stiffly at the wheel looked at Neil and smiled and winked. Still preoccupied, Neil didn't register anything at first and then came alive.

"Hey! Captain! Ahoy, there!'' he shouted, and ran up to the water's edge.

The old man was facing forward again, and Neil thought he must not have heard. He felt his shoulders slump, but the fishing smack abruptly swung to the left, away from them, and kept circling until it was heading back toward the dock. As Neil watched and Frank came up beside him, the boat, *Lucy Mae*, angled into the dock.

"That boat's too slow,'' Frank said.

"Not with this light wind and rising tide,'' Neil answered, and they watched as *Lucy Mae* coasted forward, banging first one piling and then the next, and stopping inches short of the *Lucky Emerald* only after the old fisherman had snubbed a line around a piling.

"Pretty neat, huh?'' the old man on *Lucy Mae* shouted with a big grin. "Ain't got no reverse. Makes docking a challenge. Help you, cap?''

"Yes,'' Neil said quickly. "Pirates stole our trimaran about two hours ago and kidnaped four of our people—a woman, two children.''

"You own that big three-engine spaceship?'' the old man interrupted.

"Yes.''

"Saw her sailing out of here about four thirty,''' the old man said. "Thought I'd got trapped in a *Star Wars* movie. Nice ship though, if you don't mind looking like you just got in from Mars. When I—''

"Our boat was stolen,'' Neil interjected. "We'd like your help.''

"You mean chase the pirates?'' the old man asked, scowling.

"Just help us find them,'' Neil said. "That's all.''

"I'll pay you five thousand dollars,'' Frank offered.

"These fellas got guns?'' the old man asked, squinting up at Neil.

"Yes, but . . .''

"And you want me to take you in the *Lucy Mae* and go poking around after them?"

"Yes," said Neil. "But we—"

"Well, git aboard," the old man said. "Sun's gonna be settin' pretty soon and I don't see so good at night." With a flip of his wrist he released the line from the piling and went back into the deck-house. Frank hung back doubtfully on the dock, but Neil rushed off to get the groceries.

When Neil had maneuvered the cart up to the edge of the dock, he carefully lowered it down to Frank, who was standing in *Lucy Mae*'s cockpit. Frank couldn't quite handle all the weight, and the cart smashed down onto the deck and tipped over, the groceries spilling out like a load of dead fish. Neil leapt aboard.

"Let's go, cap," he said.

"Push out my bow there, sonny," the old fisherman said to Frank, "so my bowsprit don't go and goose *Lucky Emerald*. Cap'n Rivers is partic'lar who gooses her."

Frank pushed out the bow, the old man shoved the gear into forward, and the old smack putted noisily forward, swinging around to head out toward the bay.

"I don't have the five thousand dollars, uh, ready to hand," Frank said into the ear of the old man, Captain Olly, almost having to shout over the noise of the engine.

"I don't want no money, cap," Olly said. "I ain't had a chance to get involved with pirates since . . . back in '74 I think it was. . . ."

He turned *Lucy Mae* a little to starboard to follow the channel to the open bay. "And then the pirate was me." Neil began picking up the rolling cans and other groceries and righting the cart.

"What you fellas think of this *war*?" Olly remarked to Frank, who stared back at him dumbly.

"I sort of like it," the old man said. "Hell, I was planning to die this year anyway, what with depression and gall bladders and all, but this here war makes everything interesting again."

"My wife may have been killed in this interesting war," Frank shouted back angrily.

"Well, I figure there was four or five million other wives killed today,'' the old man countered. "Probably two or three of mine. Still, nothing beats being alive now, does it?''

Frank looked at the grinning, grotesque face in stunned silence.

"You fellas got any idea where these pirates are headed?'' he asked amiably.

"No,'' Neil replied sharply. "But we've got to assume they're heading south.'' Olly nodded.

"How fast will this thing go?'' Neil shouted. Frank was standing off to the right, scanning the horizon for a glimpse of *Vagabond*. There was a big motor yacht anchored off to port and several runabouts within sight, but no *Vagabond*.

"She'll do eight knots in the morning,'' the old man shouted back, "but in the late afternoon she gets a little pooped.''

"How much fuel?''

"Ten hours' worth. With you big fellas aboard maybe only eight.''

As they churned out the channel from Crisfield, there was a large low island to their left that blocked their view to the south, and Neil strained impatiently for them to get past it.

"Do you have any binoculars aboard?'' Neil asked.

" 'Fraid not,'' the captain replied. "Don't need glasses to see fish.''

Neil had been gauging the wind and tide, and could feel hope rising. The tide was coming in, and *Vagabond* would be bucking it if she was headed south. The wind was still light, so it wasn't much help to them either. Would they try to hide in a cove or inlet to repair the propeller shaft? Would they sail between Tangier and Smith islands to get into the main part of the bay? He thought of the tactics he would adopt if he were Macklin and decided he'd just head south as fast as possible. They could work on the shaft while under way; the farther off they were standing from shore, the easier it would be to see an approaching enemy.

He took out his pistol and examined it to see if it had been damaged by the salt water. He removed the clip, cleaned it, and put it back in. There were five bullets. He hesitated, sighted on a drifting piece of Styrofoam, and pulled the trigger. The gun barked, and the Styrofoam shattered.

"You have any weapons aboard?'' Neil asked the old man.

"What?'' Captain Olly said, cupping his ear.

"Weapons! You got weapons aboard?" Neil shouted.

"Gaff. Boathook. Two knives. A harpoon. I mostly hunt fish."

"Hey, there's water coming in over your cabin sole," Frank shouted from the entranceway to the little forward cabin. He looked back at Olly and Neil in alarm.

"Well, if it worries you," the old man answered, "you can exercise that pump you got your right hand on. I don't generally pump until my bait box floats aft. You know how to pump?"

Frank saw that he had his hand on an old-fashioned manual bilge pump, and without replying he began pulling it up and pushing it down.

"You spaceship pilots don't get much chance to pump bilges, I 'spect," the old man said to Neil with a grin, "but it keeps the body in trim, it does, 'specially in a gale when you figure you're two inches from havin' more water inside your boat than out."

They had finally cleared the island to port, and Neil searched the horizon to the south. He estimated that *Vagabond* would only be making four or five knots, and they were being headed by a knot and a half tide. In two hours they would have a five- or six-mile lead at the most. With binoculars he could see that far. With the naked eye . . .

He climbed up on the foredeck and then onto the wheelhouse roof, balancing uncertainly as *Lucy Mae* rhythmically hobbyhorsed through the water.

There were dozens of boats in sight. He knew they were pouring down the Potomac from Washington and probably from the northern parts of the bay too. Patiently he focused on one distant boat after another. He hoped some emotional vibration would permit him to recognize *Vagabond*, even if it were only a white speck on the horizon. He saw nothing that registered.

As *Lucy Mae* proceeded due south and left more and more of Cobble Island behind to port Neil began to sweep the horizon off to the east southeast. It might make a certain sense to get out of the tidal flow in Tangier Sound and into the quieter waters of Pocomoke Sound. He saw what appeared to be a sloop three or four miles off but almost nothing else. The only advantage Macklin might have there was that any boat approaching him out of the main channel was likely to be up to no good as far as he was concerned. Neil stared hard at the sloop again and suddenly he saw it was *Vagabond* sailing without her mizzen.

"Hard to port," he yelled down at the old fisherman, and leapt back onto the foredeck and then into the cockpit.

"Our boat's at about east southeast," he said.

Captain Olly squinted through his dirty wheelhouse window and scowled.

"I'll take your word for it," he said.

"Get these groceries out of sight, Frank," Neil said. As Frank began to maneuver the cart down below, Neil could see to his right a spectacular wash of red spreading across the horizon, the great gray mass from the explosion now an incongruously glorious crimson. Only the undersides of a few cumulus clouds were still touched with light, and then they too turned to pink. *Lucy Mae* chugged forward at only about six knots.

"You fellows got a plan?" the old man asked.

Neil and Frank looked at each other, and when Olly saw that they didn't, he shook his head.

"You ain't got a *plan*," he said, frowning at them like a disappointed father.

"If they're becalmed, we can offer to give them a tow," Neil mused aloud.

"I don't think they's gonna be too trustful when they sees the men whose boat they just stole."

"The two of us will hide below," Neil went on. "Captain, you offer them a tow or to sell them some food, and bring *Lucy Mae* alongside the trimaran. Have one of them come aboard to make their towline fast or to check your food supplies. It'll be fairly dark by the time we overtake them. When one comes aboard *Lucy Mae*, I'll go out the forward hatch and rush the one who's still on board *Vagabond*. You and Frank jump the man who's here on *Lucy Mae*."

"Sounds good, sonny."

"Can we go any faster?" Neil asked.

"Maybe, but those fellas may have binoculars. You fellas better lie low."

"Frank," Neil said, "get a big bag of groceries and leave it out in plain sight. Stow the rest in the cabin."

Neil looked forward. The sun had set, but in the early twilight they could still see for almost a mile. *Lucy Mae* chugged steadily east southeast. Neil could no longer see *Vagabond*.

"I don't see it," Frank said from beside him.

"Where?" Neil asked urgently, misunderstanding what he'd said.

"I said I don't see anything!" Frank shouted at Neil.

Cobble Island was still to their left, some shoals to their right and dead ahead . . .

"There she is!" Neil said, pointing, and there, barely visible a mile away in the dusk, her three hulls silhouetted now against the distant shore, was *Vagabond*. Captain Olly slowed down his boat and squinted into the distance. All three of them were straining forward in the dusk as *Lucy Mae* chugged ahead loudly.

"Get below!" Olly shouted, and just then the bright white flash of a spotlight from Vagabond swept over *Lucy Mae*.

Frank and Neil ducked their heads and scrambled forward into the little cabin. The old man opened up the throttle some to increase speed back to eight knots. He switched on his running lights.

"What are you going to do?" Neil shouted over the hammering of the engine. He was peering up at the old man from the cabin entranceway.

"Same plan, sonny!" the captain yelled back and then motioned for them to be quiet. His hand trembling, Captain Olly's face was pale. With his lips drawn back exposing his gums and his few remaining teeth, his face had a slightly mad expression. He kept his little craft throbbing steadily forward, and the strange three-hulled, insectlike trimaran loomed up slowly out of the darkness. For ten minutes the two boats drew closer, Neil and Frank straightening up the grocery mess below, Captain Olly eventually singing softly to himself.

"Ain't gonna sink her till the sun sets low," he began in a low, cracking voice. "Don't care how much the wind does blow, I got a few fishies still to stow, so . . . ain't gonna sink her till the sun sets low . . . *Ahoy, spaceship!*" he suddenly shouted and Neil took out his pistol and crawled forward to undo the forward hatch cover.

Lucy Mae was only fifty feet behind and slightly to port of *Vagabond* when the old man hailed her. He slowed down slightly while he waited for an answer. There were two men in the unlit wheelhouse of the trimaran, and one of them moved into the port cockpit.

"What do you want?" Jerry shouted.

"You fellas want me to give you a tow?" Olly shouted back. "Do it pretty cheap." He slowed *Lucy Mae* down until she was going at the same speed as the trimaran, now only thirty feet away. Jerry turned back to the man at the helm.

"No, thanks," he finally shouted back.

"You fellas stay on this course and in another two minutes you'll run aground," Olly said amiably. The two men looked at each other and Macklin went forward to check the instrument panel.

"Our depthmeter shows twelve feet of water," he said loudly.

"Well, then, I reckon I must be sixteen feet tall," the old fisherman said. " 'Cause I get in my high boots and go clammin' right here every Saturday low tide and four feet of me sticks outa the water."

Macklin stared back at *Vagabond*'s instrument panel.

"Get the boat hook," he ordered Jerry.

Olly slipped *Lucy Mae*'s throttle forward and eased the boat slowly ahead, against the tide and toward the left side of the big trimaran. It was almost dark.

"Careful of the sharks," Captain Olly suggested quietly.

"What sharks?" Jerry asked nervously as he approached the side of the trimaran to test the depth.

"School of small sharks feedin' here in the shoals. Better not put your hand too near the water."

Lucy Mae was moving slowly ahead only a foot or two from *Vagabond*. Jerry looked uncertainly at the boat hook and then back at Macklin.

"You fellas sure you don't want me to give you a tow out of here? Only cost you fifty bucks an hour."

"Who the hell *are* you?" Macklin burst out and turned the spotlight on, sweeping the length of *Lucy Mae* and then holding it steady for a moment on the old man.

"Cap'n Oliver Mann," the old man answered, flashing a toothless grin up into the light. "Cap'n Olly, they calls me. Just an old geezer tryin' to earn a crooked buck. You want some Colombian pot? Or I can sell you this here bag of groceries cheap too. Cost only forty."

"That's twice what it must have cost you," Macklin barked back, turning off the spotlight.

"Cost me yesterday," the old man replied, still smiling. "Price tripled today. Be eight times that tomorrow, I reckon." *Lucy Mae* bumped the side of *Vagabond*. "Hold this line, will ya, young fella?" Captain Olly tossed a mooring line to Jerry, who instinctively grabbed it and made it fast to a cleat on the forepart of *Vagabond*'s port cockpit.

"Let's see your groceries," Macklin said, coming over to stand beside Jerry, his big gun clenched in his right hand.

"It's right here, sonny," the old man said amiably, turning on his flashlight and pointing it at the bag of groceries.

"Hand it up here and let us have a look," Macklin said.

"I ain't got enough strength in my back to lift a teacup off a saucer," Captain Olly said. "One of you young fellas'll have to come aboard and haul it out."

"Hand it up here," Macklin repeated.

"I tell you, sonny, my back won't take it."

"I'll get it," said Jerry.

"No," said Macklin, suddenly pulling Jerry back from the rail. "There's something wrong about all this. Go get the .22."

"Suit yourself, fella," Captain Olly said indifferently, switching off the flashlight, which left everyone only barely visible in the dim red glow of *Vagabond*'s portside running light. "I've made a lot of money today towing sailboats. If you—"

"Raise your hands and climb up here," Macklin snapped, crouching with his gun aimed at Olly, his eyes flicking nervously over the length of *Lucy Mae*. Jerry returned with Jim's .22 and stood beside Macklin.

"Now what you want me—" Olly had started to protest when the forward hatch cover clattered onto the foredeck. Macklin swung his gun around and fired past Jerry, and two shots exploded from Neil's gun. Macklin and Jerry disappeared behind the combing of the cockpit.

After the three sudden explosions in the darkness a silence descended on the two boats, which rocked gently side by side in the small swells. *Vagabond,* left untended, began swinging up into the wind, her sails fluttering as they luffed.

"Jerry?" Macklin called hoarsely from the other side of the trimaran.

The only answer was the rough hum of *Lucy Mae*'s idling engine and the gentle slapping of the sails. For twenty seconds, then thirty, no one spoke. Olly was crouched in his cockpit peering up at the vacant space where Macklin and Jerry had been standing. Neil stood with his head and shoulders out of the hatch, his gun aimed at the wheelhouse entrance, which he could just make out in the darkness. A small stream of blood crept down his left arm—pierced by splinters from *Lucy Mae*'s shattered hatchway.

"Your friend's dead, sonny," Captain Olly finally shouted. "Better come over here and give up."

The silence resumed. Neil, feeling certain he had hit Jerry, pulled himself quietly out onto the deck and crawled over onto the foredeck of the trimaran; he felt Macklin must be in the opposite cockpit. He crawled swiftly across *Vagabond*'s entire width forward of the cabins and crouched on the foredeck on the opposite side from *Lucy Mae*.

Olly had felt his boat rock as Neil's weight shifted to *Vagabond*, so he called out again to draw Macklin's attention.

"We got four men here with automatic rifles, sonny!" he shouted. "Better get on over here with your hands held high."

Macklin again didn't respond. Peering aft, Neil couldn't see his dim bulk crouched in the starboard cockpit as he had expected. Macklin must be close to Frank's cabin hatchway. He wondered where Jim and Jeanne were. If Macklin were to take them as hostages, they were in trouble, but even so he didn't dare risk his life now by rushing him. He crouched and waited to see the effect of the old fisherman's propaganda campaign.

"Three to one ain't good odds, sonny," Olly's high-pitched voice called out through the darkness. "If you're not over here in the next minute, we're going to come after you."

Neil could still see no sign of Macklin and suddenly had the unnerving conviction that Macklin wasn't there, that he, Neil, had miscalculated again. He glanced down behind him into the water, then over to the other cockpit, but nothing moved. He strained his eyes again to see some sign of Macklin in the starboard cockpit, strained his ears to pick up the slightest movement.

"I surrender."

The words, spoken quietly, reached Neil from the area he'd been so desperately searching.

"I'm throwing my gun across the top of the cabin," Macklin continued. Something clattered across the cabin top.

"Come over here with your hands behind your head," Olly shouted. A flashlight suddenly lit up the wheelhouse from *Lucy Mae*'s cockpit. Macklin abruptly appeared in the light, his empty hands behind his head, moving slowly. He had to step over something before he emerged into the center of Olly's light in the cockpit near *Lucy Mae*. As Neil glided over the cabin tops Frank came up over *Vagabond*'s combing and picked up the .22.

"We've got him, Neil," he called, holding the .22 on Macklin.

When Neil arrived, he saw Frank and Macklin staring down at Jerry, who lay in a pool of blood, his open eyes fixed.

"I told him not to do it," Macklin said quietly. "But he said you were going to kick us off."

Frank and Neil stared at him.

"I got that puller tool you asked for," he said to Neil.

As Frank broke away to throw back the port hatch to search for Jeanne, Neil watched Macklin.

"Are any of our people hurt?" he asked coldly.

"Your people are all a lot healthier than Jerry."

"They'd better be," said Neil, and as he heard Jeanne's voice, he began to feel relieved: *Vagabond* was theirs again.

An hour and a half later *Vagabond* lay at anchor, *Lucy Mae* still tied to her port side. After the initial exhilaration and the relief of being reunited, those aboard were in various states of disorientation and exhaustion. Jeanne, Jim, and Lisa had all been hurt resisting the taking of *Vagabond,* and Neil during its rescue. Jim had bruised ribs, a bloody nose, and cut and sore wrists where they had bound him.

Jeanne's left cheek had a swollen and bluish bruise where Macklin had hit her when she'd tried to help Jim. When Lisa had begun pounding on Macklin's back, Jerry had struck her on the side of the head with the butt of his gun. Neil had a two-inch-long, half-inch-wide wood sliver lodged in his left arm. Conrad Macklin had examined Lisa's head right after her injury and again when *Vagabond* had been sailing away and had told Jeanne that Lisa probably had a minor concussion but no fracture. He offered now to pull out the splinters from Neil's arm, but after first refusing, Neil soon concluded that Jeanne and Frank were being too gentle in their probing. He finally let Macklin coolly butcher the splinters out.

Later, after tying Macklin's hands behind him and then to the mizzenmast and leaving Jim on guard, they buried Jerry at sea. Jeanne came up on deck and saw Neil, Frank, and Olly standing in the dim light of the wheelhouse with Neil reading in a low voice from the Bible. She stood momentarily mesmerized by the weird scene, which continued as Neil stopped reading and he and Olly lifted the body up and slid it overboard. The whole experience was so unreal, so disconnected from her previous life, that she staggered down the steps to the main cabin for the reassuring sight of pots, pans, a kitchen—anything to erase the eeriness of those three dim figures in the cockpit, like warlocks chanting some incantation, and then throwing a body into the sea.

She prepared coffee, not because anyone had asked her to, but to ground herself, to reestablish everyday reality. When Frank came down, he looked anxiously at Jeanne and came over to take her in his arms again. His white sport shirt was sweat-stained and grimy, his gray hair slick with sweat. He had embraced her after the initial rescue, and she had clung to him as a brother or father, a haven from the insane chaos that was raining down upon her.

"Coffee or scotch?" Jeanne now asked Frank. Captain Olly was already sipping at a cup full of scotch—caffeine being "bad for the teeth."

"Both," Frank replied and sat down with a great sigh on the settee opposite Olly, who had slumped over sideways and was soon snoring.

When Neil appeared, he paused with uncharacteristic uncertainty at the foot of the steps. He accepted a cup of coffee from Jeanne with a mechanical smile, his severe face showing none of the warm attentiveness that it had so often throughout the day.

"We should be getting under way," Neil said to Frank, who was sitting with his back to him. Frank stared into the bronze glow of his whiskey and in a single swallow tossed it off. When Frank didn't reply, Jeanne asked, "Where are we going?"

"It's my judgment we should sail out the bay to the ocean," Neil replied, looking at Frank's back.

Frank turned on the transistor radio on the shelf above the dinette table and after a moment located a working station. As they all began listening to a radio report of the events of the day Jeanne exchanged a strangely conspiratorial glance with Neil and then sat down beside Frank, instinctively placing her hand on top of his.

The nuclear war was exactly one day old and already, although someone claimed both sides were showing "restraint," every European country and most parts of the United States had been hit. The U.S. retaliation against the Soviet Union was described as if it were even more devastating than the blows the U.S. had received. A statement by the President indicated that the war would be fought to the bitter end, no matter what the consequences. The President had said that he expected every citizen to do all he could to support the American effort to punish the Soviet Union for its unprovoked criminal aggression. A state of martial law had been declared.

Finally Frank reached and turned off the radio.

"I couldn't get to Norah," he said to no one in particular.

"No planes available?" Neil asked.

"Nothing to pay with," Frank replied. "I have no money."

In the silence that followed, Jeanne became aware of Neil's unanswered call to get going hovering over the room.

"What are we going to do now?" she asked Frank gently.

"I don't know," Frank answered.

"Macklin got hold of a puller," Neil said, "and they loosened the old shaft. Jim and I should be able to put in the new one and get the prop on in less than an hour. Then we should sail south."

Frank turned in his settee seat to look past Jeanne at Neil, who was still standing at the foot of the companionway steps.

"What about Bob?" he asked. "What about Captain Olly? What about the rest of the country?"

It seemed strange to Jeanne to hear someone asking about Bob. It was like an inquiry into another lifetime.

"Bob is dead," she said automatically.

"The radioactive cloudbank from Washington is still spreading," Neil went on. "The fallout from everywhere will get worse. I doubt we can survive unless we get east and south. Fast."

Seeing Frank's haggard face Jeanne realized with a shudder that he was in a state of shock, that he was barely there. She saw a vague flash of irritation cross his face when Neil spoke, but no comprehension.

"Then . . . we should get under way," she said softly and stood up. Looking back at Frank, she saw him turning to pour himself another small glass of whiskey.

"We've got new food supplies in Olly's smack," Neil said to her. "I'd like you and Olly to transfer them to *Vagabond* and then you can begin storing them."

"All right," she answered, aware of how gently Neil was speaking to her.

"We're running away," Frank announced in a low, husky voice.

"I hope so," Neil snapped back.

"What else can we do?" Jeanne asked quickly.

Frank tossed off his second drink, slid himself sideways, and stood up.

"When I know, we'll do it," he said. *"Hey! You!"* he shouted at the sleeping fisherman, who awoke, startled and blinking.

"You want to join us on an ocean cruise?"

Captain Olly squinted dazedly at Frank. "I got a son I want to see," Olly replied, frowning.

"Well, then, you'll have to shove off," Frank said. "We're only taking cowards and deserters." He brushed past Jeanne and Neil and up the companionway. Neil and Olly followed.

"What are we going to do with this load of filth?" Frank asked, stopping to stare at Conrad Macklin, who was sitting at the foot of the mizzenmast with his arms tied behind his back. Jim was on a settee seat guarding him, a bandaged forehead and bluish bruise on his lower ribcage indicating his wounds.

"I'm sorry we stole your boat," Macklin said unexpectedly.

"I say we dump him overboard," Frank went on fiercely, turning to Neil. "I tried to get through to the Coast Guard to come arrest him, but the man on duty said we'd have to bring him in."

"To where?" Neil asked.

"Their station at Crisfield."

"We're not wasting time going back there."

"Throw him overboard."

A silence followed. Macklin looked expressionlessly at Frank. When Jeanne came up into the wheelhouse, he turned to her.

"I'm sorry about your girl," he said. "Jerry didn't mean to hurt her. She'll be all right though."

"SHUT UP!!" Frank shouted, taking a step toward Macklin and flushing with anger.

"Ignore him, Frank," said Neil. "Jim, get into your scuba gear. We're going to put the new propeller shaft in."

While Jim went forward to change, and Jeanne and Olly began transferring the food from *Lucy Mae,* Frank sat down and put his face in his hands. Neil stayed where he was, facing Macklin.

"I panicked," Macklin went on quietly, his eyes as expressionless as always. "Jerry was convinced that without food you were going to kick us off the boat before we'd cleared the Chesapeake. When I got back with that puller, he'd already taken over the boat without me. Ask Jim." He looked up at Neil with an anguished expression that Neil couldn't quite believe was genuine. "Take me with you. I can help."

Frank erupted from his seat and grabbed Macklin by the throat, sending his head crashing back against the mizzenmast.

"Shut up! You stupid bastard!" he shouted. "You say another word, and I'll kill you!"

Neil pulled Frank away.

"Help Olly and Jeanne," he said to him quietly.

For a moment Frank stood looming over Macklin; Neil could feel him trembling.

"I can't stand that kind of talk," Frank said, finally moving away. "A man steals my boat, hits a woman in the face, has his crony almost kill Lisa, and expects us to forgive him. Jesus!"

As he led his friend over toward *Lucy Mae,* Neil couldn't respond. It was disturbing to remember that he himself had been perfectly ready to steal a boat to go chase after *Vagabond.* And would he have let Macklin and Jerry stay if he hadn't cleaned out that super-market?

Now, left alone with Macklin, Neil knelt down to loosen the large removable section of decking that covered the engine. He took a flashlight out of the tool chest lying on the shelf above the engine to examine the position of the bent shaft.

"You need me, Captain Loken," Macklin suddenly said to him in a whisper. "You need my medical skills. You need someone else aboard who's got your cold will to survive. You can use me."

Neil pushed himself back up to a kneeling position to look at Macklin in the dim light. Macklin was staring at him serenely.

"The others have too much heart to survive in this world," Macklin went on. "You can use me, you know it. I didn't want to take this boat. I can't sail. Without Jerry I'm not about to turn pirate again."

Neil looked back at him expressionlessly.

"Despite *your* cold will to survive," he said, "the helpless people with too much heart have you tied to a mast and are getting ready to throw you overboard."

Jeanne and Frank came into the wheelhouse carrying bags of groceries and disappeared into the main cabin.

"You know Frank won't kill me," Macklin whispered. "That woman wouldn't let him. Only you are strong enough and cold enough to kill me, but you need another man like me. And you need a doctor. You know it."

"With you around we'll damn well need somebody's medical skills," Neil said.

When Jim came into the wheelhouse, dressed in his wetsuit, Neil stood up.

"If Frank agrees, we're dumping you ashore at the first opportunity," he said aloud to Macklin.

"I'm a fighter, Loken," Macklin said in a normal voice. "You need another fighter."

"I can use your .45," Neil replied, nodding to Jim to pick up the new shaft. "The rest of you, no. Let's get to it, Jim."

Because she felt herself moving in a dream from which she might momentarily awaken Jeanne was partially detached from all she did. The pedestrian act of bringing groceries into the galley was slightly unhinged when she had to pass by the dark figure of Macklin, bound to the mast whispering to Neil. Later she could hear Neil and Jim grunting and swearing as they worked on the engine shaft, and as she traipsed to and fro between the two boats, she became aware that around *Vagabond* was a vast darkness. There were no lights to be seen now in any direction, and although stars shone above them, the whole northwestern quarter of the sky was ominously dark. She had managed to put away almost half the food in the galley when the propeller shaft was finally fixed, the engine tested, and the sails raised again. With the men shouting to each other on the deck above her, Olly poked his head into the galley and said an awkward good-bye. In another moment she felt the steady hiss of water along the sides of the hull at her feet; the anchor was up and they were sailing.

And then, in a casual, almost routine way, the nightmarish side of her dreamworld returned again. They had been sailing no more than a minute or two, and she was still working in the galley, now lit by a kerosene lamp, when the companionway to the wheelhouse, which had been dark, was filled with light. She heard Neil shout "Don't look!" and a moment later Frank's voice: "Get the sails down!"

She braced herself, expecting the boat to be hit as her car had been by the force of the blast. She heard and felt feet thudding across the cabin roof and again Frank's voice shouting something to Jim. The sails began to flutter and snap as they did when the boat came up into the wind. She still crouched by the galley stove, her teeth clenched, her hands clutching the counter top.

A screeching sound cut into the flapping sails—were the sails being lowered?—and then Neil's face appeared in the cabin entranceway.

"Batten everything down!" he shouted. He started to leave but, catching her blank expression, he turned back. "Big waves may be hitting us from the blast. Store everything where it can't get loose and fly around."

As she began putting the dishes and remaining groceries away helter-skelter into drawers and cabinets, Jim leapt down into the cabin.

"I'll help," he said and, kneeling, pushed back the carpet and removed a section of the floor. "We'll store the rest of the food in the bilge for now," he added.

By the time they had stowed everything away in the main cabin and come back up into the wheelhouse, the glow to the south—over Norfolk, Jim told her—was large and growing, but not as bright as the blast over Washington had been. The sails were lashed down, and the boat headed slowly north under power, its diesel engine barely audible.

When Jeanne checked Lisa and Skippy, she was surprised to see that someone had tied them into their berth to prevent them from falling out: two half-inch lines across the top of the blanket attached to fittings in the far wall and at the edge of the berth near the cabin walk space.

"Hold on, Jeanne!" she heard Frank shout, and then came a hissing, swishing sound growing closer. She grabbed the handrail of her own berth just as *Vagabond* was struck by noisy, moiling wash of water. The breaking waves threw *Vagabond* forward, swinging Jeanne around and slamming her into the wall beneath her berth.

But that was all. The rushing sound continued and *Vagabond* seemed to be surging and rocking, but the blow seemed to have been relatively harmless. Her children didn't even awaken.

Back up on deck she saw Frank, looking grim, handling the wheel and looking to his right, where she could see another boat, *Lucy Mae*, easing alongside. With Neil and Jim assisting, the two ships were tied together again, both moving slowly forward.

"I came back for dessert," Olly said to her from his cockpit and smiled an elfin smile.

Neil returned to the wheelhouse.

"We ought to make for deeper water," he said to Frank.

"You think there'll be more waves like that?" Frank asked.

"In two or three hours there may be some huge waves," Neil

replied gravely. "The water around the blast area will have been hit with tremendous force and sent rolling up the bay. These little things that are hitting us now must be from the local shock wave."

"How much time do we have?" Frank asked.

"If the waves are moving at twenty to thirty knots, probably about two hours. Maybe more."

"In that time we could get ourselves into the lee of Tangier Island," Captain Olly said.

"That would be good," said Neil.

"Let's do it," agreed Frank.

Neil and Olly were both frowning over at *Lucy Mae*.

"Olly," Neil said. "*Vagabond*'s made for big seas, but the *Lucy Mae* will be swamped and sunk if the big ones hit before we make the lee of the island. I think you ought to anchor and come with us."

"How much warning you figure we'll get?" Olly asked.

"If this light holds, we should be able to see big waves coming from quite a distance . . . about a minute's warning," Neil answered. "But Christ, Olly, we can't know even that for sure."

Olly nodded.

"Why don't we both go side by side," he said. "I'd like to try to make it."

"Okay," agreed Neil. "Stay close to leeward. If we see danger, we'll signal with the air horn and turn due north, away from the waves. You get over here and board us. Figure you have about thirty seconds. Why don't we send Jim with you to help you get ready to abandon ship if the time comes?"

"Sounds fine to me, sonny," Olly said. "How big you figure these waves'll be?"

"Too big," Neil replied.

The two vessels were soon speeding through the rough water, thirty feet apart, headed northwest to take shelter behind the northern end of Tangier Island, fourteen miles away. Jeanne could see *Lucy Mae* rolling and pitching in the short, steep waves sent northward by the local shock waves. *Vagabond*'s motion was less pronounced, since her three hulls made her more like a huge sailing raft, but the waves still smashed into the port hull with ominous crashing sounds.

After she became queasy while preparing some hot tea in the galley, Jeanne remained in the wheelhouse. Frank was steering while

Neil with the binoculars was keeping a lookout south for the anticipated larger waves.

It must have been something like two hours later—Jeanne had fallen asleep on the settee—with the two boats still running side by side, and now only a half-mile from Tangier Island and nearing the protection of its northern tip, that Frank's shout awakened Jeanne.

When she sat up, she saw Neil, at the helm, grab the air horn and shoot out four loud blasts. Frank, with the binoculars, ran into the cabin and stood beside him.

"It's a *wall of water*!" he shouted.

"Help Olly and Jim get aboard," Neil shouted back, glancing to his right, where *Lucy Mae* was already approaching. "Jeanne! Get below!"

But she simply took hold of one of the wooden supports of the wheelhouse roof and looked back at him dumbly.

"Untie me!" Macklin said fiercely, but Neil, ignoring him, slowed *Vagabond* down slightly to permit *Lucy Mae* to come up alongside. Jim threw an armful of fishing gear into the cockpit and then went back for more. Olly handed something to Frank and shouted to Jim to get off. Frank was trying to hold the two boats together as they rolled and smashed into each other's sides while Olly turned back to the wheel and tied a line to one of its spokes. When Jim had thrown the last of *Lucy Mae*'s salvageable gear onto the trimaran and boarded, Olly jumped aboard *Vagabond*, tugging on the line. *Lucy Mae*, still under power, swung away and veered off at a right angle into the darkness.

"Damn pretty boat," Olly commented as he watched her go.

All the hatches and door slides had been put in place earlier, and now everyone except Neil crouched in the wheelhouse, looking aft through the Plexiglas window at the low wall of water rising up out of the horizon behind them, the wall made visible by the huge hill of light that filled the low southern sky from the explosion over Norfolk.

"Untie me!" Macklin pleaded to Jeanne, who just looked past him at the approaching water.

Neil had opened *Vagabond*'s throttle up all the way, and *Vagabond* rushed forward, away from the tidal wave at over nine knots, but the wall still grew toward them, and they clearly heard a roaring sound as the wave smashed along the shore of Tangier Island. Neil had swung the boat slightly toward the island, but when the wave was only a hundred feet away he turned back to present *Vagabond*'s stern directly to the racing sea.

The first wave was over twenty feet high, a mound of water rather than a wall, a cap of white froth bubbling down its forward side. The roaring noise grew louder, the wave grew immense, and then was upon them, first lifting *Vagabond*'s stern, then burying it as it struck at her three hulls, a river of water ten feet high rushing across the whole boat, smashing through the rear of the wheelhouse, hurling the trimaran forward at twice her previous speed, leaving Olly, Jim, Jeanne, and Frank in a heap against the wall and hatch slide of the main companionway and tangling Olly in Neil's feet as he stood clutching the wheel.

Jeanne, crushed up against the cabin wall by the cold salt water swirling over her, choked and gasped as she struggled upward in a nightmare of drowning, clawing at the wall as the water still seemed to be pinning her down. Frank grasped her arm and pulled her, sputtering, up into his arms and wedged himself against the control panel shelf.

The water was up to her knees, and she assumed that they were sinking, but then she saw Neil looking back over his shoulder with a look of concentration devoid of dismay. The roar was still all around them and she felt they must be hurtling through the water at some fantastic speed, but even as she thought this, she saw that Neil was actually gunning the throttle.

"We'll anchor behind Tangier Island just as we planned," he shouted. "It'll take us awhile to pump her out and clean up."

The water had already fallen to her ankles, some of it pouring into the main cabin through the broken hatch slide and the rest draining out the holes of the self-bailing cockpits and wheelhouse.

Jim crawled forward to prepare the anchor, while Frank stared at the smashed fragments of plywood, Fiberglas, and Plexiglas that had been the back wall of his wheelhouse.

"Not too many boats going to be floating after *that* ripple," Olly said to Neil with an uncharacteristically grim expression.

"Check our main bilge, Olly."

"Jesus, what's the use," said Frank. "Every time we—"

"Go check your starboard cabin bilge," Neil interrupted. "Jeanne, check your children. We've survived."

Vagabond had had ten tons of water sweep over her, had shipped over half a ton in her three bilges from stove-in windows and hatch slides, the wheelhouse rear wall was reduced to splinters, but all her rigging had come through intact. In another half-hour they had pumped or bailed out most of the uninvited water and were anchored behind what was left of Tangier Island. They set up a rotation of two-hour watches and, numb, shell-shocked, exhausted to the point of not caring, all at last were permitted to sleep.

Neil didn't waken until nine o'clock the following morning and thus had five full hours' sleep, a luxury after the previous forty-eight. As he emerged from his damp cabin he felt anxious and irritated. In the daylight he saw clearly for the first time the extent of the damage to the rear wall of the wheelhouse, saw Olly's gaffs, fishing nets, oyster tongs, and other gear still lying in a heap in the starboard cockpit, saw the smashed cabin hatch slide, saw Frank sprawled asleep on one of the wheelhouse settees—it was Frank's watch—and felt a strong breeze blowing, now out of the north. The thought that they had been sitting still doing nothing for almost seven hours rankled him, and he had to stop on the afterdeck to calm himself down.

But as he gazed around the bay his irritation and impatience gave way to an entirely different emotion. A house was floating only a hundred yards to the east; on the shore of Tangier Island were the remnants of several wrecked houses and boats. On the island itself not a single building seemed to remain standing. Farther to the south was the now-familiar ghastly gray mass squatting in the otherwise clear blue sky like an ugly, swelling toad. However much he was displeased by the current condition of *Vagabond*, she was afloat; she had survived.

As he stepped down into the starboard cockpit to begin work he stopped. *Where was Macklin?* He'd been left tied to the mizzenmast. Neil leapt down into the starboard cockpit, ran into the wheelhouse, and then stopped: Macklin was sitting nonchalantly in the sun of the opposite cockpit, sipping coffee. Jeanne emerged from the main cabin and behind her he saw Lisa at the galley stove.

"Good morning," she said.

"How'd he get loose?" Neil asked grimly.

Jeanne flushed in response to Neil's unconcealed anger.

"He was free when I got up," she replied. "Can I fix you something for breakfast?"

Neil walked farther into the port cockpit and saw with a start that the .22 was lying across Macklin's knees.

"Good morning," said Macklin neutrally.

"May I have the rifle?" Neil asked.

"Sure," said Macklin. "It's of no use to me." He put his coffee cup down on the seat beside him and handed the .22 to Neil. "But look, Loken, let me sail with you. Putting me ashore would be murder."

"How did you get loose?" Neil asked quietly, noting that the .22 he had taken from Macklin was loaded.

"Child's play," Macklin replied with a sneer.

"Why didn't you take the dinghy and escape?"

"Escape, shit," Macklin snapped. "There's no escape out there. My only chance—I admit it's smaller than a flea's cock," he added parenthetically, glancing to his left at the blast cloud over the Norfolk area, "is on this ship."

"Are you all right?" Neil asked Jeanne.

"Yes. I thought you had released him."

He nodded, grimacing.

"Would you like to eat now?" Jeanne asked again.

"Thanks," Neil answered. "Use whatever's in the refrigerator first—bacon, cheese, other things that will spoil when we turn off the propane to conserve it for cooking. Don't cook potatoes, for example."

"Fine," she said, disappearing down into the galley.

"Cook for everyone," he called after her. As he looked down into the galley he was pleased to see that although the area was a mess, it was a functioning mess: Jeanne and Lisa had removed all the food from the bilge, where some of it had been spoiled by the previous night's deluge, and were inventorying and stowing it away. He noted too that Jeanne and her two children were dressed as neatly as for a quiet summer cruise, their white shorts and blouses in curious contrast to the big bluish bruise on Jeanne's cheek and the bloody bandage on the side of Lisa's head. Skippy was looking shyly up at him, clinging to one of his mother's bare thighs.

"Can you keep an eye on Skippy for me?" Jeanne called up to him.

"Of course."

But Skippy didn't need an eye kept on him, since he was content to stay with his mother down in the main cabin, clinging to her as if she were safe space in a game of tag. He ignored her suggestion that he go up with Neil to look at a comic book and limited his conversation to periodic announcements to his mother: "I'm hungry."

Lisa came up to where Neil was examining the wrecked wheelhouse wall to hand him a cup of coffee. The bandage on the left side of her face was immense and had a blot of red in the middle, but she told him that though it hurt and throbbed, she felt no dizziness.

"Here comes somebody," she added unexpectedly, squinting off to the northeast.

Following her gaze, Neil turned to see a small skiff motoring at full throttle toward them, a man standing up in the stern, steering. Neil picked up the .22 again and cradled it in the crook of his elbow. At first he assumed the man was headed toward the village of Tangier, but the skiff kept coming straight in and coasted to a halt alongside the starboard hull. A small, deeply tanned young man about Jimmy's age wearing dirty khakis and a soiled cotton sweatshirt looked over *Vagabond*'s combing at them.

"My father here?" he asked.

"Who's that?"

"Cap'n Olly."

"He's sleeping in the forepeak, I think."

"Hey, pa! *Pa!* It's Chris!" the young man shouted.

After a moment the captain poked his head out of the forward hatch and then came up on deck, his sparse white hair disheveled; he was dressed only in T-shirt and underdrawers.

"Well, you don't have to shout about it," he grumbled, looking aft, and seeing Lisa standing twenty feet away staring at him, he disappeared below to get his trousers on.

" 'Pears you had some waves come visiting last night," Chris said to Neil, nodding solemnly at the wrecked wall of the wheelhouse.

"We did," Neil agreed. "How about you?"

"Well, most of the houses on Smith Island are a few hundred feet farther north than they used to be, and there aren't many people left to give a damn." Chris glanced to his right. "Tangier must have really got socked."

"I'm afraid so."

"Good morning, ma'am," Chris said to Jeanne, who had come up into the wheelhouse.

"Good morning."

"Well, what you want?" Captain Olly asked when he came out on deck a second time, buttoning up his pants. "Getting so a man can't even escape his own family out at sea."

"I was worried about you, pa," his son said. "They said you went chasing pirates or something, and then the tidal wave last night, and you didn't come back."

"Well, I'm back," he said. "Got myself two pirates. Woulda gotten more, but there weren't none."

"Where's *Lucy Mae*?"

"I sent her into Crisfield to pick me up some pipe tobacco."

Chris looked at his father uncertainly.

"We had to cut her loose when the big wave was about to hit," Neil explained. "I imagine she sunk."

"You okay?" Chris asked his father.

"Course I'm okay. I been dying for two years now, and chasin' pirates and dodging tidal waves ain't gonna affect it none. What you been up to? You remember the mayonnaise?"

"I'm going in the Navy, pa."

"What do you mean you're going in the Navy?" the old man demanded, sitting now on the cockpit bench near his son and pulling on his socks. "Why you want to go in the Navy?"

"Because I have to," Chris answered.

"How have to? Why have to? What are you talking about?"

"The President ordered us to," Chris answered quietly. All reservists had to go. I'm taking a special bus this morning at eleven from Salisbury."

"What's the hurry?" Captain Olly said irritably. "Navy got a ship needs bailing out this afternoon?"

"I've got to go, pa," Chris insisted.

Captain Olly stood up and looked out across the afterdeck toward Smith Island. He stood silently for almost half a minute while his son watched him patiently.

"Well," the old man finally said. "Give me a good-bye kiss. Ain't every day a son goes put-putting off to get himself blown to bits." He took a step toward his son and presented his grizzled cheek. Chris kissed him awkwardly. Captain Olly straightened up but kept looking down at his son.

"One of them H-bombs come after you, you remember to get below," he said.

"You know me, pa," Chris said, smiling boyishly. "If I know one's coming, I'll want to come up on deck to get a look at it."

"Know you will, son, know you will. I figure in another week you'll come raining down into the Atlantic."

Chris stared at him.

"Don't mind me, son," Olly said, tears glistening in his eyes. "I just wish you'd a stole a boat and sailed into the Atlantic like a respectable son would do. Or at least a live one."

"I'm going, pa."

"I know you are, but I'm not going to stop talking. You're just gonna have to go, 'cause I ain't letting you go. 'F I had my druthers, I'd stay here talking to you till this boat rotted and sank. I like your face, son, and the damn sky's gonna be empty without it."

"Good-bye, pa," Chris said, and gave his skiff a gentle shove away from *Vagabond* and pulled the starting cord on his outboard. The engine purred into life.

"I know you're going, son, but you can't stop me from talking to you. I been talkin' to you eighteen years, and I ain't gonna stop now just 'cause you want to go rushing off to become a smithereen. The world's full of smithereens these days, and I don't see why you think one more's gonna make the air smell any purtier, 'specially you smelling most the time like a blowfish after flies been at it a week. Why I remember when you . . ."

His son was already fifty feet away, the sound of the skiff's engine buzzing gently back to them across the water and beginning to fade.

Captain Olly, tears dampening both cheeks, turned to look at Neil and Lisa and Jeanne, who had been watching Chris's departure from the wheelhouse. After several seconds delay he snorted.

"You got breakfast ready yet, lady?" he suddenly blurted at Jeanne. "I gotta get some eggs and coffee aboard my belly before I swamp us again with my dribble. Got any that whiskey left there, cap'n? I'm eighteen."

The three stared at him.

"Nine o'clock in the morning and I ain't even pissed yet," he went on. "You got a head aboard this boat or can I pee off the side or use a bucket like real sailors do?"

"Off the afterdeck is fine," Neil answered.

"Would you like some bacon and eggs?" Jeanne asked.

"Course I'd like bacon and eggs," Captain Olly said as he stepped up out of the cockpit to get to the afterdeck. "And toast and juice and potatoes and anything else you got cooking. A dying, orphaned man got to make the most of his last days. Least he can do is eat like a pig." Turning his back to the ladies, who went below to make breakfast, Captain Olly pissed with dignity off the aft deck.

It was thirty minutes later, after they had all finished eating breakfast and begun coasting down the bay, that Neil, on his way forward to check the genoa, placed one foot onto the little step built into the cabin wall and stopped. He stared at the cockpit deck. A thin, barely visible layer of something lay on the cockpit floor. He bent over and ran an index finger for a few inches along the deck and looked at it: a gray smudge. He looked up at the sky above him. A thin haze marred the blue summer sky. He went quickly over to the opposite cockpit: the same thin layer of ash covered the deck around the fishing gear and other salvage from *Lucy Mae*.

He felt trapped. To the south lay a thick cloud over Norfolk; to the northwest the closer, more diffuse gray fog from the blast over Washington. And on the deck at his feet the first radioactive fallout.

"Frank!" he shouted.

Still bleary-eyed from weariness, Frank left the wheelhouse and stumbled to the cockpit.

"We've got fallout on deck," Neil told him in a quiet voice.

Frank reached down to examine the ash, and then looked back at Neil.

"Everybody should go below," he said. "I'll wash the fucking stuff off the decks."

Frank and Neil sent everyone into the main cabin and ordered them to shut all windows and portholes and check for ash, wiping off and throwing overboard any they found. Since every thickness of material between them and the radioactive fallout would give some small additional protection, Skippy was put on the floor underneath the dinette table and a jury-rigged wall of plywood was used to create a cave. The table was covered with blankets and sleeping bags from the forepeak. Jeanne ordered Lisa to crawl under it too. Olly suggested Jeanne make a space next to the dagger board well and beneath the crossbeam for greater protection. Conrad Macklin went into the forepeak and covered himself with bagged sails.

On deck Frank began washing down the boat with buckets of seawater and a long-handled brush. Neil disappeared for a while and then emerged wearing full foul-weather gear, including rubber boots and a hood tied tightly around his face as if he were about to go out in a gale. He handed a full set to Frank and took over the washing down of the boat while Frank put on his gear. Jim had checked the genoa, and when he came aft, Frank ordered him below with the others. He and Neil would stay on deck.

As they set sail down the Chesapeake for the Atlantic a low-level dread hung over all of them as they huddled in the main cabin. They talked in low voices, like mourners at a wake. On the horizon to both north and south lay the ugly gray cloud masses that seemed to be creeping up the sky to kill them. One was chasing down from the north, and they were sailing south into the one over Norfolk. There was no escape.

When *Vagabond* sailed past Tangier village Neil looked dully at the wreckage. Two large fishing trawlers lay on their sides among the shells of three houses tilted crazily, as if all five were some child's toys carelessly cast aside. One of the buildings must have been the bar they had stopped at the night it all began, but even through his binoculars he couldn't tell which building it was. He saw no sign of life.

To the east the shore was too distant to reveal what had happened, but as *Vagabond* sailed out into the middle of the Chesapeake, Frank sighted the capsized hulk of a motor yacht a quarter mile to starboard. Other floating vessels became visible, a sailboat sailing south like *Vagabond*, and two other boats coming from the direction of Norfolk. With a sense of foreboding, Neil realized that on the previous day the bay had been crowded with boats, thirty-five or forty when he'd been searching for the sight of the stolen *Vagabond*. Not many had survived the explosion and the tidal wave.

It was Frank who spotted the first corpse: a limp, wet lump of clothing floating face-down less than fifty feet from *Vagabond*'s course. Frank's first instinct was to alter course to retrieve the body, but then he quickly realized that the last thing they needed aboard was a corpse. There would be more.

The two ships coming toward them remained close to the western shore and soon disappeared past them, headed up the Chesapeake to God-knew-where. That they had survived at all was a surprise. The sailboat on the same course as *Vagabond* disappeared into a cove or a river on the western shore. By late morning they seemed to be all alone on the vast expanse of the bay.

With a sense of dread and impotent anger Neil observed that enough dust would accumulate in a half-hour's time to form a visible gray film. He and Frank alternated doing the cleaning work, both of them getting overheated and exhausted in their stifling foul-weather gear on the increasingly hot day. His face dripping with sweat, one of them would plod over the entire length and breadth of the boat with a big plastic bucket and the long-handled brush, dipping the bucket into the bay, pouring it across the deck, then rapidly brushing to push everything back into the water. When he was finished he would stumble back to the other man, at the helm, and without a break the other would take up the exhausting work.

At eleven thirty Frank collapsed on the foredeck. Neil rushed forward and dragged him back, loosening his foul-weather gear. He hoped it was only heat exhaustion, and he carried Frank below where he could be undressed and cooled off. Olly took Frank's place, wearing his own foul-weather clothing. Macklin was ordered to take a turn next.

Forty minutes later Frank reappeared on deck, dressed again in full gear and ordered Neil and Macklin to go below, saying that if they rotated four men, none of them would get overheated again. Olly came up again to share the ordeal.

Down in the main cabin Neil was struck by the stuffy, close atmosphere and by the silence. The wet towels they'd used to cool Frank down were still draped over the galley shelves. Lisa and Skippy were squeezed into the "doghouse" under the dinette table, Jim was sitting back against the galley cabinets with a Styrofoam cooler and settee cushion on his lap, and Jeanne was huddled beside the dagger board well with a settee cushion covering most of her. Neil stripped off his foul-weather stuff and rubbed himself down with one of the wet towels. Macklin crawled into the forepeak cabin.

"Mommy says the rain has radioactive germs in it," Skippy said suddenly, peeking his head out of his cave. "Did you see them?"

"One or two," Neil answered. "I kicked them overboard."

"Mommy says you're *washing* them overboard," Skippy corrected.

"She's right."

Lisa also peered out.

"Is it still falling?" she asked.

"A little bit probably," Neil answered. "But we're keeping the boat so clean, you can't tell." He knew better, of course. The stuff was still falling, although even Neil thought at a slightly slower rate, and though they were a lot better off here than on land, they were still being exposed, especially those who had to work on deck.

Jeanne crawled out from her hideaway.

"You should get under the crossbeam," she said. "You've been exposed already much more than we have."

He glanced at the space, then at her. He wanted to lie down and wanted to feel better protected.

"Can we both squeeze in there?" he asked, frowning.

"No," she said. "But you go ahead."

He hesitated, but the thought of being able to lie down won out over gallantry; he realized how exhausted he must be. He stepped over Jim's legs, held Jeanne briefly as he passed her, and then crawled into her space. She covered him with her cushion and sat down beside Jim. *Vagabond* sailed on. Below, no one spoke.

It was at about two o'clock, after they had sailed twenty-four miles down the bay and to within forty miles of Norfolk, that they came upon the floating hulk of a charter fishing vessel and its passengers. There had no been no measurable fallout since Neil had gone below about an hour and a half before, so Frank had let Olly remain on duty with him rather than bring Neil up again. But when he saw the derelict he called down for Neil.

Frank had altered course when he saw the survivors waving frantically at him, and with a gloomy, doomed expression he now ordered Neil and Olly to prepare to pick them up. The hulk lay low in the water, its afterdeck crowded with fifteen to twenty people—men, women, and children—a seemingly random collection of those who had escaped the disasters of somewhere to blunder into the disaster of the explosion over Norfolk.

A large man with a blond beard emerged from the crowd to stand on the cabin roof and shout that they'd been swamped by a tidal wave and, with flooded batteries, were helpless. The two vessels rolled and pitched awkwardly in the swells, and when they were rafted together at last, their decks sometimes slammed together with a sickening crunch.

Frank surveyed the packed near side of the yacht, the dazed and anxious faces, all looking exhausted, many sick, some people with burned faces and singed hair, two or three women holding children, men elbowing their way in front of them, and he felt the same sense of despair he'd felt when Neil showed him the ash on the deck: he was trapped and about to be overwhelmed.

"We're headed out into the Atlantic," he shouted over to the other boat. "We can put you ashore at Cape Henry or take you out to sea."

Frank saw that most of the fatigued and frightened faces looked at him without comprehension. A ship had come to rescue them; if he'd announced he was sailing to Hell, they still would have come aboard.

"Bring all your food!" Neil shouted, but no one seemed to pay attention. The men began to clamber over *Vagabond*'s combing like pirates boarding a ship they planned to plunder. Only Jim and Neil tried to help the weak and injured aboard.

A scream broke from the confusion, and a pale young blond woman was soon led sobbing into the wheelhouse, her right hand bloody; apparently it had been crushed between the two boats. Neil called down to Jeanne and told her to get Macklin and the ship's first aid kit, and he had the woman sit down on a wheelhouse settee. Between sobs the woman kept calling for her cat and seemed as disturbed by its not being present as by her mangled fingers.

The big man with the bushy beard was the only one helping people to escape from the foundering *Fishkiller,* and when Frank yelled again to bring all their food and water, he ducked down into the ship's cabin and soon began passing cartons of food across to Jim.

A dog snarled at Jeanne when she brought up the first aid kit, and Neil had an impulse to throw the stupid beast into the sea. Macklin followed, wearing a raincoat. Neil could hear someone retching loudly off the afterdeck and smelled vomit.

As Macklin bent to examine the woman's hand two men began scuffling behind him and one fell against Neil, knocking him into the seated woman, who screamed in pain. The two men, arms locked around each other in a violent wrestling match, reeled against a young couple and child on the opposite settee and then bounced off them onto the wheelhouse floor.

Macklin jumped up and grabbed them both by their hair, yanked hard, and shouted at them to let go. In another half-minute he and Neil had separated them.

It took almost fifteen minutes before the sixteen survivors and skimpy food supplies of *Fishkiller* had been transferred to *Vagabond*. At last the two ships separated, *Vagabond*'s genoa ballooning out to port with a flutter and a loud pop, and the derelict wallowing in the swells behind her.

The new passengers were scattered in listless confusion throughout the two cockpits, wheelhouse, and main cabin. Dressed in suits, slacks, jeans, bathrobes, and bathing suits were two elderly men, five women, three children, one of them an infant, and six able-bodied men. Neil was aware of at least one dog and cat aboard, but in the chaos it seemed like a dozen. Suitcases, knapsacks, and shopping bags were also strewn around underfoot.

After *Vagabond* had been sailing on southward toward the mouth of the Chesapeake for several minutes, the big man with the beard who seemed to have been their leader came up to Frank, who was at the helm. He had removed his foul-weather jacket and boots, but still was wearing the red plastic pants.

"My name's Tony Mariano," the man announced loudly. "Where the hell are you heading?" He was dressed in blue jeans and a silk shirt and fancy leather loafers. He was a powerfully built man in his late twenties, and he loomed at least a couple of inches over Frank.

"We're headed out to sea," Frank replied.

"You're not taking us past Norfolk, are you?" the man persisted. "That's right into the fallout."

"That's our plan," Frank replied uncertainly.

As he watched Macklin work on the woman's crushed fingers Neil was aware that two couples in the wheelhouse were listening intently to the conversation; even the woman he was treating seemed to forget her pain for the moment.

"The law of the sea," Frank went on in a tense voice to Tony, "says that anyone rescuing shipwrecked survivors can either continue on to his scheduled next port, or put them ashore at the nearest point they find convenient. We—"

"I don't give a fuck about the laws of the sea," Tony broke in. "We're not sailing into a rain of death."

"That's right," another man said, coming up to the wheel. "Some of us are sick already. We can't take any more radioactivity." A teenage boy, an older man, and two women now gathered near Frank too. As Neil watched he could feel his anger rising.

"What's going on?" another man asked, pushing his way past Neil.

"This man is taking us south back into the fallout," Tony answered loudly.

"If you like—" Frank began.

"I thought we were going north," the second man said.

"I did too," the elderly man said. "Away from the explosion."

Several additional voices made noises indicating that they agreed. Frank stood frowning.

"But in the north—" he began again.

"Who owns this boat anyway?" Tony asked, looking around aggressively as if someone were trying to put something over on him.

"I do," Frank replied. "And I—"

"Well, get us turned around before it's too late."

A chorus of "Yeahs" resounded after Tony's remark.

Neil slid away from the crowd and found Olly organizing the suitcases and knapsacks in the port cockpit.

"Go get the .38 that's hidden in my aft cabin," he whispered to him, "and be ready to back me up. Tell Jim to get the .22."

Olly nodded solemnly, and when he had gone, Neil descended into the main cabin. Two strange women and three children were seated at the dinette, and Jeanne and Lisa seemed to be waiting on them. Jeanne looked up intently at him as he entered.

"What's happening now?" she asked anxiously.

"Chaos," Neil answered. He walked past her and took Macklin's .45 from its hiding place behind a short shelf of books. After checking the chamber he returned to the wheelhouse.

"I think we'd better head east, Neil," Frank said to him nervously as he came up the steps. "These people think that—"

Neil's gun exploded once with a deafening bang. All conversation ceased. He shoved the person nearest him and the others backed away too. Everyone in the wheelhouse and cockpits stared at Neil, who stood for a moment in the center of the crowd holding his .45 with the barrel just a few inches below his chin—where everyone could see it. He was feeling a strange mixture of desperation, fury, and determination. In his yellow foul-weather gear he looked strangely out of place among the crowd of refugees.

"All right," he began in a loud, tense voice. "I want you all to listen, and I want you to get it.

"We're at war, and I'm your commanding officer. I expect everyone here to obey me as if I were God incarnate, without hesitancy and without question. I've commanded regular Navy ships ten times this size, and I've been sailing boats like this for ten years. If anyone else on board feels he's better qualified, he'd better speak up now.''

There was a silence, and when Neil felt some people begin to stir restlessly, he plunged on.

"Good," he went on, still speaking loudly. "Frank Stoor, here beside me, who owns this boat, is first mate. You treat him as you would me. Captain Olly, the old fellow standing over there is second mate. And Jim, at the helm now, is third mate. They are the ship's officers, and their word is law. If anyone willfully disobeys any of our commands, I will personally throw him overboard. *Do you get it?*''

No one spoke. Most were falling back into that listlessness they'd had before Tony stirred them up.

"Good," said Neil after a pause, aware now of the sweat dripping down his face, of Frank staring at him uncertainly, of Tony looking at him with a mixture of fear and resentment.

"As captain I'm announcing that our course is through the fallout area around Norfolk and out into the Atlantic.''

A few groans greeted this statement, but Neil cut them off immediately.

"*Shut up!*'' he shouted. "We're heading south until I feel it's safe to make a landfall. You may feel that we ought to have a democratic discussion of what we ought to do. I don't give a shit how you feel. If you don't like this policy, I'll give you a life preserver and you can go in a different direction. You may decide later, when you're out in the Atlantic, that you wish you'd never left land. Bitch among yourselves all you like, but *obey.*''

"But what if—'' someone began.

"Anyone who willfully disobeys one of my commands will be thrown overboard.''

When Neil paused again, no one spoke.

"You're beginning to understand," Neil went on more quietly. "Now for some commands. First of all I want all weapons—guns and knives with a blade longer than two inches—turned over to the ship's officers immediately. These weapons will be returned to you when we part company. Anyone found with a weapon on his person or in his luggage ten minutes from now . . . will be thrown overboard.''

Silence.

"Second, I want this area around the wheel and around the winches kept clear. When an officer orders you to go sit someplace on the boat, you go sit there and don't move without permission. Consider where he puts you to be your battle station.

"Thirdly, anyone who brought food aboard shall immediately contribute all of it to the ship's stores. If you leave soon, it will be returned to you. We're sharing our ship, our weapons, our water, our food, and our skills with you, and we expect you to do the same with us. Anyone caught hoarding a private stash of food or eating or permitting his or her children to eat any of the ship's food not rationed out to them will be thrown overboard."

Again Neil paused, aware that Jim was watching him.

"What if we have to go to the bathroom?" a woman asked in a frightened voice.

"If a man has to piss, he goes to the leeward side of the boat and pisses into the bay," Neil replied in the same loud, tense voice. "If you don't know which side of the boat that is, you ask an officer. Knowing which side of a boat to piss off is what made him an officer in the first place." Olly chuckled, but the others were too frightened or awed to respond.

"Ladies will piss in buckets provided in the side cabins. A mate will see to it that their contents are tossed overboard."

"Aren't there marine toilets?" someone asked.

"Yes, there are. But the animal species capable of landing men on the moon and blowing the world apart has yet to develop a marine toilet that doesn't clog if you stare at it too long. While we're this crowded and while we have more important things on our minds, we won't use them."

This time when he hesitated, Neil felt that he'd gotten his point across, but perhaps too strongly.

"I sound harsh," he continued. "I intend to be harsh. I intend this ship and those remaining aboard it to survive. My experience has been that in life-or-death situations the traditional Navy way of doing things is the only one that works. This policy is not open to discussion. Are there any questions?"

The silence aboard *Vagabond* as she sailed serenely down the Chesapeake in the direction most people thought they didn't want to go was uncanny. No one spoke. Most of those he looked at simply looked numb.

"What if we have to vomit?" an elderly man finally asked.

"If you feel seasick, go to the leeward cockpit and lean over the combing. Vomit to leeward." Neil paused. "Anyone caught vomiting to windward will be . . . thrown overboard. Anyone who vomits to windward will be so covered with vomit, he'll probably be happy to be thrown overboard."

A few nervous giggles.

"All right," Neil concluded. "All weapons and food to the ship's officers. Anyone attempting to resist these commands will be shot. Olly, Frank, get the weapons first. . . ."

"Jesus, Neil," Frank said a half-hour later, when *Vagabond* was as calm and orderly as a concentration camp. "Don't you think you were a little hard on them?"

"No," Neil replied. "We're all trying to survive. Everyone on this boat, *everyone*, will lie, steal, cheat, and kill in order to survive. That speech served one purpose: to let their survival instinct know that the first thing it has to consider is *me* and whatever promotes the survival of this ship."

"It was nice of you to let me be first mate on my own boat."

Neil looked at Frank with total seriousness.

"It wasn't nice," he said. "You deserve it."

Frank stared at him.

"You bastard."

"You'd better believe it," Neil said coldly. "When I said everyone obeys my commands, I meant *every*one."

"I see."

"I hope so."

At seven that evening Neil had them anchored off the coast near Cape Charles and began ferrying refugees onto the beach with the inflatable dinghy. Neil had stated his intention of continuing south, passing within fifteen miles of Norfolk before making it out into the Atlantic, where they would remain until fallout conditions and radio reports indicated that they dared return to the U.S. coast. Three people asked to remain on *Vagabond,* including the man who had started all the fuss in the first place, Tony Mariano. The second volunteer was a woman named Elaine with a young child, and the third a small man named Seth Sperling.

Although Neil had the .45 tucked into his belt and had armed both Frank and Jim for the evacuation and the redistribution of food and weapons, the event proceeded more smoothly than had the boarding five hours earlier. Even Conrad Macklin went meekly when Neil ordered him to go with the very first group.

As he helped people down into the dinghy Frank became aware that some of those who were leaving were afraid now that they had made the wrong choice and wanted to remain on board, but when an elderly man hesitated and was clearly intending to ask to come back aboard, Frank brusquely ordered Jim to cast off and ferry the last group ashore. The beach was only fifty feet away and so ten minutes after the last trip ashore *Vagabond*'s inflatable had been pulled back up on deck and stowed and the ship was under way again.

When the sun set at eight-forty, they were still fifteen miles from the Chesapeake Bay Bridge-Tunnel. The wind was dropping and shifting as they neared the Norfolk-Portsmouth area, blowing now out of the northeast at only six or eight knots. With the tide against them now, they started up the engine.

After the sun was gone and with the half-moon not yet risen, the blackness that descended upon them was depressing. Fallout was appearing on deck again, and the only lights they could see were from fires still burning in the blast area, one in particular blazing up sporadically like hydrogen flares from a dying sun. All the navigational aids seemed to have been destroyed; the lights of the bridge-tunnel were gone. They had seen no traffic except for one tiny sailboat in the late afternoon; now at night they had seen no running lights at all. As they headed south toward the northern opening through the bridge causeway that would lead them out to sea it was as if they were the last ship on earth, sailing alone away from a doomed land into the unknown.

Leaving Olly alone at the helm, Neil joined Frank, Jim, and Jeanne in the main cabin for a conference. Although he had ordered each of them to try to sleep for a couple of hours, they all looked exhausted. The men hadn't shaved and hadn't changed clothes since the war had started. Jeanne's white clothes were dirty, her eyes red from fatigue or weeping, and her bruised cheek still ugly.

When Neil spoke, his voice was noticeably softer than it had been whenever he'd spoken to anyone on deck. He quietly laid out his plan of three-hour watches, with three watch teams, one led by each of the mates. Frank would work with the newcomer, Seth Sperling, a shy man who wore glasses and seemed uncertain of himself; Olly with big Tony Mariano; and Jim with Lisa. The third new passenger, a young woman named Elaine Booker, was to stay with her three-year-old child below in Jeanne's cabin. Olly and Seth would sleep in Neil's aft cabin; Tony in the forepeak cabin; and Jim with Frank in Frank's cabin. He himself would sleep on the aft settee of the wheelhouse so as to be always on call.

Neil said that the amount of radiation they'd been exposed to so far was insignificant, but Frank wasn't certain whether he really believed that or was merely saying it for the sake of morale. Jeanne's queasiness, Neil insisted, was simple seasickness.

When the meeting seemed to be over, Jeanne unexpectedly spoke up.

"I don't know how serious you were, Neil, but I warn you that I'll try to stop you from throwing anyone overboard," she said softly.

Startled, Neil looked at her, then his severe face broke into a small smile.

"I'd have to throw you overboard too," he said. "Then who would look after your children?"

Jeanne flushed with anger and Frank quickly cut in. "He'd have to throw me overboard too."

Neil stopped smiling and shook his head.

"I never said how close to shore we'd be when I threw someone overboard," he finally replied.

"Is that a promise?" Jeanne asked, looking directly at him.

"On the other hand," Neil went on, "the traditional punishment for mutiny *is* death. I'm afraid that is the way things are done aboard ship."

"Not my ship," Frank said.

"Let's agree then," said Neil quietly, after a pause, "that if there is a case of willful disobedience, I'll convene a court of inquiry composed of all the ship's officers and let them decide on the appropriate response."

Jim nodded, and then Frank did too.

"Jeanne," Neil went on gently, "please leave the management of the ship to me."

"Not when it involves the lives of my family."

"Your family?" Neil asked uncertainly.

"I consider everyone who comes aboard this boat a part of my new family."

Neil frowned.

"Then in that sense every decision I make involves your family."

"Then I am involved."

Frank was amazed at how serenely she stared back at Neil, her eyes glowing with rebellion.

"All right," Neil finally commented. "I understand your concern. If I seem cruel or capricious, you may complain to me, and we'll try to resolve it."

"Thank you."

"And if we don't, I'll throw you overboard."

He grinned.

"Not if I have my butcher knife," she rejoined, grinning back.

"I believe it," Neil said, standing up to end the meeting.

Back on deck in the darkness, Neil realized that the passage through the causeway, or the remains of the causeway, was going to be difficult to locate. He had taken a bearing on Fisherman's Island just before dark, but since then it had all been dead reckoning. Even after the half-moon had risen, there wasn't enough light to see anything on the horizon except the line of fires to the southwest. They would be able to see objects in the water no more than sixty feet away. Their depthmeter confirmed that they were in the big ship channel, but this by itself would give little advance warning of the presence of the causeway or the rocks of its wreckage. *Vagabond* was making toward the causeway at only about four knots.

Frank was sick, either from radiation exposure or ordinary seasickness, so Neil had Jim take his place on watch with Tony Mariano. When he ordered Tony to wash down the decks again just in case, Tony went to it quickly and energetically and finished with sweat pouring down his face and into his bushy beard. "Hell of a way to make a living" was his only comment.

"I wish we could see something!" Jim exclaimed a few minutes later as the three men stood sweating together around the helm.

"Alter course twenty degrees to the east," Neil ordered.

"What's up?" Tony asked.

"We're not going to see anything until we actually reach the causeway," Neil answered. "This way, when we do reach it, we'll know we're to the north of the channel. How are your night eyes, Tony?"

"Damn good."

"Go forward and stand at the bow as lookout. Keep an eye out not only forward but also to port and starboard."

"Aye, aye, sir."

Tony crawled forward in the darkness, and soon his huge form was visible against the distant horizon like a black sail bundle tied to the forestay. Neil ordered Jim up to wash down the aft sections of the boat and ordered Tony to do the bow again.

A half-hour later they had still seen nothing. Jim wondered aloud whether they'd miraculously sailed through a gap and not seen either side.

"Or maybe the whole causeway got blown to pieces," he suggested.

"*Object to starboard!*" Tony shouted, and Jim dampened the throttle and put her into reverse, bringing *Vagabond* slowly to a halt.

Neil turned on the twelve-volt spotlight and swung it to the right where Tony was pointing. A huge chunk of metal and some pilings appeared to be sticking out of the water. Neil swung the light in a slow arc, almost a full circle, but nothing else was visible. Although *Vagabond* was now in neutral, the tide was carrying her backward away from the strange objects to their right. The depthmeter showed they were in thirty-five feet of water—most likely on the edge of the big ship channel.

"Ease her over closer," Neil said to Jim, holding the spotlight on the huge protruding metal chunk, which seemed to get longer as they approached it. Slowly Jim maneuvered *Vagabond* to starboard and forward.

"Okay," Neil said after a while. "Back her off."

"What is it?" Jim asked, still not able to put the huge metal object and broken pilings into any coherent pattern.

"A sunken freighter."

"Oh . . . wow."

Jim backed *Vagabond* away and put her into neutral at Neil's command.

"She was either sunk by the blast or may have hit the submerged causeway. All we can do is ease forward some more, but we may be near it or on top of it." Neil left Jim to climb up on the cabin roof to see better.

It was ten minutes later that they spotted the causeway. It emerged in front of them like a long spit of land, which it was, as solid as the rocks that it was made of. Their spotlight revealed, however, that the roadway was shattered and dozens, even hundreds, of burned-out cars gleamed brightly in the ship's spotlight. No living being responded to their presence.

Neil had Jim swing *Vagabond* to starboard, and they motored south about two hundred feet from the causeway, Neil and Tony watching for the break in the wall that separated them from the sea. The air was still, and the sight of the endless line of blasted cars, motionless bodies sometimes visible inside them, made the humid air seem even more oppressive. They were all in full foul-weather gear, except that Jim had pushed back his hood.

Tony spotted the end of the causeway first and shouted the information back to Neil, who still kept *Vagabond*'s heading due south, as if they were going to motor right past it. But when the changes of depth registered by the depthmeter indicated that they were definitely in the middle of the big ship channel, Neil was sure the gap hadn't been created by the explosion.

"Take her through," he said quietly to Jim. "And on the other side alter course to due east magnetic."

"What about speed?" Jim asked.

"Slow her down to five knots. We don't want to hit something now that we're so close to getting out."

As they began motoring through the opening—now the other end of the causeway was also visible in the spotlight off starboard—Jim became aware of the gentle swells of the open sea, lifting *Vagabond*'s bow like a mother's gentle hand and then lowering it again, the ship pitching so gracefully that it was like a rocking cradle.

"What's that?" Tony shouted, pointing now to his right.

When Neil swung the spotlight in that direction, something huge appeared to be thrashing around in the water, sending gigantic bubbles bursting up to the surface not far from the end of the causeway. As Neil held the light on it, they all stared until finally Jim realized what it must be: air escaping from a hole in the undersea automobile tunnel directly beneath them must be bubbling up to the surface. Neil shut off the light with a grim nod.

As Jim slowly altered course to due east, he smiled to himself with the excitement of breaking free. Except for the unlighted buoys, sunken ships, derelicts, fallout, and further explosions, it was all clear sailing from here, he thought almost gaily. Ahead of him he could see only darkness, Tony even now not visible.

Lisa came up out of the main cabin with three cups of water and handed one to Neil and another to Jim.

"Thanks, Lisa, we're sweltering up here," Jim said, smiling down at her. "But we're out of the bay."

"We're in the ocean?" she asked him.

"Yep. And no new fallout either."

Seth Sperling suddenly appeared in the darkness beside them.

"Where are we?" he asked, staring at the dark shape of the causeway still visible astern and off to port.

"That's what's left of the northern section of the causeway of the Chesapeake Bay Bridge-Tunnel," Jim replied, looking forward to where he could just make out Tony crouching at the bow. "We're out in the ocean."

"And what's that boat coming toward us?" Seth asked next, as casually as if they'd been in a crowded, well-lit harbor.

"What?" said Neil, wheeling to face where he saw the little man staring.

A motorboat without its running lights on, which must have been hidden on the seaward side of the causeway, was angling in at them from the darkness of the causeway.

"Get the guns!" Neil hissed at Jim. "Aft cabin. Lisa, get below. Tony!" He shouted forward to the dim figure at the bow.

"What's up?" Tony asked as he began to amble back aft, stopping near the mast to retrieve the spotlight.

"A boat coming!" Neil snapped back. "May be pirates."

Neil squinted into the darkness and suddenly saw the motorboat now only thirty feet away and closing fast, its big outboard motor now audible over *Vagabond*'s diesel. When it was obvious that the smaller craft had no intention of standing off to identify itself, Neil threw the throttle full forward, and *Vagabond* slowly responded. Jim returned with the weapons.

"Keep the .22," Neil whispered fiercely to Jim, taking Macklin's .45, "and take the helm. Seth, can you use a pistol?"

Wide-eyed, Seth shook his head "No."

"Then take it forward to Tony. Quick!"

Even as he spoke, he could see the motorboat was already only a few yards away, a twenty-footer with three or four men aboard. Neither boat was showing running lights, and the men on the motorboat had not hailed them or signaled to them in any way. Neil shouted at them but there was no answer.

Crouching in the wheelhouse doorway and certain of danger, Neil fired a warning shot above *Vagabond*'s combing and over the launch, which had now moved so close to *Vagabond* that he couldn't have hit it from the wheelhouse if he'd tried. The thump as the launch careered into *Vagabond*'s port hull was both heard and felt.

"Get down, Jim!" Neil whispered, watching the combing for the outline of a human figure. He could still hear the roar of the outboard outside the line of his sight, less than fifteen feet away. Crouching down, Jim swung *Vagabond* sharply to starboard for the moment, tearing the two boats apart. The launch, speeding along on its earlier course, came in sight twenty-five feet off *Vagabond*'s port side, and Neil fired a second shot, this time to kill, but Jim had swerved back again, throwing off his aim. Feeling sure he hadn't hit anyone, he watched tensely as the launch quickly closed on *Vagabond,* disappearing behind her combing.

"Stay below!" Neil suddenly shouted, fearful that Jeanne or Frank, awakened by the shots, might emerge right in the line of fire. Then, again acting instinctively, he ran in a crouch across the wheelhouse out into the opposite cockpit and crawled onto the deck beside the entrance to his aft cabin. As he stared through the blackness at *Vagabond*'s port side, he suddenly realized that the motorboat had dropped back into *Vagabond*'s wake and . . .

The *bam-bam-bam-bam-bam* of the automatic rifle sent Neil rolling off the deck back into the side cockpit, the slugs slammed through the forward Plexiglas windows of the wheelhouse, and Jim swung the trimaran sharply into another evasive turn to starboard.

Trembling, Neil quickly crept back up to peer astern, but the launch was no longer in their wake; from the sound of the outboard it seemed to be returning to the port side.

Two quick shots rang out from forward, sounding like Tony with the .38, and a vicious *bam-bam-bam-bam* answered from the automatic rifle.

Jim swerved again, this time into the launch, and the two boats collided with a crash that elicited a scream from one of the attackers. Jim held the trimaran at full port rudder, the two boats crashing together again, and a man suddenly pulled himself up onto the deck behind the port cockpit and fired two shots at Jim as he crouched at the helm.

Hearing rather than seeing what was happening, Neil leaped aft to get around the wheelhouse, saw the man with the gun, shot him once, and then kept running across his cabin top to fire his last three shots down into the launch, which was speeding along, locked together with *Vagabond.* Then he dove into the port cockpit, rolling away into the wheelhouse. Jim, squatting down, pulled the wheel now full the other way; *Vagabond* swept off to starboard.

Trembling and tingling with fear again, Neil crawled behind the wheelhouse settee for protection, listening for the sound of gunfire, his shoulders and back waiting to feel the thud and sting of a bullet. Then, in the silence, he realized that the launch was no longer bumping *Vagabond*'s port hull. He dared to raise his head to peer out the shattered Plexiglas window, but could see nothing. He ducked around into the starboard cockpit again, staring astern, but again could see no sign of the attackers. Although he knew he must have hit some of them in the boat, he was afraid Jim's maneuvering had disoriented him and even now the attackers might be about to pick him off.

"*Seth! Tony!*" he called forward. "*Come aft!*"

He needed a weapon now that his .45 was out of ammunition. He thought he had hit two of the three dark figures in the speeding boat, knew he had hit the man on *Vagabond*'s deck—looked over to make certain he was still lying where he had been hit.

Tony thumped down into the cockpit beside him.

"Seth is hit," Tony said. "But that boat is buzzing off."

"Where?" said Neil.

"It's way off the other side," Tony replied. "I think I hit a couple of them." Even in the darkness Neil could see Tony's eyes were wide with excitement or fear. For a half-minute he remained crouched down, listening for the sound of the outboard, but he could no longer hear it.

"Are you all right, Jim?" he then whispered.

"Yes," Jim answered, his voice cracking, "but they really wrecked poor *Vagabond*." The forward Plexiglas windows were shattered in five or six places. They'd have to check for other damage.

"Head us back east," Neil said. "Keep us at full throttle."

For a minute more *Vagabond* surged through the darkness, beginning, at almost nine knots, to smash into the swells with loud booming reports. Neil, Tony, and Jim stayed where they were, then Neil walked beside Jim and turned off the engine.

In a few seconds the noise of both the diesel and of *Vagabond*'s hull plowing through the swells had diminished to nothing, and Neil strained his ears to hear the outboard. There was no sound of it. Jim suddenly left the helm and vomited into the sea from the port cockpit. Expressionlessly he returned.

"Okay," said Neil, feeling for the first time since the skirmish had started a measure of calm. "Get her going again, Jim. Come on, Tony, let's see about Seth."

In another thirty minutes the sense of danger had passed. *Vagabond* was almost four miles from the causeway and was now sailing before a light breeze. The night was dark, the engine switched off now, and she was both invisible and inaudible to any potential attacker, except at very close range. Neil and Jeanne did their best to treat Seth Sperling's bullet wound, but they knew it was beyond their limited skills. Seth had been struck by the first burst of automatic rifle fire, a slug tearing through his left thigh and imbedding itself in his right thigh. The artery hadn't been severed, so all they did was clean the wound, staunch the flow of blood, and give Seth some antibiotics.

Later, when Neil came up on deck, he realized that the man he had shot was still lying on the afterdeck. He went and knelt beside the body, that of a slender man, and searched his pants pockets: wallet, handkerchief, some change, several loose bills, a business card. Then he rolled the man over to look at the face. In the dim light from the aft cabin, where Jeanne was still sitting with Seth, he could see little, but something looked strange. He asked Frank to shine a light over and then he saw: the man's face was disfigured with recent burns. Neil wondered if the whole boatload of attackers was equally disfigured.

He briefly recited from memory the concluding verses from the Navy burial service and then rolled the body into the sea.

At dawn Neil, sleeping in the back of the old wheelhouse area, was half-awakened by something. Lying on his back, he had the vague feeling of still being in a dream. He was disoriented. In the dream he had been lying where he was lying now, but Jim was at the helm, and another figure, also himself it seemed, was seated a few feet away on the port settee. The third figure in the wheelhouse was both himself and an intruder, and he struggled in his half-awakened state to determine who the other person was. In the dream the figure began to take on a more ominous emotional significance; Neil began to have the nightmarish feeling of struggling to awaken himself in order to deal with impending danger.

He sat up with a groan, awake at last. Jim was standing at the helm, as in his dream, and to his left, seated with characteristic calm, was the thick, compact figure of Conrad Macklin. He was sipping a cup of tea.

For a brief moment Neil felt himself back in the dream, then realized with a sinking feeling that he was facing reality. Conrad Macklin was back on board.

He looked steadily at Macklin, who gazed back without expression.

"Would you like some hot tea?" Macklin asked.

"Where'd you come from?" Neil finally asked.

"I never really left," Macklin answered. "I stowed away in some kind of storage area up front."

"How did you get back aboard?"

"Swam out, mostly underwater, right after you put me ashore," Macklin replied. "Pulled myself up the anchor line while you were loading the last bunch onto the dinghy."

Neil continued to stare at Macklin coldly, then released a long sigh. "A man is wounded," he said. "I suppose you'd better take a look at him."

"Good," said Macklin.

"I doubt it," said Neil.

An hour later, awake but with his eyes closed, he realized that all night long, even before the dream, something had been missing, something he ought to be feeling but was not. *Vagabond* was cutting cleanly through the blue waters; dead ahead the sunlight sparkled like diamonds on the whitecaps. He had escaped to sea; the horrors of the land were receding. At such times he should feel elated. But he didn't. Something inside him must be telling him that this time there was no escape: the tentacles of land had reached out and even now lay heavily on his deck. He was at sea, but that ninety-eight cent lump of earth called man was still with him.

PART TWO

ASHES

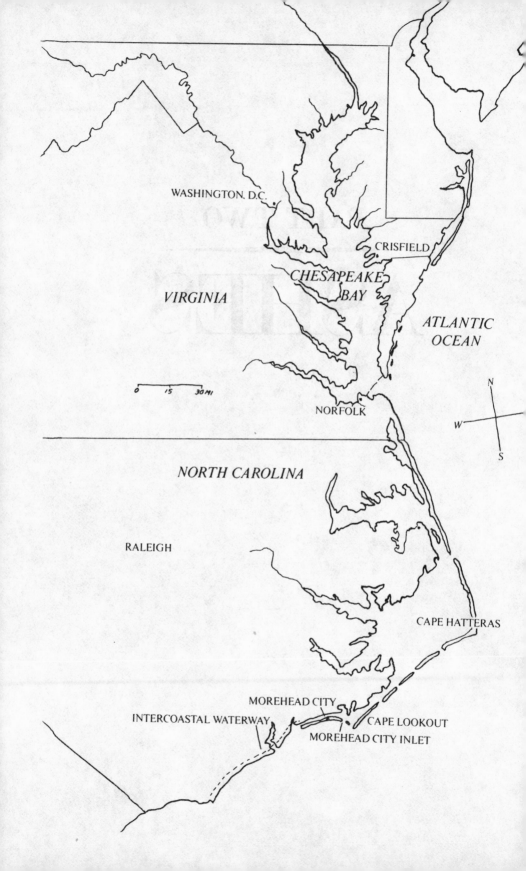

THE moon, now almost three-quarters full, lit up the sea to port like a giant nightlight. It was after midnight, and Neil had enjoyed the last hour more than any since they'd fled the Chesapeake three days before. *Vagabond* was now rushing through the night at eleven or twelve knots, and Neil was feeling that exhilaration that only a sailboat tearing through the sea at night could give him.

Behind were three trails of phosphorescent white, bubbling out so fast it seemed *Vagabond* must be doing twenty knots, no matter what the speedometer read. Ahead Neil could see almost nothing. The trimaran charged into the blackness, as if totally confident that nothing could halt her queenly progress.

They were now about a hundred miles east of the North Carolina coast, and Neil held his course at due south by lining up the cluster of stars that made up Orion's belt with the upper port shroud. He had let Jim and Lisa, whose official watch it was, continue sleeping, rather than wake them for their midnight to three A.M. watch. *Vagabond,* plunging forward through the night, was just on the edge of being over-canvased, and Neil kept checking to feel if the wind was getting too strong for the sail area. So far it hadn't, and part of his joy arose from the feeling that he, *Vagabond,* the wind, and the sea were in total harmony.

With moderate seas he had been able to adjust the mizzen so that *Vagabond* was steering herself. He could wander out of the wheelhouse into either cockpit to stare at the stars or watch the moonlight on the sea, and *Vagabond,* like a giant puppy unleashed and glorying in a midnight romp, hurtled forward by herself through the night. At moments like this she seemed to be human, and he loved her, urged her on in his mind, congratulated her when, after an errant wave had pushed her bow off course, her mizzen slowly pushed her stern around to get her back on course.

All the troubles of the day were flushing away in *Vagabond*'s bubbling wake. Although the familiar gray cloud masses, which had seemed to be permanently pursuing them, had dissipated two days earlier, Neil, Frank, and Olly had all suffered from radiation sickness. Frank was still nauseous after three days, and Olly still suffered from diarrhea. Although the men had told the others it was seasickness, they all knew that none of them were ever seasick except in exceptionally heavy seas. Neil himself had been queasy for two days and once—only he knew it had happened—vomited off the afterdeck. His sickness frightened and depressed him, but on this third day it appeared to be gone.

In addition, listening to reports of the war had been a depressing and divisive experience. Although a Pentagon spokesman that morning had made a vague report about the great devastation that had been wreaked upon the Soviet Union, about a decisive naval victory in the Indian Ocean, about the grudging way allied forces were giving ground in what was left of Europe; the idea that the U.S. might win the war seemed irrelevant in the face of a report that most of the population east of Cleveland, north of Philadelphia, and south of Boston was fleeing from the effects of the war—lack of food, water, electricity, and the reality and fear of radioactive fallout. It was implied that half the northeast might soon be uninhabitable for all except a tenth of its former population. Other sections of the country were equally endangered. How people were evacuating when all fuel was requisitioned by the military and the public transportation network had ceased to exist was not explained.

"They're jogging," Frank had commented, not mentioning that his wife and a daughter might still be alive and among the fleeing millions.

Neil wandered to the back of the cockpit to adjust the drag on the trolling rig that was jammed in place there. Although they rarely

hooked anything at night, especially at ten knots, Neil had asked Olly
to try. As he set the drag and checked the tension, he remembered
that it was Jeanne who had finally gotten them out of their oppressive
mood. Earlier that evening she had browbeaten them into a singa-
long. It had started out as lugubriously as a funeral dirge, but ended
with giddy silliness. Captain Olly taught them a blatantly obscene sea
chanty, and though Lisa blushed, little Skippy sang along loudly and
triggered the last burst of laughter by announcing that he liked songs
about pussies.

Pressing the rod back into place, Neil smiled at the memory. The
world of the last several days had been one emotional somersault
after another: the gloom of thinking about the war and personal losses
alternating with the delights of sailing or of eating their meager meals
or bringing in a fish. He wished he could control the lows. In the
Chesapeake they had endured seemingly hourly threats to their survival, but now, ninety miles from land, he felt it was his task to
create for them a new world of order, routine, and dependability. As
he came back to lean against the entrance of Frank's cabin and look
forward, he thought of his watch teams.

Frank and Tony, Olly and Macklin, and Jim and Lisa were now
working out well. At first he'd tried Tony with Olly, figuring Olly
might need Tony's extra strength, but it hadn't worked. Tony was a
huge athletic man of twenty-eight, outgoing, ebullient, used to running things—a former football star and successful salesman. He'd
had trouble getting along with Olly. Although Olly never appeared to
order Tony around, he assumed control of *Vagabond* as naturally as
he had of *Lucy Mae*. He treated Tony as a minor tool, a winch handle
perhaps, and didn't tend to listen when the winch handle talked back.
Once when Tony finished a brilliant analysis of why loosening the
genoa sheet and altering course three degrees had increased their speed
a half-knot, Olly responded with a brief silence, a puff on his unlit
pipe, and the suggestion that Tony should tighten up on the genoa a
bit and alter course three degrees back again. At the end of their first
day at sea Tony had taken Frank aside to complain.

"The old guy's senile," he had said when they were off in the
port cockpit after Olly had retired into the aft cabin to nap. "I don't
think he relates to people anymore."

"Only when he wants to," Frank replied.

"He spent an hour on watch today talking about the various positions he used when he was screwing his third wife. Claimed there were twenty-seven and started mumbling and swearing when he could only remember twenty-two."

Frank smiled.

"You get a free stand-up comic every watch," he said.

"I don't want a stand-up comic," Tony exploded. "I want to talk with someone who speaks English."

"I'll take it up with Neil," Frank said.

"Why the hell can't you change the watches?" Tony went on. "You own the boat, don't you?"

"I own it," Frank replied evenly. "And Neil is captain. I'll speak to him."

"Let me work with you," Tony said. "Macklin is exactly the quiet sort that Olly will love."

"You're probably right," Frank had said, smiling, and when he had reported the conversation Neil had laughed and changed the watch teams as suggested.

Jim and Lisa were an unexpected gift. Lisa hopped around the boat with the nimbleness of a cat, and although she had to be reminded to wear a life jacket when she went forward to change a sail, she otherwise followed orders quickly and well. Intensely serious most of the time, she seemed to glow when working with Jim, as if the physical work liberated her from her seriousness.

For a moment Neil was brought out of his reverie by the appearance of a light off the port bow, but he decided it was just the moonlight reflecting off a distant whitecap. He wandered from the starboard cockpit through the wheelhouse with its unattended wheel to the port side to get a better look and to take a piss off the afterdeck. As he approached he was startled to see a head and shoulders silhouetted against the reflection of the moonlight on the water. It was Jeanne's profile, silent and motionless compared to the swirling, rushing roller-coaster ride of *Vagabond* through the ocean.

He stopped unnoticed a few feet away and looked with her out over the water; the night breeze stirred her long hair away from her face.

"Oh!" she said, turning her head as she became aware of his presence.

"Incredible, isn't it?" he asked softly.

She turned away again to look out at the river of moonlight that sparkled across the ocean, flowing toward them from the east.

"Yes," she said.

Neil stood close behind her, steadying himself with his right arm on the wheelhouse roof and smiling, in love with *Vagabond*, the sea, the night, the moon.

"Who's steering?" Jeanne asked, turning briefly back to him, her face in darkness with her back to the moon.

"*Vagabond*," he answered. "She told me she wanted to handle things herself for a while."

Jeanne rose slightly to stare past him into the wheelhouse and saw the unattended wheel. Then she looked up at the sails and aft at the three white rivers of light bubbling out behind them. Finally she looked back at Neil.

"Amazing," she said.

"As long as there are wind, sails, and sea, the world won't be all bad," he said.

"For *you*," she commented.

"For me," he agreed quietly.

"I'm still not comfortable out here," she said. "The idea that there's a mile of water beneath me and no dry land within a hundred miles is a little terrifying. I'm sorry."

"If it weren't a little terrifying," Neil replied after a pause, "it wouldn't be so beautiful."

She also took some time before replying.

"For a while I thought you weren't emotional about anything" she said.

"I guess I'm not," he replied, "except about the sea."

"Millions can die, but a good wind cures all," she said, not sarcastically but rather questioningly, as if trying to understand him.

"If I can't save the millions," Neil replied cautiously, "then I'm willing to enjoy a good wind."

"But what if you can?" she countered.

"Then I'd like to know how."

She turned away and stared out into the darkness.

"No, the millions are lost," she finally said. "And I have to admit you're good at saving the single digits."

Still standing behind her, Neil didn't reply.

"A ship's no place for children," Jeanne went on quietly. "Especially with reduced rations . . . no definite destination, people sick . . . their whole previous lives . . . gone forever . . ."

"I know," Neil said, "but children who've just . . . lost their father, seen their mother beaten up, been hit on the head with a gun butt, aren't likely to be comfortable in any new place." He paused. "But Lisa's doing great out here," he went on. "Skippy will too. Give him time."

"I suppose so," she said, "but the portions of food you're making us dole out are so pathetically small, it's frightening."

"I know," Neil said, then had to grab the back of Jeanne's settee as a swell sent him staggering. "But just ask yourself how you're going to feed Skippy two weeks from today."

She grimaced, nodded, and finally managed a small smile.

"I keep forgetting that the next supermarket may be a decade away."

"If we're lucky," Neil replied. The radio reports made it clear that on the mainland supermarkets had ceased to exist even in the "untouched" areas. Everything—even in farming country—was being confiscated and rationed by the military. Food was going to be their major worry for a long, long time. He and Jeanne had set aside an emergency food supply on their second day at sea, good for ten days at half-rations, but not counting that emergency cache, they had enough food even at their present low rate of consumption for only four or five more days. Catching fish was their key to survival.

A random wave slapped loudly at the speeding hull and sent a fine spray up over them in the cockpit. As he stood there he suddenly got a strong sense of Jeanne's fear and loneliness.

"I'm afraid stability and the familiar are gone forever," he said quietly.

She was still looking out over the sea. "Even on land there's no place left to stand," she said in a low voice.

In a shattering rush Neil was aware of her as a woman, filled with the desire to hold her, protect her, care for her. He released his grip on the wheelhouse roof and took a stride toward her just as an unexpected swell lifted *Vagabond*'s port hull and then lowered it with a slam, sending Neil tumbling forward and down onto Jeanne. After clutching her right leg to steady himself, he ended up sitting beside her on the cockpit seat.

"What's happening?" she asked him urgently. "Are you all right?"

Neal laughed softly. He could see her face clearly for the first time in the moonlight. The bruise on her check was almost gone, and she looked beautiful.

"I wanted to come over and comfort and protect you," he said, smiling. "Instead I almost knocked you overboard."

Gazing wide-eyed at him, she took awhile to absorb what he'd said.

"Maybe you'd better get us life preservers," she commented, smiling.

For Neil the world was reduced to her eyes gleaming in the moonlight. He pulled her gently toward him, cradling her head against the side of his face, simply holding her close. He only noticed the stiffness of her initial response after he felt her suddenly sag against him, relax, and sigh.

"Oh, Neil," she said, and he felt her arms tighten around his back, her powerful hug surprising him. After a long moment they drew apart, and Jeanne tilted back her head to look with her large glowing eyes into his. Their faces came together as slowly and inevitably and perfectly as *Vagabond* correcting her course; their lips touched, wetted, parted, kissed. Neil lost track of time and place, and when the kiss ended and Jeanne gasped for breath, he instinctively glanced at the sails and sea to assure himself that his ship was still on course.

Jeanne sighed.

"Well," she said, blinking her eyes and looking a little dazed. "Well."

"How beautiful you are," said Neil. She looked up at him uncertainly.

"Neil! . . . Neil!"

When Jim's voice invaded their world with cruel abruptness, Neil released Jeanne and stood up.

"Over here, Jim," he said, looking into the wheelhouse and dimly seeing Jim standing by the wheel.

"Oh, there you are," Jim said, rubbing his eyes. "I just came up to go on watch and saw there was no one at the wheel and panicked."

"*Vagabond*'s sails are balanced," he said. "She's self-steering."

"Really? That's fantastic," Jim said, coming toward Neil. "Isn't it about time for me to take the helm. I thought you said . . . Oh! . . . Hi, Jeanne."

"Hi, Jim," Jeanne said.

"It's about twelve thirty," Neil said, glancing at his watch. "Since *Vagabond* was doing the job by herself, I thought I'd let you and Lisa sleep."

"Thanks," said Jim. "Wow. Look at that moon."

Neil turned to follow Jim's gaze out to the east, his eyes just meeting Jeanne's briefly.

"It's quite a night," Neil agreed.

"I feel great," said Jim. "I think I needed the extra sleep."

"Do you want me to fix you some coffee?" Jeanne asked.

"Oh, no, I'm fine," said Jim. "Besides, Neil says we can't have any coffee at night except under pressure conditions."

" 'Pressure conditions'?" Jeanne inquired, looking up at Neil.

"I think it means no coffee unless we're sinking," said Jim, grinning.

"I doubt we'll be able to get any more coffee unless we end up in South America," Neil commented with his usual seriousness. "It's now a delicacy. Sorry."

"Our Captain Bligh," said Jeanne, smiling.

"He was a marvelous seaman," Neil rejoined.

"But unpopular with his crew," said Jeanne.

"*I* like Neil," said Jim solemnly, and Jeanne and Neil both laughed.

A sudden violent snapping and flapping from the bow sent Neil rushing past Jim over to starboard. The genoa was luffing, and *Vagabond* was veering off course upwind. He turned the wheel to port, and when he saw her swinging back on course he realized that the genoa sheet had come loose.

"Winch the genny in," he said to Jim, who had followed him over to help. As he steadied *Vagabond*'s course, he watched Jim pull in the line controlling the genoa, first by hand and then with three turns around the winch.

"Far enough?" Jim finally asked.

"A little more," Neil said.

When the genoa was sheeted to Neil's satisfaction, and *Vagabond* once again contentedly galloped southward through the night, Neil turned the helm over to Jim.

"I think she'll steer herself still," Neil said. "But you may have to adjust the genny or mizzen sheets to get it right. Do you remember how I showed you?"

"Sure. I've got her now."

"Good."

Neil turned to see if Jeanne was still there and saw her standing next to the entrance to her cabin. He walked over to stand behind her, just touching her, their backs to Jim, looking out to sea.

"How strange it is," she said softly after a long pause. "Here my husband is dead, millions killed, millions more doomed, and all I can think of is wanting a man I've known for just a few days in bed with me."

Startled, he turned to her.

"Jeanne—" he said.

"But I can't—"

". . . Jeanne," he whispered again. "Life doesn't offer us much these days. . . . We should take what we can. . . ."

They were only a few inches apart; she turned to look up at him, the moonlight full on her face, his in shadow.

"No, Neil," she said softly. "There are others. And, my God, only four days . . . I think I owe it to Bob, and to . . . Frank . . . to you even, to assume it's just . . . temporary insanity."

"Would we were always insane like this," said Neil.

"No, Neil," she said and, squeezing his hand once, disappeared down her cabin steps. Vaguely Neil thought she might also have whispered a "Good night." He reluctantly slid her hatch closed and, feeling exhilarated and alive, headed back to the wheelhouse. Jim was sitting on the edge of the other cockpit combing, staring forward.

"I'm going to rest here in the wheelhouse," Neil said to him. "And if you fall overboard," he went on, noting Jim's somewhat precarious perch on the side of the boat, "remember to leave a forwarding address."

"An island in the South Pacific," Jim responded immediately.

Stretching out on the cushions, Neil yawned.

"You'd better be in good shape," he commented.

"Good night," he heard Jim say to him.

"That's my impression," said Neil, smiling to himself, until the sudden image of Frank chilled him.

Vagabond, indifferent to it all, plunged forward through the night.

After Neil had fallen asleep on the cushions in the back of the wheelhouse, Jim was forced to take the helm. The wind had picked up and was heading them more; he wasn't able to get the sails adjusted so that *Vagabond* could steer herself anymore. Even though he looked forward to her company on their watch, he decided to let Lisa sleep a little longer. He wanted time alone to think.

Although Jim had disagreed with his father at the time, Jim admired him for trying to get back home to Oyster Bay to try to save his mother and Susie. Jim knew that Frank had a fierce loyalty to his family, a sense of family pride that often made him act too severely toward his children. Now that he himself was all the family that his father had left, Jim felt a sense of responsibility toward him he'd never felt before. This sense of caring was increased by his realization that, more than any of the others on board, his father still appeared to be in a state of shock.

Jim knew he had been hurt by Neil's taking command of *Vagabond,* and that of course his radiation sickness must be depressing him. Jim could see that Frank lacked his usual dynamic energy. When Jim had been helping him tear down the remains of the shattered rear wall of the wheelhouse and replace it with a sailcloth awning that could be raised and lowered, Frank had been enthusiastic about the task for half an hour and then had lost interest, wandering away and leaving the project for someone else to finish. The only person who seemed to be able to bring him back to life was Jeanne. When she'd suggested that all the men should take a turn working in the kitchen, he had smiled at her and argued playfully, "What's the sense of surviving if I have to wash the dishes?" but nevertheless had cleaned up the galley more cheerfully than Jim had ever seen. When Jeanne had become impatient with Skippy's clinging, Frank had spent close to an hour playing horsy and card games with him. Since he knew that his father *cared* about Jeanne's feelings, the way that Neil and Jeanne had been whispering together in the side cockpit earlier made Jim uneasy. For though he'd been too caught up in the rush for survival over the first four days to feel grief for his mother and Susie, now, when he was aware of his father's problem, he felt a sense of loss. He would never be able to express his love and appreciation for his mother; she had been cheated out of the love that both he and Frank would have given her had she survived to be with them now. Jim's feelings for his father were reinforced by this sense of having failed his mother. But how could he help him?

Lisa stepped from her mother's cabin out into the moonlight and then into the wheelhouse.

"It's our watch," she said. "Why didn't you wake me?" She was wearing jeans and a blue Windbreaker, her hair, dark and long like her mother's, tied into a ponytail. Since none of them could wash with fresh water, everyone's hair was getting stiff and straggly.

"Until the wind got too strong, *Vagabond* was self-steering," Jim replied in a low voice, motioning toward Neil. "Careful, Neil's sleeping."

"Oh," she responded, glancing to her right.

Jim felt a little burst of happiness at her nearness as she came to stand beside him at the helm. He took her hand in his. Even though they had flirted with each other the previous summer and were even closer now, since the horrors of the war, Jim had felt almost asexual, as if anything too pleasant must be obscene. But they needed to touch each other, and they often held hands while on watch.

"Mom's pacing woke me up," Lisa said softly. "She was going up and down like a subway shuttle."

"I'm glad you're here," Jim said, thinking of Jeanne and Neil embracing but not wanting to tell Lisa. For a moment they stood silently, *Vagabond* plunging and hissing through the night. "*Vagabond*'s really moving, isn't she?" Lisa said.

"It's great," Jim whispered back.

"You want something to drink?" Lisa asked.

"No, I'm okay."

"Did you check on Seth?"

"Oh, no, I didn't."

Lisa took a flashlight and went aft to Neil's cabin to see if Seth needed anything. Seth's right thigh had become infected, and whether the antibiotic Macklin was administering would clear up the infection still hadn't been determined. Seth had tried to make a joke of the whole thing by saying, "That's the last time I come up on deck to find out what's going on."

As Lisa pushed back the hatch and started down the short ladder she was startled to see a dim light and the figure of Conrad Macklin sitting in the darkness beside Seth, who seemed to be sleeping.

"Oh!" Lisa said, frightened.

"Can I help you?" Macklin asked quietly.

"I . . . I didn't know . . . I was checking on Seth."

"He's alive," Macklin stated indifferently.

"What . . . what are you . . . ?"

"You ever tried sleeping up forward?" Macklin answered. "I was bouncing like someone was dribbling me."

"Oh," said Lisa, noticing a red glow, indicating Neil's radio was on, and that Macklin had some papers in his lap.

"I'm sleeping back here," Macklin went on, "until your boyfriend stops trying to smash my skull against the forward cabin roof."

Lisa left; the surge and sway belowdecks had left her feeling slightly nauseous, and her encounter with Macklin made her uneasy. On her way back to the wheelhouse she noticed a light in Frank's cabin, and she mentioned to Jim that Macklin was with Seth and that his father seemed to be up.

"Dad's not sleeping well," Jim said. "He's still sick."

"I know," said Lisa, taking Jim's hand in hers. "Do you think . . . it's . . . ."

"I hope it'll go away in a few days," said Jim. "Neil and Olly don't seem too bad, and they were exposed almost as much."

"Mom thinks he's a little depressed about losing . . . your mother."

Jim merely nodded, staring forward into the darkness.

"Do you think she's dead?" Lisa asked softly.

"Yes," said Jim.

"My dad's dead too," said Lisa. "Sometimes it seems like he never lived . . . Everything is . . . so changed." Lisa released his hand and steadied herself against the control-panel shelf.

"It's strange," Jim said, putting his arm around her waist. "Everything I used to be interested in, you know, sports, music, cars, seems sort of far away. I tried listening to some of my favorite tapes and I started to . . . you know, I felt like crying. It was pretty funny."

Lisa didn't reply but gently moved closer. She wanted to put her arm around him, but felt awkward and left her hands on the molding.

"I'm glad you're here, Lisa," Jim went on very softly. "I get kinda lonely with my dad . . . sick and Neil all wrapped up in the boat. You're about the only part of the old world that seems . . . all right."

"I . . . I'm glad you're here too," she said, letting her head rest against his shoulder. "We will be all right, won't we, Jim?" There was a wistful quality in her voice that Jim felt viscerally.

He hesitated, all the horrors, past and still possible, clamoring for his attention.

"Yes," he replied simply, pulling her more tightly against him and ignoring the clamor. "But not unless we take down the genoa and reef the main."

She looked up at him, puzzled.

"The wind's gotten too strong," he went on. "I think the number-one watch team better reduce sail."

She smiled and took over the wheel from Jim, who smiled back and went off to get his safety harness and go forward.

By midmorning of the following day Neil's midnight romance had become unreal. Reality was upon him in the form of a crowded wheelhouse and thirty-knot winds out of the east southeast. A little after dawn Jeanne had gotten up to prepare the watch of Frank and Tony a breakfast and given Neil a polite, perhaps warm smile, but with no more apparent passion in it than the one she gave to Frank.

After breakfast he and Frank had listened to another appalling news summary. Refugees were flooding southward all over the world and being resented and rebuffed by the local populations in the traditional ways of treating war refugees. Cuba, the Panama Canal, and Venezuelan oilfields and refineries had all been struck by some sort of nuclear weapon; the Caribbean too would be a disaster area. It wasn't even clear who had attacked Venezuela, since she, like all the rest of South America, had loudly declared her neutrality and was refusing to sell oil to the United States.

And later, at eight A.M., with the wind now beginning to screech through the stainless steel rigging and Tony cracking a rib in a fall while trying to bring in a torn jib, reality had regained its usual harshness. In the crowded wheelhouse, under an overcast and darkening sky, Skippy was whining about the taste of fish, Lisa had just vomited up her breakfast on the wheelhouse floor, and Jeanne, feeling queasy herself, was trying to deal with them. For Neil, battling at the helm, there was no room for romance with a torn jib, an injured crewman, rising winds and seas, and Frank and Tony arguing with him about their course.

By dead reckoning from their noon position of the day before Neil calculated that they were about a hundred miles east southeast of Cape Lookout, North Carolina, a spit of land that tipped the long sand barrier that stretched south of the notorious Cape Hatteras. Without consulting the others, Neil had been maintaining a southerly course, partly because he was considering a run to the Bahamas and the West Indies rather than trying to put in again on the mainland. Frank had complained the previous afternoon that they seemed to be staying unnecessarily far off the coast and suggested they angle more to westward. Now with large angry swells sweeping up against them from the south and the wind still rising, a choice was being forced upon him. They could either continue to work their way south, or they could turn and run back toward land.

They had been unable to pick up a radio station in the Morehead City–Pamlico Sound area of North Carolina, and they had no way of knowing what conditions would be like there.

Reports from the Bahamas about the West Indies were discouraging. The Bahamian government had declared a state of emergency and martial law, warning Bahamians that the food imports on which they had depended for more than eighty percent of their normal supply had been cut off by the war. Foreign ships, by which Neil knew must be meant American ships, were urged to go elsewhere. After panic buying had eliminated most of the island's stores of food, the Bahamians were not welcoming the sudden influx of sick, injured, and foodless Americans fleeing from the two nuclear explosions over Miami and Cape Canaveral. There had been at least one ugly racial incident already, or so Neil concluded from Radio Nassau's report that five American "yachtsmen" had been killed by several unapprehended black Bahamians "in a street fight." If *Vagabond* had to bypass the Bahamas, they would run desperately short of food and water before they could hope to reach Puerto Rico or the Virgin Islands. Jim and Lisa's success the last two mornings at hooking three big fish was encouraging, but they were in the Gulf Stream now; if they continued south, in another day or two they'd be east of it and the fishing less dependable.

As the wind freshened and storm clouds gathered on the southern horizon like thick black smoke, Neil had to admit that he was also worried about *Vagabond*: she was badly overloaded. A good trimaran normally sails faster than a good monohull because of its light weight, which permits it to skip over the water rather than plow through it.

But *Vagabond* was now almost two thousand pounds heavier than the ship they had sailed north and was moving two or three knots slower, which made her pound heavily into the huge seas that were rolling at her.

Although altering course to run before the storm would put an end to this slamming, which was the greatest source of anxiety for Neil and discomfort for the crew, Neil knew that even then the buffeting of the wind and seas would continue to drain the energy from everyone aboard. In his own experience thirty-five-knot winds and twelve-foot seas were bearable, but for most of the others they represented a danger far more immediate, palpable, and unpleasant than anything on the mainland. Everyone was seasick except Neil, Tony, and Elaine, and since none of them were the type to go cleaning up other people's messes, most of the cabins were beginning to stink of vomit. With Seth's bullet wounds, Tony's cracked rib, and general seasickness, their crew was considerably weakened.

But despite the problems he hated the thought of turning back toward the fallout and explosions and people-evil of the land. A storm at sea was something he could deal with; the effects of man's madness on land were not.

As he made the rounds of the ship before meeting with Frank, Tony, and Macklin to discuss their course, he knew that to continue southward against these seas would create serious morale problems. It might be exhilarating to escape from explosions, pirates, and radioactive fallout, but with those dangers now distant and remote, the endless slamming, the awful whine of the wind in the rigging, the woeful roll, pitch, and plunge of the trimaran, the seasickness, and worst of all, he knew, no indication of any safer haven to the south than to the west was depressing most of the ship's company. Only Elaine and Tony had complained directly, but the averted gaze of Jeanne and the sardonic humor of Frank and Seth revealed similar feelings.

He, Tony, Frank, and Olly gathered around the dinette table at eleven thirty that morning, the four of them swaying and bumping in their seats as *Vagabond* plunged and smashed forward through the huge seas. Jim was at the helm while an almost useless Conrad Macklin sat miserably on the little seat in the corner of the cabin. Everyone else was below in a berth. Frank, pale and weak from vomiting, and Tony, seeming as energetic and healthy as ever, had both been urging Neil to change course for several hours.

Even before they could begin their discussion, *Vagabond* struck a big roller with a savage smash that spilled silverware out of a drawer and toppled a half-dozen books out of the dinette bookcase. Neil went immediately up on deck and instructed Jim to bring *Vagabond* around ninety degrees to head due west while they had their discussion. As he watched and instructed Lisa in adjusting the sheets of the storm jib and double-reefed mainsail, Neil felt immediately how much easier the motion of the boat became. *Vagabond* now began surfing along and down the big swells instead of having to plow through them, and though the noise of the water and wind was scarcely diminished, the actual strain on the boat had probably been halved.

When Neil returned to the main cabin, Frank and Tony looked pleased.

"What a different feeling," Tony announced triumphantly. "Thank God we didn't wreck poor *Vagabond* before we changed course."

"Yes," Neil commented dryly. "How lucky."

"Are we going to hold course back toward land?" Frank asked.

"Not necessarily. That's a decision that I've decided should be made by the four ship's officers," Neil replied.

"What about the rest of us?" Tony interjected. "Don't Seth and me and Jeanne count for anything?"

"That's right," said Frank. "I'm not sure it's fair not to include all the adults."

Neil glanced at Olly, who was leaning back with his eyes closed holding his unlit pipe in his mouth, and at Tony, also sitting opposite him, who was flushed with excitement.

"Are you prepared, Frank," Neil countered, "if outvoted by Tony, Seth, Macklin, and Elaine, to surrender the ship's fate to a majority decision?"

Rubbing his big hands in front of him, his face sweaty from seasickness, Frank scowled.

"No, I guess not," he answered slowly. "We should consult with everybody, but the decision should be made by the four officers." He didn't look up at Tony.

"Well, Tony," Neil said neutrally to Tony, who had flushed at Frank's decision. "What do you advise?"

"You know what I advise," Tony answered angrily. "That we stop beating our brains out and get back to land. You promised us in the Chesapeake that we'd be landing back on the U.S. coast. You can't go back on that."

"Would you feel that way if we began to run into fallout?"

"Of course not," Tony snapped back. "But we should try to get back. Especially when the damn boat is getting smashed to pieces."

"Frank?" Neil asked quietly.

"We should run before the storm and get back to land," he said, again not looking up.

"Olly?"

"Whatever you want, cap, is all right by me," Captain Olly replied promptly, without even bothering to open his eyes. "I like it out here, but if you feel we ought to go unload a few landlubbers, it's okay by me."

Neil smiled and stood up.

"I'll go consult the others," he said.

Five minutes later he returned.

"Jim and Seth say they'd rather I decided," Neil announced quietly as he resumed his seat opposite a now-dozing Captain Olly. "I—"

"What the fuck is this shit?" Tony exploded. "You got everybody but me and Frank under your thumb?"

"I doubt it," Neil replied. "I'm sure that if Macklin here had the strength to comment he'd want to return to land."

"You're damn right," Tony said. "And what about Elaine?"

"She was sleeping, but I'm sure she'd vote the way you do."

"You're damn right."

"And Jeanne?" Frank asked softly.

Jeanne's vote would have been decisive for Neil, but fortunately— or unfortunately—she had been as ambivalent as Neil himself. She was miserable with her seasickness, her own and Skippy's, and frightened of the crashes of the waves against the seemingly flimsy plywood of the hull, but she had at first joked by urging Neil to "take me away from it all" and to "take me someplace where I can die in peace." But just before he left she had clutched his arm and said earnestly, "You've saved me and my children twice already. I'd be a fool to question how you plan to do it a third time."

"Jeanne essentially left it up to me also," Neil finally answered Frank.

"None of this proxy shit," Tony persisted. "The fact is that most of those with minds of their own know we ought to be getting back to the mainland."

"Frank votes your way, and Jim and Olly abstain," Neil went on quietly. "My personal decision—"

"I insist you consult the others," Tony interrupted.

"My personal decision," Neil went on, "is that we continue on a course to close with the mainland until the weather moderates or we encounter the danger of radioactive fallout."

"It's only fair that— what?" Tony said, taken aback by Neil's decision.

"Frank, when you and Tony go on duty an hour from now," Neil said, turning to his friend beside him, "try the transistor radio every hour to pick up news about conditions along the North Carolina coast."

"Fine," said Frank.

"We're about a hundred miles off the coast now," Neil continued. "At this rate we'll close with the coast during the night. We've got to find out if the big navigational lights are in operation."

"They've got emergency generators," Frank said.

"I know. They *should* be working. However, I'd prefer not to sail onto the Hatteras or Lookout shoals to find out they're not."

"We're going back to the mainland?" Tony asked, still adjusting to his unexpected victory.

"If the mainland will have us," Neil replied, rising again. "I'm going to check with the shortwave to see if I can find out more about this storm. See you later."

After Neil had left, Olly announced that he was going to take a nap and went forward to lie down. Frank poured himself and Tony a tiny amount of whiskey in water and sat down again.

"Well, we won that one," Tony said.

Startled, Frank looked up at him.

"I think Neil realizes," Tony went on, "that he can't run this boat without our support. He's made himself captain, but in effect we have veto power."

Frank sipped at his drink.

"And I want you to know, Frank," Tony went on, leaning forward and putting one of his hands on Frank's arm, "that if push ever comes to shove, I'm behind you one hundred percent. You understand?"

Frank stared at his drink.

"One hundred percent," Tony repeated, standing up. "As far as I'm concerned you already are the captain." He paused, staring down at Frank, who didn't look up. When *Vagabond* surfed down a big wave, Tony staggered forward, steadying himself against the wall behind Frank.

"I gotta take a piss," he concluded and disappeared into the small head located opposite the stove.

Frank stared at his drink another ten seconds, then, grimacing, tossed the rest of it off. The grimace continued until, looking sick and swearing irritably under his breath, he went hurriedly up the hatchway steps for fresh air.

When Tony came out of the head, Conrad Macklin was seated at the dinette and had poured himself a shot of whiskey. Tony sat down opposite him.

"I thought you were too sick to drink," Tony said.

"I'm only too sick to stand watch," Macklin answered indifferently, looking coolly at Tony and pouring the other man a drink.

"You hear what I said to Frank?" Tony asked, holding his plastic cup of whiskey.

Macklin nodded and took a short swig from his cup.

"But you know, Tony," he said after a short silence, "Frank will never be captain of this ship."

"No?" said Tony, steadying the bottle when it slid a few inches after *Vagabond* surfed along the face of a wave.

"He'll be dead in a month," said Macklin. "And, besides, he hasn't got the guts to be captain."

"Well, all I know is that Loken makes like a dictator."

Macklin nodded and sipped gingerly again at his drink, his round eyes examining Tony without expression.

"Sooner or later, Tony," he went on softly, "he's going to kick you and me off the boat."

Tony looked up quickly.

"You, maybe," he countered. "But why me? I'm as good a sailor as he is, maybe better."

Macklin smiled and nodded meaningfully.

"That's exactly why he has to get rid of you," he said to Tony. "He knows you're the only other man aboard with captain potential."

Tony looked at Macklin uncertainly, the sway of the kerosene lantern creating shadows that made it difficult to decipher Macklin's expression.

"Sooner or later," Macklin went on softly, "either you'll get kicked off . . . or you and I will have to take over the boat."

"No one's kicking me off anything," Tony snapped back.

"That's right, Tony," Macklin replied, nodding. "That's right."

Macklin held his half-filled cup toward Tony, and after a pause Tony understood. The two men clicked their cups together and drank.

When the rain began falling that afternoon, Neil called out all hands that had the strength to come up on deck to catch and store as much water as they could. Because the winds were gusting by then to over forty knots and the double-reefed mainsail couldn't be used as it normally could to channel rainwater into buckets, Neil had his crew use a small jib and two nylon Bimini covers instead. They caught as much as they could in these, then channeled the water into buckets and at last into the main storage tanks and their large plastic containers. With the winds making their nylon collectors difficult to control and his crew never having tried this maneuver before, there was much swearing and quite a bit of spilled rainwater. However, Neil had also stopped up the drainage holes in the cockpits so the water could be scooped up later. By late afternoon they had gathered almost fifteen gallons, more than half of it quite clear, and even the water that was rescued from the cockpits was potable. Because they were at last headed back toward land and many were seasick, Tony and Elaine and a few others complained it was all an unnecessary game, but Neil kept them at it for two hours. By dusk there were quite a few grumblers.

For Jeanne the day seemed endless. The smell of vomit permeated her cabin, and though the horrifying blasts of the sea against her cabin wall had ended, *Vagabond* still seemed to be thrown around like a tiny dinghy. Elaine, although thoroughly frightened most of the morning, had been reassured by a solicitous Tony for over an hour in the early afternoon and emerged from their tête-à-tête quite cheerful and as oblivious of the rolling and plunging of *Vagabond* as a globecircling sailor. Her daughter, Rhoda, was sick, but nothing seemed to disturb the bland Elaine, who, unable to concentrate on anything for more than a minute or two, was another source of misery for Jeanne.

A delicate wide-eyed blonde, Elaine let her child take up most of her time and was helpless at any job assigned to her. Jeanne had become so exasperated with her when she was sent to help in the galley that she and Lisa had decided to ask her to stay topside. Jeanne had offered Elaine and Rhoda the use of her berth and usually slept on the floor herself, but at night Elaine sometimes would wake her up to ask her to get Rhoda a cup of water since Jeanne "was already up," namely on the floor. The child was cranky and slept poorly. Her toys and Elaine's clothes and toiletries could never be confined to the cubicles Jeanne asked her to use but ended up sprayed all around the cabin as if by a particularly violent explosion.

Elaine was off somewhere with Tony now, and while Skippy, somewhat recovered from his seasickness, played on the cabin floor a few feet away Jeanne lay on her back staring at the ceiling and wishing she could express her fears to Neil and be reassured and comforted. She hated feeling so helpless, hated being unable to focus her thoughts on the war or on her feelings for Neil or on anything except the dizzying, nauseating motion of the ship.

Frank came down three or four times to comfort her and see if there was anything he could do, but when he tried to clean up some of the vomit, he himself became sick again and had to hasten topside.

Neil appeared only twice, once to ask her opinion on their course—

an opinion she was reluctant to give since her mind felt like mashed potatoes still being beaten in the blender—and a second time in the afternoon. He suggested she try to come up and assist with the rain catching.

That time she had struggled out of her berth, stood weakly for about thirty seconds, and then fallen woozily into his arms. He had to pick her up and lift her back up into her berth.

"I hope you're not blaming the captain for this," he said.

"I'm beyond blaming," she replied wearily, realizing sadly that she wished he would go away so he wouldn't see her looking like a drowned cat, and smelling worse.

"You'll be over it by tomorrow," he suggested. "Get some sleep."

"I'll never be over it," she moaned. "I'll remember this moment as long as I live."

"Since it's so special, I plan to try to see to it that you live a very long time," Neil said.

She looked over at him, tried to smile, and feebly squeezed his hand.

"I'm sorry I'm letting you down," she said.

"Never," he said. "I just hoped the fresh air might help." Neil released her hand and wiped the perspiration from her face with the edge of the sheet. Frank came twice more, but she didn't see Neil again until the next day.

The final indignity for Jeanne came that evening as the storm seemed to be getting even worse. Elaine came cheerfully down into the cabin and told her that Jeanne could sleep in Elaine's berth that night, with little Rhoda. Elaine was going to be with Tony. So Jeanne, miserable, was left to babysit while Elaine spent the night being "comforted" by Tony.

She was too sick to be angry. She barely had the strength to wonder where the two lovers had had a chance to become lovers in the crowded boat. Someday she'd have to ask.

They picked up the light at Cape Lookout on the North Carolina coast at midnight. By two thirty A.M. they had left it on their starboard beam while making for the Morehead City inlet. The storm, Neil had concluded, must be coming directly at them. The winds, instead of becoming more northerly as he had expected if the storm was passing out to sea, were in fact becoming more southerly. The storm center must be moving right up the coastline. In any case, the winds were still blowing at about forty-five knots, with stronger gusts, and the seas remained between eight and ten feet. To turn south now would be impossible.

Fortunately the Morehead City inlet was wide, deep, and well marked. Immediate protection was available as soon as they got inside it and made for the turning basin. Neil had entered the channel on half a dozen occasions, and although he hated approaching land in storm conditions, he was not particularly worried under the circumstances, not with a boat and a crew he had confidence in.

As they neared the inlet it was Frank and Tony's watch. Lisa and Jim, who had just come off duty, remained on deck more out of excitement than necessity. Still sailing under storm jib and double-reefed main, they had already picked up the white flashing sea buoy that marked the beginning of the big ship channel when Neil turned on the transistor radio. He wanted to try again to pick up local news about conditions in the Morehead City area. The best he could do was a station from Charleston, South Carolina. A voice announced that they were going to repeat the President's address to the nation that had been broadcast at eleven o'clock that evening—four hours before.

With Frank handling the helm and the radio placed on the shelf to his left, the other three men and Lisa lined up along the front of the 'wheelhouse, peering through the Plexiglas windows with their half-dozen bullet holes out into the darkness and listening to the President's voice.

"Good evening, my fellow Americans," the voice began, slow, somber, and sincere. "It is my sad duty to speak to you on this fifth day of this horrible conflict. Our nation, a victim of an unprovoked attack by the Soviet Union, has suffered immense devastation. So many of our cities have been destroyed that, as you know, our ability to communicate with each other has been considerably reduced. The ability of your government to deal with the chaos and suffering, which have overtaken many parts of our land, is extremely limited. It is the task of our military forces to continue to wage war on the Soviet Union, not only to avenge the horror they have inflicted upon us, but also in order to try to destroy their nation before the freedom of all peoples has vanished from the earth.

"Those of us who have survived the initial Soviet onslaught must always keep in our hearts that we are fighting on now both for our individual survival and for the survival of the very idea of freedom. Mankind is at a terrifying crossroads: whether we shall all fall under the yoke of Communist dictatorship or live on with our cherished principles of individualism and freedom intact. I urge you all to do everything in your power to contribute to this struggle.

"I have unleashed the full power of all our military forces against the Soviet Union. I am happy to report to you this morning that though more than half of our great nation lies in ruins, even more of the Soviet Union has been destroyed. We have received no further reports of effective enemy action in the last twenty-four hours. The Russian people are also suffering for the crimes committed by their masters.

"However, despite our successes, I'm afraid that this morning I must issue a momentous warning that will take the form of an executive order. I have been advised by our best scientists working with the National Security Council that all Americans still living in certain areas in the northeastern part of our country must evacuate immediately. I am speaking now to the people of eastern Ohio, New York, Massachusetts, Connecticut, Rhode Island, Pennsylvania, New Jersey, Maryland, and Delaware. Within ten days to two weeks the radioactive fallout from the war will have accumulated to such a degree that its effects will make life in these areas almost impossible. Residents are to move as quickly as possible either to Canada or areas in the far north of the region, or south at least as far as North Carolina. United States military forces will provide all the assistance at their disposal, but airplanes and vehicles are in extremely short supply. In most cases you will have to provide your own transportation.

"Do not be deceived if your area has not yet received significant radioactive fallout. All indications are that radioactivity and its effects will spread and become worse, causing not only death to humans immediately, but contaminating water and food supplies, which will make these areas uninhabitable in the future. Thus, I hereby direct all citizens . . ."

The President's voice went firmly on, reporting next on the greatly reduced level of fighting in Europe caused by the high casualties sustained on each side and indicating that he considered the stalemate to be a victory for the forces of freedom, although the destruction of most of Europe was, of course, a great historical tragedy.

He also indicated that he had sent a stern note to the governments of all thirteen nations of South America. He threatened grave consequences if they continued to profess strict neutrality in the world conflict. Although most of these governments were fascist dictatorships, they were still historically part of the free peoples of the American continent and their refusal to permit United States military forces to use certain ports, air bases, and fuel depots for repairs and resupply was hampering the war effort. In particular, the decision of Venezuela and Trinidad-Tobago to stop selling oil to the U.S. was tantamount to an act of war and would not be tolerated. He also condemned the governments of Mexico, the Bahamas, and several unnamed South American countries for their unjust, shortsighted, and sometimes cruel treatment of American refugees. He concluded his address with the announcement that with Congress unable to meet, he was using powers granted to him as Commander-in-Chief under martial law to order all Americans between the ages of eighteen and forty-five to report immediately for military service. His last words were an appeal to his fellow Americans to stand tall in this great crisis.

When the President had finished speaking and a commentator began summarizing his address, Neil turned off the radio. Jim and Tony went and sat down on a settee while Frank remained at the wheel; Neil sat down opposite them. They all became aware again of the sound of the wind and of *Vagabond* rushing down the seas in the darkness.

"It all seems so impossible," Frank finally said, still staring forward. "The President talks about the depopulation of the whole northeast as if they were evacuating a small town because of a gas leak."

"I wonder why the big cities got hit so bad," Tony mused. "I thought I read someplace that Arizona and North Dakota were the places that were going to get clobbered. You know, our missile sites."

No one answered.

"I wonder what 'standing tall' means?" Tony went on in a low voice.

"It means we're all drafted," Neil commented.

"Except for Frank," Tony commented.

"I may not be drafted," Frank said from the wheel, "but there'll be things for me to do too. Our country needs us all now."

Again no one spoke. *Vagabond* surged and roller-coastered forward in the darkness, rolled and surged again. The three men behind Frank sat silently staring at the deck between them, swaying with the ship's swoops and swerves. Neil stood up for a moment to look forward and then sat back down.

"I'd like to fight," Tony burst out after a while. "But where the fuck are the Russians? Are they supposed to invade?"

"I don't imagine either side sees much of value left to invade," Neil replied after a pause.

"What about Cuba?" Tony asked. "Are we going to take Cuba?"

Neil didn't answer.

"I hope everyone just stops fighting," Jim said.

"Not until we've won," said Tony. "The Army needs us. They'll find something for us to do."

"I'm sure they will," said Neil ironically.

"What's that mean?" Tony shot back, sensing the cynicism.

"It means I can't imagine what good a bunch of civilian draftees inducted now are going to be in the final stages of thermonuclear war."

"There're a lot more useful things a man can do than run away," Frank said. After a brief, awkward silence, he added: "Here's the number three red-flashing bell. We're in the channel."

Fifteen minutes later, in quiet water for the first time in four days, *Vagabond*'s sails were down and she lay drifting on the incoming tide awaiting a launch from the Coast Guard cutter that was idling nearby, with its cannon manned by three sailors, barely visible in the darkness.

The launch party consisted of a lieutenant and four men, two armed with pistols in holsters and two with automatic rifles.

"Who's the captain of this vessel?" asked the lieutenant, a short, stocky man with a neatly trimmed mustache.

"I am," said Neil. "What's the problem?"

"Where are you headed?" the officer rejoined.

"Morehead City obviously."

"Your purpose?"

"Get out of this storm, put some passengers ashore, take on supplies," Neil answered, finding the interrogation bordering on the ridiculous.

"How many draft-age persons do you have aboard?" the officer persisted.

"Three or four," Neil answered.

"They are to report to the induction center on Main Street within twenty-four hours," the lieutenant said, looking around at the five men. "How much diesel fuel do you have?"

"About fifteen gallons," Neil answered, lying for some reason he didn't understand yet.

"Unless you've got a special exemption, we'll have to requisition that fuel later today. Do you have weapons?"

"Only an old .22," Neil replied quietly.

"All weapons are requisitioned. We'll take your rifle now." The officer stared at Neil. "Also," he went on, his gaze not wavering, "my men will search your boat." He nodded to the bos'n, who divided the four crewmen into two teams and began a search.

"Jim, you can go get the .22 for the nice men," Neil said, then turned back to the officer. "What's the trouble? Why can't we keep our rifle?"

"Civilians are going around shooting each other for food, fuel, fallout shelters, you name it," the lieutenant replied. "The only way the military can regain control is to make unauthorized possession of a weapon illegal."

"How are we expected to defend ourselves?" Tony now asked.

"That's the trouble," the officer countered. "Everybody's been defending themselves so vigorously the morticians can't keep up with it. Leave the defending to the Army, Navy, and us."

"Couldn't someone authorize us to keep the .22 aboard?" Frank interjected.

"I doubt it. If you want to waste time, the district military headquarters for this region is located about six miles outside Morehead City."

"What's the food and fallout situation here?" Neil asked.

"We haven't had any fallout since a small amount came down on the third day of the war," the officer said, peeking down into the main cabin. "This rain has some, but it's not supposed to be a problem."

"And food?" Neil asked.

"All food distribution here is administered by the U.S. Army. If you want to eat, you'll either have to be in the military or go to a refugee center."

"Nothing special, sir," the bos'n reported to his superior as he returned with the other three. "Just a few fishing knives."

"Good," said the officer with a tired smile. "Okay, captain, welcome to Morehead City." He motioned to his crew to return to their launch. "And by the way," he added, turning back to Neil and the others, "without written permission from Colonel Nelson, no draft-age men are allowed to set out to sea."

"What's that?" Jim exclaimed.

"No vessel is permitted to go to sea without the permission of the local military commander," the lieutenant replied. His eyes narrowing as he looked at Jim, he added, "We had to sink three ships who didn't think we meant it."

And he left.

Vagabond then proceeded slowly up the channel toward the small town of Morehead City, which lay in almost total darkness, and in another hour she was anchored a hundred feet off the main line of docks. Neil wanted them all to be able to get some sleep before they had to confront the world that awaited them on shore. Although it was four thirty, and dawn should have been breaking, the storm system kept the sky as dark as night.

As the boat was being anchored Jeanne came up on deck and went down to make hot tea for Neil, Frank, and Tony, who soon joined her in the main cabin. She was pale, with a gray puffiness under the eyes from her long bout of seasickness, but now that *Vagabond* was merely rocking gently in the gusting blasts of wind and not playing at roller coaster, she was feeling better. Olly was already slumped asleep in the little corner jumpseat in the forward end of the room.

"I could use a drink," Tony announced, staring irritably at his tea. "Aren't we supposed to celebrate a landfall?"

"Do you feel like celebrating?" Neil asked.

"I don't feel a damn thing," Tony answered, taking the bottle of brandy Jeanne put on the table. "I'm too beat."

"Thank God we've made it back to land," Jeanne said softly, standing with her back to the seated men. Neil, Frank, and Tony looked up at her, and then Frank stood up and went over to her. While the other two men looked on silently, he embraced her.

"Will we be able to find a place to live?" Jeanne asked Frank, looking up at him.

"They have a refugee camp," Frank answered.

"Is . . . is that where we're all going?" she asked with a surprised frown.

"It looks that way," Frank said.

"All the men aboard except Frank and Olly have to report for military service," Neil said.

"But why?" Jeanne asked, freeing herself from Frank's arms and again looking surprised. "What possible use can any of you be in the Army?"

"We're at war, Jeanne," Frank replied, sitting back down opposite Neil.

"No, we're not," Jeanne responded passionately. "This isn't a war. It's . . . it's genocidal suicide."

They all looked up at her.

"We're at war, Jeanne," Frank repeated. "Our country has been attacked."

"Neil, you don't believe in this draft, do you?" Jeanne said, looking flushed with anger or excitement.

"I suppose it's like this ship," Neil answered after a long pause. "In a survival situation everyone has to belong to a military hierarchy, or there's chaos. Drafting everyone is the government's way of keeping us out of mischief."

"And we'll be needed in the Army too," Tony said. "They're not calling us up just to keep an eye on us."

"They'll need *everybody*'s help . . . if the war lasts long enough," Frank suggested.

The silence was not a happy one.

"I'm not going, dad," said Jim, appearing unexpectedly on the companionway steps.

"What do you mean, Jimmy?" Frank asked, frowning.

Jim came down the three steps and stood a few paces behind his father. Lisa appeared in the cabin entrance.

"I can't report for military service," he said nervously. "I won't go."

Frank turned to look at his son and then returned his gaze to Jeanne, who had sat down opposite him.

"I'm afraid the President has ordered almost all of us to serve," he said.

"I know, dad. But I won't fight in this war. Not unless the Russians land troops."

"No one likes fighting nukes," Tony said, "but we've got to serve."

"It's not the nukes and radiation anymore," Jim said. "It's just that I've decided this war is all wrong, no matter—"

"What about your country?" Frank interrupted, not looking at his son.

"I just think . . . I don't know . . . I want to sail south with you, dad. Help Lisa and Jeanne and—"

"What about your country?" Frank repeated stonily.

"I know. I know," Jim said, a flicker of anguish on his face unseen by his father. "I owe my country a lot. I know that. But the war seems so insane, the kind of killing so wrong . . . I don't see how . . ."

"Jim can't save the country," Jeanne said as Jim trailed off.

"But he's goddamn well going to try!" Frank spat out angrily, banging his fist on the table and tipping over the mostly empty bottle of brandy. As Tony righted it, old Captain Olly's body jerked upright, and his eyes blinked open. "Huh?" he said. "What say?"

Frank swung his head around to look at Neil.

"Are you going to report for duty?" he asked.

"What I do isn't relevant," Neil answered. "With my naval experience in theory I can be of service, but untrained teenagers would only be cannon fodder. If Jim thinks the war is all wrong, he shouldn't go. And I may not go either."

Frank felt a strange sinking feeling and glared at Neil.

"I should have known," he said. "You've taken wishy-washy positions so long you've forgotten a man's duty to his country."

"I know my duty to my country," Neil snapped back. "I just happen to believe that my country is now located primarily on this boat."

"That's inconvenient," said Frank, "because in that case I'm kicking you out of your country." He felt both a senseless rage and an urge to cry. "In other words you're fired." The words seemed hollow even as he spoke them.

"Are you going to force Jim to be in this war?" Jeanne asked.

"He's in it whether he likes it or not."

"I'm not going to report, Dad," Jim said, now more steadily. "I'd like to help sail everyone south."

"You need Jim," Jeanne said softly to Frank. "In this world if we're lucky enough to have any children still with us, the last thing we should do is let them go."

Frank stared at the cushion between Jeanne and Neil and unseeingly added more brandy to his empty teacup, his eyes wet. A siren wailing off in the city a half-mile away underlined the silence in the cabin. Captain Olly again awakened.

"Don't recommend telling grown kids what to do," he said.

"No one asked you," Frank muttered.

" 'S okay," Olly replied. "I don't mind volunteering good advice. People who ask for advice generally made up their minds anyhow."

Jeanne rose from her seat. "I'm going to get more sleep," she said. "Good night, Captain Olly, Tony. Good night, Neil." She paused. "Good night, Frank." She leaned down and held his head in her arms and pressed her face against his hair for several seconds. "You're a good man, Frank, a . . . but you're absolutely wrong about Jim." And she left.

"That's one sweet lady, that is," Captain Olly said. "Ain't met a woman like her since my last wife. She married?"

The ship's clock on the forward wall of the cabin struck six bells, and Neil glanced at it.

"We should set a watch this morning, Frank," he said. "We haven't seen the last of the pirates. I'll take the first two-hour watch and wake Jim for the second. We can all get up at ten."

Frank looked up dully.

"You still trying to run things?" he said, then let his head fall forward.

Vagabond was back on land.

Morehead City, over one hundred and fifty miles distant from the nearest nuclear explosion, a small town in the middle of a rich farming and fishing region, had, in a way, like most of the rest of the country, ceased to exist. Its restaurants, bars, drugstores, service stations, movie theaters, supermarkets, grocery stores, gift shops, banks, and most retail stores were closed. The only traditional commercial enterprises open for a few hours each day were the clothing and hardware stores, and one bar: all had become unofficial bartering centers.

The town had electricity, at least in theory, but the military authorities were systematically disconnecting electric service to all except businesses or institutions they considered necessary. The town had food, at least in theory, since a few fishermen still brought in their catches and neighboring farmers still had chickens, pigs, cows and a few early summer crops. But fuel was unavailable for either the fishing trawlers or farm machinery, and harvests from both sea and land were diminishing. No food arrived from outside the county and all food inside it was being requisitioned for distribution and rationing by the Army; much of it was being shifted to areas where the need was greater. More than half the arable land was planted in tobacco.

Since no private vehicles were permitted on the road without authorization, most normal social life had ended. Local draft-age adults had disappeared either into one of the services or into the faceless masses of refugees fleeing even farther south. Those remaining consisted mainly of men over forty, the sick and the maimed, and women and children. Few people other than farmers and fishermen were still able to practice the same occupation they'd been in a week before.

All newspapers and television stations had ceased operating. Only one radio station went on the air on a limited schedule, its sole function being to transmit official information and instructions from the national government or local military authorities. There was no music. The national networks had ceased to exist, but the government was able to use satellites to transmit messages to all stations at once.

All manufacturing not directly related to military needs had ceased. All large department stores had sold out of basic items in the first three days of the war—flashlights, generators, batteries, coolers, knives, hatchets, tools, guns, fishing equipment, camping gear, cooking fuels, and so on, and now, filled with useless nonessentials—television sets, phonographs, cosmetics, fashionable clothing—they remained closed, unguarded, and unlooted.

The churches alone were booming. Most held services of one sort or another every day, and streetcorner end-of-the-world preachers gathered small crowds around them immediately, people who listened apathetically and then wandered away.

The little town had received an influx of refugees from the areas around Washington and Norfolk, the first wave arriving by car and truck, those in the last few days by foot, bicycle, horse and cart, and by boat down the Intracoastal Waterway. Many were suffering from burns, blindness, and radiation sickness.

When the survivors on *Vagabond* were awakened by Jim at ten o'clock, they saw that boats were jammed into every available space, rafted two and three deep in places. Neil eased *Vagabond* in against an apparently unoccupied luxury yacht, the only space large enough to take the fifty-foot trimaran alongside.

After a reconnaissance ashore in the gusty wind and rain, it was clear that most of the boats had either been deserted for want of fuel or crew or were owned by people determined to get farther south. Some hoped to continue down the Intracoastal Waterway, and a few were planning to go out the inlet. Whether the latter would be carrying passengers who had been officially called to duty and forbidden to leave was unclear: most people were tight-lipped about their plans and personnel.

Posted prominently on several dockside telephone poles were

posters, printed by hand and Xeroxed, warning mariners that no ships were permitted to leave the inlet with any male of military age aboard without written authorization from the district military commander.

Looking out toward the inlet, Neil could see two U.S. Navy vessels, one looking badly damaged, moored in the turning basin. He had never known warships to use Morehead City, but with the naval facilities at Hampton Roads near Norfolk destroyed, the Navy's options were clearly reduced.

As the morning wore on Neil became increasingly frustrated by his inability to get any reports on the fallout situation in the southeast. There were only three stations left on the whole AM dial, each broadcasting only sporadically. Official statements never indicated what people in the Carolinas could expect.

He was depressed too by the breakup of the ship's family. Jim was determined not to go into the Army, but he had only a few hours to come up with a workable alternative. After breakfast Jim and Lisa had spent forty minutes talking quietly to each other on the docks in the rain. Jeanne said little about her plans. After talking to Frank, she seemed to take it for granted that the refugee center was her only alternative. Although Elaine chatted pleasantly about being back on land—as if they'd just returned from an interesting cruise—Jeanne was silent. She finished packing, cleaned up the galley, and sat down in the wheelhouse with Skip.

As the boat-weary, war-weary, weather-weary crew of *Vagabond* gathered themselves together that late morning the wind moaned through the shrouds, halyards slapped rhythmically against masts, the rain drummed down on the decks and cabin tops. Although the seasick appreciated the lack of motion, all were exhausted by thirty-six hours of storm at sea. Tony was the first to leave, escorting Elaine and Rhoda ashore to find the refugee center. Frank and Conrad Macklin left a few minutes later carrying Seth on a makeshift stretcher made from two oars and the last section of the jib they had used to jury-rig the awning for the new back wall of the wheelhouse. The plan was that they would take Seth to the hospital and that Frank would meet Jeanne later at the refugee center in the high school. Macklin, ineligible for the draft because of a foot shattered by a mine in Vietnam, had announced he was planning to try to get farther south by car. Neil hoped he would simply disappear.

When Olly went down into the cabin to hide the weapons and disable *Vagabond*'s engine, Neil was momentarily alone with Jeanne, but Jim and Lisa came in from the rain and stood awkwardly side by side in front of her. Jim's face was partly hidden under the hood of his yellow foul-weather jacket, from which rain was still dripping. Lisa seemed lost in the over-sized foul-weather gear she was wearing, and they both seemed to Neil ridiculously young.

"Jeanne," Jim began uncertainly. "I . . . I'm not going into the Army, and I guess I have to hide." He hesitated. "Lisa wants to come with me."

Jeanne looked at him with a strange kind of serenity and nodded once, glancing briefly at her daughter.

"Where will you go, Jim?" she asked quietly.

Jim looked uncomfortable. "Neil said last night he thought my only chance was to get a small boat and head down the waterway," he said. "I don't know."

Jeanne now looked up at Neil.

"Well, captain?" she asked.

Neil resented her addressing him as "captain."

"I'm beginning to think we were crazy to come in that inlet," Neil replied almost angrily. "Jim is trapped. If the Army is rounding up young people, sooner or later it'll round up Jim. The only haven from the government is out at sea."

"Can't he stay with Olly on *Vagabond*?" Jeanne asked.

"Yes," said Neil, "but a man on the ketch in front of us said that the military police came through earlier this morning searching all the boats along the docks."

"But why?" Jeanne suddenly burst out. "What possible use can Jim and the others be?"

"How do people like Jim eat?" Neil replied gloomily. "They have to steal to survive. If they have guns, they may end up killing. The government is trying to control chaos."

"Then perhaps Jim should just go in," Jeanne said. Neil shrugged and Jim stirred uneasily.

"We shouldn't have come here, Mother," Lisa said.

"What do *you* expect to find here?" Neil asked Jeanne in a low, tight voice.

Startled, Jeanne stiffened. "I'm not sure," she replied tentatively. "A place to help other people, I guess. A safer place for Lisa and Skip."

"Safer than what?" Neil asked.

"Safer than the Chesapeake," she answered, looking at him, adding, less surely, "safer than the ocean."

"Land will never again be safer than the sea," he replied.

"We're here, Neil," she countered quietly.

"I hate your going . . . back . . . out there," Neil said in almost a whisper.

Conrad Macklin suddenly burst in from the rain, stamping on the floor, seemingly unaware that he might have interrupted anything, and announced that all private housing had already been taken over either by the military or by earlier refugees. There was absolutely no food being sold anywhere. The hospital they'd taken Seth to was so overcrowded they were treating people in tents and garages, or rather not treating them—hundreds of victims of burns, radiation sickness, and retinal blindness were not being treated at all as far as he could see. Frank had stayed behind to try to get medical attention for Seth. There were no vehicles available for going south and roadblocks on every major highway. Macklin ended his report and went below to change and dry off.

Jim and Lisa were left standing in the center of the wheelhouse with Jeanne, her face averted, staring at the floor.

"Look," Neil said, striding forward so Jim and Lisa could see him. "I'm going to find out from the Army or the Navy what the food and fallout situation is going to be here. If I'm needed in the Navy, I'll serve. But I don't think, Jim, that you and Lisa should go anyplace by yourselves. Hold up a bit. Stay here on the boat with Olly. Lisa, at least for now, you should go with Jeanne to the refugee center."

"Why can't we all stay on the boat?" Lisa asked.

"Because—" Neil began.

"Because we can't run forever," Jeanne replied. "Our duty is to find a place here on land to live and work. There's both farming and fishing here. It must be better than most places. And the only way we can get more food is at the refugee center."

"What about Captain Olly?" Lisa asked.

"He'll stay here to guard the boat," Neil answered. "In case . . . we need it again."

Lisa looked up at Jim to see what he was deciding.

"All right," said Jim. "I'll hide here for a while. Lisa . . . you . . . better help your mom . . ."

"When . . . when . . . ?" Lisa began.

"We can visit the boat, honey," Jeanne said quietly. "We're all just finding out what the new world has in store for us. Nothing is final."

Lisa took Jim's hand and, after exchanging a look with him, stared down at the floor.

"I'll risk helping you take your things to the high school," Jim said. Together he and Lisa began to gather up the duffel bags and small suitcases and transport them to the docks. After they'd left the wheelhouse, Jeanne stood up and went over to Neil, who was standing with his hands gripping the stainless steel wheel.

"I wish . . . we didn't have to go," she said.

"You don't," Neil answered.

"I mean . . . but you too . . . have to leave *Vagabond*."

"I don't *have* to go," Neil replied quietly.

As Jeanne gazed at him she realized that he was making a subtle appeal to her.

"But . . . what would we all do on *Vagabond*?" she asked after a pause, Skippy holding on to her skirt.

"We would sail south out of the probable path of the fallout," Neil answered. "To the West Indies."

Jeanne visibly flinched.

"They wouldn't let you and Jim out of the inlet," she said softly.

Neil hesitated. "Cowards and lovers will always find a way," he said.

Jeanne gazed at him, flushed, and then impulsively threw herself into his arms. She squeezed him, burying her head against his chest. She felt his arms tightening fiercely around her. After half a minute, aware of Skippy tugging gently at her skirt and murmuring her name, she looked up, tears in her eyes.

"I don't want to go," she said.

"Then don't," Neil whispered to her.

"Everything okay, Jeanne?" came Jim's voice from close behind her. Still in Neil's arms, when she turned and saw him, the image of Frank in his boyish face reminded her of all the complications and uncertainties involved in her staying with Neil.

She looked back up at Neil, saw his feeling for her, but pulled herself roughly out of his arms.

"Good-bye, Neil," she said and brushed past Jim out into the rain.

After she had gone, Neil turned to see Macklin sitting behind him with a cynical smile.

"Well, captain," he said softly. "Nothing like a little pussy to turn a solid upstanding Annapolis man into a deserter, is there?"

Neil went at him, his fists clenched, but when Macklin ducked and cowered on the settee, he checked himself and strode to the back of the wheelhouse to watch Jim and Jeanne drift out of sight on shore. She was gone. He stood there silently for half a minute.

"I thought you said I lacked heart," he finally said.

"Oh, you do, you do," Macklin agreed affably, "but I never said you lacked cock."

"Thank you," said Neil and then went quickly down into the main cabin to find Olly.

He wanted both to be rid of Macklin and also to advise Olly on taking care of *Vagabond* before Neil himself reported for duty. He had decided to proceed directly to one of the ships in the turning basin and find out what the military situation was and whether he was really needed or not. For him, as for Jim, the war was madness and both sides insane, but the U.S. Navy, insane or not, was his team, and if the game were still being played, he had reluctantly decided it was his duty to take the field.

Even Captain Olly seemed depressed as Neil went over the boat with him. Neil had requested, and the others had agreed, that the remaining food aboard should stay aboard for at least the next few days. Neil told Olly where Jim had hidden their emergency food supply. He also showed Olly where the two pistols were hidden behind the partition in Jeanne's cabin; he showed him the five-gallon jerry jug of diesel fuel lined up with the water containers and now labeled "Water." Since pirates were still a threat, Olly had disconnected the battery cables from the engine and hid both the cables and the two ignition keys, letting only Neil know their hiding place. In addition,

Olly decided to stash one of the two pistols in the galley where he could reach it on short notice.

When they had finished going over the boat, Olly stopped in the rain in the side cockpit and began chuckling.

"You sure don't act like a man who's leaving his boat forever," he said.

"I wish I weren't," Neil said.

"You joining the Navy?"

"If they need me."

"Who's gonna decide? Them or you?"

Neil shrugged.

"Me," he answered.

"Then I'll keep the tea water hot," said Olly, smiling.

"Cynical old bastard, aren't you?" Neil shot back, smiling in spite of himself.

"I figure you got too much sense to get involved in a war where if you don't shoot till you see the whites of their eyes, you'll die of old age without firing a shot."

"I already fought in that kind of war," Neil said.

"And loved it, didn't you?" Olly said, ducking into the wheelhouse out of the wind and rain, leaving Neil to face a rush of gloom.

Frank, already depressed by his confrontation with Jim and by his lingering nausea, was overwhelmed by what he found on land. His first encounter with chaos and panic came when he and Macklin, carrying Seth between them on the stretcher, left *Vagabond* late that morning. Frank, in the lead, had not even gotten his feet on the dock when a man in a wet, wrinkled business suit, his graying hair plastered to his forehead, accosted him.

"Are you the owner of the trimaran?" the man asked. A woman and three children stood behind the fortyish man watching intently.

"Yes, I am," Frank replied as he waited for Macklin to lower himself and his end of the stretcher onto the dock.

"I want to book passage for myself and family on a boat going south," the man said, his drawn face belying his calm voice.

"I can't help you," Frank answered dully. "We're not going south, and if we were, we'd have a full boat already."

"I have gold," the man said, lowering his voice. "Fifteen thousand dollars' worth. You'll need it wherever you're going."

When Macklin put his end of the stretcher momentarily on one end of a bench, Frank rested his on a nearby railing and looked at the man with surprise.

"Well, you're fifteen thousand dollars richer than I am," he said. "But I still can't help you. A trimaran can't take the extra weight." Despite the rain, five or six other people had clustered around and were listening to this exchange.

"Then take just my wife and children," the man said. "They don't weigh much, and they can sleep on deck."

"No, Harry," the woman interjected. "I'm not going anyplace without you. I won't."

"We're not going south, I'm afraid," Frank repeated, depressed that a man should be so desperate to leave this place that he was willing to sacrifice himself to get his family on a boat. Depressed too that he couldn't help.

"Let's go try somewhere else," whispered the wife.

Harry, sensing Frank's sympathy, kept staring, the woman tugging at his arm, the youngest child tugging at hers, the rain streaming down everyone's faces.

"How about me, captain?" another man asked. "I'm all alone. I'm a good—"

"Me, too!" shouted a woman from the back of the small group. The crowd pushed toward Frank, shouting and holding up money, but picking up the stretcher, he and Macklin plunged roughly through the crowd and strode away.

At the hospital Seth was put on a mat on a garage floor. No doctor or nurse or administrator seemed to know who was responsible for the patients in Barnaby's Ford Garage, and so none of the seven patients lying around the room, some on mats used by the mechanics to work under cars, were being treated. They were out of the wind and rain: that was their treatment.

Macklin had quickly disappeared, and Frank crossed the street to the main hospital grounds to find a doctor. He saw a bulldozer digging up one whole section of the side lawn in the rain, an act which struck Frank as senseless. He assumed it was part of some long-range construction program. There were large tarpaulins covering what he thought were building materials, until he saw two soldiers carrying a body on a stretcher out into the rain, across the still untouched section of lawn, and then dumping the body unceremoniously in the mud next to the tarpaulin. An hour later, when he finally left the hospital, the cover had been removed and a pile of corpses was being bulldozed into a muddy hole.

Inside the hospital he discovered there were only three doctors left for all of Morehead City. All the other local doctors had been called up by the Army to serve elsewhere. One doctor was asleep, having just put in his fifth consecutive nineteen-hour day, or close to it. The second was a surgeon working in the OR on those with serious injuries, mostly burns. The third was a pediatrician, who was acting physician for the other thousand or so patients located either here or in the refugee center.

Frank appealed to the nurses and paramedics for help. At one point when he was exploding in anger at an indifferent and unresponsive nurse, he was dragged away by two military policemen whose purpose was to maintain order in the hospital. In the end the best he could do was to see a nurse write down Seth's name and location and tell him that Seth was "sixteenth on Mr. Umberly's list." Mr. Umberly, he gathered, was one of two paramedics.

On his way back to Seth he wandered by mistake into a room where the authorities apparently were putting patients who had been exposed to severe and presumably lethal doses of radiation. About ten people were lying against the walls or on the floor of what must normally have been a custodian's room, some groaning, one screaming, and at least two of them already dead. The room reeked of vomit. All of those sprawled on the floor were badly burned, and one man who had no eyes and whose face was hideously burned, the skin dangling down one cheek, begged in a singsong chant for water. Frank fled.

When he finally returned to Seth, he found him flushed and breathing rapidly. He explained about the shortage of medical help but withheld the other horrors he had witnessed.

"Well, they warned us," Seth said in his high-pitched, self-mocking tone.

"Who warned us about what?" Frank asked, kneeling down beside him.

"Books," Seth said, bright-eyed with fever. "The marchers. The protestors. They all warned us that a nuclear war would be inconvenient. Too many sick and wounded, too few surviving doctors. I should have known better than to get involved in a nuclear war."

Frank stared down at him where he lay on an inch-thick mechanic's mat covered by the sailcloth they had used for the stretcher. He couldn't tell if Seth was delirious or not.

"It wasn't the Russians and their missiles that got you," Frank said. "It was . . . an American."

"I know," said Seth. "They warned us about that too. Someone predicted the Russians would win a full-scale nuclear war because their citizens were unarmed and thus unable to wipe each other out." He grinned up at Frank as if it were all a good joke.

"I . . . ah . . . I'd like to go to the refugee center and check on Jeanne," Frank said. "You think you can . . . ah . . . handle yourself okay until the doctor comes?"

"Of course," Seth replied, still smiling. "I have exactly those qualities that will guarantee my safety in this world."

"What's that?" asked Frank.

"I'm useless and destitute," said Seth. "I'm even less likely to be visited by a pirate than by a doctor."

"I . . . I've got to go," Frank said.

For the first time Seth was silent, staring past Frank at the ceiling, his grin frozen and lifeless.

"Will you come back?" Seth asked in a low, totally different voice.

"I . . . Sure," Frank answered. "I'll come back this evening."

"I'd like that," said Seth, still looking past Frank at the garage ceiling.

"So I'll be seeing you," said Frank.

"Please come back, Frank," Seth whispered desperately through gritted teeth, and Frank, somber, rose and left.

Jeanne had no illusions about the difficulties she would encounter as a refugee in a strange town, but as she had told Neil, the sea was no home for her; every moment she'd been aboard *Vagabond* her heart had been eyeing the horizon for land.

Although she had anticipated scarcity and crowding, when she entered the long, low, modern high school building, she knew that her expectations weren't going to make it any easier. The hall she entered with Jim, Lisa, and Skip was crowded with people as wet and weary-looking as themselves. The hard floors were covered with mud and water. Some were shouting, a round man with a red nose and blood-shot eyes was trying to herd people into a line, and twenty-five or thirty confused refugees stood or sat against the walls, a few crying, many looking sick. Four or five had visible burns. Skippy was pulling at Jeanne's belt and periodically asking her questions about nothing. She could feel a numbness creeping into her, as if her life were again being threatened. With all the sick people around she wondered whether Jim had brought her to the hospital by mistake rather than the refugee center, but on the walls were the familiar official graffiti of a school: "Seniors taking SATs report on Tuesday to Mr. Owens," "Graduation rehearsal at 3:00 on Thursday," and "Support your Tigercats!"

"Mother, let's not stay here," Lisa said, looking frightened.

"There's no place else to go, honey," Jeanne answered mechanically.

"We should have stayed on the boat," Lisa insisted.

"We've got to try this," Jeanne replied, fighting off the panic she could feel invading her as it had Lisa. The boat was a refuge of last resort—it had only a few days' worth of food left. This was now how people lived on land: it was necessary to try.

It took more than an hour before they were "registered" and assigned to a room. Jim said an awkward good-bye to Lisa, leaving her stricken and silent, and left to sneak back to the boat. They hiked down the hall to find their room, where a large matronly woman welcomed them "to the third grade."

Forcing a smile, Jeanne stood tentatively in the doorway and finally urged Skippy and Lisa ahead of her into the room, which was occupied by four other families, though there was only one adult male among them. Each group had carved out a little space for itself by arranging the desks into a low wall. Although no mattresses were available, most families seemed to have sleeping bags or blankets, as did Jeanne. The lights were off, and with the wind and rain slashing against the big windows, the interior of the room was dark and depressing. Skippy, however, seemed to relax in the presence of desks and toys and began to play by himself with some blocks not far from another child his age, who seemed reluctant to leave his family's walled-off space. There were seven children in the room.

For the next few hours, Jeanne left Lisa to watch Skip so she could tour the building and talk with her fellow refugees. She began to realize how lucky she had been. Many had been a hundred miles from the nearest blast and had still been overtaken by radioactive fallout and radiation sickness. Whether they were sick or not, most of those she talked to seemed confused and numb rather than terrified, and manifested a debilitating passivity. They accepted instructions, food, friendship, and hostility with a numb equanimity that she knew was a symptom not of spiritual maturity but of surrender.

She was appalled when a young woman who was caring for those with radiation sickness told her that only one doctor was available to come to the center and then only for an hour each day. Most of the sick were too weak to go to the hospital and had been instructed to stay in the school, where conditions were, in fact, better.

"Are you an official here?" Jeanne asked the young woman, almost afraid to look at the line of ashen, slumped figures propped up against one wall of the large fifth-grade classroom.

"No," the woman answered. "I'm just doing what I can to help. My name's Katya."

Katya was a petite, ashen-haired woman in her early twenties wearing jeans and a sexy peasant blouse with a deeply scooped neckline that seemed strangely inappropriate in a roomful of sick and dying people. She wore no makeup, and she was not so much pretty as she was striking, especially her dazzling green-blue eyes.

Although Jeanne was still a little shaky from the aftereffects of seasickness, she worked for almost two hours with Katya lugging buckets for potties, cleaning up vomit, relaying messages, bringing water and food, and answering questions. At first she was disturbed by Katya's indifference to and even disobedience of the various officials who appeared sporadically throughout the afternoon—one even ordered them to leave the room because "you aren't sick or dying"—but she soon came to feel that the only worthwhile things being done were being done spontaneously by volunteers rather than as a result of any official system.

After they had fed patients who wanted to eat anything, at six o'clock Jeanne went with Katya to get Lisa and Skip, and they all headed for the school cafeteria with the other refugees. A tall, skinny young man with glasses, apparently Katya's boyfriend, joined them at their table.

The food was fried fish, onion soup, and water. The cafeteria was packed, and the refugees elbowed into line as if they were scrambling for tickets to a first-run movie.

"I've been here almost three days," Katya said when Lisa asked her about the food. "We had some meat the first day, but since then it's been all eggs, fish, and a few vegetables, mostly onions. I think we had some apples the second day, but otherwise no fruit."

"And the portions keep getting smaller," commented the young man, whose name was Sky. He cleaned his plate of fish away with amazing rapidity and eyed Jeanne's plate with interest.

"I'll give you a joint for half your fish," he offered.

It took Jeanne a moment to absorb the suggestion.

"No . . . thank you," she replied. "What I don't finish, I plan to save for my children."

"That's cool," said Sky, although he was clearly disappointed.

"Where are you working?" Jeanne asked him, more to make conversation than out of genuine interest.

"What do you mean?" asked Sky.

"Katya and I are working with the people in the fifth-grade classroom," she explained. "I wondered—"

"Oh. No. Katya likes to keep busy," Sky said. "I like to take things easy."

"Oh," said Jeanne.

"Actually I volunteered to help in the kitchen," Sky continued brightly. "But they had enough people there already."

"What . . . what about military service?" Lisa asked.

"Medical disability," Sky answered.

"Oh."

"My mind's all screwed up," Sky explained.

Katya was eating quietly as if she were indifferent to the conversation.

"Do you plan to stay here?" Jeanne asked, trying to address her question as much to Katya as to the young man.

"Long as the food holds out," Sky answered, grinning.

"Not me," said Katya, her eyes flashing. "The first two days I felt safe here. No more. I'd be out in a second if I could figure a way."

"Where would you go?" Jeanne asked, scraping the last of her fish from her plate onto Lisa's. Skippy was having trouble finishing his.

"As far away from where the bombs are going off as I can get," Katya answered. "If it's like this now," she went on, motioning at the crowded cafeteria and by implication at the whole refugee center, "I hate to think how bad it will get."

"Perhaps we've already seen the worst," Jeanne suggested.

"All I know," Katya replied, "is that the *alive* people seem to leave this place after only a day or two. Most of those who stay have already given up."

"What about me?" asked Sky with a sly smile.

"You gave up so long ago you can't even remember when."

"Thanks."

"But . . . then why do you work so hard here?" Jeanne asked.

"Where there's work to be done, I do it," said Katya.

"Where there's work to be done, I avoid it," said Sky, grinning.

Frank suddenly appeared at their table, standing behind Katya and across from Jeanne; on his face was a look of relief that he had located her.

"Jim's been drafted," he announced. "No punishment, but they were marching him through the street when I was on the way here. I ought to be happy . . . I feel like shit."

"Where will they send him?" Lisa asked, looking up wide-eyed.

"No one knows," Frank said. "He's alive, he's being fed, eventually he'll be able to serve: that's all that counts."

"How can we see him?" Lisa asked. Frank glanced at her painfully and shrugged.

"Sit down, Frank," said Jeanne. "I'll go get you something to eat."

"It's too late," said Sky. "They're closed up for the night. You've got to get here early." He turned to grin up at Frank, who merely walked around the end of the table and came over to Jeanne. "You okay?" he asked, after a cold glance at Sky.

"I'm tired," she said. "I'd like you to meet the woman I worked with most of the afternoon. This is Katya. Katya, this is Frank."

"Glad to meet you," he said.

"You own the trimaran, right?" Katya asked immediately.

"Yeah, I do. How'd you know?"

"Jeanne's been telling me her adventures," Katya replied. "If you decide to sail again, I'd like to join you."

"I'm afraid I don't think we're going to be sailing."

"You plan to stay here?"

"It seems that way," said Frank neutrally.

"I'm getting out of here if I have to crawl," said Katya, her eyes again seeming to flash angrily.

Lisa and Skip had gotten up by now, and Skip was pulling his mother's hand to lead her away. As they started to leave, Sky looked up at them glowy-eyed and grinned.

"Never knock a place that serves free food," he said.

"The class of '71, is it?" the officer asked. He was a tired-looking, sloppily dressed man about Neil's own age who had come from the damaged destroyer.

"Yes, sir," said Neil. "If you have anyone aboard from '70, '71, or '72 they'll probably know me . . . or know of me."

"Know *of* you, huh?" the lieutenant said, eyeing Neil speculatively. "Are you famous for something?"

"It was a suggestion," Neil said, sidestepping the question. "I don't have my papers with me."

"There are . . . were half a dozen Academy boys aboard this ship, but none that I can think of from your time. Maybe Captain Cohen. You know him?"

"No, I don't."

"Then you're out of luck, I guess."

"Could I see your commanding officer?" Neil persisted.

"I'm afraid Commander Bonnville wouldn't appreciate being disturbed by something as—"

"Bonnville?" Neil interrupted. "Greg Bonnville?"

"That's right," the lieutenant said, looking surprised. "You know him?"

"I served with him for eight months in Nam."

The lieutenant hesitated, his exhausted face screwed up in a frown.

"Maybe you should see him."

"I'd like to."

In ten minutes Neil had been escorted aboard the destroyer *Morison*. The *Morison* was a mess. All its topside paint was blistering, its portholes and bridge windows shattered, bloodstains still evident, damaged weapons and debris everywhere. The petty officer who received him aboard looked sick, exhausted, or both. It took almost another ten minutes to make contact with the duty officer and receive permission for him to see Commander Bonnville.

Greg Bonnville had been Neil's group leader for ten months in the South China Sea off Vietnam. He had been a fierce, dedicated, by-the-book officer who had made Neil for that first year in Vietnam a believer in going by the book. Two years later, when he'd learned that Neil planned to resign his commission, he had telephoned from Manila, where he was then stationed, to urge Neil to change his mind. As Neil was being taken to the bridge to see him again he felt a pleasant stirring of excitement, which was sickeningly crushed the moment he saw Bonnville.

His friend was only ten years older than Neil, but now he looked twenty. Slumped behind his desk in his cabin, he was gray-faced and hollow-eyed. His formerly eye-catching mane of dark hair was gone; he was almost bald. Scar tissue marred his forehead and one cheek. He trembled when he stood up to greet Neil, his lanky body badly stooped.

"I'm afraid I can't say welcome aboard, Neil," Greg Bonnville said. "The *Morison* is a deathship."

Neil stood facing his friend uncertainly. Greg's quarters were strewn with clothes, books, and papers. The ship's logbook lay on the floor, propped up against one leg of the desk. Greg sat back down with a groan.

"What happened?" Neil asked.

"Wrong war," Greg answered gloomily, not looking up. "We were steaming south fifteen miles off Cape Henry, probably thirty from Hampton Roads, when *boom,* we got . . . permanently decommissioned."

"Did you . . . personally get hit?"

"I look it, don't I?" he replied. "I got some mild burns and cuts from the initial blast, but it was the radiation all that morning that clobbered us. The only men who might come out of this all right are the engine-room crew. Anyone who had to be out on deck or on the bridge that night is probably . . . not going to make it."

"Including you?" Neil asked softly.

"Obviously including me."

Neil turned and paced over to the shattered porthole and stared out over the waters of the turning basin toward the ocean.

"Is the ship still contaminated?" Neil asked quietly.

"It's pretty clean except in the aft hold, which we've closed off," he said. "They almost wouldn't let us put in here till they got their own geiger counter man aboard and cleared us."

"May I sit down?" Neil asked.

"Please," Greg responded. "You make me sad standing up so straight." Neil sat down on the edge of Greg's berth. "What are your orders?" he asked hesitantly.

Greg looked up blankly and then snickered. "Stay here and die."

"You're kidding."

"Absolutely not. And damn good orders they are. This ship is dead, and the engine-room crew has been transferred to the *Haig*. The rest of us will stay by ourselves with our little individual time-bombs. Whoever can walk off in a week will be reassigned."

"Living Jesus," Neil muttered.

"Quite an end to a distinguished career."

"There's nothing you can do?" Neil asked, looking up at his friend as if he were appealing for himself.

"Remain on standby and if, by some miraculous stroke of luck, a Soviet sub should amble up the Morehead City inlet, go down with my ship."

"I see," said Neil, getting up and walking back over to the porthole, where pieces of shattered glass were resting like a cache of diamonds on the circular sill. "Look, Greg," he went on, turning back to his friend, who was slumped forward at his desk, staring down. "What do you know about the overall military situation?"

Greg lifted his head, and the two men gazed at each other.

"All I know is what I can read between the lines of the radio communiqués and orders."

"That's something," said Neil. "What do you think?"

"I think we're planning to evacuate all remaining naval personnel from the whole East Coast. I think it's rapidly becoming a war of individual initiative, just the kind we always wished we could be in."

"But where's the enemy?"

"Ahh," said Greg, straightening up with a grimace. "That's the new twist. The enemy is in the sky, in the food chain, in the rain, in my bloodstream."

"And the Russians?"

"They've shot their bolt," he said. "There've only been two or three incoming missiles since the second day. Their Mediterranean and Indian Ocean fleets are gone. Their population has been decimated. Whatever fighting's still going on is nothing more than the last twitching of two corpses. The Russians and us will probably both be fantasizing to our last breaths that we're just about to snatch victory from the jaws of mutual destruction."

Neil looked at the sunken face of his friend and saw no sense of triumph.

"We . . . ah . . . we've won?" Neil asked, feeling feeble and foolish.

"If we've won, it's the way the *Morison* has won . . ." He looked dismally around the room.

For a third time Neil walked over to look out the shattered porthole. Outside he saw the Coast Guard launch begin its turn to sweep back out the channel in its systematic patrolling of the inlet.

"I've been ordered to report for duty," he announced with his back still to Greg.

"Here?" Greg asked, astounded.

"No. To report somewhere. All men are supposed to report."

"How'd you happen to end up *here*?"

Turning around to face him Neil gave a brief account of his voyage on *Vagabond*.

"And you're all leaving her for *here*?" Greg asked in a low, sad voice.

Neil shrugged. "The law—" he began.

"Neil, I told you," Greg said, leaning painfully back in his chair and almost glaring at Neil. "This has become a war of individual initiative and . . ."—he grimaced and groaned once—"and the enemy," he continued, "the sole enemy . . . is death."

"And the U.S. Navy?" Neil asked softly.

Greg slumped forward again.

"Wrong war," he replied in a low voice.

After Neil had left Captain Bonnville, he searched out the infirmary and drug dispensary. There he found a sailor kneeling in front of two open drawers and a clutter of bottles and little cardboard cartons strewn around him on the floor. When the sailor looked up at him, Neil saw that he was stoned. He was probably searching for some sort of dope—morphine or codeine or barbituates, judging from the dull look in his eyes. Slowly a look of bewilderment made its way onto the young sailor's round face as Neil stood stiffly over him, dressed in jeans and a T-shirt.

"All right, sailor," Neil said firmly. "I don't have to ask what you're doing here, but I want you to find me any antibiotics that are still around."

The small, weary-looking young man, his face pale and his eyes bloodshot, hestitated, still in confusion.

"I'm Captain Loken, sailor," Neil barked in the traditional manner. "And I gave you an order."

"Aye . . . aye, sir," the sailor finally replied, wobbling to his feet. "Uh . . . antibiotics don't work against radiation sickness."

"I know."

"Nothing works."

"I know. Find them."

The man stared around the room and then walked over to the opposite wall and began going through drawers. Neil came up beside him and began searching also. Eventually he found two vials containing liquid penicillin and a bottle labeled Tetracyclin with a hundred capsules. He located two syringes in a glass cabinet. The sailor was now staring dreamily into an empty drawer.

"Is there still morphine available, sailor?" Neil asked loudly.

The man lazily shook his head and smiled. Neil made a further search for pain-killers, found a small amount of codeine, and left.

He decided that since weapons had been officially removed from the *Morison*, his only hope was to search the petty officers' quarters. There he encountered, in the four separate staterooms, one corpse, two dying men, and two men listening lugubriously to a newscast. He asked them about weapons, but they stared back at him as if he were mad, or they were stoned. In the last stateroom, empty of its occupants, he discovered in a bureau drawer a nine-millimeter pistol—the official Navy sidearm—and a half-full box of ammunition. From this same room he also stole a bottle of aspirin, matches, razor blades, suntan lotion, and a small cache of cocaine. When he found himself tempted to steal Kleenex, he felt he was becoming a kleptomaniac and hastily left.

Later, as he was leaving the dockyard, Neil ran into the petty officer who had originally heard his story.

"Well, Mr. Loken, are you going to join us?" he asked.

Neil hesitated only a moment. "It doesn't look that way," he replied. "It appears I've been given . . . an independent command."

And he left.

At ten P.M. that evening, after he had filled out forms, had been given a perfunctory physical exam by a corpsman, and been issued a uniform, Jim and other recruits of the last three days were rounded up and marched to the Rialto movie theater. There about one hundred and fifty new soldiers, some without uniforms, stood at attention between the rows of seats, most of them sweating profusely in the stuffy theater, no longer cooled by air conditioning. Jim stood at the right rear, uncomfortable, resentful, curious. For fifteen minutes the men were kept standing like this. Finally a major marched out onto the stage in front of them.

"At ease, men," he shouted down at them, and a great groan broke from the group as the soldiers relaxed, many of them collapsing into their seats. The relaxed hubbub lasted for less than five seconds.

"*Atten-shun!*" the major unexpectedly bellowed.

Surprised and confused, the men struggled back up to attention, a few, not hearing the new command, having to be urged up by those around them.

"At ease, men," the major shouted at them after less than twenty seconds.

This time the relaxation was much less pronounced; most of the men remained standing, looking at the major suspiciously, not talking among themselves this time as they had before. Jim himself stood exactly as he had been when he was supposedly standing at attention, staring up at the major with resentment. About twenty seconds passed this time, then thirty, and a few of the men began to whisper to each other, one or two to sit down.

"*Atten-shun!*" the major bellowed a third time, and again the men responded, many sullenly, until the noncoms spread out around the auditorium began to enforce the major's command.

"All right!" the major shouted, pacing off to the left of the platform, his compact body moving with suppressed power, his dark face and neatly trimmed mustache accentuating his smartness and correctness compared to the ragtag bunch of men in front of him. He glared down at his audience.

"You've just demonstrated the single most important attribute of a soldier: obedience. I don't give a fuck if you don't know your right foot from your left foot, an antitank gun from a .22, or a platoon from a spittoon, but if you know how to obey, you'll make one hell of a soldier."

He paused and paced back over to the center of the stage.

"In this war, especially with the losses we've already sustained here on the mainland, it's absolutely necessary that everyone pull together, that we all work to get the country back on its feet again. And the only way that can happen is for the President to point, the officers to lead, and the rest of you to fall into line. . . ."

The major wiped sweat from his brow, but his bushy eyebrows and trim mustache still kept glistening under the row of bright lights.

"The Russians haven't landed yet," he went on in a loud voice that seemed just on the verge of cracking from the effort. "We hope they never will, but there are already enemies loose in this country, and it's our job to stop them. The enemy is anyone who thinks they know better than the President, anyone who selfishly puts his own interests above those of the whole nation. It's the Army's job to keep our country functioning, keep the food, medical, and military supplies flowing. Your officers will determine how this can best be done, and then you and they will do it.

"And I don't want any of you assholes to try thinking you know better than your officers. There's only one right way to do things in the Army, and that's the way you're ordered to do them. . . . And don't you forget it. . . ."

He paused, glared, sweat again pouring down his face, and Jim watched him with a feeling of dull dread and hopelessness. He felt like he was trapped in a small room.

"Any day now some of you may be sent on assignments that involve our using the muscle against misguided bastards who think their personal asses are all that count. I don't want any shilly-shallying. If you are ordered to shoot someone, you shoot him. There's no time for you to complain that you haven't heard the guy speak Russian. Anyone who disobeys an order from a superior officer is a traitor and deserves to be shot. Don't you forget it. . . .

"All of you men here have just become part of this army. You are idiots, ignoramuses, assholes, zeroes. Don't pretend you're anything else. We'll teach you to be soldiers. You'll learn. But right from the beginning I want you to know that there's really only one lesson: obey. . . . And don't you forget it. . . ."

Later that night, as Jim spread out his sleeping bag next to Tony's on the floor of a double room in the Moonlighter Motel—their temporary barracks—the other six men in the room, all of whom had been "in" since the second day of the war, were loose and joking. There were three blacks, two of whom were big men and the third a little runt of a man, and three middle-aged whites. They had all been at the theater and heard the major's talk.

"Sheet, man, we're the *kings,*" one of the big black men said as he spread his sleeping bag out on top of a double bed. "Ain't no way you gonna get me outa this army. In here they look out after your ass. Out there it's everybody's ass for hisself. Ain't no way."

"I don't like shootin' no *peo*ple," the little black man said sullenly as he prepared to crawl into his sleeping bag, also on the floor. "You shoot anybody they ask you?"

"Sheet, I shoot my *mother,* man, if they says to," the first black man countered. "That's the way it *is,* man. This is *wah!*"

The other three men, the older whites, remained silent, two of them preparing to sleep on the second double bed and the third, a plump, red-faced man, bedding down near Tony and Jim.

"If they ask us to shoot somebody," Tony announced loudly in the brief silence, "you can be damn sure that guy deserves to be shot."

Jim, uncomfortable, unconvinced, was quietly unlacing his GI boots.

"Well, at least we won't starve to death in the Army," the plump man said with a hesitant smile.

"They feed us, they give us guns, and when a bomb comes, they tell us to duck," one of the other white men said. "Compared to what I was facing four days ago, this is heaven."

"You're damn right," the man next to him echoed.

Jim placed his boots and his fatigues in a neat pile at the head of his sleeping bag and, in his underwear, crawled into his sleeping bag.

"What this wah is, is a great big mother-fucking urban renewal program," the big talkative black man said as he undressed. "Now Manhattan and Washington and Boston all get to look like Harlem." He laughed.

The others were silent. Jim linked his hands behind his head and closed his eyes. He could feel the floor swaying underneath him, its motion the counterpoint to *Vagabond*'s during the last two days at sea.

He felt isolated, alone. Tony appeared to feel at home in the Army; Jim felt he would be lucky to last a single day. He tried to think about what he could do and where he could go if he escaped, but he was tired, the three blacks were laughing about something, and the two white men in the other double bed were whispering together. He heard Tony getting into the sleeping bag beside him.

"Don't mind these shits," Tony whispered to him. "Tomorrow we'll be assigned to a platoon, and it'll be a whole new ball game."

Jim didn't reply. He didn't think the league he was stuck in now was going to be getting any better for a long, long time.

For most of his fifty-eight years George Cooper had thought that he would defend his country to the death. He had fought in the Korean War; two of his sons had fought in the war in Vietnam. So it was with some degree of confusion that he found himself standing behind a barricade of farm machinery, oil tanks, and hay with eighteen other farmers and a few of their teenage sons, preparing to fight a company of soldiers from the Army of the United States. Every decision he had made during the week that followed the outbreak of war had seemed logical, but there was nothing logical about what was happening now. His own government seemed about to kill him and his sons and friends because they felt they ought to be able to keep some of their farm animals and produce for their families and friends.

When four days earlier an officer had come and told him the Army needed all his eggs every day and all his spring corn, George had still been too stunned to resist. But when some of his neighbors began to complain that the Army was taking everything, and then yesterday a new officer came to requisition the rest of his spring vegetables and forty chickens, George began to feel that his country had already been invaded; it was just that the uniforms weren't the color he'd expected them to be.

George understood that food was now gold and that he and his neighbors were millionaires in a poverty-stricken world. He understood that with real money almost meaningless he would have to give away most of his food without compensation so that others wouldn't starve to death. What he couldn't understand and couldn't accept was that he had to give up *everything* to the government and depend on feeding his own family on what the government planned to give back to him.

Eggs and corn he could spare. But his chickens, or Bart Hasler's cows, or Fred Lapp's hogs, these they couldn't give up without endangering their own families' survival. Taking their animals away was like tearing down small factories.

The officer had arrived that morning for the chickens, and George had refused to surrender them. The officer had left, announcing he would return with reinforcements. He had. About sixty soldiers with automatic rifles were standing around three troop carriers parked two hundred feet away on the road. The chickens were in the henhouse behind them. About half of Bart's herd of sixty cows and most of Fred's hogs were in the big barn to their left. A large store of recently harvested vegetables was in the cellar of the main house. The women and smaller children were staying over at Fred's farm a mile away. All the young men were in the service someplace, one of them, John Simpson's son, Cal, standing with an automatic rifle among the sixty soldiers confronting them.

When the officer shouted at them through a bullhorn, the other farmers chose George to go out and speak to him. The soldiers began to fan out around the barns and henhouse, and Bart, who was in charge of tactics, had posted men in various defensive positions around the barn and henhouse to keep the soldiers at a distance. Their orders were that if any soldier got within fifty feet of the barns they were to fire a warning shot at the ground in front of them.

The officer in charge was a Captain Ames, a tall, skinny fellow with a nervous twitch on one side of his face. He didn't seem too sure of himself. George wasn't too sure of *him*self. He'd left his shotgun back with the others and ambled slowly out to talk to Ames.

"We've come for your chickens, Mr. Cooper," Captain Ames said in an unnaturally loud voice. "My orders are to confiscate all edible livestock in this area."

"All of them?" George asked in surprise. In the morning the order had been for just forty of his chickens.

"All of them." Captain Ames held out a piece of paper, presumably containing written authorization for the confiscation.

"Can't give 'em up, captain," George replied, staring unseeingly at the paper but not taking it from Ames's hand. "Until people are starving to death, I figure I can best take care of 'em here."

"You're not the one to do the figuring," Ames countered. "The Army knows what's needed, and we need chickens."

"Can't do it, Captain."

"I've got sixty men here that says you can."

"If that henhouse catches on fire, and that barn," George replied, squinting back at his farmyard and watching the circle of soldiers grow tighter, "then nobody's gonna eat the chickens. Or the hogs or anything else. Why don't you go back and talk it over with your general or with whatever asshole sent you out here?"

"My orders were clear and irrevocable," Ames said nervously. "I am to bring back the requisitioned food supplies from this area this afternoon and use whatever force is necessary to do so."

"You can't bring 'em back if we burn down the barns."

Ames flushed.

"Why would you do that?"

" 'Cause we don't like having our property stolen."

"Your country's at war," Ames shot back. "The President has declared martial law. If the Army orders something requisitioned, that's not stealing."

"I don't figure the President had my chickens in mind when he declared martial law."

"But he did," Ames countered. "He had everyone's chickens in mind."

"Well," George said after a pause, "I'm not too good at arguin'." He stared off at a group of soldiers in back of the barn. "Fact is though if your soldiers get within fifty feet of our barns, bullets will hit three feet in front of them, and if they get within forty-five feet of the barns, then they'll bump into our bullets. And if they get into the barns, then our boys will set the barns on fire. We figure there ain't no way you can carry out your order."

Captain Ames, seeing that his men were within seventy or eighty feet of the barns in some places, shouted out an order to halt and the noncoms passed it on. Ames told George to wait where he was, went over to the back of one of the trucks, and got on the radio back to headquarters in Morehead City. When he returned five minutes later, he looked pale and shaken.

"Look, Mr. Cooper," he said with an anguished, pleading note in his voice. "The colonel says to get what food I can, no matter who gets hurt. He says radioactive fallout is coming this way, and all your animals will be useless as food in less than a week. The Army will be evacuating the area, and we've been ordered to take all the food we can find with us. You people should evacuate too. We'll leave you plenty of food for your families, but most of it we'll have to take."

George Cooper squinted at the captain. The fallout bit might be an excuse or it might be true.

"You plan to kill us for a few chickens and pigs?" he said after a pause.

"I will have to kill you if you disobey the orders of the military commander of this region."

"For a few chickens?"

"You seem to be all ready to destroy your barn for a few chickens."

"My barns are useless without anything to put in them," George said slowly. "I figure that you and your colonel can survive without my chickens."

"Ten minutes, Cooper," Ames said with a grimace as he glanced at his watch. "If you don't put down your weapons and let us take what the local military commander has ordered requisitioned, my men will attack.''

George Cooper looked numbly back at Captain Ames.

"Seems like a pretty shitty thing to do,'' he said.

"May be,'' said Captain Ames, flushing. "But I'll do it.''

George turned and walked slowly back to his friends behind the tractors, examining as he walked the positions of the soldiers around his farmyard. A few of them back of the henhouse seemed awfully close to fifty feet away from the buildings.

Bart, Fred, and two more of the older men met him by Fred's harvester, and he began to recount his conversation with Ames. He had just gotten to the Army's claim that fallout was coming their way when a shot rang out. Then two others. George wheeled to see Captain Ames crouched down next to one of the trucks, and the soldiers near him throwing themselves down onto the grass. Off to the left two soldiers were running away. To the right, a squad of eight or ten soldiers, in a crouch, were running toward the henhouse. A fusillade of shots erupted from the teenagers there, and one of the soldiers fell. Then the real firing began.

As he sat exhausted in his cabin and fiddled with the shortwave radio Neil was feeling baffled. The day and a half since his visit to Greg Bonnville when he had made his separate peace, had been frustrating. He'd found it easy enough to bluff his way out of the two confrontations with the authorities challenging him about his not being in uniform—he put on his captain's demeanor and Navy lingo and said he was on special assignment from the *Morison*—but had found it difficult to learn what was really happening in the world.

Official radio announcements indicated that Morehead City was a safe area. Army policy was that refugees should stay put. They were offering no assistance to people who wanted to move farther south. As long as there was no danger in staying where they were, he didn't feel he had any right to take Jeanne and Frank back out to sea, much less to help Jim desert. Although he himself no longer felt an obligation to serve his country, the transformation of Greg Bonnville was not an example he could use to persuade others. It was too personal. He himself felt the only safety lay in escaping the mainland to sea; to others this seemed to be simply his mania.

Conrad Macklin had disappeared while Neil was on the *Morison,* and since he had stolen some food from *Vagabond,* Neil assumed that he'd seen the last of him. But he'd returned thirty hours later— just four hours ago—to inform Neil that though the Army had roadblocks up to prevent civilians from fleeing south, a caravan of Army vehicles with both military and civilian passengers had been streaming south on Route 17. Macklin had hung around and learned that the Army was having problems manning its roadblock units because some of the troops were panicking at the sight of so many others going south after they had been ordered to stay put. Macklin urged Neil to take *Vagabond* out to sea immediately, whether Jeanne and the others came or not.

Neil knew that if he didn't take *Vagabond* out soon, Macklin would find somebody else who would. That meant he not only had to worry about choosing the correct course of action but about Macklin's trying to hijack *Vagabond* again. With Olly often aboard alone there wasn't much to stop him. Neil had tried to delay any precipitous action on Macklin's part by telling him he planned to decide on his plans tonight. He had visited Jeanne, Frank, and Lisa at the refugee center briefly late that afternoon and had been discouraged to see that they seemed to be settling in; both were working hard, making friends, feeling they were making a contribution. Lisa had spent much of the day trying unsuccessfully to see Jim and had just returned in tears, so Jeanne was in no condition to make decisions. Her response to Neil's announcement that he wasn't going back into the Navy was a brief stricken look, as if she were frightened by the implications for her own life. Frank told Neil that he could take *Vagabond,* as if for Frank the struggle were over and Morehead City High School was now home. Neil had left frightened and depressed at their state.

"There was more fallout today. The total's more than an eighth of an inch since we first got some four days ago. Some of the farmers are trying to get it off the leaves of the corn and squash and beans, and Pat Nerron reports the wind blows it off the wheat and rye, but it's killing some of the plants even lying in the soil.''

The voice over the shortwave radio was that of the ham radio operator from east Tennessee who Neil had last listened to the evening the war started.

''Henry Tickney says his geiger counter shows it's up to three roentgens in his soybean fields, which isn't healthy for either him or his beans, but supposedly it'll drop off every day unless we get more. Like most of us, Henry says he only goes out for a half-hour a day.

''Three new shelters were started yesterday and one's already finished. Eight people moved in with enough food for two weeks. We put in Jesse and Marge Williams and their two kids, Gor and Hilda Lafson and their son Leo, and the Barletts' sick girl, Tina. The Williams run the Exxon station east of town and are sick and don't have anything they can do, and the Lafsons paid for all the material and labor on the shelter. Like I said, the Williams and Tina Barlett are pretty sick from the radiation, and we figure they need the protection. Course I guess we all do.

''Martha Peterson died yesterday. After her sons went away, we couldn't get her to stay in the cellar.

''The Linkletters and Potts moved south today, using the Linkletter's team of workhorses and a wagon Tim built out of an old truck flatbed. They're the sixth and seventh families to leave. Most all of the young people are gone of course. Most of the old people have chosen to stay. We don't know whether we'll make it or not, but most of us decided it'd be better to die here than live in those camps they've set up in northern Louisiana and Arkansas. I suppose if we had kids, it might be different. That's why we help those who feel they have to go.

''It's kind of sad though. You know you'll never see each other again. The people leaving feel kind of like traitors, and the people staying feel kind of like fools . . . Still, we do what we got to do . . .''

After the frequency went dead, Neil turned off the set and continued to sit in the darkness of his cabin. He became aware of the faint glow of his wristwatch lying at the base of the radio. It was almost midnight. They were dying in east Tennessee, what?—perhaps six or seven hundred miles away. Not even that far.

Sighing, he turned the set back on, adjusted the earphones, and began a slow sweep of the ham frequencies. The first voice he brought in reported increased radioactive fallout and radiation sickness in southern Mississippi, with thousands fleeing out into the Gulf of Mexico. Military authority had ceased to exist; soldiers as well as civilians were stealing boats, commandeering barges and helicopters to get away. The voice speculated that to the west, toward New Orleans and Galveston, there were few survivors. Those fleeing east across the Florida panhandle would probably be overtaken by the lethal fallout. He mentioned some towns whose names Neil didn't recognize, but when he checked his small atlas he concluded the broadcast had come from somewhere less than a hundred miles east of Pensacola.

Neil moved the dial, bringing in a ship, the *Athena,* three hundred miles out of Boston, asking for medical advice on the treatment of radiation sickness.

He brought in a station in Bermuda warning of starvation facing the islanders there.

Then his ear caught "Raleigh, North Carolina" on a frequency filled with static, and he tried to tune it in more clearly. Raleigh was about two hundred miles west of Morehead City. The voice, clearer now, a woman's with a strong southern accent, was announcing that she was taking over for her husband, who was sick but who wanted her to keep up his daily reports. The radioactive fallout in the last day had increased tenfold, and now everyone was trying to stay belowground. Those who ventured out for more than a half-hour took sick quickly. Those who stayed in cellars or shelters did better. The ground was covered with ash, thick, black, ugly. They were drinking only bottled water, but most had only a limited supply. Electric pumps could no longer be used. They couldn't figure why there was so much fallout, where it was coming from, and it was scary. They hoped it would stop raining soon.

When Neil switched off the radio this time, he was trembling with a great, deep dread, almost desperation. They were all doomed. Shelters, putting out to sea, joining the Army, the Navy, all seemed equally futile.

No, that was a lie. He knew it was a lie. Safety lay far to the south and out to sea. He knew that, could see that for a certainty now. Morehead City, bucolic, innocent, unimportant Morehead City was doomed. In a few days it would be overtaken by the fallout. So too would the rest of the East Coast. But the ocean and a run to the south represented hope and life, for him, for Jeanne, for Frank, for Olly, for all of his remaining friends. Only out there, where the fallout would be swallowed up by the insatiable sea, was there hope for survival, and he knew it was up to him to get them all to act, and to act now. The Army was lying. There was no safety left on land.

Having made his decision, he stood up, carefully turned off the radio, disconnected the batteries, and went up on deck. Captain Olly was sitting in the darkness of the wheelhouse talking in a lively monologue to silent Conrad Macklin. Olly stopped talking when Neil appeared.

"I'm taking *Vagabond* back out to sea," he announced quietly after sitting down opposite the old man.

"Good," Captain Olly replied. "Been wonderin' how long it would take you."

Neil turned to Macklin.

"To get out the inlet we'll need another boat to act as decoy," he said. "A boat with just enough fuel to get to the inlet and create a diversion. I want you to find one, devise a plan for stealing it, and when the time comes, steal it."

Macklin stared back at Neil.

"You want me to be on one boat while you and the rest are sailing out the inlet on this?" he asked, scowling.

"One of us will be with you," Neil answered. "And, if possible, think of a plan that won't mean your hitting or killing anyone."

"If possible?" Macklin said with a sneer.

"Olly, about how many gallons of diesel fuel do you figure we'll need to get two boats out into the ocean?"

"It's three miles from here?" Olly asked.

"Yes," Neil answered.

"Six or seven."

"That's what I was afraid of," Neil went on. "Since they took all but five gallons this afternoon, we'll need more. Macklin, keep an eye open for another three gallons of fuel. Or more."

"Like everyone else in the world," Macklin commented.

Neil, staring past Captain Olly with his eyes half-closed in concentration, ignored the comment.

"We leave tomorrow night at ten," he finally said.

"Who's coming with us?" Macklin asked.

"We'll see," said Neil, and he got up to return to his cabin to sleep.

Neil arrived at the refugee center and located Frank at four o'clock the next afternoon. As he moved through the halls he became distressingly aware that he was entering a little world that, no matter how dislocated, was permitting people to assume that they and this little world could continue to exist. This was a center where people came to be safe and to be taken care of, and the men and women in the halls had the look of those who saw danger as something they had survived in the past rather than something that might still be looming over them.

Neil himself was anxious and tense. He strode down the hall with the feeling that every moment they delayed might be fatal, that even now lethal clouds of radioactivity might be only hours away.

Frank was in what used to be the principal's office supervising the relocation of some of the refugees. A harried-looking Army lieutenant was standing behind Frank, looking alternately commanding and bewildered. As Neil paused in the doorway he watched people come up to Frank for instructions, saw him consult the chart on the desk in front of him and then send the person running off on some errand or another while Frank carefully made a chalk mark on the chart.

Neil pushed his way through three or four people and stood in front of the desk. Frank looked up abstractedly, as if Neil were an old college friend who had turned up unexpectedly.

"Fallout's coming this way," Neil said as quietly and unemotionally as he could. "We've got to leave, sail—go south. You and Jeanne have got to come."

Frank emerged from his abstracted state and looked at Neil with a tired frown.

"You're running?" he asked.

Neil flinched.

"Everyone in Morehead City will probably have to relocate," he replied, aware of the half-dozen faces watching him attentively.

"Says who?" Frank asked.

"Frank, let's talk this over in private," Neil appealed.

"Look, mister," the Army lieutenant cut in abruptly. "If there's any danger to this area, the Army will let people know."

Neil looked up at the man coldly.

"You'll be lucky if they let *you* know," he said.

"You think we should all evacuate Morehead City?" Frank asked. He spoke heavily, as if the thought of moving again depressed him.

"Yes. Everyone."

The crowd around the desk began murmuring.

"No one goes nowhere," the stubby lieutenant burst out a second time, "unless the Army says so."

"I want you to help me to save Jeanne and her children," Neil went on desperately, ignoring the lieutenant.

"Another ocean voyage?" Frank asked. He gazed at Neil a moment more and then turned to look at the refugees around the desk, who were looking at him as if he were about to hand down the verdict on their fate. Then he peered sullenly down at his chart.

"It's up to Jeanne," he said in a low, husky voice.

"Frank, please."

"No one's going anywhere," the lieutenant said.

Neil found Jeanne working alone in a small room with a dozen elderly women. She was serving them cups of water and giving them instructions on the routine of camp life, the location of the bathrooms and so on. She looked tired, her hair, tied back in a bun, was damp with perspiration. She had on jeans and a green sweatshirt. Surprised and smiling, she came out into the hall with him.

"What's the matter?" she asked, sensing his urgency.

"There's massive fallout coming," he said in a low voice. "We're sailing out the inlet tonight. You, Lisa, and Skip have got to come with us."

As she looked up at him he could see the fear and uncertainty in her eyes. She slowly shook her head.

"I . . . can't believe it," she said.

"Jeanne, it's a life-or-death decision. No one who stays in this camp will be alive in another two weeks."

"You . . . Isn't it illegal for you and Jim to leave?"

"Everything is illegal now except staying here and dying."

"How are you going to get past the Coast Guard?"

"I don't know," he continued in a whisper as two women passed by. "I just know we have to do it."

"But . . ." she began, gazing numbly down the hall after the women as if she expected them to help her somehow. "Why . . . tonight?"

"Because the sword may fall at any moment."

"If fallout's coming, they'll warn us, won't they?" she asked him next, resisting the decision that would force her to run again. "They'll bus us south, or put us on a train."

Neil grabbed her fiercely. "They won't," he hissed at her. "There *are* no buses or trains, except for the Army."

"Oh, Neil," she said, twisting in his grasp.

"Don't you trust me?" he said sharply, still holding her. "Do you think I'm lying to you?"

She searched his face for certainty and saw with a shock that if she didn't leave, she would die.

"Oh, Neil, of course I trust you," she said, and found herself trembling violently as she accepted their danger.

"Then come," said Neil with relief, taking her arm. "Let's get the others."

After they picked up Frank, they started back to Jeanne's room to get Lisa and Skip.

"What about Jim?" Jeanne asked Neil as they hurried along.

"We'll get him," Neil answered.

"Tony? Seth?" she asked.

"If they want to come."

"How about Elaine?" Frank asked. "She's here in the building."

"No," Neil said firmly. "I'm practicing triage. Having her on the boat might mean that sooner or later someone else might have to die."

"You don't know that," Frank said.

"No, I don't. But she can't come."

"There's another woman who wants to join us," Jeanne interrupted as they began walking again.

"No. No one else," Neil replied promptly, striding on.

"But I promised her—"

"No," Neil repeated as they entered the third-grade classroom. Lisa and Skip looked up at their mother. "Where's your suitcase?"

"It was stolen," Jeanne replied as she went over to Skip and gave him a hug. "Get our stuff together, Lisa. We're going back to the boat."

"What about Jim?" Lisa asked, not moving.

"We'll get him," Neil said.

"Go!" Jeanne said sharply to Lisa, who hurried back to the corner where she had been reading. "Neil, you must speak to this woman," Jeanne added.

"No more," said Neil. "Come on, let's get going."

But as the five of them were leaving, Neil's path was blocked by the small, defiant figure of Katya.

"I can sail, sew, cook, and I'm tough," she said without introduction. "I want to go with you."

"We're overloaded," Neil replied automatically, looking down at her, stopped by her almost comical fierceness.

"But, Neil—" Jeanne began from beside him.

"I weigh a hundred and six pounds," Katya countered. "Pound for pound I'll be the best crew member you've ever had."

Neil smiled in spite of himself, then shook his head.

"Look . . . we simply can't take on any stranger who wants to join us," he said. "If you're tough, you'll understand that."

"I understand that," she replied. "But you need another woman aboard. Jeanne can't handle everything."

Neil hesitated, thinking of Jeanne's seasickness, of Elaine's banishment.

"I can sail, I can sew, I can cook, and I can fuck," Katya went on firmly, looking Neil in the eye.

"A Renaissance woman," he murmured, wishing she hadn't alluded to her sexuality, since he knew he'd already made up his mind when Katya had reminded him that Jeanne needed another woman's help.

"All right," he said firmly. "Jeanne needs you; therefore, we need you."

"Thank you," she said, reaching up on tiptoe to kiss him quickly on the lips.

"But try to remember that it's your first three skills we're taking you for and not the fourth," he said, moving on past her.

"Please, let's get Jim," Lisa pleaded.

And they hurried on.

"The Battle of Cooper's Henhouse", as one rather stoned corporal had dubbed it, had a gloomy effect on the men of C Company. None of them had been killed and only three of them wounded, but Captain Ames had made it seem like it was all a mistake. Four of the farmers had been killed—three of them teenagers—and seven wounded before the officers got the shooting to stop. The henhouse had burned down, but most of the chickens had escaped. The soldiers had had more trouble rounding up the chickens and hogs than they had winning the battle. Ames had radioed for an ambulance for the wounded but was told to bring them back in the trucks instead. With the farm animals and wounded taking up two of the trucks, most of the company had to march back the fifteen miles to Morehead City.

Tony Mariano was a member of C Company, and he was goddamned angry at Ames and some of the others. He knew the farmers had started the shooting because the first shot had kicked up dust five feet away from Tony himself. And even before the soldiers had fired a single shot, one of the men in his squad had been hit as they were running forward to hide behind a big fallen tree trunk about thirty feet from the back of the henhouse. So if a few farmers had gotten killed, they had only themselves to blame. The captain's going around trying to find out who had advanced without orders was a waste of time.

But though Tony thought his company's actions had been justified, he still found the whole business as unpleasant as most of the others. Tony himself had been wounded in the left side, but was laughed at by the other soldiers when the corpsman who examined the wound and extracted the bullet announced that it was a pellet from a BB gun.

"Hey, Mariano," his corporal had shouted at him. "Aren't pellet guns outlawed by the Geneva Convention?" and the whole squad had laughed. Tony had seen the fifteen-year-old that had been killed: the young body and face chewed up by at least three slugs from someone's automatic rifle. Tony hadn't killed him—at least he didn't think he had—but he had sure blasted the henhouse pretty good before Sergeant Viagio had yanked the gun out of his hand and shouted for him to stop.

By the time they had marched back to Morehead, it was almost seven o'clock and he, like the rest, was exhausted and starving and filthy from wrestling with hogs and chickens. In the mess hall they were served another meal of fish and eggs, but with two or three cans of beer apiece, thank God. Jim Stoor was there, and he told Jim about the battle, trying to explain that it was a serious and necessary business, but he could see that Jim was appalled. Goddamn it, there was a war on!

At eight, when a soldier told Jim that his father was outside, Tony went along to see what was up. Frank and Neil were standing in the dusk at the side of the former restaurant that now served as the mess hall for the garrison. Frank quickly explained to his son about their decision to try to take *Vagabond* back out to sea.

"I'm coming," said Jim.

"What the fuck," Tony burst out. "You're deserting? And you, Neil, how come you're not in uniform?"

"Wrong war," said Neil, echoing Greg Bonnville's words. "Do you want to join us?"

Tony looked at Neil uncertainly, his loyalty to his country battling with the fear aroused by the sight of others fleeing an approaching danger.

"I'm no deserter," he finally said sullenly.

Neil turned away.

"Let's go," he said.

"Hold it!" Tony shouted. "If you take Jim now, I'll be an accessory or something."

The other three stopped and turned to face him.

"If everyone acted as selfishly as you guys, our society would be doomed," Tony continued aggressively. "It's my duty to report you to my superiors."

"Come with us," Neil said gently.

"You won't make it," Tony countered. "The Coast Guard won't let you put out to sea. Don't go, Jim. They're shooting deserters."

"I was going to desert even if the fallout weren't coming," Jim said. "I'm going."

"I'm not letting you guys—" Tony began, but then Neil's fist slammed into the side of his face. He staggered backward into darkness.

The night was overcast, as Neil had hoped, although on the northern horizon a few stars could be seen, which indicated an approaching high pressure system. With the wind blowing out of the east at fifteen knots, the passage out the inlet would be rough.

By midnight they were putting the plan they'd developed into execution. Conrad Macklin had stolen a small abandoned fishing vessel named *Moonchaser* and enough fuel to get it to where Neil wanted it. They had tied and tacked *Vagabond*'s blue carpets along her white port sides and decking to reduce glare and the chances of being seen by the Coast Guard's searchlight. They had even packed mud on the lower part of the masts to cut down reflection.

Neil and Jim were on board the fishing smack, which was towing *Vagabond*'s dinghy with its outboard motor tilted up. Frank was at the helm of the trimaran, with Olly, Macklin, Jeanne, and Lisa as crew. Skippy was asleep in the port berth, Katya was on call, and Tony was tied up in the forepeak.

Neil had taken Tony back to the docks because he'd feared that he would get the authorities to investigate *Vagabond*. He had planned to leave Tony behind at the last minute, but Macklin had argued vehemently that Tony might still raise the alarm and, besides, was the best sailor they had for a long voyage. When Frank agreed, Neil decided they could abandon Tony in the Bahamas if he wanted off or didn't work out.

The escape plan was for Neil and Jim to scuttle *Moonchaser* on the eastern side of the inlet, at Shackleford Point, to draw the patrol launch over while *Vagabond* would motor along the western side of the inlet a quarter mile away, pick up Neil and Jim, who would cross the inlet in the dinghy to join them, and make a run for it.

As Neil steered the sluggish *Moonchaser* toward the inlet a light rain began to fall. Neil had decided that he and Jim should take the decoy vessel, because he had confidence they could do the job and because if *Vagabond* were seen and stopped, without them aboard the Coast Guard might let the ship proceed, simply removing the deserter Tony. Of course he hadn't told Macklin or Tony this line of thought.

As he brought *Moonchaser* to within three-quarters of a mile of the patrol path of the cutter he realized that with the rain falling he could no longer depend on seeing the unlighted buoys and stakes that he'd planned to use to stay out of the main channel to avoid being spotted. Now he'd have to stay in the main channel, hoping the rain would cut visibility so much that he could get the old fishing smack scuttled before the Coast Guard came close enough to see them taking off in the dinghy.

Jim stood beside him in the little wheelhouse, his face wet with rain from peering around the salt-streaked window trying to pick up the channel buoys and look for signs of shoal water. He could barely make out the flashing red light of the next channel marker, but beyond that he could see neither the running lights nor the searchlight of the Coast Guard patrol. Neil was keeping *Moonchaser* to the left of the main channel, motoring slowly forward against the incoming tide. Then, at a little after one, he opened up the throttle and headed for Shackleford Point and the planned scuttling.

Jim still saw no clear sign of the Coast Guard except for brief flashes of white that Neil said were the searchlight. The wind had picked up and seemed to be blowing the rain and seaspray directly into his face. Although it was a warm rain, he was shivering. He had on a foul-weather jacket, but his legs were bare and cold beneath his swimsuit. Then he saw what Neil had said would be the last two lighted buoys before the point: "a flashing red and a flashing green." He had to yell now over the noise of the engine.

"I'll take us just to port of the red one," Neil shouted back. "Get its number. And watch for the cutter."

They seemed to approach the blinking red light on the red bell with aggravating slowness, but once they were there, Neil steered to within a few feet of the loud mournful gonging and Jim verified that it had "16" stenciled in white paint on its side. Almost the moment he looked forward again after they'd passed the bell, he saw the green starboard running light and sweeping searchlight of the cutter. It seemed to be a quarter mile off in the blackness and wet wind, almost dead ahead. It was moving west across the channel—away from Shackleford Bank.

Jim shouted this to Neil, who brought *Moonchaser* to a complete halt in the water, waiting while the cutter moved farther west and away from them. Once the light swept in their direction and played over the smack, but rapidly, without pausing. Though the glare temporarily blinded Jim, the cutter apparently didn't notice the black hull. Jim saw Neil look at his watch, grimace, and increase speed. The rain was only sporadic now, but the wind was gusty and blew in sweeping bursts of spray against the windshield. Ocean swells made the boat pitch from side to side as they approached the open water of the ocean.

In another two minutes the cutter was a little more than halfway across the inlet and still heading for the far side. Neil gave the boat full throttle, his face knitted in tense concentration, and *Moonchaser* pounded forward at seven knots into the tide and the ocean swells.

The small boat rose and smashed down on one big swell that seemed to rear up out of the darkness like some living sea mammal to lift them up momentarily and then toss them back into the water. Jim was thrown hard against the control panel, and Neil was swung around—still holding the wheel—to bang against the ship's combing.

"We may really need that Mayday," he shouted with a grim smile. Jim, shivering, felt a fearful exhilaration. He peered ahead and could see two flashing white lights, one after another—the lights of a range that normally guided ships down the center of the channel, but that Neil would use to guide them onto the sands of Shackleford Bank. The Coast Guard cutter was off to the right someplace, but Jim couldn't make it out.

"Bring the dinghy up closer," Neil shouted to him, and Jim stumbled aft, falling against the stern combing when *Moonchaser* plunged down another swell. Righting himself, he hauled in the towline to the dinghy until it was only a few feet off the stern, where he recleated it. Returning forward, he stared out into the rain and blackness again and realized Neil was easing the boat toward shore.

"Hold on!" he shouted. "Here we go!"

With a harsh, grating sound, the fishing vessel ran aground, slowing down at first and then, as Neil killed the engine, stopping abruptly. Jim grabbed the deckhouse shelf and held on, looking to Neil for orders. As *Moonchaser* seemed to sit contentedly in the sand, Jim turned to get into the dinghy; a wave smashed broadside into the boat with a tremendous crash. Jim was flung against Neil, and the two men smashed into the side of the deckhouse, then against the combing, and then they were in the sea.

It happened so suddenly and the chill water of the ocean was such a shock that Jim didn't realize clearly what had happened at first. He was standing in four feet of water that suddenly became seven feet of water when a swell surged past.

"Get the dinghy!" Neil shouted from somewhere off to the left. Jim could barely make out *Moonchaser* heeled over in the surf a few feet in front of him, but he struggled over to her stern and felt for the rubber dinghy. It was there, bobbing and tearing at the towline like a wild horse. As he reached for it, the edge of the protruding outboard struck him on the shoulder. He swore, reached again to control the dinghy, and was submerged by a huge swell that slapped him in the face like a lazy porpoise flipping its tail. He spit out salt water and felt a sudden panic. He couldn't *get* the dinghy. It danced away from him, then swung its engine shaft at him like a club.

"Cut the line!" Neil shouted, appearing beside him and handing him a knife.

Jim swam the few feet to *Moonchaser*'s stern, pulled himself up, and slashed the towline. In an instant the inflatable pulled its line out of Jim's grasp, surged away on a breaking wave, and was swallowed up into the darkness.

"Get it!" Neil screamed, and Jim plunged away after it.

"Mayday! Mayday!" Olly's voice crackled urgently as Frank stood by, operating *Vagabond*'s radiotelephone. "Damn engine went and killed himself. I'm aground on Shackleford Point. Mayday! Mayday! Do you read me? Over."

Frank switched to receive, deciding that Captain Olly's unprofessional way of sending a distress call was probably more credible than the scenario he himself had planned. He leaned backward to look up at Macklin in the wheelhouse, who was expected to keep *Vagabond* heading steadily into the tide barely inching forward. He nodded at him in reassurance.

"Roger, Mayday," a distant static voice said from the radio. "This is the Coast Guard station at Fort Macon acknowledging Mayday. Identify yourself and your position. Repeat. Identify your vessel and your position . . . . Over."

Frank switched the button and nodded at Captain Olly.

"This is Cap'n Olly," he said irritably. "*Moonchaser* is banging on the beach here at Shackleford Point and getting swamped. I'm at Shackleford Point just south of the range. My ship is beginning to . . ." Captain Olly banged his fist down on the console and shouted: "Jesus! Help! We're foundering! Help!"

Frank cut the switch, and they listened for the Coast Guard's response.

"This is Fort Macon Coast Guard calling *Moonchaser*," the voice said with more urgency. "Please repeat position and clarify. Over."

Frank shook his head no to Captain Olly and kept the button switched to receive. After twenty seconds the voice came through again.

"This is the Coast Guard calling *Moonchaser*. We have received your Mayday. Will send assistance. Do you read me? Over."

Frank shifted the dial to the frequency he knew the Coast Guard usually used for routine traffic. For twenty seconds there was nothing, but finally the same voice crackled out, calling the cutter *Avenger*. After they had established contact the voice said: "A vessel called *Moonchaser* radioed a Mayday. Ship reports being aground and foundering off Shackleford Point. Can you provide assistance? Over?"

"Roger, Macon. Affirmative. Are you sure it was a genuine Mayday? Over?"

"Affirmative, *Avenger*. Sounded real to me. Over."

"Okay, Macon. *Avenger* headed for Shackleford to provide assistance . . ."

"I'm going up and get us moving full speed to the rendezvous," Frank said to Captain Olly. "Keep listening."

After Frank went up on deck, Captain Olly lowered his head toward the radio. For a minute or so there was nothing. Then: ". . . *Avenger* now only about three hundred yards off Shackleford. No sign of a vessel aground. . . . Okay, Macon, we've got our light on a fishing smack aground and partially submerged. . . . She's taking a pounding. . . . *Moonchaser?* . . . It's *Moonchaser*. . . . No sign of anyone aboard. We're sending the launch to investigate. Stand by."

As the seconds ticked away Captain Olly realized that *Vagabond* was beginning to pitch and smash into the ocean swells as she rushed at full speed toward the inlet. He heard Frank saying something loudly to Jeanne but couldn't hear what. Two minutes passed before the voice spoke again from the radio.

"This is *Avenger*. There's no one aboard *Moonchaser*, Macon . . . When was your last radio transmission from the vessel? Over."

"Just before we radioed you, *Avenger*. Over."

Another long silence ensued, broken once by Fort Macon Coast Guard Station asking *Avenger* if it still "read me."

"Affirmative, Macon. I'm waiting for my launch crew to report. . . ."

Another silence. Captain Olly realized that *Vagabond* had slowed down and become stationary again. She was pitching and slamming more steeply into the swells. They must be at the rendezvous point.

After another minute, the voice returned: *"Avenger* to Macon. Something strange going on here. Launch reports there's no radio aboard *Moonchaser*. How could she send a Mayday. . . ?''

Bewildered by the nightmarish suddenness with which he had been pitched into the ocean and had the dinghy torn out of his grasp and flung into the turbulent darkness, Jim had dived clumsily into the water and struck out after it. He took six or seven strong strokes and saw no sign of the dinghy, when its rubber hull bumped the back of the head as if teasing him. He grabbed a trailing line just as another wave rolled indifferently over him. He found he could stand and, holding the dinghy and bracing himself for the next wave, called out into the darkness, "I've got it! Over here!''

There was no answer, and Jim could see neither the boat nor Neil. He shouted again.

"Neil! I've got it! Over here!''

". . . Jimmmm!'' came an answering yell from off to his left and slightly closer to shore. Jim began struggling through the water toward where the voice seemed to come from and was startled when a huge fish splashed almost on top of him.

"Help me,'' he heard Neil's voice say, and realized that it was Neil. He reached out with his free hand and grabbed hold of him. After a wave passed, Neil suddenly stood up, choking and gasping for breath and clinging to Jim.

"My arm,'' he said, grimacing. "My elbow's killing me. I can't use it.''

The two men stood in three feet of water and braced themselves as another hill of water swept over them, slamming them a foot closer to shore.

"I'll hold it now,'' Neil gasped out. "You get in. *Get in!* '' he shouted.

In a lull between waves Jim quickly hauled himself over one side of the dinghy and plopped into the middle. It was filled with five or six inches of water. As he got onto his knees, he heard Neil shout, "Start the engine!''

He turned around and groped for the release lever that would lower the prop into the water. A wave smashed into the dinghy, jerked it sideways, and spilled Jim over against the left side and almost overboard. He struggled to his knees again and groped for the lever. When he found it, the engine fell with an abruptness that pinched his first finger and he gasped out a Franklike oath as he pulled back his hand and grabbed the starting cord. He jerked it once, but the engine didn't start.

"Start the engine!" Neil shouted again from someplace in the water near the bow.

Jim remembered the second time to pull out the choke and tried again. No catch. Again. The engine sputtered and died. Again. No catch. Again: sputter, sputter—he pushed the choke in—roar: the engine came alive.

"Help me in!" Neil shouted, now bobbing up right beside the dinghy; he could only throw one arm over the bulge of inflated rubber. "Grab the back of my belt!"

As Jim throttled down the outboard another wave broke over them and smashed them into even shallower water. Neil was then in only two or three feet of water, and his torso fell across the starboard side of the dinghy, permitting Jim to grab his belt and haul with all his strength to get him up and in. The next wave seemed to scoop Neil up and splash him down into the pool in the bottom of the swamped inflatable. Jim shifted into forward and pulled out the throttle.

The outboard roared, and the dinghy exploded against the next wave, plowing partly through it like a submarine rather than over it, then surged through fifteen feet of calm water before exploding through the next wave. Even with two men aboard and six inches of water, the dinghy was able to nose forward at four or five knots. Jim had no sense of direction, except the impulse to get out of the surf and back into deeper water. Crouched low in the plunging dinghy, he couldn't see any channel lights and had only the vaguest idea of which way was west.

"Steer by the swells," Neil shouted to him, kneeling beside Jim in the middle of the dinghy, one arm limp and held awkwardly in front of him. "Keep them coming at you on the port beam."

Jim had been heading into them, but as soon as Neil spoke he realized that their destination was simply straight across the swells at a right angle. He swung the dinghy to starboard, squinted into the rain and spray, and steered at full throttle toward where he hoped to find *Vagabond*. A giant white eye suddenly peered at them from almost dead ahead, then swept away to the right. The Coast Guard cutter was coming directly at them.

". . . Strange going on here. Launch reports there's no radio aboard the *Moonchaser*."

Captain Olly heard shouts from up on deck and felt something thud against one side of *Vagabond*.

"Okay, Fort Macon," the voice from the *Avenger* went on. "We're leaving our launch here to check for survivors, but *Avenger* is now resuming normal patrol duties. Something's not kosher about this. Over. . . ."

Captain Olly hurried up the cabin steps and bumped into Frank, who was scrambling across the wheelhouse to get to the controls and get *Vagabond* moving. Jim and Neil were barely visible in the darkness, hauling up the dinghy into the starboard cockpit.

"Coast Guard's coming back," he said to Frank, who simply gave him a wild look and put *Vagabond* into full ahead. Neil stumbled into the wheelhouse and collapsed with a groan on the cushioned seat. Jeanne followed and knelt beside him, then called Macklin over.

Captain Olly went to help Jim with the dinghy. He was pulling it off the open deck aft, up over the cockpit seat and into the cockpit. After the two of them had got it down into the cockpit, Jim asked, "Can we leave it here for now?"

"Sure. I'll lash it down," Captain Olly said. "Go help your dad."

Jim took a long stride over the slightly squashed inflatable, went into the wheelhouse, and stood beside his father. Jeanne ducked past them into the main cabin, and then Jim leaned out to peer ahead into the rain.

They were motoring at full speed south along the western side of the inlet, headed directly out to sea. They were already far to the right of the big ship channel and pounding into the steep swells that rolled directly at them. Jim's glance at the depthmeter told him it read four feet, which meant they were in only seven or eight feet of water. *Vagabond*, with her dagger board up but heavily loaded, probably drew a little less than four feet. There was a terrific slam and shudder as a big breaking wave smacked into all three hulls at once. *Vagabond* slowed seemingly to a halt and then surged forward again.

"Have we passed the point yet?" Frank shouted at Jim. "Look out your side!"

Jim stared out into the blackness off to his right, remembering that the point on which old Fort Macon and the Coast Guard station were located was the last land to starboard before the open ocean. He thought he could see a few lights, probably the Coast Guard station, slightly aft of their starboard beam.

"I see lights at about four o'clock," he said to his father. "I can't see anything directly abeam."

Another breaking wave crashed into the trimaran, slowing her almost to a halt before she recovered and made good headway again.

"Two feet—*dad!*" Jim shouted to his father when he saw the depthmeter flicker at two feet, then zero, then three, then zero. "Zero feet!"

White-faced and grimacing, Frank swung the wheel to bring *Vagabond* around toward the channel and deeper water, but also back toward the Coast Guard cutter.

"It's just turbulence!" Neil shouted from behind them. "Does it stay steady at one or zero?" he asked.

"It says zero now," said Jim, frightened. "And just occasionally two or three."

"It's turbulence," Neil said, staggering up between Jim and Frank to look at the controls while Jeanne seemed to be trying to hold something against his arm. "We should swing her southwest now. Away from the cutter."

"I'm not running her aground," Frank said urgently, holding his course back toward the channel. He stared down first at the depthmeter, which fluctuated erratically between zero and now four or five feet, and then at the compass, which showed them on a southeast heading.

"We're free, Frank!" Neil insisted, grimacing in pain. "We're out of the inlet. Head her southwest, even west. They'll *see* us if we stay on this course."

Frank, frowning, his face, like all of the others', wet with rain and sweat, looked once briefly, fearfully at Neil.

"Are you sure?" he asked.

"Head her west!"

"Six feet!" Jim announced.

Frank turned the wheel back to the right, and *Vagabond* swung to starboard, first heading south, then southwest, where Frank straightened her out. As they surged into the blackness, taking the swells now on their port side, Jim took a long look aft and saw the light sweep along Fort Macon Point, then out toward them. A white beam blinded him as the wheelhouse filled with light, and then the light moved away out to sea.

None of those standing in the wheelhouse spoke, and Neil joined Jim in watching the subsequent movement of the light.

"They didn't see us," Neil said quietly. "Take her full west, Frank."

"I'll keep her on southwest," Frank said, not looking at him.

"I tell you we're free!" Neil shouted.

Frank didn't answer.

"Five feet," said Jim. All three men now looked at the depthmeter, which held at five feet for a few more seconds and then went on to six, seven, then ten feet. Frank eased the wheel a little to starboard, and slowly the boat swung more to the west until, after a half-minute, Frank steadied her at 260 degrees, ten degrees south of west.

And again the light, less bright now, exploded into the wheelhouse as the distant cutter swept the sea with its searchlight. Again it did not hesitate or return to *Vagabond,* which sliced and plowed away at full speed. For two or three more minutes the depthmeter read between ten and twelve feet, and then began climbing rapidly through the teens. Indeed, they were free.

PART THREE

WATER

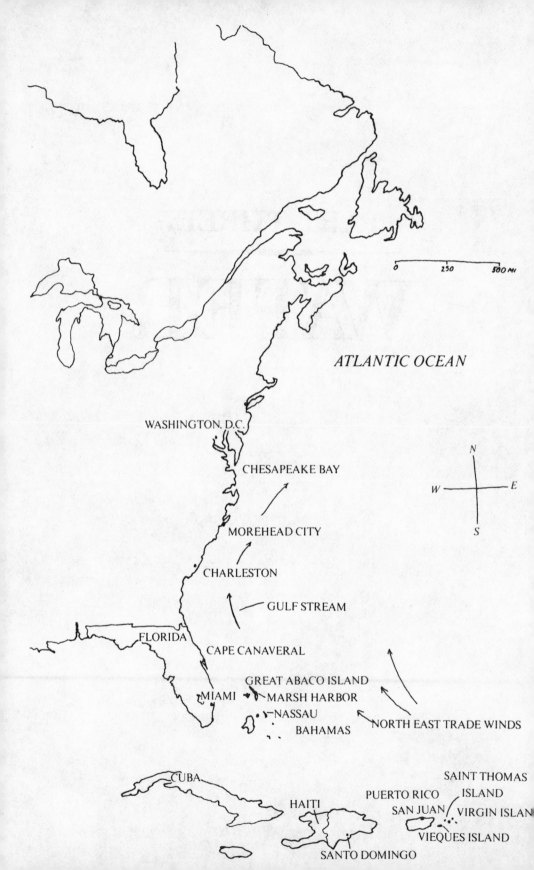

ATLANTIC OCEAN

N

W —•— E

S

WASHINGTON, D.C.

CHESAPEAKE BAY

MOREHEAD CITY

CHARLESTON

GULF STREAM

FLORIDA

CAPE CANAVERAL

GREAT ABACO ISLAND

MARSH HARBOR

MIAMI

NASSAU

BAHAMAS

NORTH EAST TRADE WINDS

CUBA

SAINT THOMAS
ISLAND

PUERTO RICO

HAITI

SAN JUAN

VIRGIN ISLAN

VIEQUES ISLAND

SANTO DOMINGO

0   250   500 MI

FREE. Except for the threat of radioactive fallout, of storms, of pirates, of their overloaded trimaran breaking apart, of death from thirst or starvation or disease, of mutiny, of the antagonism that the whole rest of the world now felt for the white people of America and Russia, both of whom they blamed for the war, those aboard *Vagabond* were free to do as they pleased. They sailed south.

The war sailed with them. Although they increased their distance from the coast as they moved south and the threat of fallout receded, the bodies of at least two of their crewmen—Frank, Olly, and possibly others—had already absorbed the poison. Frank looked much more haggard than anyone else, had lost ten pounds, and was sick again after a three-day remission. Olly was better but still "feeling poorly." Even Neil still felt unaccountably nauseous once or twice.

Nevertheless, at sea, after a whole day of adjusting sleeping accommodations, mealtimes, and rations, they settled into a routine. Their watches remained the same, except that Katya sometimes spelled Lisa and shared a watch with Jim. Macklin and Tony berthed together in the forepeak, Katya was in with Jeanne, and Olly slept either in Neil's cabin or on the dinette settee.

Tony, in his bluff, self-confident way, had made himself thoroughly at home again. Although he spoke loudly the first day or two about being forced to let his country down, after they heard a report about heavy radioactivity over Morehead City and the mass evacuation of everyone who could move, he didn't raise the subject again. He flirted with both Jeanne and Katya, helped them in the galley more than any of the other men, and turned out to be an excellent cook, especially good with fish, which was their principal food. He was also, Neil admitted to himself, the best all-around sailor on his crew.

Katya and Jeanne got along well together, and though Katya wasn't a cook, she let Jeanne, Lisa, and Tony instruct her. She was, as she had advertised, a good sailor and tough; she usually volunteered to help with sail changes on any watch when she was awake. When Tony and Macklin began to come on to her, she handled each of them in his own style. With Tony she was casual and playful; with Macklin quiet and direct. Neil never knew precisely what passed between her and Macklin their second evening at sea, but he saw him speak to her in the side cockpit with a tight smile, saw her flush and speak to him angrily. He sneered, said something back, and wandered quietly away. If Katya was good at ''fucking,'' she apparently was in no hurry to prove it, at least with Macklin.

Macklin himself rarely said or did anything to draw attention to himself. He blended in. On land he had stolen a case of canned fruit, a carton of cigarettes, and five six-packs of beer. Though the fruit was relegated to emergency rations, they worked their way through the beer at a rate of two a day, dividing it up and sipping at it as if it were fine champagne. When asked where he had gotten these items, he had simply shrugged and said he'd ''stumbled across them in some guy's cellar.''

Their destination was the West Indies, initially Puerto Rico. But with the southeast wind forcing them to sail directly south, by the end of the third day Neil felt they were already so close to the Bahamas that they should make a landfall on Great Abaco Island. There they might barter for more food and water, even, if they found the right conditions, try to settle. However, Radio Nassau reported debilitating food shortages throughout the islands, and Americans were not welcome. If their principal food was fish, they might as well remain at sea.

Fishing was, in fact, the focus of every morning and evening's activity. They had two ocean rods and reels with good line, but only five lures, one of which they lost on their second day. At dawn and dusk they usually trolled with both rigs, one from each cockpit. The rods were usually jammed into place with a strong drag on the reels so that no one had to sit and hold them all the time. When a fish was hooked, the helmsman would bring the boat up into the wind to slow it down, and someone would stand by with both a gaff and large net while the other man on watch duty, who was responsible for the rods, would begin to reel in the hooked fish.

Because this type of fishing was new to most of them, and because, ultimately, their lives depended on it, bringing in a fish was a major community event. They caught two bluefish their first evening, a twenty-pound tuna the next dawn, two dolphins and a tuna at dusk, then inexplicably lost two hooked fish and a second lure at dawn the next day. The third evening, however, they recouped their losses with another dolphin and a barracuda.

Neil was still wearing his arm in a sling after cracking his elbow on the *Moonchaser* and couldn't help with the fishing, but it interested him to watch the different styles of bringing in and gaffing the fish his crew had evolved.

When Frank was in charge of the gaffing there was shouting and confusion and irritability before Frank could get the man controlling the rod and reel to position the fish properly for gaffing. Once the fish was flopping around in the cockpit, there was always a delay and more shouting before Frank, looking pained, would knife the fish out of its misery.

When Olly was in charge everything proceeded as quietly as a silent movie, the only sound being Olly's soft crooning to the fish. Olly never told the man with the rod or the helmsmen what to do, but by talking to the fish—"Come on in a little closer, fella, my back hurts and I don't like leaning down none"—the man with the rod would know exactly what to do. When he had gaffed the fish, Olly would say something like "Up you go, sonny, easy does it," as if the fish wanted to come aboard, and all of them were involved in a cooperative enterprise. Then, after the fish was flopping on the deck, Olly would take a minute to praise the fish to all the onlookers. "Look at those colors, will you? I ain't seen anything as pretty as that since my second wife bought herself that new dress," or "Now isn't that a big fella. Must weigh twenty-five pounds and not an ounce of fat. Bet he was an Olympic champ down below. . . ."

And when Olly killed, he always began talking to the fish again.

"Okay, big fella, afraid we got to quiet you down. I gave you time for your prayers but if you got anything else you want to say you better say it now . . ." The fish would flop violently in response to this, or once, so everyone agreed, made some distinct grunting sounds, and then Olly with one neat slice would quiet the fish forever.

"Don't he look beautiful?" Olly would conclude. "Just hope I look half as good when the Big Fisherman hauls me in and lays me out. I'm damn sure I won't taste as good."

Conrad Macklin on the other hand gaffed and killed a fish with a fierce scowl, as if he were involved in a life-and-death combat with a lifelong enemy.

When Jeanne participated in the fishing, Neil found himself focusing more attention on her than on the fish. Her glistening dark skin and full lithe body distracted him considerably from the problem of boarding the fish, especially as she wrestled with the rod and reel or stuck her behind in the air to lean down to gaff a fish, clad as she usually was only in shorts and a bikini top. She and Katya seemed to have the same effect on Tony, Macklin, and Frank. Lisa's budding body, perhaps because of her shy dignity, was less observed, except by Jim.

They were adapting to a world of scarcity. Neil had decreed that their remaining two gallons of diesel fuel could only be used to charge the three batteries. Oil was unavailable everywhere now except to the military. To avoid having to charge the batteries any more than necessary, Neil used them solely for the shortwave radio. For illumination they used kerosene lamps and, if necessary, flashlights. They had only four gallons of kerosene, and that too might never again be easy to obtain. The two dozen candles aboard Neil stored as light of last resort. Even matches were scarce. Fortunately, no one smoked except Jim, who smoked marijuana and was abstaining, and Macklin, whose cigarettes had been confiscated by Neil to use in the West Indies as barter.

But the bleakness of the land world and of shortages Neil and Frank and Olly kept to themselves. For all of them the sea represented a haven, a relief from the terrors and suffering they had experienced on land, and Neil wanted to try to keep it that away. For the first time there began to be casual joking among them that had been missing before.

On the second afternoon Neil had overheard Captain Olly teasing Frank about *Vagabond*.

"Yep," Captain Olly was saying. "You got a good ship here, Frank. All you got to do is take off those two side boats you got, and unstep the masts, and put a bowsprit on her and paint her black, and she'd be right pretty. Might not even have to paint her."

Frank laughed as he sat down in the wheelhouse with a small cup containing his daily ration of beer.

"Thanks," he said to Olly, who was at the helm with his own cup.

"Don't be embarrassed your boat don't look like a boat," Olly went on. "Brazen it out. Pretend you got yourself a beginner's boat. You know, a three-wheeler so you won't tip over."

Frank laughed again, and Neil realized that it was the first time since the war had begun that he *had* laughed.

"I tell people I got a special three-for-the-price-of-one deal that I couldn't pass up," Frank said.

"Yep. Good story. Good story. Got to tell them something, that's for sure, so they won't know you're nuts," Captain Olly concluded.

While Neil assumed responsibility for the sailing of the ship, Jeanne began to assume responsibility for the way they interacted with each other. At dinner their second day out she suggested that at every evening meal they observe a half-minute of silence before eating, and if anyone wanted to offer thanks for the food or for life, he or she might. Jeanne usually spoke, occasionally mentioning some specific individual she wanted to acknowledge. Often Katya or Jim or Frank would also add a brief word, more rarely Tony or Neil.

That night too she embraced and kissed each of the others who were still topside before she went below to her berth. Although all she said was "Good night" and the person's name, Neil could see the physical contact breaking through the isolation each of them tended to feel. Even Conrad Macklin flushed and looked pleased. Among the men, at Jeanne's insistence, there were more "Good job, Frank," and "Thanks, Jim," and "That's good, Tony," where before there had been either cold correctness or nothing.

Captain Olly had the most trouble adapting to the more affectionate routine that Jeanne kept urging upon them. When Neil relieved him at the helm at the change of watch and said "Nice job, Olly," he testily replied, "Can't expect me to run aground in five thousand feet of water." When Jeanne gave him a goodnight kiss the second night, he grimaced and grinned. " 'T warn't much of a kiss," he said. "If you want to get laid, you got to do better than that." Jeanne looked surprised and then smiled. "Don't worry," she had said, her eyes flashing. "When I want to get laid, the man will know it."

Most of them found the meals repetitious and skimpy. They were rationing themselves severely on the last of their canned foods and some remaining fruits and vegetables, and salting and drying some of their fish steaks for later. They were cooking in salt water and had cut their fresh water intake to a quart per person per day. The six adults were experimenting with drinking a cup or two of sea water every day.

To help avoid unnecessary gloom Neil became a censor. He permitted only Frank and Olly to listen to the shortwave and transistor radios with him. The violent antiwhite, anti-Americanism he was picking up from stations in the West Indies they kept to themselves. The probability of mass starvation within a month on many of the islands they did not mention. Officially they were sailing for a chain of islands that were still untouched by the war. In his heart Neil knew that no place and no one and nothing would ever be untouched by this war.

Shortwave and AM reports from the U.S. mainland raised a new specter on the third day at sea. A summer flu that seemed to be afflicting many people in the west and southwest had already caused an unusually high number of fatalities. One ham operator speculated that a biological warfare laboratory had been destroyed, and that part of its stockpile of disease germs was responsible for the epidemic. In any case it now seemed to be killing more people than fallout. Typhoid had also become a problem. Of the fighting itself there was little news. The superpowers were still technically at war, but now they were more like two exhausted and glassy-eyed fighters who had landed such devastating blows in the first round that they now seemed barely capable of standing up, much less hitting each other. Thus it seemed that each day the ramifications and elaborations of the world disaster spread a little further, like a spilled bottle of black ink slowly soaking along a paper towel. Cuba had been heavily bombed with conventional ordnance early in the war, and when the Cubans tried to take the naval base at Guantánamo, the U.S. had used a tactical nuclear weapon to destroy most of the enemy forces. Cuba's air force and navy had allegedly been destroyed, but no effort made to invade the island. Guantánamo was being evacuated.

Although nuclear explosions had destroyed the Panama Canal, Miami, Cape Canaveral, American forces in Central America, and the oil refineries in Venezuela, the Caribbean area had been spared since the third day of the war. Some rich Americans were flying to Puerto Rico and this influx of the privileged was deeply resented. Depsite the presence of the U.S. Navy, which, with the losses of its other Caribbean bases now had its largest facility outside San Juan, pirate attacks were reported against both private and commercial ships, both small and large. Food riots occurred on a regular basis in San Juan and smaller cities although officially there was as yet no famine.

It was to this island that *Vagabond* was supposedly heading, but in the new world that they all had experienced over the last ten days, no one aboard really expected anything. Neil set a course, they sailed on. In this new world the future was something that could only hurt or terrify or kill. To look beyond the next wave was dangerous. Neil set a course, they sailed on. To hope for more could only be done in whispers.

On their third night at sea Lisa and Jim had the ten-to-two watch, with Neil awake in the wheelhouse. Near midnight Jeanne fixed them some hot tea, one bag for three cups. *Vagabond* was still sailing due south with a good easterly breeze. An afternoon squall line seemed well behind them. With Jim now at the helm and Lisa watching the trolling rig in the side cockpit, Neil and Jeanne sat kittycorner across from each other a few feet apart in the unlit wheelhouse, sipping at their weak tea.

"Do you think about where we're going to end up?" Jeanne asked him unexpectedly.

Neil did think about it, frequently. It made for depressing thinking.

"Yes," he answered.

"Will we be able to settle in Puerto Rico or the Virgin Islands?" Jeanne asked after she saw that he wasn't going to go on.

"Perhaps," Neil replied, doubting it very much. As he looked at her he wished he could share his fears, but he wanted even more to spare her the burden. Even though the sky was mostly overcast, the nearly full moon shed light on *Vagabond*'s decks and allowed Neil to see the outline of Jeanne's face and body. She was very still, her teacup held in her lap. The afternoon squalls had dampened the seas, and for a change, *Vagabond* wasn't pounding but rolling gently through the water.

"I suppose, ultimately, it has to be South America, doesn't it?" she went on. "Some place untouched, where the . . . infrastructure of civilization is still solid."

Neil sipped at his tea. He'd heard a report that half a dozen South American countries had set up internment camps for American refugees. The threat of the mysterious plaguelike disease that was spreading from the western U.S. was increasing their fear and resentment of Americans.

"Yes, I guess it will," he said, without elaborating.

"That was a strange time we had that other night, wasn't it?" she asked unexpectedly in her low, intense voice. Neil suddenly realized that Jim, at the helm, eight feet away, and Lisa were both within earshot. "That other night" in the side cockpit had been . . . my God, almost a week before.

"It was more than that," Neil answered.

For a half-minute, as Neil stared at Jeanne's indistinct face, neither of them spoke.

"There aren't any rules anymore, are there?" she said after a while. "We have to create our own."

"There are rules," Neil said. "Blowing up the world didn't get rid of them."

"I mean . . . some of the old ones can't be applied anymore."

Like what? Neil wondered. Like widows and a period of mourning? Love leading to marriage? Love leading to bed?

"Like what?" he asked. He noticed Lisa coming in from the port cockpit to talk to Jim.

"The old rule that you could go to bed with a man for enjoyment," Jeanne said in a low voice.

Startled, he waited for her to go on. It wasn't an old rule he had expected her to come up with.

"In the new world," she continued softly, glancing toward the wheel, where Jim and Lisa were also talking in low voices. "In *our* new world, in this small world of *Vagabond*, that rule won't work. My sleeping with . . . a man would transform our universe."

"Yes, it would," Neil said.

"Frank wants me to sleep with him," she announced.

"I see," he said in a voice so low he wasn't sure she could hear it. Then, louder: "Rather popular, aren't you?"

For a moment the only sound was of the water rushing past *Vagabond*'s three hulls. In the darkness Jeanne was only a vague silhouette.

". . . Neil . . ."

The sound of anguish in her soft voice made Neil move to the edge of his seat, and leaning toward her he started to speak, but knew that even whispers would be heard by Jim and Lisa. He slowly lifted his right hand in the darkness to touch her unseen face. When it reached her cheek, she held it against her face with both hands, turning to kiss his palm.

"I see," Neil said in a normal voice.

"I hope you see," she answered in a low voice, but still loud enough that Jim and Lisa could hear.

"What I see," said Neil slowly, caressing her face with his hand, and fully aware of the absurdity of the conversation, "is that you are still temporarily insane. Am I correct?"

"Yes," she said softly.

"And you see that I am still temporarily insane. Correct?"

"Yes. I hope so. Yes."

"And now you're telling me," he went on in a low voice, barely able to contain his joy and laughter, "that Frank has become temporarily insane too. Is that right?"

"Yes." She giggled softly.

"How about Jim? Is *he* insane?"

She laughed again.

"I don't think so," she said.

"Well, *I* think so," said Jim suddenly from the wheel. "I can't tell *what* you two are talking about. You sound *nuts*."

"Mother, you *are* being silly," Lisa added with a childlike primness that Jeanne thought she'd lost since the war began.

As Neil and Jeanne stopped laughing Neil could feel Jeanne tense, her hands still gripping his.

"Oh, Lisa," she said, "you missed it all. We're joking about the insanity of trying to create a new world in South America, but that's where all of us—Frank, too—think we have to end up."

"Not me," said Jim. "I think we should head for the South Pacific."

"See," said Neil, grinning in the darkness. "You were right, Jeanne. Jim at least is still sane."

"Thank God," said Jeanne.

"Right," said Neil.

"Around Cape Horn," said Jim, and Neil and Jeanne's laughter burst into the wheelhouse again, Jim and Lisa turning to stare at them in slight bewilderment.

"Christ, how do you expect me to sleep?" Frank's voice cut into Neil's giddy world like an executioner's sword.

Pulling away from Jeanne, he turned to see Frank's gaunt body outlined in the entranceway behind him.

"I'm sorry, Frank," Neil said quickly. "We got a little silly, I guess."

"You sure as hell did," Frank said, still looming in the entrance ten feet away. "You sounded like a couple of loonies out here."

Jeanne stood up.

"It was thoughtless of us," she said. "Forgive us, Frank." She walked over to him and put her arms around him. Neil saw him respond stiffly at first and then put his arms around her and lower his head to rest on hers.

"You make it kind of tough to hold a grudge," he said.

"I hope so," she said softly.

"What were you doing, anyway?" he asked.

There was a brief silence.

"Flirting with Neil," she answered. "I'm trying to get out of even-day garbage detail."

"Try flirting with me," Frank said. "I *own* the damn boat."

Jeanne stretched up and kissed Frank on the cheek.

"Good night again," she whispered and moved off toward her cabin.

"You might pay a little attention to the boat," Frank said to Neil. "Every now and then, for appearances."

"I pay attention to this boat every second of every day and you know it," he snapped back.

Jeanne had stopped at her cabin entrance, and Jim and Lisa, who had withdrawn from all this, were still standing at the wheel.

"Yeah," said Frank after a strained silence. "I guess you're right. I'm sorry, Neil."

Neil waited a moment before responding.

"Don't worry about it," Neil said. "I'm sorry about the noise."

"Yeah. Good night. Good night, Jim. You, too, Lisa."

Frank moved away again to his cabin, sliding his hatch closed behind him. Neil walked over to where Jeanne was still standing at her cabin entranceway.

"I'm sorry," he said to her softly.

She looked up at him in the darkness and then away.

"I . . . think I love you, Neil," she said in a low voice. "But it's no good. We're a family. Our . . . love would be . . . a kind of incest."

"You're not my sister," he replied almost sharply.

"Ahh, but I am," she said softly, looking up at him. "Don't you see, you and Frank are brothers, and Frank and I are brother and sister, so you . . . we're all too close, Neil."

"I see that Frank would be hurt if we made love," he said after a pause. "And I don't want to hurt him. But he'll be hurt by our love whether we . . . act on it or not."

She turned away her face, barely visible in the dark, and glanced toward Jim and Lisa.

"In this world . . . in our new world, no one must be alone," she said.

"Does that mean no two can ever be together?" he asked, pulling her gently against him.

She turned to look at him, then again turned away.

"Oh, Neil, I don't know," she whispered. "I've got to get things right with Frank. You must see that."

Neil stared down at her barely visible face.

"I'm not sure that's possible, Jeanne," he suggested quietly.

When he tried to lift her head to look at her she pressed her face against his shoulder, refusing to budge. He could feel the wetness of tears on his bare shoulder. He held her, stroking her hair against her back; his smile faded, and he suddenly had a clear image of himself on a ship racing through the night away from a universe of death to the north. A second image, of Frank angrily looming up in the wheelhouse entrance, returned to him, and he felt a great sadness.

"It's no use, Neil," Jeanne finally whispered. "We're not free."

In the wheelhouse after Neil and Jeanne had gone off to their separate cabins Jim and Lisa carried on with the task of keeping *Vagabond* on course. For many minutes neither of them spoke. Lisa left Jim to check on the trolling rig and spent two minutes reeling in the lure to look for seaweed. She cleaned off the lure and let it back out again, adjusting the drag. When she returned to Jim at the helm, they were both silent. They didn't touch each other.

A muffled sobbing from Jeanne's cabin cut through the silence, and both of them stiffened. After another minute in which every groan of a line stretching, every slap of a halyard, rustle of a sail, whine of wind in the rigging, seemed for a brief second to be the sound of a woman moaning, Jim finally spoke:

"Are you all right, Lisa?" he asked quietly, touching her briefly on her shoulder, then letting his arm fall.

"It's so sad," she said in a small voice.

"It's hard on my father too," Jim replied. "He . . . ."

"I know," she said.

"Everyone seems so alone," said Jim. "It makes me feel lonely." He had to put both hands on the wheel as *Vagabond* slid off the face of a swell.

Lisa took his arm and hugged it, then put her arms around his waist and pressed her head against his shoulder.

"Don't feel lonely, Jim," she said. "Don't ever feel lonely."

Jim released one hand from the wheel to put his arm around her. Still facing forward, he hugged her to him. He was grinning.

"Hey," he said, looking down at her until she raised her head to return his gaze. "I wish I could kiss you."

"Why can't you?" she replied, looking up at him seriously.

"I thought you wanted us to be the best watch team Neil has?" Jim asked.

"I do," she said. "But a good helmsman should be able to steer and kiss too."

Joyously Jim bent and kissed her, *Vagabond* almost immediately racing slightly off course, and after fifteen seconds she slammed into a wave with a boom and shudder, effectively interrupting their embrace.

As Jim wrestled the wheel with both hands to get *Vagabond* back on course Lisa clung to him, her head buried against his chest.

"I love you, Jim," Lisa whispered. "Please love me, please love me."

Jim squeezed her against him, his heart pounding, his eyes facing forward but seeing nothing.

"I do," he whispered down at her.

"And I want you to make love to me," Lisa said. "Before we die, I want you to make love to me."

"We're not going to die," Jim said.

"Yes, we are," Lisa said. "Oh, Jim, hold me, hold me. You're the only solid thing left in the world—"

Jim hugged her to him with his left arm and held *Vagabond* roughly on course with his right.

"Make love to me, Jim," Lisa whispered hoarsely. "I so much want us to make love."

"We will," he said. "We will."

"We're so alone. . . ."

Frank lay on his berth, staring up at the white overhead, where the reflection of sunlight off the water danced like cold white fire. He'd gone to sleep about a half-hour after coming off watch at six that morning, and he figured it must be getting close to noon.

He didn't feel rested. He felt bone-tired. There was a dull ache in his lower back that had been bothering him off and on for the last several days. His belly ached. An occasional wave of nausea swept over him like a pestilential fog. He wanted the voyage to be over. He loved *Vagabond* and was completely at home on her, but his ship, like the rest of life, was slipping out of his control. As long as he had owned her—three years now—he had loved her partly because she was *his*, his creation and his to control. Now she was no longer his. She belonged to . . . to everyone who needed her. If he didn't like to see Skippy's comic books lying around, or Jim taking over half his cabin or playing his guitar up on the foredeck, or Neil always sitting or standing around in the wheelhouse as if it were his personal command post, he was no longer free to say so. It was their boat too. If he tried to have everything run to please him, everyone else would be miserable. So instead he had to be miserable.

Vagabond was getting junky. No matter how often he and Neil spoke about it, no one ever seemed to clean the blood and fishscales from the side cockpits, ever remembered to pick up the lures and leaders and line that always seemed to be lying around. The wheelhouse was always cluttered with comic books, towels, paper cups, books, bits of food, or somebody's shirt or socks. Bullet holes in the Plexiglas. The aft wall now a sail. The blankets and sheets were starting to stink. Jeanne and Katya kept the galley and dinette in good shape when they were around, but at other times Olly, Tony, and Jim left little messes. Neil and Macklin were neat, he supposed, but Neil didn't seem to be trying to control the others.

And he hated the way Neil made all the decisions without even the pretense of consulting him. He felt like a passenger on his own boat. He knew he didn't have Neil's experience or instincts, but he knew his boat, had handled her more than Neil had, and resented being shunted aside. He felt he had the right at any time to override any of Neil's decisions, but hadn't yet found the issue that was right for reasserting his control. Neil didn't even seem to be aware of the ways he was ignoring his skills, advice, and rights as owner.

And Neil seemed to be starting to flirt with Jeanne. Jeanne. There was the fucking rub. Frank wanted her closeness, needed her closeness to protect him from the shocks that were coming at him from all directions, felt that she needed his closeness and comfort, but suddenly, out of nowhere, there was Neil. He himself had known Jeannie since before Skippy's birth, and in the past few years had become damn fond of her. It wasn't so much sexual attraction, except on occasion, just a strong feeling of warmth, affection, longing even, that he found hard to express to her, but which he felt she sensed. Shit, maybe he was in love with her and had been for a couple of years.

And now Bob was dead, and he needed her, and suddenly there was Neil. It wasn't fair. He rolled from his back onto his stomach and wrestled angrily with the pillow.

When he'd finally told Jeannie of his feelings two nights before, he'd felt subtly rejected. She'd admitted that she'd sensed his affection and appreciated it, and said she had admired him over the last year for not creating conflict for her by approaching her overtly and forcing her to respond. She seemed to think it was okay now for him to express his feelings, but wasn't at all sure about herself. Events had moved so fast that she didn't think she could depend on *any* of her emotional responses. But now he wondered if it was all just bullshit to cover up the fact that she was turned on by Neil.

"Turned on": Jesus, that phrase made him sick. His feelings for Jeanne went far beyond just being turned on. So Neil was younger and had muscles like a gymnast and always stood around looking like Patton in his underwear: what kind of a relationship could you have based on that?

But what could he do about it? What could he do about anything? *Vagabond* hissed and plunged forward as if she were an independent creature fleeing for herself southward through the sea, he and Neil her obedient servants. Would Puerto Rico solve his problems? Neil's getting pressganged back into the Navy would certainly solve one problem . . . but even the idea of Neil's leaving saddened him. Although Neil had become self-absorbed lately, normally he was the only one he'd ever sailed with who appreciated *Vagabond* the way he did, could communicate with a glance what a blast it was sizzling along at thirteen knots or swinging at anchor in a squall . . .

But even sailing these last few days didn't inspire him with enthusiasm. Nothing did. A part of him felt he was dying and he needed someone to talk to, but she always seemed too busy. He felt lonely and alone, his two best people, Jeanne and Neil, beginning to sail away from him on a different tack. He wanted to alter course, stay with them, but in the nightmare world he was inhabiting he couldn't find the sheets or, finding them, had no sense of whether they should be pulled in or eased. Rudderless, his life raced through the night and he, its captain, no longer knew his position or his course. He was lost. And his fucking back ached. And he wanted to puke. And it was noon: his and Tony's watch again.

The nice thing about Neil's insisting on a tight, rigidly maintained watch schedule was that every six or eight hours it forced you to stop thinking and act. Frank pushed himself heavily up off the berth and lowered his feet to the floor. Action. Action. Slowly, painfully, he began putting on his boat shoes.

That night in the forepeak Jim and Lisa finally found the place and time to make love. Olly and Macklin were on watch, and Tony, who also had a berth forward, was talking with Katya up in the wheelhouse. The others were asleep in their cabins. For Jim and Lisa it was the only place they could find to be alone.

The motion of *Vagabond* into and over the swells alternately accented and interfered with the motions of their lovemaking in ways that made Jim and Lisa giggle. Everything—even their awkwardness—was a delight. The few couplings Jim had known, burdened with the pressure of performance and the absence of love, hadn't prepared him for the unexpected joy of being with Lisa, who, inexpert, shy, and passive, made him feel that his every touch was a miracle of perfection. When he first entered her it had been painful for her; his first climax a disappointingly minor event, soon forgotten in the midst of rising pleasure and the excitement of the continuing play of their hands and lips and words. They were naked and sweating, suppressing their noises and giggles, and enraptured with the discovery of so much happiness. When Jim had climaxed a second time, they lay side by side facing each other, grinning, laughing, trying halfheartedly to raise their conversation above the level of the idiotic.

"You did too squeal," Lisa insisted. "And it was nice."

Jim shook his head, smiling. "*I* didn't hear a thing."

"Do I make noises?" Lisa asked.

"I was too busy to notice." Again they laughed, until a noise behind the curtain reminded them that they were only a few feet from the main cabin. They lay quietly, staring at each other, listening. They heard Tony swear and Katya laugh.

"Do you think they might come in here?" Lisa asked.

Jim grimaced and nodded. "They might," he said.

"Should we let people know?" Lisa asked. "You know, about . . . what we're doing?"

"No," said Jim. "Our parents have enough to worry about without—"

"I know," said Lisa. "After Frank and mom had that long talk after dinner tonight, I found her crying in her cabin."

"Really? I don't understand what's happening with them all, do you?"

"I think—"

Katya abruptly ducked underneath the curtain and poked her head up only a few feet away.

"Oh!" Katya said. "Hey, I'm sorry. I must have the wrong room." She laughed briefly and just as quickly stooped down to disappear behind the curtain.

As they heard Katya and Tony begin arguing, Jim grabbed his swimming trunks and pulled them on, and Lisa scrambled for her shorts and blouse.

"What is this?" Tony said, suddenly pushing past the curtain. "Neil gives me the worst berth on the boat and even then it's not mine."

"I'm sorry," said Jim, whispering. "Would you please keep your voice down?"

"I can't even *talk* in my own cabin?" said Tony.

"Oh, shut up," Katya whispered from behind him. "Leave them alone."

"We're leaving," said Jim. "And I'm sorry we . . . used your bed."

"It's not mine, it's Conrad's," said Tony. "But it's the principle of the thing."

"Tony, you've got as many principles as an eel," said Katya.

"Come on, Lisa," said Jim.

"Do your parents know you're screwing?" Tony asked.

"Not yet," said Jim. "And I'd like it if they didn't."

"Sure," said Tony. "I dig it. I don't imagine your dad would be too hot about your fucking with Jeanne's baby. Hey, you know, it's statutory rape! How about that?!"

"Go," said Katya to Jim and Lisa. "Tony, you're an ass."

"Statutory rape. Army desertion. I'm witnessing all sorts of crimes."

"You witness a crime every time you look in a mirror," said Katya. "Good-bye, kids. I'm glad you're lovers."

Jim and Lisa left, the shame and uncertainty that Tony had stirred not dispelled by Katya's blessing. They stopped for a drink of water in the galley and then soberly climbed the steps to the wheelhouse.

Olly was snoring on a settee while Macklin stood at the wheel, the light of a cigarette casting a brief reddish glimmer on his face. Jim was aware that Macklin had been ordered not to use up any of the cigarettes, and he automatically stopped and looked closely at him.

Macklin didn't speak, simply returning Jim's gaze, then looking at Lisa, then back at Jim. Lisa left to go to her cabin with Jeanne. Macklin exhaled a cloud of smoke toward Jim, but the rush of air from the port entranceway blew it aft.

"Have a good time?" Macklin asked.

Jim returned his stare a moment longer and then walked past him and out of the wheelhouse toward his own starboard cabin. His futile rage at Tony and Macklin had him trembling.

Down in the cabin Frank was awake, staring at the ceiling.

"Where you been, Jim?" he asked.

Jim went to the little sink to wash the sweat off his face.

"With Lisa," he answered after a moment. "Talking . . ."

His father didn't say anything for a while. Jim wiped off his face and chest; the salt water still left him sticky.

"I'm glad, Jim," Frank said. "I mean you and Lisa getting together. Being friends. It's good."

Jim, his back to his father, felt a wave of emotion flood him—gratitude to his father, love for Lisa, sympathy for his father's troubles.

"Thanks, dad," he said, wiping his face and chest.

"You know," said Frank, still invisible on his berth, "Jeanne and Lisa and Skip are really part of our family now. We've got to take care of them . . . take care of them just as we would . . . your mother and Susan."

In the darkness Jim put the washcloth and towel down on the sink and went to his narrow berth forward of Frank's.

"They . . . they're good people," Jim said as he climbed up onto the foam mattress.

"They're family," said Frank. "Lisa's your sister."

Jim pulled the sheet up over his damp, sticky body and pulled off his swim trunks. He felt a chill when his father referred to Lisa as his sister, fearful that Frank was thinking in terms of his relationship with Jeanne and not seeing Lisa as separate, as . . . a woman.

"Good night, Dad," he said.

"All of us . . ." Frank seemed to be saying softly, but Jim didn't know what he meant, and in another minute he could hear the heavy rasp of his father's breathing as he slept.

Lying in her berth beside Katya the next morning, Jeanne thought about Neil and about Skippy's not eating enough and of how gaunt Frank was beginning to look, and about Neil's thighs and Skippy's fascination with fish guts, and about Lisa and Jim, and about the planet withering with the plagues unleashed by the war, and about how tired she was of dealing with it all, and about Neil. At times their voyage seemed hopeless; at others selfish and narcissistic. Part of her felt that she ought to be suffering and dying on the mainland with the rest of the world, not falling in love. She wanted to be a nun ministering to the suffering victims of war; she wanted to be naked in Neil's arms. She wanted to devote her life to bringing up her children so that the world they created would be free of the evil that her generation had unleashed. But she wanted a house, a big double bed, with a supermarket and restaurant next door. She wanted Frank to stop loving her and Neil never to stop. She wanted the world to stop surprising her with its ability to kill people; she wanted to die. No, she wanted to live, to live, to live.

She slipped abruptly out of her berth, and though it was still forty minutes before she was due to feed the two watch teams, she began to dress.

"Hey, what's the problem?" Katya asked her unexpectedly. "You've been tossing and turning as if you were trying to solve the whole world's problems in one long think." Resting on one elbow, Katya was looking sleepy-eyed at Jeanne, who stood a few feet away, buttoning her blouse. Katya spoke in a low voice so as not to disturb Lisa and Skip, who were still asleep in the adjoining berth. At five the light was just gathering in the east.

"Restless," Jeanne answered.

"Men *do* have that effect, don't they?" Katya remarked, not accepting the evasive answer. Jeanne stared back but didn't reply. "Frank and Neil are both coming on to you," Katya went on, "and you're interested in Neil. What's the problem?"

Jeanne leaned down to put on her boat shoes. Although she liked Katya, she was not used to confiding in another woman, especially one she barely knew.

"I don't think my emotional problems are worth talking about," she finally said in a low voice.

"They're worth talking about if you plan keeping me awake every night thinking about them," Katya replied. "Hey, come on, I'm exactly the person you should talk to."

Jeanne walked softly to the forward part of the cabin to check that Lisa and Skip were asleep. When she got back, a gentle swell rolled under *Vagabond*, making her three hulls tip, slide, and roll with a queasy sideways motion that always made Jeanne feel a mild dizziness.

"Have you slept with Neil?" Katya asked after the silence continued.

Unused to such bluntness, Jeanne did not even turn around to face her.

"If you'd like me to vacate this berth and take Skip off your hands today so you and Neil can be alone, I will," Katya said. "I mean getting it on with a lover on this boat is going to involve a major logistical effort. It's worse than a girl's dorm."

Jeanne turned back to Katya.

"You . . . and Tony?" she asked.

"Oh, me and Tony are the types that could make it in Grand Central Station . . . if that's what I wanted," Katya replied, smiling sleepily. She sat up and stretched, the sheet sliding off and revealing her small breasts with their long nipples.

Jeanne looked away. "It's not a problem of privacy," she said softly.

"Well, tell me what it is," Katya said. "I promise to give you bad advice, which you can ignore. It's the telling that will help."

Jeanne glanced again at her sleeping children and finally, with a rush, began talking.

"Oh, Katya, I love Neil, but it's no use. It can never work out. It's so mixed up. I'm fond of Frank too. We're all a family now, and I can't do anything that's going to make Frank bitter and divide us. I just can't do it."

Katya, now sitting up and leaning back against the partition between her berth and Lisa and Skip's, was brushing out her curly ash-blond hair. When Jeanne stopped talking, Katya frowned.

"So don't sleep with either of them," Katya concluded, looking puzzled. "Most men survive. Or they find someone else they can bury their sorrow, and other parts of their anatomy, in." She looked at Jeanne questioningly.

Jeanne was depressed by this advice. It was excellent advice, but had the flaw of asking her to stay away from Neil.

"Or sleep with both of them," Katya went on, watching Jeanne carefully.

"No, I can't do that," Jeanne said simply.

Katya swung herself out of bed to begin dressing. As she reached into a cubby to get her shorts, she suddenly became irritated.

"You think too much, Jeanne," Katya said. "If you and a man love each other, that's it, that's first. The rest of the world doesn't count. Family doesn't count. A woman friend doesn't count. Grab it."

She stepped into her shorts, then grabbed a yellow T-shirt and pulled it over her head, shaking her hair and brushing it down when her head emerged.

"Everyone else does," she added and, with Jeanne staring after her, she climbed the hatchway steps, slid back the hatch, and was gone.

According to Neil's noon sunshots, *Vagabond* was now about fifty miles north of the reef and cays off the northeast coast of Great Abaco Island. Sailing at about seven knots, *Vagabond* might come within sight of land a little before sunset.

The thought gave Neil little satisfaction. He found himself approaching this landfall warily. He and Frank had already argued that morning about whether it was absolutely necessary to take on additional food and water before sailing on for Puerto Rico. Frank was concerned about cutting their rations in half for up to two weeks, while Neil felt that starvation was not their primary danger. The Bahamian government had announced that it was impounding any foreign vessel that landed in Bahamian waters without first clearing customs at Freeport or Nassau. All weapons aboard any ship were being confiscated. The rash of piracies that were infesting Bahamian waters could be stopped only by the rigid enforcement of these rules. All food was strictly rationed by the authorities. Foreigners unable to pay with gold, silver, or barter for their food were being forced to join labor gangs or—those who had them—give up their boats as exchange.

If the wind direction had not made a landfall on Great Abaco Island their most logical choice, Neil would have preferred to stay out at sea, away from the dangers he foresaw in closing with the land. The sun was shining brightly, the sky a deep blue, and the sea sparkled with small whitecaps from the twelve-knot breeze still blowing out of the east southeast. Frank, at the helm, was pinching *Vagabond* a bit east of south, because when they came to the reef they would have to proceed southeast alongside it until they decided if, where, and when to take *Vagabond* into land.

It was a little before the changing of the watch at two o'clock that Jeanne spotted a ship with the binoculars. At first this was all she could be sure of. Ten minutes later she and Neil, trading off the large pair of binoculars, had determined that it was a sailboat heading north, but without any sails up. A minute later, when the sailboat altered its course to the west, Neil thought that it, like the only other sailing vessel they had seen on their trip south, was starting to flee from them. Then he realized differently.

"What is it?" asked Jeanne.

"It's a drifting sailboat," he replied, handing back the glasses. "Probably abandoned, a derelict." As she began studying the mysterious ship, Neil walked out into the port cockpit where Frank and Tony were looking through the smaller glasses.

"Alter course," Neil said to Tony at the helm, "We're going to take a look."

"What the hell for?" Tony asked.

"There may be survivors," Neil replied. "If not, there may be supplies we can salvage."

"Anybody still alive on that boat we can do without," Tony commented. "This close to land the ship's probably been sacked already."

"We're going over," Neil said.

Within a half-hour *Vagabond* had come to within a hundred yards of the derelict. The ship's white paint was blistered and peeling, fragments of the mainsail lay loosely along the boom, and a halyard was slack and swinging idly back and forth with the rocking of the boat. There was no sign of life.

"Ahoy, *Windsong*!" Neil shouted as Tony brought *Vagabond* so close to the wind that all three sails luffed and she was almost dead in the water ten yards away from the forty-foot ketch.

"Hit the horn," Neil said to Tony, who gave one loud blast from the air horn on the control panel shelf.

"Are you going to board?" Frank asked Neil.

Just then a figure emerged from the cabin into the ship's cockpit. Crouched and blinking in the bright light, a small, unshaven man in his forties wearing only a bathing suit stared at them.

Neil and the others stared back, stunned.

"Can we assist you?" Neil asked loudly after the shocked silence.

"Water," the man said hoarsely. He was hollow-eyed. "Water," he repeated more loudly.

As Jim ducked below to get some of their precious water and the man peered down into his own cabin, Frank came up to Neil.

"What are you going to do?" he asked.

"Take him off," Neil answered, staring glumly at the stricken *Windsong*. "Back her off a bit," he added to Tony, "then bring her up to the port side. Get the fenders."

"There must be others aboard," Jim said, returning with the water. "He can't be alone."

"The guy's practically dead," Tony said, easing *Vagabond* alongside *Windsong*. Neil and Frank moored the two boats side by side, with the fenders cushioning their impact.

"Do you want to abandon ship?" Neil asked. "We can take you aboard."

The man, the bones of his ribcage protruding grotesquely beneath the skin of his emaciated body, lowered his head and stared at the water.

"We're all dying," he answered. "I don't know."

"Radiation sickness isn't necessarily fatal," Neil said. "You may recover."

The man looked back up at Neil. "I know," he said. "That's what's hell. But my wife and daughter . . . are almost dead. They'll never make it."

Jim handed a plastic jug of water across to the man who, with sudden agility, grabbed it and hugged it to his chest.

"Let me go below and . . . decide what we'll do," he said and made his way less nimbly down into the cabin of his boat. Neil, Frank, and Tony were left in the side cockpit waiting.

"What is this shit?" Macklin said, suddenly appearing beside them, looking sleepy, the hair on his chest glistening with sweat. "You bringing more people on board to raid our food and water?"

Neil didn't reply.

"If they're all dying," Tony said, "it'll just be a waste. You said yourself that prospects of finding food in the Bahamas don't look good."

"I know," Neil said.

"What happened to your fucking principle of triage?" Macklin interjected.

Neil didn't answer. The four of them stood silently in the gently rocking *Vagabond,* awaiting the reappearance of the dying man. What had happened to triage, thought Neil, was that at sea you didn't abandon a fellow sailor.

The man emerged from the cabin.

"I'd appreciate it if you could take us off," he said. When they stared at him, he finally added, "I'll need help."

"Mac," said Neil, "get aboard and give the man a hand."

"Go yourself," Macklin said and stalked away.

"I'll go," said Frank. He boarded *Windsong* ahead of Jim but suddenly noticed along the combing and in the corners of the cockpit a fine gray ash. He first took it to be sand, but with a stab of fear realized it was radioactive debris. He clambered quickly on board *Vagabond*, pushing Jim back ahead of him.

"Jesus Christ," he told Neil. "There's fallout on deck."

Neil looked and frowned.

"This is ridiculous," said Tony. "Let's get out of here."

Neil hesitated again, then turned to Frank.

"I'll get on board and help them off," he said.

"I'll help you," said Jim.

"You stay here," Frank said gloomily to Neil, grabbing his shoulder. "With your bum arm you're the wrong man for the job."

After Frank boarded *Windsong,* Jim quickly followed. Ducking below into the main cabin, Frank saw that there were two women lying under dirty sheets on opposite sides of the main saloon on what normally would have been settees. The cabin was a jumble of pails, towels, open cans of food, dirty dishes, clothing, blankets. The stench of sweat, urine, and excrement was stifling. The small hollow-eyed man stood apologetically next to his wife.

"They can't walk, and I can't lift them," he said.

Frank pushed himself over to the older woman, bent over, and tried to force himself to smile. But when he saw the gray-faced, frozen apparition that was staring up at him, the "Hi" he had been about to speak froze in his throat. He gasped. Without any further efforts at sociability he leaned over and picked her up and headed back toward the gangway. The woman was almost dead. She was wearing nothing under the sheet, and the contact of his hands with her naked flesh after seeing death on her face horrified and disgusted him. He wanted to run up the stairs, but Jim appeared, on his way down.

"Bring the girl and get out quick," he said sharply.

Teeth gritted, his face showing his fear and disgust, Frank climbed the cabin steps, went quickly over to *Vagabond* and, refusing Jeanne's offer of assistance, thrust himself from one boat to the other.

"Where are you putting her?" Jeanne asked.

"Frank's cabin, I'm afraid," Neil interjected. "All three."

Frank carried the woman below.

Jim had suffered the same sickening shock at the sight and smell of *Windsong*'s cabin as, with face averted, he gently slid his arms under the daughter and lifted her up. She was small and light. As he took her in his arms, he noticed that she turned her face away from him.

"Come on," he said to the man and started back to *Vagabond*.

"Are there things we can salvage from *Windsong*?" Neil asked Frank, who was coming out of his cabin after lifting the woman up on his double berth and instructing Jim to put the girl in beside her. Macklin stood nearby, glaring.

"No," Frank snapped back. "Let's get away now, fast."

The skeleton of a man, standing slightly bent over in the starboard cockpit a few feet away, grimaced.

"We've got a few emergency rations that you can have," he said. "It's stored—"

"Let's go!" Macklin said sharply to Neil. "That ship's contaminated. Everything on it may be carrying death. Let's go." He brushed past the man and untied the aft line that kept *Vagabond* rafted to the other ship, and then hurried forward to get the other line. In just a few seconds *Vagabond* fell away, her sails filling, then surged forward and past the stricken *Windsong*.

The owner turned and looked at her as *Vagabond* steadily moved away, then the man moved slowly to the hatchway to go below.

Frank stepped trembling into the wheelhouse to stow the fenders Macklin was handing back to him.

"Take it easy, Frank," Neil said.

"We've brought death aboard," Frank said grimly.

Neil, staring forward past the little transistor radio that lay on the control panel shelf, was as tight-lipped as Frank.

"I know," Neil replied. "But when was he *not* aboard?"

The presence of the three apparently doomed refugees upset *Vagabond*'s company. Having three dying people aboard was a disturbing reminder of their own danger and gave rise in some to a guilty resentment of the new burden of stricter rationing and more limited space. Frank now had to sleep in the wheelhouse, Jim aft with Neil. Frank found himself resenting mild Sam Brumburger as if he were a boorish guest who'd crashed a previously enjoyable party. He was naturally appalled by his resentment. He realized that if they had abandoned Sam and his family, he would have felt worse.

He was annoyed, too, with Jeanne for showing so much solicitude for the refugees; she seemed to spend the whole afternoon in endless trips down into the hellhole of his cabin to minister to their needs. None of the men had any appetite for that sort of thing, although Olly went down and spent an hour talking with Sam.

"Wife's just about dead," Olly said to Frank afterward. "The daughter's not going to make it either. Sam thinks now he should have scuttled his ship."

"Sam looks pretty bad too," Frank commented.

"Yep. Tough way to go," Captain Olly said. "Prefer a quick sinking myself."

"Me too," said Frank.

The rescue of the Brumburgers had cost them more than two hours, so that when the wind fell away to nothing at dusk they were still fifteen to twenty miles from land.

Sam Brumburger told his story after dinner that night.

Sam, his wife and daughter, and two male friends had set out from Miami to bring their boat north for the summer. On the night the war started the ship was shaken by a tremendous blast. With his two friends on watch, Sam was with his family below. He was thrown off the settee berth onto the floor. Recovering, he staggered up and hurried topside. Although there was a terrifying brightness to the southwest that lit up the night, he couldn't at first see anything wrong. He called to his friends and got no reply. Then he saw one of them lying across a seat in the rear of the cockpit. His friend's body was smoking. He had been literally burned to death.

The other friend had disappeared, presumably thrown overboard by the blast. His wife, sleeping in an upper berth forward, had been badly burned on the stomach and upper thighs. He and his daughter had escaped direct injury from the blast.

That morning, when fallout began to fall onto his deck, he got his engine going and motored to the northeast for eleven hours, skirting north of Grand Bahama Island until he ran out of fuel. Meanwhile, he, his wife, and his daughter had begun to vomit.

On the fourth day Sam spotted a fishing boat and fired a flare and the boat came over to investigate. It was a beat-up twenty-five-foot runabout with an outboard that was on its last gasp. There were two black Bahamian men aboard and one white man. They looked shocked at the sight of Sam and his boat and Sam's wife. At first Sam was afraid they were just going to motor away. But they decided to stay. They locked Sam in the forepeak, looted *Windsong*, and took turns raping his daughter on the settee berth, three feet away from her dying mother. Since then *Windsong* had been drifting helplessly.

When Sam told his story, Frank found it strange to listen to a man who knew he was dying, accepted that he was dying, and who looked at everything with emotionless objectivity. His manner was also strangely apologetic, as if the needs of a man who was going to die were futile and irrelevant. Commenting on the war, Sam seemed to speak from some other world that he alone had moved into. "I never thought we could spend a trillion dollars on something without sooner or later demanding our money's worth."

Later that night, after everyone but Neil, Frank, and Jeanne had gone below, and Vagabond was wallowing in a dead calm, there was a strange scene. Jeanne had just returned from another visit to Frank's cabin to clean up after one of the Brumburgers and had stopped, after washing out a towel in salt water, to take a look at Neil's elbow. Frank was steering, and Jeanne sat beside Neil on the wheelhouse settee and adjusted the kerosene lantern to get a good look.

The swelling on Neil's elbow had gone down considerably. He could move his lower arm about forty-five degrees without pain, although there was still redness over a three-square-inch area. They had not used antibiotics and were depending on Neil's immune system to handle the infection by itself.

Neil tried to joke lightly with her about his arm and her ministrations, but she seemed solemn and withdrawn.

"You're sure you want to keep trying to do without the sling?" she asked after they'd finished the examination and wrapped the elbow again with gauze.

"Yes. I think that's the best way to put pressure on myself to use the arm more normally."

"All right. But the infection's still there."

"For Christ's sake," Frank suddenly interjected. "Put some mercurochrome and a Band-Aid on it, and let him be. People *dy*ing all over the world and you're worrying about Neil's sore elbow."

Jeanne looked up at Frank, who kept his back to them, and then glanced fearfully at Neil. She moved away from him and stood up.

"She also spent half the day with the Brumburgers," Neil said to Frank's back.

"At least *they*'re dying," Frank shot back, half-turning. "Can't you take care of yourself anymore?"

In the awkward silence that followed Jeanne gathered up the medicine kit and hung the lantern back from the roof.

"I promise either to heal myself or to go terminal as soon as possible," Neil finally rejoined.

"And you, Jeanne," Frank said, ignoring Neil's remark and stopping her on her away down to the main cabin. "Don't waste so much time with the Brumburgers. You're got your own life to live."

"I thought I *was* living it," she replied coolly.

"You're not," Frank countered loudly. "You're spending all your time with Lisa and Skippy and cleaning up vomit and mothering Neil and not a second on yourself."

Neil saw Jeanne watching Frank closely, seeming to study him.

"I'm sorry, Frank," she said. "I suppose I am compulsively doing things whether they need doing or not. I'll try to relax."

Frank stared at her, seeming as surprised as Neil by her abrupt acquiescence.

"Well . . . it's just that I want you to be happy," Frank finally said.

"I know," she replied. Then she stepped down into the main cabin.

Later, after she'd gone over to her own cabin to sleep, Frank stopped Neil as he was headed for bed.

"That's one incredible woman," he said to Neil.

"Yes," said Neil.

"If I don't accomplish anything else in the rest of my life except see to it that she's been taken care of, I think I'd be satisfied."

Neil looked into Frank's intent, confiding face and felt a distant stab of fear.

"She . . . she's a fine woman," he said.

"I hate to see her martyring herself," Frank went on. "She's working much too hard."

"Maybe it's better for her now than thinking," Neil commented.

"Maybe," Frank said and took a deep breath. "Jesus, what a world. Just when things were beginning to look good, we get three breathing corpses."

"I know what you mean."

"You think it'll ever end?"

Neil looked into Frank's face, less intent now and somewhat distracted, and without thinking answered simply, "No."

And he went to bed.

At dawn the next day Sam came up from his cabin to report that his wife and daughter were dead. He made this announcement to Neil apologetically, as if he were confessing that he'd broken someone's teacup. He and Neil discussed their deaths briefly and concluded that they should be immediately buried at sea. Land was visible four miles to the south, and Neil was worried about both pirates and Bahamian government boats.

By six thirty everyone except Jim and Katya, who were in their berths after an early morning at the helm, had finished a spare breakfast and was ready for the burial. Jeanne, concerned about the effect on Skippy of seeing bodies tossed casually into the ocean, asked Lisa to keep him occupied in the forepeak.

The adults gathered self-consciously in the cockpit outside Frank's cabin and looked morosely at the covered bodies of the two women, which were stretched out along the cockpit seat. Jeanne had wrapped them together in a clean sheet, and Neil weighted the bodies with an old dinghy anchor.

Sam Brumburger was Jewish, but his wife was not, and he had told them he had no strong feelings about how she should be buried, only that he wanted to say the words over them before they were committed to the sea.

As he watched and listened Neil was struck by the grotesqueness of this funeral. Everyone, including Sam, was dressed in bathing suits or cutoffs or jeans and either bare-chested or wearing T-shirts. *Vagabond* was sailing along under cloudless blue skies through sparkling blue water. Only an unpleasant odor—either from the bodies or Frank's cabin—reminded him of death.

Sam spoke again with that almost painful objectivity that his own death seemed to give him. He talked emotionlessly of the troubles he and his wife and daughter had had, their weaknesses, his, as if they were traditional parts of a eulogy. He was like an historian summing up a doomed civilization. Sam seemed to be not just burying his wife, but himself also. He was summing up before the Lord his being, offering it without apology.

"Human beings don't plan to die," he was saying. "They get picked up, incredulous and protesting, and leave the stage like a vaudevillian getting the hook. In some ways Ingrid and I've been lucky: we got to say our good-byes, sing our final song, and walk off the stage under our own power, knowing precisely where we were going.

"So, Lord, we commit Ingrid's body to the sea. I thank you for her life. I thank you for her death."

At first when Sam stopped speaking, Neil was not sure that he was really finished. Then he nodded at Frank, and Neil joined Frank in lifting up the shrouded bodies, first to the edge of the combing and then, with a quick thrust, into the sea.

Sam had stood with his head lowered as they did this, and he did not raise it to watch the bodies swirl astern, slowly sinking. Jeanne came up and gently embraced him, held him for five or six seconds, and then wordlessly went back into the wheelhouse. Neil, surprised by his mild revulsion at seeing Jeanne hugging the dying man, then went up and put his hand on Sam's shoulder.

"That was fine, Sam," he said, feeling awkwardly that he sounded as if Sam had just done a good job hauling anchor.

The others, too, after saying a brief word to Sam, moved onto the central part of the boat. It was Neil who, turning back to adjust the mainsheet, saw Sam Brumburger climbing up out of the cockpit. Neil *saw* him, one leg already over, straddling *Vagabond*'s combing, moving clumsily and weakly, *knew* what he was doing, *knew* he could stop him, but didn't. As he watched, Sam pulled his other leg up onto the combing, looked down into the water rushing past, then pushed himself off into the sea.

"*Hey!*" Frank shouted from behind Neil and then rushed past into the cockpit.

Sam's head bobbed up briefly in the wake of *Vagabond*'s starboard hull, then disappeared. Frank stared after him.

When Neil turned into the wheelhouse, he saw Captain Olly steering *Vagabond* as if nothing had happened.

"Good man, Sam," Captain Olly said, staring forward. "Got himself a good death too."

For Neil, Olly's wisdom made only the smallest dent in the horror.

The low smudge of land lying on the horizon dead ahead grew slowly toward them through the hot, still morning. They had listened at eight to news of destruction and starvation throughout the world that made their recent losses and current privations seem insignificant, yet Neil sensed that his ship approached the land reluctantly, with more fear than hope. They'd had no rain and foresaw none through the next day anyway, and Neil felt they had to try to duck into an outer cay for water if the opportunity arose. Jim was reading a guide to the Bahamas, trying to determine which islands had fresh water and which didn't, but the writers of the guide had never anticipated anyone's wanting to get water on uninhabited islands when it was available at any port. Neil doubted that any of the small islands would have springs or wells. Any hope they'd had earlier of sailing into Hopetown or Marsh Harbor for supplies had been dashed by the government edict that all foreign vessels had to clear customs and surrender their weapons in Nassau or Freeport.

At eleven that morning they observed a small plane flying south. It circled low around *Vagabond,* which made Neil uneasy, and he called everyone together to discuss tactics for repelling pirate attacks. They had only three weapons, the 9mm pistol with four dozen bullets, Macklin's .45 with two dozen bullets, and the .38 revolver with two bullets. They were "short on artillery," as Olly had phrased it. They decided their flare gun could appear to be a fourth weapon. They talked about the possible ways they might be attacked, and Neil assigned them to various defensive positions with standing orders on how to respond in various contingencies.

By one o'clock they were only about a half-mile off from the ragged line where surf was breaking against the outer reef. They were sailing south-southeast along this barrier, and low islands were visible across the emerald lagoon beyond the reef. When they came within clear sight of an abandoned lighthouse, Neil was able to verify their

252 · LUKE RHINEHART

landfall: they were off Man-of-War Cay. The next opening in the reef was six miles down and led into Marsh Harbor, the most populous town on Great Abaco. Neil knew that they had to land for food and water, but before he decided on whether to try to sneak in for supplies, or sail to Nassau, or bypass the Bahamas completely, he hoped to be able to talk to someone on one of the local boats.

An hour later the gloom that had accompanied the first hours of their fresh contact with land deepened when they sailed past the marked channel leading into Marsh Harbor. They could see the town and a few boats anchored in the cove and at the dock. They sailed past. They were outcasts.

After another mile Neil ordered Jeanne to bring them about to head offshore and avoid the reef. As soon as they had tacked, he noticed a launch speeding toward them from the Marsh Harbor inlet. Neil ordered them to take their prearranged defensive positions: Jeanne, Lisa, and Skippy below amidships with smoke flares, Neil standing in the aft cabin hatchway holding Macklin's .45, Frank in the forepeak hatch with the .38 revolver, Jim in the starboard cabin hatchway with the Navy 9mm pistol, and Tony in the port cabin hatchway with the flare gun. Captain Olly was with Katya at the helm. They all kept their meager weapons momentarily out of sight, their intent being to create the illusion of having four heavily armed men on guard at four widely separated points.

Neil, standing on the second step of his cabin, with his head and shoulders sticking out above the cabin opening, clutching the .45 in his right hand, watched the launch approaching them from the left. It had a machine gun mounted on the foredeck, manned by two black men. As the launch slowed down he saw in the cockpit two additional black men, one studying *Vagabond* through binoculars. When the launch swung up behind them, Neil saw that the second man in the cockpit, who was wearing white shorts and shirt in contrast to the khakis and jeans of the others, smile a big, white-toothed smile at *Vagabond*. Neil had the momentary absurd idea that he was about to shout, "Welcome to the Bahamas!"

Instead the launch pulled up broadside to *Vagabond,* holding off about thirty feet. For perhaps fifteen seconds the men on the two ships contemplated each other, their two vessels slicing serenely through the water, side by side, at five knots. Captain Olly broke the silence.

"Hi, there, fellas," he shouted amiably. "How they hanging?"

As far as Neil could tell, the launch was manned only by the four black men already visible, all of whom looked back at Captain Olly blankly.

"We need some food and water," Captain Olly went on. "You fellas know where we can get some?"

"Where you headed, mon?" the officer, whom Neil had seen grinning, shouted back.

"Puerto Rico," Captain Olly replied. "Where you fellas headed?"

"You have permit for Bahamian waters?" the officer asked.

"Shit, no," Captain Olly replied. "We're heading for Puerto Rico."

"No weapons permitted in Bahamian waters," the officer shouted. "You have weapons aboard?"

"No weapons," Captain Olly replied, heading *Vagabond* into the wind and slowing her up some.

"We will board you then for routine inspection," said the officer, grinning.

"You try to board us," Captain Olly replied in the same easygoing tone, "and we'll blast you all to kingdom come."

The white-toothed smile disappeared from the Bahamian's face.

"We ain't got no weapons," Captain Olly shouted as the two vessels continued slicing through the water side by side. "So you don't got to inspect us." Olly grinned. "Course if you *do* try to board us, we'll have to sink all four of you fellas."

The officer turned to the shorter man at his side and they whispered together urgently. The two men with the machine gun were staring back looking for orders.

"What you have to pay for watah, mon?" the officer shouted.

"Got a good Johnson outboard," Captain Olly replied. "Got some cigarettes."

"You have gold? Silvah? Jewelry?"

"Maybe," said Captain Olly. "You selling water?"

"We sell you fifteen gallons of watah," the officer replied. "You pay in gold, silvah, or diamonds."

"Can't we sail in to one of these here little islands and get some water?"

"Not without permit," the officer replied, grinning. "For permit you must go to Nassau and surrender all your weapons."

"Need a permit for water, huh?" said Captain Olly. "Seems a little shitty to me."

"You have gold? Silvah?"

Olly frowned and looked aft at Neil, who shook his head slightly in the negative.

"Not a drop, sonny," Captain Olly said. "Got some fancy clothes, though, you fellas might like. You like fancy clothes? Also got a bottle of whiskey."

"I think maybe we go trade, right, mon?" the tall officer said and flashed his smile.

"Right, sonny, but you tell those two fellas with the peashooter to point it forward, okay? I get indigestion staring at the open end of a barrel."

After the two men manning the gun moved aft, the two boats eased in closer to each other, Captain Olly bringing *Vagabond* up into the wind. He instructed Jeanne to come up and help Katya prepare the fenders, the four other men maintaining their defensive positions.

When the two ships were secured, Olly went down into Frank's cabin and brought back up two of his dress suits while Jeanne brought two packs of cigarettes and a half-full whiskey bottle from the main cabin. After the goods were spread out on the cockpit seat, negotiations began. The launch crew had brought up on their deck five three-gallon containers of water. While the grinning officer came aboard to finger the material of Frank's suits and hold them up to his body to check the size, Captain Olly dipped a finger into each of the water jugs to see that they were fresh and potable. They all tasted heavily chlorinated but drinkable. Olly grimaced each time he sampled the water.

"Worst water I ever tasted, sonny," he said to the Bahamian officer. "This horse piss or what?"

The black man just grinned.

"Two suits, whiskey, and cigarettes for nine gallon watah," he said.

"No sale," Captain Olly replied. "I'll give you that blue suit there for all fifteen gallons, including the jugs."

The black officer laughed and slapped his brown bare thigh below his clean white shorts.

"You crazy, mon," he said, glancing at Katya with a grin. "Watah is gold. This suit's just pretty shit. No way it's gold."

"Take it or leave it, fella. We got to get on to Puerto Rico."

The black man glared.

"I sell you good watah, mon. You pay me whiskey, cigarettes, and suits. You want me arrest you?"

"Now, now, fella," said Captain Olly, his wrinkled face breaking into its toothless grin. "I got an army of sharpshooters in all four cabins. Unless that there peashooter can shoot in four directions at once you ain't arresting nobody, least not on this boat."

The black man still glared, puffing out his chest and breathing heavily. The other three men looked on from their cockpit indifferently. The officer's eyes abruptly narrowed and he scrutinized Captain Olly carefully.

"I sell you fifteen gallons without the jugs, for this blue suit, the whiskey, and the cigarettes."

"With the jugs."

"With two jugs, mon. I cannot give you more."

"Okay, fella, you got yourself a deal."

Captain Olly grinned and stuck out his hand. The officer grinned back, and they shook hands heartily. The three men in the other boat began laughing and talking, the whole atmosphere abruptly changing. Olly asked Katya to bring up three empty plastic containers to transfer the water from the three jugs, and the Bahamian officer called one of his men over to admire his beautiful new suit. Both men took a slug of the whiskey and then handed the bottle over to the two blacks who were still aboard the launch.

"Well, now, tell me, cap," said Captain Olly to the officer, after taking a slug of whiskey himself when it was offered to him. "Why's your government so fussy 'bout our landing and getting a little water?"

"I don't know, mon," was the reply. "Too many you Yahnkees, s'pose."

"But you got plenty of water here, don't you?"

The man frowned.

"Watah, yes, mon, but not food. Ships want food and can't pay for it. They take our women too. You bettah keep your guns, mon, or you won't have your women." He looked over at Jeanne and Katya and grinned.

"Your government have other boats southeast of here likely to bother us?" Captain Olly asked.

"Doan' know, cap'n," the officer answered. "But it's not us you 'av to worry about, it's *pi*rates. South of here the pirates so thick you can walk across their decks all the rest way to Puerto Rico. You ought to get to Nassau quick, mon. Pirates stay clear of Nassau."

"Who are the pirates?" Olly asked, frowning.

"Everybody, mon!" the officer shot back, grinning broadly. "Everybody who's got a boat. 'S only way a mon can make an honest living."

Olly frowned again.

"Well, thanks, cap," he said, and stuck out his hand again to the Bahamian officer. "We 'preciate your help."

"That's all right, mon," said the officer, shaking hands and then getting back onto his launch with the others. After putting his new suit down neatly on a seat, he turned and gave Olly a big grin. "Welcome to the Bahamas, mon!" he said loudly, spreading his arms out wide, one holding the whiskey bottle. "Right?"

And the two vessels parted.

As the Bahamian launch withdrew toward the entrance to Marsh Harbor, Neil emerged from his cabin, ostentatiously wielding his pistol. The others soon joined him in the starboard cockpit next to Olly at the wheel.

"Well," Neil said. "We've just survived our first pirates."

"Shall we go to Nassau?" Frank asked, shaking his head and pursing his lips in disgust.

"We can't risk it, Frank," Neil replied. "It's still on to Puerto Rico."

"With only twenty gallons of fresh water?" Frank said, startled.

"If we go to Nassau we'll never get out. They'll take our weapons, make us barter away our equipment for food, and all we'll get is extra water and two hundred extra miles of fighting off pirates. It's not worth it.''

"But who knows if it's any better in the Virgins or Puerto Rico?" Tony asked, joining them.

"Puerto Rico's a lot larger," Neil answered, "and they're both presumably more friendly to Americans.''

"Isn't there a chance Puerto Rico will have gotten involved in the war?" Jeanne asked. "We've got naval and air bases there.''

"And we can sail to either of them from Nassau almost as easily as from here," Frank added.

"Not if they've taken our weapons," Neil shot back, tight-lipped. "We'd be sailing a thousand miles through a sea of pirates armed with Olly's gaff and a boathook. I'd prefer to die of thirst.''

Frank shook his head and paced into the wheelhouse and then turned around and came back.

"In Puerto Rico you'd be a draft dodger and Jim a deserter," he reminded Neil.

"In a war in which all the fighting will be over," Neil replied, "I doubt that by the time we get there anyone will care.''

"But can we go on much longer with so little food and water?" Jim broke in. "You told me yesterday we've got enough dried fish and water left for only three more days.''

Neil frowned, frustrated at facing three unacceptable alternatives. "I suppose we could try sneaking into one of the out-of-the-way cays," he mused aloud.

"And if they catch us without clearance, they confiscate the boat," Frank said. "There's no way we should try that.''

"Can't we land on an island at night, get water, and get away before daybreak?" Jeanne suggested.

"All the cays are buffered by reefs," Neil replied. "We can only get in and out during daylight, when we can see the shoals and find the channels.''

"And we'd be spotted during the day," Frank added. "The Bahamians probably have air patrols as well as cutters.''

No one spoke. They seemed to have reached an impasse. Frank paced into the wheelhouse, this time sitting down when he got there. Jeanne looked at him and then at Neil, finally at Olly, who stared forward humming lightly to himself.

"We should keep going," she said quietly. "God's put us in the middle of the biggest supermarket in creation, and if we can't learn to eat and drink what's out here we don't deserve to live."

When she stopped speaking, Frank ran his two hands through his thinning gray hair and stood up. He stared absently at Neil.

"The West Indies," he said almost to himself. "Jesus, I bet by the time we get there, we'll decide we have to go to Brazil." He smiled mournfully at Jeanne.

Neil moved for the first time since the discussion had begun. He lifted up one of the new water jugs.

"I think we might begin planning on it," he said.

"Well, Mac," said Tony a few hours later. He loomed over Conrad Macklin, who was sitting in the side cockpit at the trolling rig. "How do you feel about our captain's latest decision? You going to enjoy starving to death?"

Macklin looked up at Tony neutrally, then idly tested the drag on the nylon line. "Yes, I am," he answered quietly.

"You are?"

"I enjoy starving," Macklin replied, which made Tony stare at him uncertainly. "Considering the alternatives."

"I still think we should try to dock in here and try to get some food."

"Be patient, Tony," Macklin said, looking up at him and smiling. "The thing you don't understand is that sometimes retreat and lying low are the best strategy. Our Loken's no fool: he's not afraid to do that."

"Yeah?"

"Just like us, Tony," said Macklin, still smiling. "Just like us."

———————————————————

And so they sailed on, past the white-sand beaches and gleaming emerald water of the eastern Bahamian cays and out to sea to the east, having to make long tacks against the southeast wind while Neil wished it would shift, hoped he could guess which way it would shift, and sailing on, to either San Juan or the Virgin Islands, whichever the wind and the radio reports made a more feasible haven.

And a new intensity took hold of the voyage. After their first escape from the mainland a certain exhilaration and hopefulness had accompanied them southward. They had food and water, and though both were rationed, it was something of a game, merely "contingency planning."

But now they had been turned away from a place they had seen as a source of supplies; now they had been sailing almost a week without a landfall, and the contingency was upon them. There was no way to buy additional food; no sure way to get water. For at least another week the ocean was the only store in business and the skies the only source of water. Now they would sail successfully to Puerto Rico or the Virgins within two weeks or perhaps die. Now the billowing white clouds that flowed lazily above them represented not beauty but potential rainfall; the color of a sunrise was watched for signs of an approaching low-pressure system that might mean rain or a shift from the tradewind pattern they were heading into.

Now fishing was as serious an undertaking as war, and when some huge fish snapped through the wire leader, took off with Jim's best lure, and left them with only three, he was as pale and shaken as if he'd lost an important hill in battle. Now that they were out of the Gulf Stream, the fishing was much less dependable. In the first five days after picking up the Brumburgers they caught only two fish.

Now they began the monotonous, unpleasant, bone-jarring bashing to windward, straight into the seas that the tradewinds seemed to be building malevolently against them. Since it was his decision that they sail on past the Bahamas with insufficient food and water, Neil became obsessed with the struggle to sail *Vagabond* to windward as fast as possible. Although one of his basic sailing principles was never to criticize the wind, he found himself cursing quietly each time he awakened to find it still on their nose. He began to view the wind and waves as opponents he was fighting, an uncharacteristic attitude that he tried to check. When he observed Lisa's thinness, Frank's weakness, and recognized a certain lethargy in everyone's movements—including his own—this filled him with a rage to drive *Vag-*

abond eastward to a safe landfall where they could rest and eat and replenish their depleted stores.

He searched out the boat for useless weight as he might have searched for spies. Overboard went the portable television set, overboard some rusted chain, overboard two dozen of the ship's trashy novels, old magazines, half-finished cans of paint, some junk wood, and nine or ten heavy bolts that might have been useful for something, though Frank had no idea what that could have been.

They also discussed removing *Vagabond*'s diesel engine, both to lighten the boat and to create a private berth for Olly to ease the overcrowding. With Frank concurring, Neil decided that its future usefulness in a world mostly devoid of fuel didn't match the burden of six hundred pounds extra weight. In a six-hour operation that involved all the men, Frank and Olly supervised the unbolting and winching up of the heavy engine. By the time they were done, they had had to use half a dozen jury-rigged pulleys hanging from the main boom, wheelhouse roof, and mizzenmast. When the engine, from which they had removed the alternator, finally rolled off the afterdeck into the sea, the men let loose a long cheer and, dirty and sweaty, appropriated a beer each as their reward. It was the first successful mutiny on *Vagabond,* and Neil, clutching his own bottle, accepted it with a smile. The trimaran gained an inch on her waterline aft, and her trim was now much better.

With the engine gone and no generator aboard, the batteries were unhooked from everything except the shortwave radio. Olly and Jim began trying to develop a man-powered generator out of the diesel alternator, but with three batteries aboard this project didn't seem pressing.

However, after the camaraderie of removing the engine, the smashing to windward began to take its toll.

They all were being weakened by occasional seasickness and the scantiness of their diet. They were now primarily eating the fish steaks they had dried a week before. They opened one can of fruit a day— for ten people. They boiled or baked two potatoes a day. For liquids there was only occasional tea or powdered orange drink. Except for one six-pack they were saving for "an appropriate occasion," the beer was gone. They drank water.

The tensions among them were building. Everyone needed more

privacy than was available, and for some the small ship had become a claustrophobic trap. Tony exploded at Neil for assigning equal rations to everyone, arguing that a big man like him needed twice the food that Lisa and Skip needed. Neil replied that Tony still had twice the body fat and that until someone showed symptoms of malnutrition, the rations would remain the same. Both Tony and Macklin complained about sleeping in the forepeak, and Neil gave them permission to use his cabin or the dinette settee when either was free. Macklin complained continually of seasickness, but still somehow managed to eat his share of rations. Katya sometimes took his place as crew on Olly's watch.

When Jeanne reported that a can of peaches was missing, Neil did nothing, but when she discovered that a small can of chicken spread had also disappeared, Neil laid down the law: if anyone was caught stealing food, he'd be put on half-rations and abandoned at the first landfall. Tony got angry again because Neil seemed to be directing his remarks primarily at him and Macklin. Neil said the rule applied to everyone.

Neil felt increasing irritation at such scenes, but he knew that if he could work things out with Frank and Jeanne, his other burdens would be more manageable. Although he and Frank treated each other with politeness, Frank's jealousy remained fierce. By words and glances he showed his anger or disapproval of any intimacy between them while he himself showered Jeanne with attention—in the galley, helping with Skippy, inviting her to crew with him and Tony. Although Frank felt better than during the first ten days—he was now keeping food down and showing more energy—he still *looked* sick, and Neil couldn't bring himself to do anything to hurt him.

But his relations with Jeanne, already sobered by the deaths of the Brumburgers and the bypassing of the Bahamas, and dampened by his obsession with getting *Vagabond* east to a safe landfall, were further restricted by Frank's jealousy. Neil could feel a barrier going up between himself and Jeanne.

He wanted to be with her, touch her, speak gently to her, but somehow such opportunities never seemed to arise. The few times they'd managed to be alone had found Neil absorbed in some nautical problem and unprepared for intimacy: tongue-tied, abstracted.

The claustrophobic mood of the boat affected everyone. Jim and

Lisa, depressed by the invasion of their privacy by Tony and the leers of Macklin, withdrew from the others on the boat, becoming an island unto themselves. Their love was obvious to everyone, and accepted, but they found it difficult to be alone. They resented the tensions between their parents and Neil, yet found themselves unable to break the knot of secrecy that they felt was oppressing them all.

Vagabond sailed on, the mood of her ship's company heavy. The paltry meals, unvaried, sparsely seasoned; the stink of the fish steaks drying in the sun; the stiffness of clothes washed in salt water; the familiar grizzled faces and unkempt hair of one's fellow crewmen day after day; the constant surge, sway, and smash of *Vagabond*; the constant hunger, and the suspicion that others were somehow eating more; the depressing reports from the outside world of war, disease, starvation, and violence spreading faster than they could escape them—all these oppressed them. Olly, who usually spent an hour every day telling stories to Skippy, now puffed violently on his unlit pipe. Katya and Tony were lovers, then fought bitterly, then were lovers again. Lisa and Jim, like two beings from some other planet, moved gingerly among them, doing their work, then retreating to Jim's guitar, Lisa's diary, long whispered conversations on the foredeck. Neil, Frank, and Jeanne, caught in a tense tangle that couldn't last, lived each day according to the rules of routine and decency, then each retired to loneliness.

They sailed on. The squalls that hit them four days after leaving Great Abaco eased the water problem. To gather water all the self-bailing cockpits were stoppered and even the inflatable dinghy was brought up on the foredeck and partially inflated to catch water. They gathered two and a half gallons in the first ten-minute downpour and close to six additional gallons in the two heavier showers that followed.

After the squalls the wind shifted to the south, the seas grew calmer, and *Vagabond* began a long tack directly toward San Juan. With the reduced weight of both man and material—the ship's company had already shed almost a hundred pounds—*Vagabond* began to race toward San Juan at almost a hundred and eighty miles a day.

A week after they left the Bahamas, when they were less than eighty miles northwest of San Juan, the outer world, the one they were trying to escape, the one they were trying to rejoin, paid them another visit. It was after one A.M. when a sudden glow lit the distant horizon ahead of them, bloomed briefly like a bright flower, and warned the watchers that man had again unleashed his madness on man.

They reacted to this explosion over San Juan not with terror but with a kind of bewildered automatism. It seemed somehow so wrong, so unjust, that after fleeing for almost three weeks and for over two thousand miles they should find *ahead* of them still *more*; they could feel no emotion except despair.

Jim and Lisa, on watch, turned *Vagabond* off the wind to sail away from the explosion, Lisa going crisply to the winches to let out the sails—as if responding to this explosion were a normal part of their nautical duties. At Jim's call Neil came hurriedly up on deck, saw the light, which was now astern of them, and went to the helm to check the course. Disoriented, he took a half-minute to realize that it was probably San Juan that had been hit. After calculating their approximate position, he ordered Jim to alter course back to the east. They would have about two hours before the tidal wave would reach them; only then would they turn to run before it. Because of the immense depth of water he guessed that the wave wouldn't be breaking and would probably be less of a threat than the wave in the shallow Chesapeake. Meanwhile they would head east, toward the Virgin Islands. When Neil took out the transistor radio and tuned it to their usual station in San Juan, they found it was no longer broadcasting.

The tidal wave overtook them in the early morning hours on schedule; a wave a little less than twenty-five feet high appeared among the three-foot seas that had been running earlier. Frank was at the helm with Tony, Neil sleeping in the wheelhouse behind; they saw it almost at the last moment, a huge wall of water glistening in the light of the moon. Frank swung *Vagabond* away to run before it, but the gigantic, unbreaking swell hit them on the aft quarter. *Vagabond* lurched violently, skidded along the wave at tremendous speed as she was carried like a toy for forty or fifty feet, and then lurched again as she toppled back to starboard at the crest and the wave rolled under her like the back of a mammoth whale. The huge sea was followed by several other large waves in the fifteen-to-twenty-foot range, but by then Frank had swung *Vagabond* downwind and she was running before them, surfing down their faces sometimes for a half-minute and setting him to grinning with incongruous exhilaration at *Vagabond*'s speed and grace under pressure. Neil awoke with a shout after the first smash and, groggy with sleep, began to shout out contradictory orders, but Frank, having survived the first awful wall of water, was not much concerned with *Vagabond*'s handling the puny little fifteen-footers. He just grinned at Neil and kept doing what he was doing.

The sunrise the following morning showed them a terrible beauty. The whole southeast became a glowing sweep of bright reds and oranges such as none of them had ever seen before. Already above them high, dark clouds were spreading out across the sky, tinged now with the most delicate pink but, as the sun rose higher, shading to tannish yellow, then brown, then a brownish gray, and finally and simply to the all-pervading, thick, dull gray that they had so hated and feared over the Chesapeake.

By nine A.M. San Juan was about seventy miles to the southwest. Sailing east, they were moving in the opposite direction from the high altitude flow of radioactivity, which was westerly. Yet even sailing at eight knots, they didn't gain on the expansion of the cloud; it spread outward from its center faster than they could flee. When the familiar terrifying ash first appeared on their decks, Neil once again ordered everyone below and had Tony dress in foul-weather gear to sweep the decks clean. By the time he had finished just the first cleanup, he was collapsing from the heat and, calling out weakly, had to be helped down into the main cabin. Neil had developed a technique of steering *Vagabond* by compass from below, since the steering cables passed down from the wheel at the rear of the main cabin and could be pulled alternately to adjust *Vagabond*'s course. The decks could be swept down every twenty minutes or so by someone as well-protected as Tony had been, but no one dressed for the Arctic had to be on deck to steer.

By noon, three hours after the first traces of ash had been discovered, they were no longer able to see any evidence of additional fallout. The dark cloud was mostly west and south of them, only a thin gray layer directly above.

It was Captain Olly who seemed most disturbed by the latest explosion. Neil discovered him late that afternoon sitting forward on the starboard hull, staring blankly out at the gray water to the south-east of them. Neil realized he must have been sitting there for hours.

"What's happening, old fellow?" Neil asked him, holding on to a stainless-steel shroud for balance. *Vagabond* was rolling and plunging uncomfortably as she reached eastward in the southerly wind.

"Feeling a little poorly," Olly answered after a brief pause.

"Your stomach?" Neil asked, concerned about radiation sickness.

"My heart," said Olly.

"My God, what's the matter?"

"Not *that* heart," said Olly irritably. "I mean . . . I mean that dust gets me down."

"I know."

"I don't mind explosions or tidal waves or fires or big winds. A sailor's meant to have to deal with those. But when it *rains* death, how do you reef for that?"

Neil didn't answer. They stared out at what seemed to be an ugly gray sea beneath the cloud bank to the south.

"And the ocean . . ." Olly went on in a low voice. "For fifty years I been figuring that no matter how much man ruined the land, the one thing he'd never destroy, no matter how hard he tried, and I *knew* he'd try his damnedest, would be the sea . . ."

Neil let the silence hang briefly and then said softly:

"It's not destroyed yet."

Captain Olly removed the perpetually unlit and empty pipe from his mouth and tapped it idly on the deck.

"No," he said after a while. "It ain't. But I seem to have under-rated man's talent for making a mess of things. All these years I been depending too much on man's weakness and stupidity. I figured he was just too dumb to mess things up totally." He looked up at Neil, his grizzled face and red eyes looking tired and old. "I just pray the Lord God will save us from man's intelligence."

Neil looked at him for a long moment and nodded.

"Amen," he said.

PART FOUR

LAND

ATLANTIC OCEAN

PUERTO RICO
←

TORTOLA —

SAINT THOMAS ISLAND

CHARLOTTE
AMALIE

CANEEL BAY
PLANTATION

SAINT JOHN
ISLAND

SALT
POINT

DOG'S ROCK ISLAND

RAM HEAD

VIRGIN ISLANDS

ANGUILLA
→

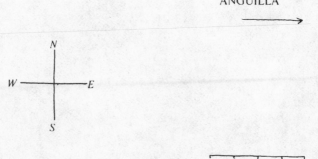

N

W   E

S

0 1 2 3 4 MI

JEANNE had slept while the men anchored *Vagabond* during the early morning hours, so that when she came up on deck a little after six, she looked out on the boats floating nearby, the quiet, smooth water of the harbor, and the white buildings of the town blossoming up the hillsides in the distance as a child might at her first big city. For more than two weeks she had known only the constant motion of the sea; now *Vagabond* lay as still as if she were imbedded in concrete. In all that time they had seen no more than four ships, one at a time; now as she slowly swept the horizon with her gaze she could see twenty, thirty . . . more. For the last two days—since the explosion over San Juan—she had felt continual low-level anxiety; now, surrounded by motionless white hulls, with white houses sleeping in the early dawn light less than a mile away, she felt that anxiety disappear. There was no exhilaration, no joy: simply a sense that here, for the moment at least, was a safe space.

She moved into the wheelhouse and saw Neil stretched out on the cushions asleep, his bearded face and tousled hair showing his exhaustion even as he slept. She wondered if he'd collapsed there, too tired to bother to go aft to his own cabin. He must have fallen asleep after they anchored, only hours earlier.

She slipped quietly down into the galley to prepare herself a cup of tea, then remembered that they had no more tea or coffee. She poured herself a small cup of water. Back in the wheelhouse, sitting opposite the motionless, leaden body of Neil, seeing the slanted rays of the early morning sun sparkling on the golden hairs of his thighs and legs, she felt a wave of longing, tenderness, and pride: they had come through, they had made it. But as she felt love welling up within her she thought too of Frank, and then the beautiful body of Neil, so still in front of her, made her sad.

It was too much for her. They were too much for her. There was no way she could create a world where all of her loved ones could be happy. Although she herself was beginning to feel at home on the water, her children needed the land. But the men, all of them really, seemed unenthusiastic about any of the permanent alternatives that they might find on any of these Caribbean islands. Here they were in Charlotte Amalie in the American Virgin Islands, as far as she could tell as safe and unhostile a place as there was within a thousand miles, and four of the men had spent two hours the previous evening discussing the supplies they would need for another two-week voyage and getting depressed because it seemed hopeless. She had tried to talk about what they could expect from St. Thomas, and though Frank had shown interest, Neil had done no more than give her a book to read.

"What's that, mommy?" Skip suddenly asked, coming up from his cabin and standing in front of her in his tiny red swimshorts and staring out at the fleet of anchored boats and the distant houses.

"That's . . . that's land, honey," she answered in a soft voice so as not to disturb Neil. For a week now Skip had been asking "When are we going to get to land, mommy?"

"That's land?" Skip asked, looking puzzled.

"Yes. That's the city of Charlotte Amalie on an island called St. Thomas. We may live here for a while."

"On a boat?"

"No, on land, in a house."

"Like the one in Washington?"

"No. Smaller. But nice."

As Skippy pulled himself up onto the cushion beside his mother he was silent, still staring at the distant town.

"They don't look like real houses," he said.

"They don't? Why not, honey?"

After a pause he said, "They just don't."

Neil stirred, adjusted a forearm under his head and chin, and then resumed his deadman pose. He had begun to let his beard grow and was in that halfway land of looking scraggly and down-and-out. As she looked at him, affection and desire mingled with her sadness.

"Do they have a McDonald's?" Skip asked.

"What?"

"Can we go to McDonald's today?" Skip repeated.

"Oh. No. I'm afraid not. I don't think they have McDonald's."

"What about a Big Whopper?"

"I don't know, honey. We'll see."

Hamburger: it, too, will have disappeared. On the islands there would be no beef or lamb, perhaps a little pork and fowl, but mostly fish. She smiled to herself as she realized that she was imagining herself having to announce to Skip the death of the hamburger. Could he take it at such a young age?

Maybe she should sleep with both of them, she thought. She wanted to sleep with Neil, but could never do so "publicly," could never slap Frank in the face like that after he had been so fond of her over the last two years. Perhaps she could become a seafaring camp follower, availiable to whichever officer was officially on watch, the way Katya seemed to have anticipated before they set out.

But she knew she couldn't, and the tension that existed between Frank and her and Neil was painful. This landfall might represent escape from the waves and starvation and fallout, but there was no escape from themselves.

When a customs launch arrived at eleven, Neil was up, but the other men had to be awakened. Most joined Neil and the others topside, all haggard and grizzled or bearded, even Jim. They looked like the collection of refugees they were. Katya's hair was tangled; she had lost several pounds from her already slight frame, but still looked healthier than the men. Lisa was a woman now, but because of her frailness she looked more like a child than she had a month earlier.

Although they were nervous about the arrival of the customs launch, they had heard a radio report that the island government had simply ignored the U.S. military. Apparently any attempt to draft the mostly black islanders would have led to an instantaneous revolution. Even as it was, the local government, controlled by blacks but greatly influenced by white interests, was on shaky ground.

The senior customs officer was a nervous, pudgy white man and his two-man crew, black. They searched *Vagabond* for weapons (all carefully hidden behind a false partition at the back of Jeanne's berth), asked detailed questions about their previous itinerary—they seemed to want to make certain they had been at sea nine days since the Bahamas—and, without a word of explanation, insisted on taking everyone's temperature. Just before the customs men left, Neil asked how he and his friends could expect to get food if they had no gold or silver or much else to barter with.

"Then you fish," the pudgy officer answered. "New immigrants aren't eligible for food assistance unless they surrender all their belongings and live in the refugee center out in Capo Gorda."

After the launch had motored off, their weapons not discovered, they prepared to go ashore. Jim got out the dinghy, and he and Macklin began to inflate it. Jeanne and Katya were talking about the chances of finding a home on St. Thomas when a man and a woman suddenly appeared beside *Vagabond* in a little eight-foot rowing pram.

"I say, you chaps going ashore?" the man asked. He was a round, red-faced man, his big chest and belly heavily matted with dark hair, although the flesh sagged on him as if he had recently lost weight. Both he and the woman, a bleached blonde, were in their forties and were wearing rather spare black bikini bathing suits.

"We are," Frank replied. "Why?"

"We own the little blue Wharram catamaran over there," the Englishman said, pointing. "Always willing to lend a hand to a multi-hull sailor, you know?"

"We appreciate it," said Frank.

"Philip felt you might need some advice before you go ashore," the woman said, smiling. "He's very good at giving advice."

"We've been at sea for more than two weeks," said Frank, feeling an unexpected pride as he spoke. "I guess we can use some advice about what the land world is like these days."

"It's a bloody mess is what it is," Philip replied, holding on to *Vagabond*'s combing with one of his big hands. "I know it's a bit presumptuous of me to come over here like this, but the world's gotten to be awf'ly small, and where there's a chance to find a friend, I like to take it.''

"I see," said Frank, his mood wavering uncertainly between suspicion and acceptance.

"Fact is," said the Englishman, "if you're going ashore for food and petrol and water, there's a bit you might know first, right?"

"Would you like to come aboard?" Frank finally asked.

"Don't mind if I do. Take the oars, Sheila."

The large Englishman and his petite and pretty wife climbed nimbly up onto *Vagabond* and introductions were made all around: they were Philip and Sheila Wellington of the catamaran *Doubloon*. A beer was brought up from *Vagabond*'s "wine cellar" (the bilge) and passed around to everyone sitting around the wheelhouse and sipped reverentially.

"Bloody marvelous," said Philip. "Haven't had a good warm beer in more than two weeks."

"Supplies are tight here too?" Frank asked.

"Tight?" Philip snorted. "If your whole wealth consists of your bare boat, then your food consists of seaweed, shellfish, rainwater, and fish." He looked at his wife with a warm smile. "We had no gold or silver, and we pawned Sheila's jewelry ten days ago to buy sailcloth and a week's worth of food. And beer doesn't exist here these days."

"Can food be bought?"

"Some, I suppose—with gold, silver, diamonds, jewelry," Philip replied. "And, ah, with pot and pussy. Such are at present the currency of your nation's former possession." Frank and Neil looked at him uncertainly. "You'll have to barter first with the precious metal dealers, then with the individual merchants. Very few shopkeepers will barter themselves, except a few who will deal in cannabis and a lady's favors."

"Is there much chance we can stay here, make a home here?" Jeanne asked.

Philip looked at her, grimaced, and looked away.

"Not bloody likely," he replied. "I'm afraid the world here is becoming a bit of a black-and-white thing, you know? Blacks don't seem to appreciate the fact that whites are blowing up the whole world and . . . uh . . . then the survivors running to the blacks for help.''

"But the Russians started it," said Tony from the port cockpit.

"Ah, well, I'm not certain too many blacks are sure of that.''

"St. Thomas is all black?'' Jeanne asked.

"Pretty much so," Philip replied. "And most of the refugees are white or now Puerto Rican. The rich whites who live here are holed up in various enclaves—those that haven't already left, that is.''

"What are *your* plans?'' Neil asked abruptly from his seat in the corner of the wheelhouse.

The big Englishman frowned. "The bloody war's gotten too close," he said slowly. "I suppose you know San Juan got hit? . . . We've decided to leave. We want to be part of a convoy.''

"A convoy?'' Neil asked.

"Pirates. You can't go twenty miles in any direction without having them all over you. Bloody trouble is you can't know who to trust. A friend of mine sailed off with another ship four days ago, and yesterday his ship turned up stripped and foundering while the other ship was reported sailing happily onwards a hundred miles from here. The world's not a nice place these days.''

"But where are you going?'' Neil persisted.

"Thought we might try Australia," the Englishman replied softly, staring at his hands.

"Australia!'' Frank exclaimed.

"My boat's too small, I know," said Philip, looking up intently. "But I have a friend who's got a fine old wooden sloop, fifty-five footer, she is, and—''

"But Australia . . .'' Frank said again. "Jesus. That's quite a sail.''

"It's quite a world, Frank.''

"Yes. I guess it is.''

"England doesn't much exist anymore, you know," he went on intently. "And since they bombed Puerto Rico and Venezuela, and the whites were massacred on Dominica, no one feels any too bright about this whole area. Everyone who can afford it is getting out. Food was short before on all the islands. Now it's almost nonexistent here. Things can only get worse, right?''

"Have you stockpiled much food?" Neil asked.

Philip snorted out a half-laugh in reply. "There are two types here: those who've got their gold and silver, and those who don't. The rich are selling it all to fly out of here now. And the rest of us fish." He laughed, and though his belly shook, his eyes weren't twinkling.

"What are you people planning to do?" asked Sheila, suddenly.

Frank didn't answer and a strained silence ensued.

"Survive," Macklin finally growled.

"Oh, yes, I know . . ." said Sheila. "But . . . well . . ."

"I'm sorry, Frank," said Philip. "But I suppose I've got to ask also whether in this new world you're rich or poor."

"We're poor," Jeanne said. "We only have a little food left, and none of the mineral wealth that passes for currency. We could never barter for enough food to go to Australia."

"Bit sticky for us all," commented Philip.

"I'm glad you're poor, Jeannie," Sheila said. "Anyone who has gold on his boat seems to have a lead anchor in his heart. Phil was saying as we rowed over here, 'Hope to Christ they're not hoarders.' "

"It's a paradox, I guess you'd say," commented Philip. "The way things are, if you had plenty of gold, you'd be the type that doesn't share, whereas since you, ah, haven't any gold, we'd be likely to help each other."

"How do you figure to help us?" Frank asked.

"Well, for one thing, give you advice on what you can and can't sell. For another, I've been here for almost a month, and I know not only St. Thomas but what's been happening throughout the Antilles. For example, when the war started, a few boats left for some of the islands south of here, but later starvation and revolution and civil war devastated two or three of the islands, and a lot of them came back. And now, after the explosion over San Juan, a lot of ships have put out to sea again."

"There seem still to be quite a few," Jeanne said.

Philip looked briefly out at the harbor. "About a third less than on Thursday," he said. "And half of them are motor yachts. Almost none of them has the fuel to go anywhere, even if they wanted to. Some came in yesterday from Puerto Rico."

"Is it possible to rent a house?" Jeanne asked.

"I suppose anything is possible if you have the means to pay for it," Philip replied. "But you won't be welcome."

"Can we at least get water free?" Neil asked. "We've got less than three gallons left."

"Water's rationed. You'll get some, but not enough for a voyage."

"Jesus, what's happened to traditional Caribbean hospitality?" Frank asked, frowning.

"It was obliterated, Frank," Sheila replied, her face as gloomy as the others', "the day the white man began bringing disease and death south with him instead of tourist dollars."

Her husband also frowned. "And of course the other reason is the plague," he said.

"The what?" Frank exclaimed.

"You'd best watch where you get your water from," Sheila explained. "There's some sort of mysterious disease on the islands—not many cases yet and worst on Capo Gorda—that kills about half the people that come down with it."

"Is that why the customs people took our temperature?" Neil asked.

"Yes," Philip replied. "It seems the disease is carried by Americans from the mainland, or so they say." He was frowning and didn't raise his head to look at the others. There was an awkward silence.

"Rainwater's safe," said Sheila.

There was another silence.

"When it rains," Philip added gloomily.

It only took them a few days on St. Thomas to realize that conditions were appalling. Black antipathy to white strangers was palpable in glances and gestures at every moment. In the month since the war the food shortages had already taken their toll. People looked gaunt,

walked slowly, squabbled violently over the tiniest disagreement about
food or water. They soon realized that the black men fishing at every
bridge and breakwater and along most of the docks were not fishing
for leisure, but for survival. The street vendor haggling over the price
of two oranges was haggling not because of "cultural tradition" but
out of economic desperation. The voluptuous black mother who spent
twenty minutes in the store manager's private office was not coldhearted or neurotic but only a human being gratefully cashing in her
last economic asset. In this world there were no luxuries, only necessities.

Human society on St. Thomas was falling apart. The government
was still paying its employees in paper dollars, which were no longer
being accepted by the few farmers, fishermen, and merchants who
had anything worth selling. Consequently government employees,
once the island's elite, were now working for nothing, whereas most
other workers—half the population was unemployed—bargained to
be paid in food and water. Pot-smoking and prostitution were now
public and open, since there were no facilities to jail offenders in, no
food to feed them with, and only unpaid, disgruntled policemen to
arrest and guard them. Bicycles and mules were the popular vehicles
of the new world. The airport was usually empty of both planes and
people, since most private planes had flown south and regular commercial flights to anywhere had ended when the fuel ran out or pirates
made off with the planes. The sight of an airplane over St. Thomas
two days after *Vagabond* arrived had sent such a rush of people from
town to the airport that when Neil saw it he thought he was witnessing some annual island bike race: over a hundred people pedaling out
to the airport as if their lives depended on it.

Everyone who could afford to leave either had left or was trying
to. With the food inadequate on all the islands, the poor, with nothing to lose, were beginning to demand forcefully their share of what
little was still left. On their first walk through the streets of Charlotte
Amalie Neil, Frank, and Jeanne had seen the broken and unboarded
windows of supermarkets and grocery stores, all of which were now
empty and deserted. Some downtown blocks had so many looted and
abandoned stores it seemed "the revolution" must already have occurred, and yet the local whites they were able to talk to still spoke
as if they feared a black uprising and takeover. There were four old

tanks parked along the waterfront. Except for the three white enclaves outside of town and the St. Thomas Hilton, Neil didn't see that there was much left on St. Thomas of value to "take over."

Settling on St. Thomas began to seem increasingly unlikely. In their first few days Frank was offered two different houses in exchange for *Vagabond,* but the desperation and hopefulness with which the owners made their offers sobered Frank considerably. He discussed with Neil the possibility of selling *Vagabond* to raise enough gold to fly most or maybe all of them to Brazil, but the prospect of arriving destitute in Brazil was unpleasant, and, worse, they would have to sell the boat before they could strike a solid bargain with a pilot.

And to complicate their situation still more, the news from the other Caribbean islands and from the rest of the world was dismal. Although the war seemed to be at a standstill, conditions worldwide were still getting worse. No one dared to declare the war was over. No government proudly announced victory or abjectly offered surrender, but reports of recent fighting had ceased—at least among the major powers. Battles for food and skirmishes between refugees and neutral countries trying to keep them out were increasing. U.S. government officials, still speaking from some unidentified underground headquarters, after three weeks of exhorting their fellow citizens to rally to defeat the Soviet Union, now spoke only of the steps that would have to be taken to save the surviving population. Although the government had spoken, there was no evidence that anyone was listening. From what could be gathered from the shortwave radio and an occasional newscast on the local AM station, the country seemed to be divided up into isolated pockets of survivors, each struggling independently to cope with their particular problems. Reports seemed to imply that more than two-thirds of the U.S. population was already dead.

Mass starvation on the mainland of the U.S. had not yet been reported. It was July, and survivors had plenty of natural growing things for nourishment—if they lived in areas uncontaminated by radiation—but throughout much of the rest of the world this was *the* problem.

Other diseases were now beginning to claim as many victims as radiation sickness and burns. Dysentery, typhoid, and cholera were becoming epidemic throughout those areas of the world where loss of electricity and overcrowding meant reduced and polluted water supplies. Worst of all, the mysterious disease from the western United States was spreading to places untouched by missiles, as it had to the Virgin Islands. Colombia, Venezuela, and four Central American countries had forbidden all immigration from the north, quarantining or exiling anyone caught illegally within their borders. The "flu" virus that had been talked about weeks earlier was now definitely more than a flu, but the etiology of the "plague" remained unknown. All that had been established was that the incubation period was between a week and ten days, that transmission seemed to have to be oral—through ingestion of contaminated food or water, or through mouth contact with someone infected. Flies that had been in contact with the sweat of an infected person could also contaminate food.

The prognosis was known now too. The disease began with stomach cramps, then a fever, then a high fever that might last five or six days, followed by either death or a remission of symptoms. Treatment was to reduce and control the fever—medication, ice packs, fluids, etc. Unfortunately none of them were very successful. Altogether about a quarter of the victims survived with no apparent permanent damage, and another quarter survived but seemed to be debilitated by the disease, lacking in energy and endurance, and about half died.

As a result, international travel and trade had almost stopped. Jeanne and Neil listened to a report that the Venezuelan air force had threatened to shoot down a Boeing 747 that had requested to land in Caracas after an eight-hour flight from Toronto, Canada. When the plane was almost out of fuel and circling outside the city, the air force did shoot it down. No one survived.

For the first time *Vagabond*'s crew discussed returning to the U.S. mainland, since it appeared that there they could still find enough food and perhaps a more friendly welcome. But Neil argued that radioactive fallout would be increasing for months, if not years, not diminishing. And the problem of avoiding the "plague," and of avoiding the violence of those who would fear them as carriers was also frightening. Moreover, most of the stored and growing food would already have been confiscated and controlled by previous settlers in each area, and when winter came these sources would be barely enough for them. Outsiders would not only be feared and kept away because of the "plague" but because of the burden they would place on the already limited carrying capacity of the region. Neil had listened to one shortwave report of a small renegade group of soldiers and a band of survivalists fighting a pitched battle for the food and shelter the survivalists had prepared. The broadcaster didn't know who had won, but it wasn't a game that anyone aboard *Vagabond* had any heart for.

Thus, although their stay in the harbor at Charlotte Amalie permitted them to recover from the weariness of being at sea for almost three weeks, by the end of a week a new kind of weariness was afflicting them: the fatigue of searching endlessly for some end to the threat of starvation, and finding none. Olly, with help usually from Jim, Lisa, and Katya, spent most of every day fishing—sometimes with hook and line, sometimes with a net along the shore—or raking for shellfish. Frank, possessive of Jeanne, took on with her the task of bartering for what little food was available in the city. Over the week they bartered away dozens of "useless trinkets": watches, shirts, shoes, necklaces, blouses, a transistor radio, the rest of Macklin's stolen cigarettes, Jim's remaining small supply of grass. Yet during the week they ate no better than they had at sea and had no more reserve food supply than when they had first dropped anchor. They were running to stand still.

So almost from their first day on the torpid streets of Charlotte Amalie Jeanne felt lost and uneasy. She had arrived wanting to find a home for herself and Neil and the others, for the alternative seemed to be an endless voyage from one hostile place to another. But as she talked to government officials, to shopkeepers, as she pushed her way through the devasted and littered streets or along the waterfront bartering for food, she could feel no connection with anyone, black or white, mostly just a powerful sullen hostility. She felt herself out of synch with the island and its people. By the third day she was just going through the motions. She wanted to leave.

It wasn't simply that she was white in a world that was mostly black. It was more than color. She sensed that for those who had lived on the islands for a few years anyone who had arrived after the holocaust—black, white, or Puerto Rican—was an outsider, an intruder, even, she realized with a start, a coward. To have fled one's homeland was to be guilty of selfish betrayal, even if that home had been blown off the earth and the homeland become a vast crematorium. And the anger and contempt with which most of the longtime residents responded to her and the other refugees was undoubtedly intensified by their own fear and their own desire to flee to some ultimately secure haven. A black woman whom she casually tried to befriend in the fish stall turned on her with unexpected hatred: "Go 'way, rich lady," she said fiercely. "You best fly while you can!" The woman's rebuke acted to reawaken Jeanne's own fears, made her begin calculating if she *were* still "rich" enough to flee.

It hadn't taken long to learn beyond any doubt the universality of the currency Philip had called "pot and pussy." Marijuana joints were traded as cigarettes had been during earlier wars. Bags of it were the big bills of island currency. And some women, if they were young and attractive and otherwise destitute, went to buy necessities from certain merchants quite reconciled to paying with their mouths or bodies. One merchant they'd heard about had, because of his own physical limitations, resorted to selling water or fruit or fish to certain women for "IOU's"—payment to be upon demand of bearer, who would not necessarily be the merchant himself. He, in turn used the sexual IOU's to buy things he wanted from other merchants.

The second real estate agent Jeanne had called upon, a dignified black man her own age, had offered her a month's free rent in a cottage he had at his disposal in return for her "friendship." The suggestion seemed to her not so much insulting as irrelevant, but it contributed to her feelings of uneasiness about St. Thomas.

So too did what was happening to Lisa and Jim. On their second trip ashore the two had discovered in the downtown city park a gathering of teenagers, black and white—the only aspect of local life that seemed comfortably integrated—playing guitars and drums, singing, smoking pot, even laughing, and often gathering around the latest street-corner prophet who was haranguing about doom or salvation or both. Almost every day after they'd worked with Olly, fishing or gathering shellfish, they went ashore and spent some time with their new friends. Katya sometimes went with them.

Lisa, although younger than most of the others, seemed determined to fit in with this society, which disturbed Jeanne mainly because she knew so little about them and had no control over Lisa's activities on shore. She could feel Lisa pulling away from her. Lisa and Jim would answer her questions about the Park Square people with code word replies: they were "cool, loving people," they were "nonviolent," but Jeanne felt only a dull feeling of dread at what seemed an aimless passivity in the face of starvation and disease. Katya didn't help matters when she said that Jim and Lisa were just trying to hold on to a little more of their normal lives before existence was, once again, solely devoted to day-to-day survival.

And finally the other thing that made her feel out of place in Charlotte Amalie was the absence of Neil. Since he stayed so often on the boat or off on other people's boats, she had no heart for the land. Neil was a major part of any new home, and if he was rejecting St. Thomas, then she must too.

And so, after six days, she felt that she was back where she had been on day one: on a ship without enough food to leave and without enough food to stay, unable to live with the man she loved because it would destroy the family that was her new world. And her children, whom she had vowed to save, to whom she felt she wanted to dedicate her life, grew steadily thinner, and Lisa, steadily more remote. The climax came one afternoon when Lisa was preparing to go ashore with Jim to visit their Park Square friends.

Jeanne confronted her down in their cabin as Lisa was changing from the wet clothes she'd worn earlier while seining for bait along the shore with Olly, Jim, and Tony.

"Lisa, sweetheart," Jeanne said to her. "I hardly see you these days. What do you *do* in the city every day?"

"We don't do anything, Mother," Lisa answered, slipping out of her one-piece suit and into panties and shorts. As she did, Jeanne noticed that Lisa seemed to be trying to show that she was unaffected by her own nakedness, not hiding her breasts as she'd done for most of the last two years.

"For seven or eight hours?" Jeanne asked, regretting her accusatory tone.

"There's not much to do, you know," Lisa replied, not looking at her mother. "This isn't exactly Washington."

"I know, I know," Jeanne said, trying to get away from the confrontational mood. "What do you talk about?"

"Lots of things," Lisa answered, pulling a blouse over her head.

She no longer wore a bra, partly because the only one she'd brought with her had worn out.

"But what are some of them, sweetheart?" Jeanne persisted. "I'm interested in your life, remember?"

"Oh, Mother," Lisa said with a sigh. "It's hard to tell you. About lots of things. The way you adults messed up the world. About how to scrounge for food. About what we want to do with our lives."

"How do most of your friends manage to get food?" Jeanne asked, handing Lisa the brush she knew she was glancing around for.

"Some of them fish," Lisa answered, beginning to brush her hair. "Garbage cans outside rich white people's houses. A few go house to house begging."

"Your friends beg?" Jeanne asked.

"Certainly, Mother," Lisa snapped back. "There are no jobs and no food. What do you expect?"

"Don't their parents manage to provide food?"

"Sometimes," said Lisa. "But most of us want to be independent of our parents."

"By *begging*?"

"It's better than blowing the world apart."

"I don't see how the parents here are responsible for the war," Jeanne responded, feeling annoyed by Lisa's self-righteousness.

"Some of them are white, mother," Lisa said, as if that explained it. "And Robby says all whites started it with their superrationality."

"Ah," said Jeanne, knowing she was too annoyed to enter reasonably into an abstract discussion. "I see."

"That's why music is so important," said Lisa.

"Yes . . ." said Jeanne, standing uncertainly in front of Lisa, who was ready to leave. "Tell me, sweetheart, is Jim your lover now?"

Lisa, who was about to escape, stood still, her eyes on the floor. She turned back to face Jeanne and she slowly raised her eyes. "Yes, Mother," she answered quietly, without defiance or apology.

Jeanne, who'd been holding her breath, let out a sigh. "I see."

"You and Neil—" Lisa began.

"It's all right, honey," Jeanne said, biting her lip and averting her face to look out the window. "I . . . Jim . . . Jim is . . . a fine man."

"I love him, Mother," Lisa said in a low, uncertain voice.

"I know, honey," Jeanne said and went over and hugged Lisa to her. "I know." They held each other for a half-minute until Jim's voice called to Lisa from the dinghy alongside *Vagabond*.

"But, Lisa," Jeanne said, releasing her daughter but blocking her path. "I don't want you abandoning the boat. Stay here. Make love here if you must."

"It's not that," she said, and, inexplicably, she seemed irritable again. "You don't understand. There's no life for us on the boat. Nothing but more of the violence that Neil and Frank seem to believe in. Some of the people in Amalie are different, and Jim and I are interested in finding a better world."

Jeanne felt herself stiffen again at Lisa's naive oversimplifications. It made her feel both sad and frightened that her daughter seemed to need to escape from the boat and the adults on it. Their world was falling apart. "But, honey—" she began.

"I'm going," Lisa announced and brushed past Jeanne and left the cabin. Jeanne followed, and as Lisa climbed down into the dinghy, she wanted to call her back or give her a warning of some sort, but she couldn't articulate her fears even to herself. "Lisa," she called down to her. "I . . . I want you to find a better world, but . . . just be certain it *is* a better world."

For a moment Lisa pretended to busy herself with helping Jim fit an oar in the oarlock, but then she looked up at her mother defiantly.

"It can't be any worse than the one that's sent us here to starve to death," she said.

Jeanne, feeling she had nothing better to offer Lisa, could only look down in shocked silence. Jim, smiling up at her awkwardly, shoved off and slowly rowed Lisa away.

For Neil, after a week on St. Thomas, land was again enemy territory. After their first few days anchored in the harbor he let any or all of the others go ashore to try to find food or a house or whatever it was they thought they wanted. He believed that each of them would soon realize the hopelessness of finding a welcome here. Whenever he left *Vagabond,* he was ill at ease, constantly looking back at the water toward the white, triple-hulled form of his ship, his home. Except when he was with Jeanne—then, together they carried home with them.

The idea of settling on St. Thomas went against his instincts. He worried that *Vagabond* might be hijacked, worried about the plague, worried about submitting to a governmental authority that was little better than a gang of pirates itself. His reaction to the appalling conditions on St. Thomas was ambivalent. While he sympathized with the native islanders and resented the rich whites flying or sailing off to other havens, he knew full well that he was one of the lucky ones who had the means to get away and knew he'd be happy to do it—indeed, was constantly scheming to be able to do it.

Yet that alternative, *all* the alternatives, were, as always, heartbreaking. Somehow, some way they had to take on enough food for a voyage even longer than the one they had just completed. Somehow, some way they had to get hold of the weapons to protect themselves against pirates and, eventually, Neil speculated, against foreign navies and air forces. Somehow, some way they had to find a place on the planet where they could feed themselves and be free of the great, leaning, gray weight of the nuclear holocaust. Somehow, some way. It was life.

He talked with as many sailors as he could, and although many said they wanted to escape, all were as stuck as he. The only difference was that many of them had lost confidence in themselves or in their boats and were waiting, stuck in their own stuckness. . . .

Philip and Sheila Wellington were exceptions. They were determined to get away, and since their thirty-foot catamaran's mast was cracked, they were trying to work out a deal with a man named Oscar White who owned an old fifty-five-foot sloop but had little skill or experience at sailing. Philip had become increasingly edgy over the week Neil had known him; he was convinced that St. Thomas was about to explode and that they had to get away.

On their eighth day on St. Thomas, Neil met with Philip again, this time on Oscar's sloop, *Scorpio*. The ship was an old racing boat, once queenly, now old and unmaintained, still solid, it seemed to Neil, but much of its gear was in need of repair and all its varnish and brightwork needed attention.

The three sat in the huge, airy open cockpit in front of the beautiful mahogany wheel, which alone was polished and gleaming. Oscar was an intense smallish man in his thirties, with long, wild blond hair, a big handlebar mustache, and narrow blue eyes. A former real estate broker, he had left his job, wife, and family for a fling in the Caribbean on a cheap yacht he'd planned to fix up and sail off into the sunset. The war had interrupted his idyll after less than two months.

His crew consisted of two young men who'd latched onto him in Fort Lauderdale. Gregg and Arnie were both wiry young men, much more laid-back than Oscar, and apparently happy to go along with whatever he decided. They were also friends of Jim, Lisa, and Katya. There were usually two or three young women aboard *Scorpio*, but none of them showed up for the conference, nor did Gregg and Arnie, content to remain fishing off *Scorpio*'s stern.

Philip and Oscar sat on one side of the cockpit and Neil on the other, each of them holding a tall glass of water as they once would have held gin and tonics.

"It's no use, Neil," Philip said. "There's no nonviolent way to do it. Believe me, I've tried."

Neil stared gloomily at his glass. Philip was one of the few men he'd met who perceived the situation since the war as he did: a struggle to the finish for individual survival, or rather group survival; Neil was committed not simply to himself but to Jeanne and to all who sailed on *Vagabond,* and now, although the commitment was unspoken, indeed perhaps unconscious, he was committed to Philip and Sheila too. But much as he liked Philip, he was less enthusiastic about getting involved with Oscar and *Scorpio,* although if Philip were to become *Scorpio*'s captain, he would go along.

"So what dishonest ways are there?" Neil replied. "I haven't seen much on St. Thomas worth stealing."

"I've been thinking about our situation a great deal," said Philip. "As Samuel Johnson said, 'The prospect of being hanged wonderfully concentrates the mind.' "

"And?" asked Neil.

"Both of us have two basic requirements: a large supply of food for a long voyage and weapons and ammunition," said Philip. "Without these two there's not much hope in setting out."

"Especially food," said Oscar. "We're already starving."

"Weapons as well," said Philip, flushing slightly but continuing to address Neil, sitting opposite him. "To get south we're going to have to run the gauntlet: the twenty or so islands of the Antilles, each of them home base for a pirate ship or two."

"How do you know that?" Oscar asked.

"I've been listening to the shortwave for a month. I've seen ships arriving stripped of everything but one sail. I've heard Maydays from vessels under attack. I haven't stayed here because I'm afraid of the sea or of starving. I'm afraid of the land, of the men who come from it."

"All right," said Neil, "but where in God's name can we get weapons? I thought you told me there wasn't even a black market in them."

"We get weapons, old boy," said Philip, brightening as if at last they'd come to what he wanted to talk about, "from the pirates."

Neil examined Philip's glowing face. "How?"

"I've sniffed out one of the pirate ships," he answered, becoming serious again. "It's a forty-two-foot Hatteras docked at Martin's Marina. Knowing what ships have been hit and when, and where *Mollycoddle* was at the time, I figured it out. That plus rumors in town and the unexplained wealth of her captain and crew."

"*Mollycoddle?*" asked Neil.

"A larky name for a pirate ship, eh? Yet Forester and the others, with no assets other than that ship, never lack for petrol, food, liquor, or barter goods necessary to buy women. They live like kings in a large estate they've taken over outside the city. Their sudden prosperity has only come upon them since the war began, since the breakdown of government has made piracy almost a risk-free crime.''

''You plan to get weapons from them?'' Oscar broke in.

''Precisely. We'll hit their ship,'' Philip replied.

''Is this Forester, Michael Forester, an Englishman?''

''I believe so.''

''Jesus Christ, count me out. That guy and his gang are killers. I mean they've shot people on the streets of Charlotte Amalie, and no one does a thing. Even the blacks are afraid of them.''

''I can understand your concern,'' said Philip, flushing, ''but when you've heard my plan, perhaps you'll change your mind.''

''You plan to raid their ship?'' Oscar persisted.

''Yes.''

''They'll outgun us three to one,'' said Oscar.

''Not when there's only one or two men aboard.''

''When is that?'' asked Neil.

''Every night the ship's in port,'' said Philip, again looking at Neil. ''They live on their estate. They always leave a guard on *Mollycoddle,* often two, I think, but I don't consider one or two overconfident guards an insurmountable obstacle.''

''Do they have radio contact with the estate?'' asked Neil.

''I believe they probably do, yes, in fact,'' agreed Philip.

''You think they keep their weapons aboard?''

''Some certainly,'' said Philip. ''Some on the estate. But the ship will be much easier to hit.''

''Food?''

''I'm sure the *Mollycoddle* is kept well stocked.''

''You steal the ship's weapons and food and then what?''

''We sail off into the sunset!'' said Philip triumphantly.

Neil frowned, considering all this.

''You're crazy,'' said Oscar. ''There'll be a dozen well armed pirates with a twenty-two-knot Hatteras chasing us to give us a cheery good-bye.''

''We scuttle the Hatteras,'' said Philip confidently.

''They have other boats,'' suggested Oscar.

"They're not certain who hit them," countered Philip.

Oscar shrugged, scowling.

"Let's hope so," said Neil.

"Also, we are now two boats, both armed to the teeth, sailing side by side. A rather unappealing target."

"Not when someone's mad," said Oscar.

"True," said Philip, flushing, "there *are* risks involved in piracy, my boy."

Philip was looking at Neil, his face glowing with excitement, while Neil watched the two young crew men aft getting excited as one of them reeled in a fish.

"It's too dangerous," said Oscar.

"There *are* risks involved in piracy," Philip repeated, looking at Neil, "but not as many as in being the victims of piracy."

"Screw it," said Oscar. "Those guys won't bother me. I haven't got anything worth taking."

Grimacing, Philip continued to look at Neil.

"I'm depending on you to iron out the military wrinkles in my little plan," he said to him. "I can but point the way."

"Any particular time frame?" Neil asked after a silence.

"Ah, yes, that," said Philip, suddenly frowning. "I'm afraid we may decide there's a bit of a rush. Three things. First, I heard a rumor today, just a rumor so far, that quite a few cases of that plague have appeared right here in the city." Neil stared at him in dismay.

"Not too pretty," Philip went on. "Secondly, let's face it, we're none of us getting any fatter. Our larders are already bare. I believe we should strike as soon as we can."

Neil nodded. "And the third thing?" he asked.

"The luxury cruise ship the *Norway* is scheduled to arrive here later this afternoon."

"My God," said Oscar. "How do you know?"

"Fred Turner on the *Spright* told me an hour ago. The *Norway* had been hung up in Santo Domingo since the war began, but the U.S. Navy has given her a huge supply of diesel fuel from its depot on Vieques, and the Norway is now carrying about five hundred Navy personnel."

"What's it doing here?" Oscar asked.

"Well . . . that we can only surmise. But clearly it will be taking on passengers. The sight of more rich people sailing off on a lovely white cruise ship is not likely to be greeted with enthusiasm."

"Maybe we could get aboard?" suggested Oscar.

Neither Neil nor Philip commented on this.

"It would be a lot safer than messing with Michael Forester," Oscar persisted.

"I wouldn't count on it," said Philip.

"Well, all I know is that if it's a choice of starving or tangling with pirates, I'll choose starving," said Oscar, standing up.

"I understand, Oscar," said Philip. "I respect your decision. But . . . if things work out, do you still want me to assume command of *Scorpio*?"

"You get me food and guns, buddy, and you can sail *Scorpio* for the rest of your life."

"Good," said Philip.

Oscar wandered aft to check on the fishing. "Well, Neil?" inquired Philip, leaning forward.

Neil shrugged, then smiled and raised his now empty glass.

"I'd like to see both the *Mollycoddle* and the estate," he said. "Is that possible?"

"Oh, absolutely," said Philip, grinning and standing up quickly with surprising grace for such a bulky man. "Sheila spent the morning reconnoitering the estate, and the *Mollycoddle* is moored at Martin's Marina. We've borrowed three bikes for the occasion." Philip was grinning triumphantly.

"Rather sure of yourself, weren't you?"

"You're a sailor, Neil. This hunk of filth called St. Thomas could no more hold you down than a cinderblock could hold *Vagabond* at anchor."

"You think I'll drag out to sea, do you?" asked Neil, smiling and standing up.

"Drag, old boy?" said Philip, coming forward to clap Neil on the shoulder. "No, sir. You'll *fly*."

"From the sound of your plan," he said, "I'd better."

That night Neil explained to Frank, Jeanne, Tony, and Macklin the plans they were developing for the raid on *Mollycoddle*. Although Macklin indicated approval, Tony, irritable, found a half-dozen weaknesses in the plans. Frank, looking fatigued, simply didn't feel that the possible gains justified the risks. After Tony and Macklin had gone down to the main cabin to prepare a small meal for themselves, Neil continued to pressure Frank in the darkened wheelhouse.

"No, Neil," Frank said, "I just can't see it. Someone would get killed. Your whole plan scares me."

"Frank, we've got to leave," Neil insisted. "There's nothing for us here. St. Thomas is close to exploding. Hundreds of people will leave on the *Norway* . . ."

"There's St. Croix, there's Puerto Rico . . ."

"Don't bullshit yourself!" Neil exploded. "In these islands there's only chaos, revolution, starvation, madness, and war. That's all we've found, that's all there is. It'll only get worse."

"And you think stealing another man's ship will improve things!"

"I want all of us to survive. And without food and weapons we won't make it."

Frank strode away from Neil and glared out across *Vagabond*'s foredeck at the few distant lights on the hillsides of Charlotte Amalie.

"I'm not sure I want to be an accessory to piracy," he said.

"Then you'll be an accessory to starvation and radiation sickness and death."

"We're still alive so far," he said huskily.

"By outsailing the fucking war! And that's what we've got to do now."

"And what about Jeannie and the children? They can't take the ocean. They need a place on land."

"I know that," said Neil, shaking his head and grimacing. "I know that, Frank. Believe me, I know that dragging everyone out to sea again isn't going to bring happiness, but this is probably our best chance. Philip's going to try to take the *Mollycoddle* whether we join him or not. Sailing in a convoy with him improves our chances against pirates. It would be nice if we could wait a week or a month, but we can't.''

"You're acting too fast, Neil," Frank said, shaking his head wearily. "Our food supplies are nil, our water low, and you want to solve all our problems, steal a boat from pirates, raid their estate, and put out to sea all in the next couple of days. It's too much. It's too sudden. I can't do it.''

"But you, yourself—"

"No! Leave me alone. I'm done. I'm sick. I'm exhausted. I'm going to my berth and sleep. I'm too tired to argue with you and too tired to agree with your plan. I'm sorry.'' And he left Neil to go to his cabin.

Neil stared after him angrily until Frank had slid the hatch closed behind him. Fists clenched, he walked to the opposite cockpit and was surprised to see Jeanne's hatchway open and Jeanne standing there, looking calmly up at him. Her face showed her fatigue. She was wearing Frank's bathrobe. The two of them looked at each other expressionlessly.

"So we have to leave again . . ." Jeanne mused softly.

"Apparently not," commented Neil, anger still in his voice.

"But you feel we should . . . steal some food and weapons and sail away.''

"Yes," Neil answered quietly, realizing that she had listened to the whole loud argument. "I'm sorry. I just don't see how we could make a home anyplace in the West Indies.''

Jeanne was still staring up at him, absently pulling the lapels of her bathrobe closer to her neck. She glanced across to Frank's cabin on the other side of the boat.

"Come down to my cabin," she said, turning and walking down the ladder. Neil swung himself into the opening and went down after her, sliding the hatch shut behind him. She stood facing him halfway down the narrow floor area of her cabin between her berth and Skip and Lisa's. Skip was presumably asleep in the darkness, Lisa ashore with Jim. Being alone with her sent something warm stirring through him, although the present situation was distinctly nonerotic.

"Frank's a gentle man," Jeanne said.

"I know."

"And Jim's withdrawal from the boat and his . . . relationship with Lisa has upset him."

Neil nodded, wishing he could see her face more clearly.

She hesitated. "And . . . us . . . that upsets him," she went on. "He . . . he's in no condition to make such an important decision, especially on such short notice. He's an awfully good man, but at the moment . . ."

"Yes?"

"I think you should go ahead with your plan without him," Jeanne concluded quietly, looking up at Neil. "I'd like to help in any way I can," she went on. "And I think it's important that Jim be part of it. And Lisa. And Katya."

"If they'll come," Neil said sullenly.

"They'll come."

Neil watched her carefully. She stood there, clearly exhausted, but with the same air of regal authority she always seemed able to maintain.

"It'll mean a long two-, three-, or even four-week ocean voyage," he said. "A lot of it like the one we had from the Bahamas, slamming, slamming, slamming. There won't be any escaping it."

She looked back at him and smiled. "I'm used to it." Then she shrugged a tiny shrug, her chin falling down. "But someday . . ." Tears had formed in her eyes.

Neil held her close and caressed her hair.

"Jeanne . . ." he said, holding her tightly. "When an animal is being chased, after a while all it wants to do is lie down and let the dogs take it. It wants it all to end."

At first she held herself stiffly in his embrace and then collapsed against him, her arms returning his hug, her hair pressed against his cheek. Although she made no sound, in her fierce hug he could feel the tiny tremors of her crying.

". . . Run . . ." she said.

"You keep running," Neil said. "Later, if you make it, you can have the leisure to worry about what *kind* of a life you want to lead. Right now, for us, the dogs are still at our heels.''

Jeanne nodded, but she looked sad and beaten.

"I love you," he said softly in her ear.

"Oh, Neil, how I wish we could . . .''

As she looked up at him Neil bent to kiss her, and as they kissed, lifted her up to put her on her berth.

"No . . .'' she said mechanically.

He climbed up beside her on the berth, wishing he could see her face, her eyes. Groping at the head of the bed, he found a flashlight and turned it on, letting its light fall against the far wall. She was staring upward, not looking at him. Her expression was tense, withdrawn.

For a long time, resting on one elbow he stared down at her.

"Hey," he finally said. "My name is Neil. I'm in bed with you.''

Tears welled up in her eyes, then she closed them and a grin appeared on her face.

"I guessed as much," she said.

"The least you can do is say hello," he continued, loving her smile and bending to kiss the tears in the corners of her eyes.

"Go away," she said, reaching up to put her arms around his neck and hold him close.

"Never," he replied, coming over on top of her. "Never," he whispered.

From the moment Jeanne drew Neil down on top of her and opened her mouth to his kiss, their desire, so long restrained, exploded in a series of passionate caresses and couplings that followed one another without words, thought, or conscious intent. The necessity of silence imposed by their unspoken concern for the sleeping Skip and the more distant Frank seemed to add to their sensual intensity. Occasionally they would emerge from their sexual universe to find themselves nose to nose staring at each other as if each had awakened from some unbelievably joyous dream. Their eyes would speak a brief acknowledgment of their jointly created miracle, but their mouths, as if afraid to break the spell, remained wordless. Then they would lose themselves again in fierce intertwining.

"Living God, Jeanne. . . .'' Neil finally whispered when exhaustion finally left them sated but still joined, back in a more normal world.

Jeanne, again beneath him, simply smiled up at him.

"Yes. . . ." she said.

Up in the wheelhouse Tony and Macklin sat by themselves in the dim light falling from the kerosene lamp, Macklin smoking, Tony sipping at some rum he'd bartered for earlier. Frank and Olly were below, sleeping. Although Katya had returned, Jim and Lisa were still ashore. Tony and Macklin had seen Neil follow Jeanne down into her cabin, but for the last fifteen minutes they had been talking about Neil's plans for the raid.

"The trouble is," Tony complained, "even if we raid the pirates and get some decent food, it just means more endless sailing." In the month since the war Tony had lost all his fat and was now muscular and slender. His boisterousness had given way to almost constant irritability. He and Katya had quarreled again a few minutes before, and it didn't help matters that she had compared him unfavorably with Neil. To give Jeanne and Neil privacy, Katya had gone aft to sleep in Neil's cabin.

"That's all there is, Tony," said Macklin quietly. "We'll never be safe until we're in the Southern Hemisphere. *Vagabond*'s the only way for outcasts like you and me to get there."

"Maybe," said Tony, "but I'm not sure I want to spend the rest of my life as a cabin boy."

"Oh, yeah, that," said Macklin, grinning. "That we can probably change."

"I'm getting a little tired of waiting," said Tony, starting to pace back and forth.

"As long as Neil and Frank are together you and I will be cabin boys," Macklin went on. "Let's face it, right now no one needs us. They have Neil. He's hardass enough to get them to save themselves. Without him they'd flounder."

"Without him they'd need me . . . us," said Tony.

"Yes, without him."

Tony stopped in front of Macklin, who was sitting with his accustomed heavy composure.

"I don't notice us doing much about it," Tony said.

"They'll do it for us," Macklin replied quietly, "if we give them enough time."

"Do what?"

"Split the boat apart. Send Neil packing. You don't think Frank is going to let Neil stay on board once he finds out he's balling Jeanne, do you?"

Tony looked uncertain.

"I don't know," he said. "Frank likes Neil, and if Jeanne went with him . . ." He paused. "He'd sure enough be pissed though."

"Unfortunately," said Macklin, "Frank seems determined not to see what's going on."

"Why don't we tell him?" asked Tony.

Macklin sat very still. Then he took out a cigarette, lit it, and took a long toke.

"Beats me," he replied.

Frank, bone-weary, nevertheless staggered out of his berth when Tony told him there was some trouble between Neil and "a woman." Confused, half-asleep, he had felt an instant flash of anger, convinced that Neil was hitting on Jeanne, but before he could ask for further clarification, Tony had disappeared.

Slipping on a pair of shorts and taking a flashlight, he stumbled up out of his cabin and went aft to Neil's cabin. He knocked on the hatch, then slid it open. Flashing his light down the ladder, he was startled to see Katya's bare legs and then her questioning face. She pulled a cover over the rest of her body.

Frank's first take was relief: so Neil was balling Katya, he thought. He was glad. But when he saw that the man in the berth was Olly, snoring peacefully, Frank blinked uncertainly.

"I'm . . . ah . . . looking for Neil," he said.

Katya blinked up at him. "He . . . went topside to check on . . . the anchor," she replied.

"Oh."

Frank closed the hatch and walked into the wheelhouse.

"Have you seen Neil?" he asked Macklin, who was sitting against the mizzenmast with his feet stretched out on the settee. "Tony said something about some . . . problem."

"He's in bed," said Macklin.

"No, I just checked there," Frank said.

"In bed with Jeanne," said Macklin indifferently.

Frank stayed where he was, turning the light off to leave himself in relative darkness. He felt fear. Unexpected and powerful fear. He walked reluctantly to the port cabin, hesitated, and then banged his fist down three times on the sliding hatch, like a judge gaveling for order. There was no response from inside. In a small burst of breeze *Vagabond* swung slowly off to port in the darkness, swinging on her anchor. Frank hammered three more times on the hatch.

"What is it?" he heard Jeanne finally say.

"I'm looking for Neil," Frank said harshly, even as he entertained a strong momentary hope that Macklin was wrong. Then he heard the sound of someone landing with a thump on the cabin floor.

He waited.

In another few seconds the hatch slid forward and away from him, a figure came quickly up the ladder and stopped on the top step, three feet away. It was Neil. After a pause he came out into the cockpit and confronted Frank. In the wheelhouse behind them Macklin was turning up the kerosene lantern, and its dim glow fell across Neil's bare chest. He was wearing only his swim trunks. Frank stared at him, Neil returning his gaze steadily. Then Frank saw on his shoulder a long black strand of Jeanne's hair.

"You goddamn son-of-a-bitch," he said automatically.

"No, Frank," said Neil. "I'm . . . sorry . . ."

Frank swung his fist with the same instinctive rage that had brought out the curse. The blow struck Neil solidly in the side of the head, sending him reeling to his right and tumbling into the cockpit seat. There he sat for a moment, stunned, his body turned sideways to Frank, touching the left side of his face.

"You heartless, selfish son-of-a-bitch," Frank said, his fists clenched at his side. Neil looked up at him, anger in his eyes too.

"Selfish, Frank, not heartless," he said.

"How *dare* you take advantage of that woman when she . . . she . . ." Frank wanted to say "she's mine," but the words stuck in his throat and he felt an urge to cry.

"I'm sorry," Neil said. "But sometimes something becomes more important than loyalty to a friend."

"A goddamn fuck!?" he shouted at Neil.

Neil looked up at him sadly. "Yes," he answered quietly.

Frank lunged at Neil to grab him by the throat, but this time Neil fell to one side to avoid the charge and grabbed Frank's left arm to pull him over and send him crashing into the back of the cockpit seat. Frank turned and reached for Neil again, but he pulled himself away. Blindly Frank got up to come at him a third time.

"Look, Frank, this is ridic—"

As Frank swung at him Neil ducked under the blow and slammed into Frank's chest, sending them back against the cockpit seat, Frank crushed hard against it by Neil's weight. The wind was knocked out of him, leaving him momentarily dazed. He felt Neil push himself to his feet and step back again, into the middle of the cockpit. Both men were gasping for air.

Frank looked up at him, feeling both a hatred that seemed to be unwinding out of control and a sad-little-boy impulse to cry, as if Neil were the neighborhood bully picking on him.

"Look, I know—" Neil began.

"You ever go down in her cabin again and I'll kill you!"

Neil stood uncertainly a few feet away, his fists clenching and unclenching at his side, sweat matting the hairs on his chest.

"Don't say that, Frank," Neil said softly. "You don't—"

"I said it! I mean it!" he shouted back. *"Stop betraying me!"*

Neil flinched at these words. Jeanne appeared behind him in her cabin entranceway, looking at Frank with a pained, frightened expression. Frank's heart ached for her: how he wanted to protect her, care for her.

"It's not Neil you should be angry with," he heard her say to him.

"Damn it, Jeanne, how could you!?" he asked huskily. Again he wanted to cry.

"Get below, Jeanne," Neil said, pushing her back with his left arm. Frank saw now that Katya, wearing Neil's robe, was standing in the wheelhouse beside Macklin and Tony, watching. And Jim and Lisa had returned, too, and were also staring at him. He felt beaten. Slowly he brought himself to a standing position.

"Have . . ." he began, but had to clear his throat. "Have I made myself clear?" he said to Neil with as much coldness as he could command, the sounds coming out huskily, like the words of a dying man.

"Yes," said Neil.

"Good."

The images of the others were blurred, barely distinguishable—later he realized that he must already have been crying—as he moved past Neil, shoved himself between Katya and Tony, and returned to his cabin. He had lost everything.

Guiltily, unhappily, Jim and Lisa escaped *Vagabond* with Katya, in theory to barter for some additional food out at a commune at Salt Point, but in reality to get away from conflicts they couldn't handle. They sailed with Oscar, Gregg, and Arnie and two young women from *Scorpio*. One was Oscar's girl friend, Janice, a plumpish woman of thirty with short curly brown hair. The other was a slender, nervous young girl named Mirabai who was vaguely connected with Arnie. Both women—and the men, too, he realized—struck Jim as frighteningly passive and apathetic. None of them seemed to have any ideas about how they might survive what was happening. They were vaguely hopeful that the commune might feed and take care of them, and only Oscar seemed interested in joining *Vagabond* and sailing farther south. Gregg and Arnie, often stoned on grass, seemed indifferent even to the prospects of the commune.

The old racing ship moved sluggishly, and Jim noticed how tentatively Oscar and his crew handled her. He was worried by the small anchor they threw overboard, especially when they paid out so little scope that a fresh breeze might well blow them out to sea. Oscar explained that their big anchor had been stolen. When Jim suggested that it might be advisable to put out another hundred feet of anchor line, they thought it was a swell idea.

By the time the three from *Vagabond* rowed ashore at Salt Point with Oscar and Janice, it was after four in the afternoon. Then, as they were pulling the dinghy up onto the beach, Gregg's shouts from *Scorpio* indicated that, even with the additional scope, *Scorpio*'s anchor was dragging with the rising wind. Oscar and Jim left the three girls and began rowing full speed back to the sloop. The three women were left to investigate on their own.

Salt Point was a barren peninsula stretching out from one of the three white enclaves that still survived on St. Thomas. It had become the unofficial home of a small group of homeless young whites and blacks.

As Lisa followed Janice and Katya into the low shrubs on their way across the peninsula toward the cove where Janice said the barter boat was reported to come, she moved reluctantly, unhappy at being separated from Jim. On the other hand she needed to be away from the tensions of *Vagabond* and looked forward to checking out the commune. Big Robby, the leader, preached that the end of the world was upon them—just three more weeks or something like that—and that all should take joy in the last days.

When they were halfway across the peninsula, they saw in the distance three or four rather dilapidated one-story wooden structures and some people. As they came nearer Lisa saw that two of the women in one group were bare-breasted and a man leaning back against the wall of one of the shacks was completely naked. Several people were smoking, and when they arrived at the clearing, she could smell the sweet odor of pot. A man with a bushy blond beard and long hair tied in a bun behind his head emerged from a shack near them. He was wearing cutoff jeans.

"Hey, welcome, good sisters," he said. "I'm Thunder. Don't think I've seen you around here before." He grinned at Katya.

"We're just visiting," she said.

"We heard good things about you," Janice added. "Thought we'd check it out."

"That's great, man, great," Thunder said, smiling and looking from one to another and then back at Katya. "We're getting dozens of new people every day. The last days are here and I guess everyone's finally learning to groove."

No one responded immediately to this, and in the pause Lisa introduced everyone to Thunder. A naked white man and a black girl walked by holding hands, the girl's long hair falling down her back. Lisa noticed how skinny they both were and that the girl's bony bottom was covered with a light coating of sand.

"We're not much on clothes here," Thunder went on, smiling. "Everyone's free to do what they want. Bare-assed or tuxedo, it's all cool here."

"But bare-assed is cooler," Katya commented, and Thunder laughed and reached out a bony hand to pat her on the shoulder.

"You're right there," he said. "Especially in this heat."

"Is there someplace to get something to eat and drink?" Lisa asked.

Thunder's face clouded. "There's a cistern about two hundred yards past that last house. Just follow the path. But it's getting low, so we have to ration. Our next meal's about dusk—only an hour—but I doubt the girls are back from buying the fruit and fish."

"We'll survive," said Lisa, tossing her dark hair away from her face.

"Yes . . ." said Thunder, looking at the three of them with a frown. "Hey, you know, I don't want to preach, but you cats ought to loosen up a bit, enjoy yourselves. This is the peninsula of love, man, and Robby's message is that we should *joy* in these last days. You folks appear a little down. Loosen up, man. Do what you will, but joy!"

They stared at him.

"We're a little done in by our sail," said Janice.

"Sure, man, I dig that. But you got to know that within a month the whole earth will be destroyed," Thunder elaborated, his bearded face strangely expressionless as he spoke.

"Things don't look too good," Lisa agreed tentatively.

"You got to *joy,* man. These are the last days. Let go!" He smiled at them and gave Janice an awkward hug. "If you want to get stoned the communal pot supply is in this first shack here. I'm afraid it's rationed too."

"No thanks," said Lisa.

"Joy, brothers and sisters," Thunder pronounced, opening his arms in a belated welcome. "Joy in all you do. The last days are here."

"Joy to you too," said Lisa shyly in a soft voice as Thunder strode away after two women who were following a path off to the left.

"May the last days find you soon," said Katya, so low that only Lisa could hear.

"Hey, Oscar asked me to get some pot," said Janice. "You go on ahead. I'll join you later."

Lisa and Katya walked on. When they emerged several minutes later from the shrub oak onto the beach they found themselves surrounded by six or seven other young women and girls and one man, all but two of them black, all watching a long powerful motor yacht slowly approaching a large mooring about forty feet from shore. The black women were wearing blouses and shorts, both so frayed in some cases they were almost in rags. The hot wind was blowing offshore at this point, and the water, despite the strength of the breeze, was calm.

"Excuse me," said Katya to the lone white girl, who was wearing only a bikini bottom, her small naked breasts a light stripe in her brown torso. "Where can we get something to eat?"

The girl frowned. "The boat," she said, pointing. "They bring it on the boat."

Lisa could see that two men had successfully tied their yacht to a mooring about fifty feet out.

"I say, are you girls coming or not?" one of the men yelled from the bow of the yacht.

"Bring us the little boat, mon!" one of the black women shouted back.

"Oh, no," the man shouted back, grinning. "You can swim out today. The exercise will be good for you."

"Put the boarding ladder down!" shouted a pudgy black girl, slipping off her brightly colored but tattered blouse, and putting it down neatly next to another woman's basket. The woman then ran four or five strides into the water, made a clumsy dive, and began swimming out to the yacht.

"Ah, shit, I can't swim," one of the other black girls said as two more prepared to swim out.

"Hey!" shouted the white girl to the man standing on the bow watching the swimmers. *"I can't swim!* How about a lift?"

"Later, sweetheart," the man replied. "We'll let these ladies row in with what they buy."

"Oh, shit," said the white girl to herself. "By the time we get there they'll be tough to bargain with."

"Who cares?" said a black girl. "We'll eat anyway."

"Shit, rotten mangoes and fish."

"It food, I eat it."

Lisa and Katya stood just behind these two, watching the three women who had swum out to the yacht. One by one they climbed up the boarding ladder on the starboard side and stepped down into the huge cockpit. The yacht's bow was pointed directly at them, so Lisa couldn't tell what was happening on board. The man who'd been on the bow went aft when the women began climbing aboard.

Three of the women still on shore now moved off along the beach and seemed to have lost interest in the yacht, leaving only Lisa, Katya, and the black girl who was desperate for any kind of food. When Lisa looked out again, she saw two of the men peering over the top of the high windshield and examining her and Katya through binoculars.

In another few minutes a dinghy appeared from astern, and a black woman climbed down into it and paddled toward shore. The girl in front of Lisa and Katya walked down to the water's edge to meet her.

"Fucking white pigs!" the returning woman said, throwing the oar up the beach. She retrieved a small cardboard carton half-filled with mangled fish from the bottom of the dinghy and came toward them.

"You want food," she said to Katya as she approached, "go get it. They tol' me to tell you they feeling generous. They like white girls."

Lisa began to walk down the beach to the dinghy. As she did she noticed the men had tied a line on the dinghy's stern, which was attached at the other end to their yacht. Katya had been slow in following, but now she stood beside the dinghy just as the last black girl had sullenly climbed aboard.

"Coming?" she asked Katya gloomily.

Lisa looked at Katya.

"Who are these men?" Katya asked slowly as if calculating.

"They bring food and stuff every few days," said the black girl.

"Is there ever any rough stuff?" Katya asked.

"Why they use rough stuff?"

"Do they have guns?"

"I never seen none. You, June?"

"Oh, they got guns," said the women who had been on board. "They pirates, mon."

"Pirates?" Lisa echoed.

"My God, that's the *Mollycoddle*," Katya exclaimed suddenly, remembering Neil's presentation the night before.

"Sure. They *famous*," said the black woman.

"You stay here," said Katya to Lisa. "I'm going out to take a look."

"Shouldn't we wait for Jim?" Lisa asked.

"I'll be all right," said Katya. "The only thing I've got they might want to take can't be permanently removed." She laughed nervously and then walked down the beach and after a long hesitation dove into the water.

As Lisa watched Katya's slow progress the last black girl was having trouble pulling the dinghy into the water; Lisa helped her and, when the boat was afloat, impulsively jumped in beside her.

Katya had swum past the boarding ladder to examine the yacht's transom—to verify that this was indeed *Mollycoddle*—so that Lisa and the black girl arrived before her. When they boarded, they were greeted by two white men, dressed neatly in blue Bermuda shorts and clean white sport shirts, and immediately offered a lit joint. The older of the two, a pale white man in his late thirties with sideburns and a baseball cap, paid special attention to Lisa. One of the two black girls still aboard was lounging topless on a cushioned chair in the huge open area aft, smoking woozily. She seemed disoriented when the joint was passed to her. When Katya pulled herself up the ladder, her wet T-shirt clinging to her breasts, the other man looked at her with frank interest.

"I say, you look better clothed than most women do naked," he said to her. "I'm Michael."

Katya shook her curly blond hair and with both hands squeezed the water out of most of its length.

"Hello," she said coolly, looking carefully around the boat. "We'd like some food."

"Why certainly, darling. What would you like?"

Katya accepted the proffered joint as Lisa had done and took a distracted puff. "What have you got?" she asked.

"Over here," said Michael.

"How old are you?" the man with the baseball cap asked Lisa. He was short and thickset, with powerful forearms, and though Michael seemed to have an English accent, this man was American.

"Fifteen," said Lisa, feeling self-conscious under his frank appraisal of her figure.

"That's nice," the man said. "You been in the commune long?"

"No, I'm just visiting."

"You'll love it," he said, grinning. "Everybody loves it."

With Katya and the black girl looking into some cans and boxes on the other side of the deck, Lisa became aware of a loud male grunting coming from the main cabin forward. A woman's suppressed little half-screams occasionally accompanied the grunting.

"Sounds like Robert must be selling the whole stock," Lisa's admirer in the cap joked to her.

"I'd like as much of the fruit as you can spare," said Katya. "You can keep the fish."

"Why certainly, darling," Michael said. He was tall, slender, and clean-shaven, with hard blue eyes that glittered happily. "How much fruit would you say we can spare, mate?" he asked his shorter friend.

"Quite a bit," said the other.

"I think we might be able to part with all the rest, don't you think?" said Michael, not actually paying much attention to the older man.

"Certainly."

"Thank you," said Katya. "May I take the basket too?"

"I think that might be arranged," said Michael.

"Fine," said Katya, abruptly lifting the straw basket of fruit and striding back toward the boarding ladder. "Let's go, Lisa."

Michael grabbed her arm in mid-stride, and as Katya spun sideways, a few oranges spilled forward onto the cockpit floor. Katya remained in a half-crouch, holding the basket clutched to her chest and staring at the fallen oranges, Michael still holding her arm.

"Payment, darling," Michael said quietly. "The matter of payment, don't you know?"

Katya slowly lowered the basket to the floor and then straightened up. She looked slowly over at Lisa. Now the sounds of the woman's gasping screams, whether of pain or pleasure—Lisa, frightened, couldn't tell—came sharply from the forward cabin. In the silence of the confrontation between Katya and Michael the screams seemed horrendously loud and obscene.

"You got to pay them," the sullen black girl said.

"It's only fair," said the other black girl drowsily.

"Besides, darling," the man named Michael said, seeming to ease his grip on Katya slightly. "These are the last days, remember? Nothing matters. Take joy in all you do."

"That's right," said the sullen black girl gloomily.

"Of course," said Katya, shaking her head as if clearing it. "I'm new here and just didn't know." She smiled at the man, whose big hand still held her arm. And then she added in a voice so soft and husky and sexy it startled and frightened Lisa, "How do you like it, Michael? You name it, I'm good at it."

Lisa thought that even Michael looked surprised at the sudden sexual power Katya seemed to be turning on him.

"Don't forget me," the older man said nervously.

Katya turned to the other man. "I'll take care of you too," she said huskily.

The noises from the cabin had ceased.

"But what about these other girls?" she added, still in her new husky voice. "Don't they get some food too?"

"Certainly," said Michael. "Help yourselves, girls. Take the dinghy ashore with your food. It's been lovely seeing you again."

"Oh, no," said the man in the baseball cap. "I've got a little girl here who wants to pay too, right, honey?"

"Go, Lisa," said Katya sharply.

The older man grabbed Lisa firmly by the arm.

"And miss the fun?" he said, smiling.

With a swiftness that caught everyone by surprise, Katya pulled a short mahogany boathook from its staple near the control panel shelf and whacked the older man a vicious blow on the side of his head, forcing him to release Lisa and stagger away.

"Swim!" shouted Katya, turning to swing at Michael who was approaching her in a crouch.

Lisa took two steps toward the yacht's combing and glanced back to see Michael duck under the boathook, tackle Katya, and send her sprawling while the third man was coming at her with a pistol. Then Lisa hopped over the combing and into the water. As she surfaced and began swimming for shore she heard a man shout, then Katya scream.

Lisa slipped once as she staggered out of the water and, seeing two men getting into the dinghy to pursue her, broke into a run toward the shrubs. Even as she darted down the trail across the peninsula she wondered if she should turn back to try to help Katya. It was getting dark, and she decided to get off the main trail and find a place to hide. She tripped once and fell, immediately springing up to run forward. Seeing a small fire and a shack ahead of her, she ran for help.

When she appeared in the firelight, an old black man who had been sitting beside the fire leapt up.

"Git away!" he shouted. "Go!"

Lisa stood frozen, trembling, almost unable to speak. "I . . . I need help," she finally blurted. "Some men—"

"Go 'way!" the old man shouted, then turned to look at the shack ten feet away.

A young white man and woman were crawling out of the entrance, their eyes red and watery.

"Water," the man called feebly. "Please help us. Water . . ."

"Get back in there!" the old black man shouted and brandished a heavy stick at the two feeble specters. "Back! Back!"

Lisa gasped as she suddenly realized that the two were sick, feverish. Glancing back in terror for a sight of her pursuers, she ran on. She hadn't gone more than forty feet when she came upon the burnt-out remains of another shack, the white bones of three skeletons gleaming in the dim light of dusk.

Whimpering, she ran on, no longer aware of exactly what she was fleeing, only needing to run, to escape the horrors that seemed to explode into her life in an unending series.

At dawn the next morning Jim reported to Neil that Katya and Lisa were missing. Earlier, after he and Oscar had finished reanchoring *Scorpio*, they had begun looking for the three women, but found only Janice. They traced Katya and Lisa to the beach where the barter boat had been moored and then . . . nothing. A black girl on the beach told Jim that the men on *Mollycoddle* had motored off with "de sexy white girl" but that she thought the younger white girl must have escaped. Although Janice and Oscar had abandoned the search when it got dark and returned to *Scorpio*, Jim had kept looking another four hours, finally stealing a bicycle to ride the ten miles back to Charlotte Amalie, and then had swum out to *Vagabond*.

For Neil and Frank and Jeanne it was clear that now they *had* to raid *Mollycoddle* and probably the estate too. Katya—if she were still alive—was probably either on the boat or out at the pirates' estate. Lisa had either shared Katya's fate or had escaped and was already back on *Scorpio* or making her way to *Vagabond*. Neil suspected that Lisa would have tried to find Jim if anything untoward had happened, and thus would have tried to make her way back to *Scorpio*. Through binoculars they soon determined that *Mollycoddle* was moored at her berth at the docks, but that *Scorpio* hadn't returned yet. They guessed that Oscar was too timid and inexperienced a sailor to try to sail the ten miles back to Charlotte Amalie harbor in the dark.

Neil ordered Jim and Tony to go back to Salt Point and contact *Scorpio*, hopefully to find Lisa there. In any case they were to help sail *Scorpio* back to join *Vagabond* in Charlotte Amalie. After Katya and Lisa were both safe—God willing—and additional food and weapons had been garnered from the raid, the two boats would set sail together for southern waters.

Jeanne's concern over the disappearance of Lisa was mostly assuaged by Jim and Tony's departure to search for her, and Neil next signaled the Wellingtons with the air horn to begin final plans for trying to save Katya and Lisa and, once again, themselves.

Eight hours later Jeanne walked slowly along the dock, holding a wide-brimmed straw hat on her head with one hand to prevent its being blown off by the wind. Ahead of her and to the left was *Mollycoddle,* tossing in the rough seas that were rolled in by the storm, its stern facing her, the wind blowing it a few feet off the dock, its mooring lines taut. She was wearing a black bikini top and a blue denim skirt, the skirt necessary to hide the small automatic strapped to the inside of her right thigh: the brief bikini top was to guarantee a friendly reception by *Mollycoddle*'s guardians. Neil's last stern-faced words to her after he'd helped her strap the gun to her thigh were, "Don't let anyone feel you up."

At this moment he was, Jeanne hoped, in *Vagabond*'s dinghy, hidden six boats back. Philip was casually fishing from the dock a dozen yards behind her. Olly and Conrad Macklin, with binoculars, were seated in the park area "admiring the boats." Neil had asked Frank to remain on board *Vagabond,* telling him that if Neil himself were killed, Frank had to be safe to take over leadership. He was to join them only after they'd succeeded.

As she neared the stern of the pirate yacht she saw no sign of life. Neil said they were certain there was at least one man aboard and Philip thought there were two, but whoever was aboard was below. Perhaps the hot wind from the distant hurricane had discouraged them. Or worse, perhaps Katya was there with them, and Lisa. . . .

Timing things carefully, she waited until she was exactly opposite the open cockpit of *Mollycoddle* and then released her hold on her hat. It went flying off toward the yacht, Jeanne uttering a little scream. The hat sailed into the cockpit as planned, but then bounced on a seat cushion and flew out the other side, no, hit a metal strut and dropped back into the cockpit. She stared at it wide-eyed. In theory a guard was supposed to come out, rescue the hat, engage her in conversation, and ask her aboard. Nothing happened.

Glancing up and down the dock and trying to look upset and pathetic, Jeanne walked over to the edge of the dock and contemplated either hailing *Mollycoddle* or going aboard after her hat.

"Ahoy in there!" she said in as helplessly feminine a voice as she could muster, the rushing of the wind in the rigging of nearby sail-boats effectively drowning her voice. No one responded. There was four feet of open water between the dock and the combing of *Molly-coddle,* an easy jump for Jeanne, if only the gun didn't work loose. Steadying herself on the dock, gauging the distance carefully, she leapt into the yacht's cockpit, letting herself fall forward with a crash onto her left side, screaming a good loud scream and lying there contorted and moaning.

In a few seconds the cabin door opened and a large, bare-chested man holding a pistol appeared, staring at her fiercely, then looking up along the dock.

"What the hell are you doing here?" he asked with a distinctly American accent.

"My hat," said Jeanne, grimacing in pretended pain and pulling down her skirt and adjusting her legs so that her armament wouldn't show. Then, sitting up, she gestured at the straw hat lying on the other side of the cockpit.

"And you jumped after it, huh?" the big man said, now grinning, his handlebar mustache flicking up at the ends.

Jeanne nodded, rubbing her left ankle, which she decided she had twisted. But not badly. She didn't want to be carried.

"Need some help?" he asked, stuffing his pistol in between his belly and his shorts.

"No, no, I'm fine," she said, holding up a hand to restrain him. "I'm just a little bit in shock, I guess." She looked up at him and smiled wanly. He stared at her breasts.

"You want a drink or something?" he asked.

"Oh, no, I don't want to bother you," Jeanne said, standing awkwardly. "Although come to think of it, a drink would be nice."

"Hey, Mike, can the lady have a drink?" the big man asked, and Jeanne saw a tall, slender man wearing a neat beige sport shirt and shorts standing in the cabin door. He was eyeing her coldly. She smiled at him. He smiled back.

"Certainly, Bart," he said. "We wouldn't want her to leave in pain. She might sue us."

Jeanne laughed prettily.

"Come in, darling."

"Said the spider to the fly," said Jeanne as she limped past Bart and Michael and into the luxurious main saloon of the Hatteras. There was no one else there.

"Wow, this is something," Jeanne said as she paused in the middle of the plush carpet and looked around, still half-hoping, half-fearing to discover signs of Lisa's presence.

"What would you like to drink?" asked Michael. "Please sit down."

"Thank you," said Jeanne, sitting down in a leather chair and quickly crossing her legs. "Gin and tonic?"

He laughed. "How about some rum?" he asked.

"That's fine too."

"Bart?"

"Sure, Mike," said Bart and went forward into the far part of the galley.

"I'm Michael Forester," said Michael.

"I'm Jeannie Wilkins," she said after an awkward hesitation.

"And what brings you tumbling into the *Mollycoddle*?"

"Stupidity, I guess. My hat blew onto your boat."

"A likely story," said Michael. "Are you sure it wasn't because you noticed my handsome face in the street and followed me here out of uncontrollable lust?"

Jeanne smiled, again awkwardly. "If I'd seen you before, I might have!" she managed, smiling more broadly.

"Are you often overcome with uncontrollable lust?"

Jeanne felt a bit overwhelmed. At the rate this conversation was going, Michael would have her in the sack before Neil had paddled halfway here.

"Only on hot, stifling days when there's no wind," she answered.

"Ahh," said Michael. "What disappointing weather then, no?"

Bart entered with the drinks, handed them around, and kept a bottle of beer for himself. He sat down on a second easy chair in the saloon.

"Cheers," said Michael.

"Anyone aboard?" a loud voice came from the dock outside.

"See who it is, Bart" said Michael, frowning.

Jeanne tensed. This was the proverbial it. She uncrossed her legs and straightened in her chair. She wished she'd practiced drawing the gun. Bart arose, put his beer down, adjusted the gun in his belt, walked up the two steps, into the cockpit, and looked to his left.

"What is it?" she heard him say to Philip.

"Have you a gaff I can borrow?"

"You seem nervous, Jeannie," she heard Michael say and saw him staring at her with a suspicious frown. "What's the matter?"

"That man's voice . . ." she said uncertainly.

"Yes? What about it?"

The yacht lurched as if a sudden new weight had been added. Michael and Jeanne both saw Bart standing in the center of the cockpit but facing away from the door now with his arms raised.

"Don't shoot, buddy," Bart said loudly.

Michael leapt up, rushed past Jeanne, and opened a drawer from which he drew a pistol. He then crouched behind her chair, facing the cabin entrance. Jeanne was stunned by such a piece of bad luck: Michael had chosen the one place where he would inevitably see her if she tried to draw her gun.

Neil and Philip appeared in the cockpit, Neil nudging Bart, who, with arms raised and empty-handed, was coming down into the cabin.

"He's got a gun on me, Mike," Bart said when he saw Michael's pistol trained on them.

"All right, lady," said Neil. "Get into the galley with your hands behind your head."

"You move, lady," hissed Michael, "and I'll kill you."

"Go ahead and kill her," Neil said evenly. "She's none of our business. *Move, lady!*"

Slowly Jeanne stood up and, appalled, terrified, walked slowly toward the galley area.

"What do you want?" Michael asked tensely.

"All we want——" began Neil.

"Don't turn around," interrupted a voice from behind Neil and Philip. "Throw your guns on the rug."

Someone Jeanne couldn't see had come into the cockpit behind Philip and Neil and had a gun on them. Neil, after a brief hesitation, threw his gun onto the rug between Bart and Michael. Philip threw Bart's gun and his automatic after it and Jeanne reached down, lifted her skirt and, her hand trembling, pulled out the loaded .38 automatic. She remembered to press the safety as Neil had instructed her to and held the weapon in front of her, hidden by the counter that separated the main part of the galley from the saloon.

Bart picked up their guns and Michael stood up behind the leather chair. A third man, black, pistol in hand, appeared in the cabin entrance behind Philip and Neil.

"Who in bloody hell are you two?" Michael hissed angrily. He thrust his pistol violently into his belt and crossed to the couch to retrieve his barely touched glass of rum. He glared at Jeanne, not really seeing her. Neil didn't reply.

The black man behind Neil and Jim spoke: "Okay, mon, you get over against that wall there. Bart, you search them."

Neil and Philip walked slowly over to the wall on the other side of the main saloon. Bart dropped Philip's gun onto the couch behind Michael and ambled over to Neil and Philip. Michael and the black man both took their eyes off Jeanne to watch what was about to happen.

She froze. As soon as she spoke and showed her gun they'd turn and shoot her. Three to one. And then Neil and Philip. She was unable to raise her gun.

"They're clean," Bart announced after his search.

Michael turned to Jeanne.

"Perhaps you had better check the lady too," he said.

Jeanne stared at him, wide-eyed with fear. As Bart came toward her she reacted instinctively: she crouched and raised her gun to her eye level, aiming it directly at the black man whose pistol was still pointed at Neil.

"Drop it!" she snapped, so sharply it astonished her. Her eyes were wide, hysterical, only her head and the gun barrel were visible above the galley shelf. Bart stopped and all of them watched her, motionless and uncertain.

Then the black man swung his pistol at her and fired, and Jeanne pulled the trigger, the gun jumping in her hand, two shots following one after another in less than half a second. Neil leapt on the man who had shot at her, ripping the gun from his hand, and Jeanne shifted her aim to Michael, who was standing only eight feet away, his hand frozen on the butt of the gun in his belt.

"Don't shoot!" he screamed.

Neil took Bart's weapon and stood behind him with two guns, one in each hand. The man who had shot at her had been hit and was sitting on the floor, clutching his shoulder and looking at Jeanne with both surprise and pain, as if she had committed a social faux pas by shooting him. Philip began retrieving the weapons on the couch and the rug.

Michael slowly turned to look at the wounded black man, now slumped back against a chair, at the bewildered look on Bart's face, at Philip now complacently pointing a .45 straight back at him, and finally at Neil, who was smiling at him tensely.

Finally, slowly, Michael looked back at Jeanne. He stared at her with frank hatred.

"You bloody bitch," he said quietly. "Are the boobs fake too?"

"I'm afraid that information is classified," Neil answered, coming up behind Michael to remove the gun from his belt.

"You'd better pray I never get a chance to find out for myself," Michael said.

Jeanne, feeling safe at last, lowered her gun onto the counter top and leaned against the counter. The big war might be over, but the small wars seemed to be getting worse.

In planning their raids on *Mollycoddle* and the pirate's estate Neil and Philip had felt that the storm passing south of them could work to their advantage. Normally the easterly trade winds made it difficult to sail east from the Virgin Islands, but the counterclockwise rotation of the storm system would give them a southerly wind as it moved westward. What they had failed to consider was the unexpected size of the storm and the leisurely pace with which it moved to the west: the waves it was sending northward were huge, much larger than they had anticipated, as was the wind: thirty knots and gusting to forty-five.

Standing with Philip on the dock beside the captured Hatteras, which Olly, Macklin, and Jeanne were busy ransacking for everything of value, Neil could feel doubt and fear blowing through him with the hot wind. Events were moving too fast, involving too many people, too many variables, too many unknowns, to permit him to deal with all that had to be done. The wind and seas were rocking the boats at the dock, and Neil watched the swells rolling into the supposedly protected harbor with increasing anxiety. The noise of halyards and lines beating against masts, the wind whining in the rigging, and the waves slamming against docks and boat hulls were unnerving. As they tried to discuss their plans Philip had almost to shout to make himself heard.

"I don't like this blow," he shouted. "I'm not sure we have the time to raid the estate before dark."

For Neil the initial purpose of the raid—food and weapons—was no longer worth the risk. But there was the question of Katya and Lisa. Neither had been aboard *Mollycoddle*, and Michael and the others wouldn't tell them who was at the estate.

"We need food," Neil replied loudly to Philip. "There's too damn little on *Mollycoddle*." He was watching the waves rolling in at them; at times froth blew off the tops in a horizontal saltwater rain. The Hatteras had already produced two automatic rifles, a small shotgun, four automatics, at least two pounds of marijuana, four bottles of rum, but only a small cache of food. Either Michael and his men bartered for food on a daily basis or their food supply was at the estate.

"I know," said Philip, "but this wind . . . I don't know. Is it worth it? There's the girl, of course."

"The girl's worth it, Phil," Neil answered grimly, feeling a disturbing lethargy and dread, as if nothing were worth the effort, and as if any enterprise they set off on now were doomed from the outset. "And Lisa might be there too. I know we're going to have a hell of a time getting out to sea in this, but . . . I *have* to go out there. If you want to—"

"No, no. If that's the case, let's get on with it."

So they went ahead. Bart and the wounded black man were tied up in the forepeak of the Hatteras while Michael was to accompany the raiders to the estate. The plan was to use *Mollycoddle* right up to the last minute to tow *Vagabond* up over her anchors and get her out of the harbor against the strong winds. *Scorpio* too would need a tow if she returned; she was already overdue. Neil only hoped that *Vagabond* didn't drag anchor before they got back out to her. It was already past four thirty: only two and a half more hours of daylight.

They divided into three groups. Frank and Olly were to barter some of *Mollycoddle*'s marijuana and surplus weapons and other "useless" valuables for food while Neil's raiding party went up to the estate. Sheila and Conrad Macklin would remain to guard *Mollycoddle* and continue to try to make radio contact with *Scorpio* while waiting for her return. The "raiding party" consisted of just Neil, Philip, and Jeanne with their hostage, Michael. They rode bicycles.

Neil felt frail and vulnerable on a bicycle, and the gusty wind increased his feeling that events were moving too quickly, decisions being made too hastily. He wondered how many officers had led their troops into battle on a bicycle. Although the three others had ten-speed bikes, Neil rode a cumbersome old one-speed and had to labor to keep up with his prisoner. Both of them were periodically blown several feet to one side by a gust of wind.

The estate was a large rambling summer house overlooking the water. It had a swimming pool on one side and a set of swings and a slide on the other. Its only landscaping was a few low shrubs and flower beds. The grass was dry and brown from lack of water. In the driveway was an old Ford station wagon with its hood up.

Michael was ordered to hold his empty pistol and pretend that he and Neil, who was armed with a loaded automatic rifle, were guarding Philip and Jeanne, who preceded them up the gravel walk to the front door with their hands clasped behind their heads.

A little man with glasses opened the door, gun in hand, to Michael's knock and hail. "What's all this?"

"Some new booty," Michael answered sullenly.

Philip and Jeanne pushed their way in past the little man. Michael, with a tense glare back at Neil, followed them.

"I say, who are you?" the little man asked Neil.

"Michael's cousin," Neil answered, smiling and holding the automatic rifle casually pointed at the little man's stomach. The living room had two couches, some handsome carved wooden chairs, and a piano.

"Oh, really? Where'd you come from?"

No one else appeared to be in the room. Neil saw Philip lower his hands, remove the revolver he had wrapped up and tucked in as part of his belly, and move toward a doorway at the far end of the room. When the bewildered little man turned to watch, Neil hit him in the neck with a karate chop and dropped him to the floor.

Neil crouched back against the closed front door watching Philip approach the doorway at the far end of the room. Jeanne came up to him.

"My gun," she said softly to Neil, and he remembered and pulled the automatic out of his belt and handed it to her. At the far end of the room Philip disappeared through the doorway, and there was a bang that made Neil swivel his gun to the right: the wind had blown a shutter loose and it had banged alongside a window there. As he watched, still tense and trying not to tremble, it banged again. Philip came back from the far room.

"Kitchen," he said. "I'd say it's quite well stocked."

"Call your friends," Neil said to Michael. "Ask them to come down here."

Michael glared at him without replying. Neil swung his rifle toward his stomach.

"Jeanne," he said. "Go into the kitchen and start getting the food into boxes and bags. Michael, I'm waiting. Call your friends."

Michael turned and walked slowly over to a second doorway off the main room. As Neil followed he saw that it led off into a hallway with a closed door and a stairway to the second floor. Michael stopped near the stairway and called:

"I say! Larry! Rick! Tolly!" he shouted. "Come down and have a chat! It's me, Mike."

A door opened upstairs.

"Welcome home, old buddy," an American voice said. "What brings you back so soon?"

"I brought you a lady, Rick. Tall, dark, long hair. I know how fond you are of long hair."

"Be right down."

"Ask who's around," Neil whispered to Michael, the muzzle of his rifle digging into his back.

"I say, Rick, who's here today?" Michael yelled up the stairs. "Is

Tolly around?'' A silence followed, then Rick's voice puzzled: "What d'ya mean, 'Is Tolly around?' You know that Tolly . . .'' The voice stopped and left only an ominous silence.

Neil raised the butt of the rifle and slammed it into the back of Michael's head; he crumpled in a heap on the floor. Neil ran up the stairs two at a time and burst into the room the voice seemed to have come from. A skinny young man, apparently Rick, was standing at a bureau, groping in the top drawer.

"No! Don't!" Rick yelled and dropped the gun back into the drawer. Neil flattened himself against the wall inside the door.

"Who else is in the house?'' he asked. Rick looked around nervously, first at Neil, then at the door.

"There's Arthur, I think, and Larry and the Pussycat—''

"Arthur's a little man?'' Neil asked.

"Yes?''

"Where's Lar—''

Two shots rang out from downstairs. Neil ran to the door, then turned back on Rick, who still stood frozen but now with both arms stretched toward the ceiling.

"Don't shoot!'' he said again.

Enraged by the delay, Neil walked over to where Rick was standing and drove his fist into his face, sending him crashing back against the bureau and to the floor. He grabbed the pistol from the drawer and, carrying the automatic rifle in one hand like a handgun, rushed back to the head of the stairs.

"Phil!" he shouted down.

There was no answer. Michael's legs were still visible at the foot of the stairs. The silence brought forth from Neil a low moan of anguish. Two shots and silence: Philip must have been hit by some newcomer. He edged over to the railing at the top of the stairs and peered down. Still no sound.

"You down there,'' Neil shouted. "I . . . I . . . I know you got Phil, so I want to surrender. I never wanted to be part of this . . .'' Neil wanted to get the man—Larry was it?—to talk, to focus his attention on Neil. Perhaps he didn't know Jeanne was in the kitchen. Oh, dear Lord, please don't let him have shot Jeanne.

"Throw your gun down the stairs!'' a deep male voice commanded from the living room.

Neil took out Rick's gun and tossed it down the stairs. It bounced twice and came to rest near Michael's feet. Neil noticed that the door to the other downstairs room was now open. Come on, Jeanne, he's talking to me. Shoot the bastard.

"Now come down with your hands up over your head," Larry commanded next.

Exactly when will he be able to see me? Neil wondered. He took a step down the stairs. Then another. Where are you, Jeanne? he wondered, prayed. A third step. Two more and my legs will be in sight. He won't shoot until he can hit my belly. A fourth step. No more. Something, pray it's not death, must be stopping Jeanne from shooting from the kitchen. He had to get Larry to move. He took a fifth step down, then took the last seven steps in two long strides and lunged through the farther door in the corridor, rolling away from the doorway. Two shots whizzed past him, pounding into the wall by the stairway.

Neil got to his knees, glanced quickly around the room, and stopped, stunned. Katya was sitting on the bed only six feet away, naked. She looked at him with as much surprise as he guessed he must be looking at her.

"Can you see anyone?" Neil whispered. She responded with a barely perceptible nod. "Is Lisa here?" he asked next.

Katya shook her head and whispered, "They never got her."

Remembering the layout of the living room, Neil added, "Is he behind the couch near the front door?" Again Katya gave a barely perceptible nod.

Positioning himself by the doorway, he steadied the rifle with both hands, then reached around the corner and sprayed off a three-second blast toward the spot where he remembered the couch to be. He heard a muffled scream, then the sound of movement.

"He went toward the kitchen," Katya whispered.

Neil stood up, took two quick strides across the hallway to the living room, and hesitated. As he started to peer into the room the *bam-bam-bam* of three quick shots blasted out from the kitchen area. He ran into the living room, rifle at the ready, and crouched behind one of the ornate wooden chairs. He saw two bodies on the far side of the room near the kitchen, one partially hidden behind the end of the second couch, only its bare legs visible. The first, he realized sickeningly, was Philip, and for a horrifying moment the bare legs of the second looked female. A movement at the kitchen door caught his eye, and Jeanne stood there, her automatic at waist level, her eyes on the man she had apparently shot, blood spreading in a wide red splotch on the shoulder of her white cotton blouse.

From the minute he and Olly began trying to barter for food, Frank sensed that something was wrong. As they made their way up from the docks the streets seemed strangely empty. The few people in the doorways of houses or bars or on street corners all seemed to be standing for the sole purpose of staring at Frank and Olly as if they were enemy agents. Black food vendors with whom they'd bartered a half-dozen times were now either gone or refused even to talk to them. They went into a bar to find out what was happening.

Even at five in the afternoon Bosso's was packed. People were standing two and three deep at the long bar along one wall, and the dozen small tables across the room were all filled. Almost everyone was drinking water or a special postwar punch spiked with rum. Imported alcohol had disappeared. Frank and Olly stood awkwardly in the crowded space between the bar and the tables. Everyone in the bar was white except for three black men at the far end surrounded by a halo of conspicuous space. Many of the patrons kept glancing nervously at the entrance as if expecting an important but formidable visitor.

Most of them talked in low voices or whispers, as if they were in church. There was no boisterousness or joy. The one loud drunk who made an effort at jollity seemed to be deranged and soon lapsed into gloomy mumbling. Captain Olly wedged himself between two customers to press against the bar.

"Say, fella," he asked the nearest bartender, "who died?"

The bartender, a big man with thick glasses and a cowboy hat, came toward Olly with a frown. The other patrons grew even quieter at Olly's loud outburst.

"What d'ya mean, 'Who died?' " the bartender sullenly asked Olly.

"The way I figure it," Captain Olly replied, "everyone's mother just got run over by a steamroller. Never been in such a dreary place. You got a law against talking in a normal voice?"

"You a stranger here?" the bartender asked belligerently. The two other bartenders, although still mixing drinks, were half-turned, listening.

"Hell, I've lived here for days," Olly said. "You fellas acting as if you'd just learned that your blind date was a Russian missile."

"You want a drink?" the bartender asked.

"The price of drinks these days being what it is, I think I'll make water last into my next incarnation."

The bartender shrugged his big shoulders and moved away to another customer. Olly turned to the tall, slender man on his left.

"What's bothering everybody, fella, huh?" he asked. The man turned and looked coldly down at him. He shrugged. "The blacks may be going to riot," he said.

"I see. What's their gripe?"

"I wouldn't know," the tall man said, looking away and lifting his almost empty glass to his lips.

"You don't seem much bothered," said Olly.

"I'm leaving tomorrow morning," the man said neutrally.

"Well, ain't that nice!" said Olly. "Where you headed?"

The man placed a silver dollar on the bar and then brushed past Olly and left. Olly returned to Frank.

"You give it a try, Frank," he said. "I guess I ain't got the personality I once did."

A big black man with glittering white eyes and a sweat-covered face abruptly stood in front of them. He was dressed in a neat brown suit, totally inappropriate in the sweltering heat.

"You want to know why it's so gloomy in Bosso's today?" he asked, smiling, his gleaming eyes either stoned or mad.

"Yeah," Frank said, "we'd appreciate it," and, glancing at Olly, followed the man over to the empty space that surrounded his friends. The other two men were dressed in the casual and unpretentious style more usual among Virgin Islanders, white or black.

"These people want to know what's going on," the first man said, grinning absurdly at his two friends. "I've promised to tell them."

The other two blacks, subdued and sullen compared to the man who introduced himself as Mr. Sutter, looked at him and then turned back to the bar and their glasses of water.

"Everyone's a little touchy these days," Mr. Sutter said.

"Why?" Frank asked.

"Well, you see," said Mr. Sutter, turning his glittering eyes on Frank, "the obliteration of San Juan has had a certain depressing effect on everyone. We all thought we were safe here and then, *boom*, we find we're not. Five days ago the cruise ship *St. Augustine,* loaded with almost a thousand passengers, most of them white, sailed away from the white enclave at Caneel Bay on St. Johns. Tomorrow the *Norway* does the same."

"Where are they going?" Frank asked.

"The St. Augustine is going to Rio de Janeiro, and the *Norway,* ah, the beautiful *Norway,* is sailing to, ah, yes, South Africa."

"Jesus," said Frank.

"This mass exodus of whites to South Africa is having a certain alienating effect upon some of the blacks," Mr. Sutter went on, grinning as if he were telling a dirty story. "Certain resentments seem to have arisen. A feeling, as you mainlanders would put it, of being screwed."

"Are most of the people in here planning to sail tomorrow on the *Norway*?" Frank asked.

"All but my two taciturn friends here," Mr. Sutter replied, gesturing at the two blacks next to them at the bar. "They are deficient in gold and in the belief that South Africa is nigger heaven."

"You're going?" asked Frank.

"You're goddamn right. If I'm to choose between my identity as a live rich man or of a dead black man, I've no trouble in opting for the *Norway* and Capetown. The South Africans may not like the color of my skin, but they've always liked the color of gold."

A commotion at the entrance of the bar distracted Frank: the people nearest the door began to talk loudly and, as if a plug had been pulled at the door, everyone in the room began to be sucked toward the entrance.

"They're coming!" someone shouted, and several men produced

guns. A man now stood aiming a .38 at the three blacks at the bar. Mr. Sutter, sweating, grinned grotesquely.

"I assure you," he said to the thickset white man with the gun, "I am *not* part of the revolution." The other two blacks were looking balefully at the man with the gun but appeared to be unperturbed.

"I want you three to turn around," the white man said, "and lean against the bar with your arms outstretched. I'm going to check you for weapons."

Captain Olly had left for the entrance, where the sound of gunshots could be heard, but Frank stood watching the confrontation.

"I'm sailing on the *Norway,*" Mr. Sutter insisted, trying to establish his connection with the "good guys." "And although it makes me gag, I must confess that essentially I'm on your side." None of the three blacks had moved.

"I said turn around," repeated the white man, looking nervous. "And lean forward, with your hands flat on the bar. *NOW!*" He poked his gun in Sutter's ribs and gave him a shove.

"My dear man," Mr. Sutter began, but even as he spoke, one of the other blacks had sprung forward, grabbed the man's gun arm, and began wrestling with him. The other came to his aid while Frank stood tensely in surprise and indecision. Within three or four seconds the white man staggered back against Frank, and one of the blacks was crouched down, leveling the gun at them and backing toward the rear entrance of the bar. An explosive roar from the bar sent the man staggering backward, his shirt shredded. The other black fled. Frank turned to see one of the bartenders standing behind the bar with a smoking shotgun. A distant explosion was heard from outside.

"*Frank!* Let's go!" Olly shouted from the front entrance.

"Get out of here, Sutter," the bartender ordered.

"Yes," said Mr. Sutter, and, tight-lipped and terrified, he darted out the back.

When Frank left the bar with Olly, the bright afternoon sunlight blinded him and he could only see a few figures moving rapidly from left to right, toward the docks. The gunfire was coming from off to the left and from behind the buildings across the street. There was another loud explosion and the ground trembled under their feet. Then he could see smoke rising above the boutique across the street. As he and Olly turned right to make for the docks Frank saw an ancient brown tank rumbling down the street toward them, a handful of soldiers running at a crouch alongside and behind it.

He and Olly scrurried along the sidewalk, watching the tank and the half-dozen soldiers—mostly black, Frank noted with surprise—head past them in the direction of what Frank assumed were the black rioters. A small Datsun heading toward the docks with a cracked windshield careered up onto the curb nearby to avoid the soldiers and tank; the white driver, bleeding from a head wound, looked terror-stricken.

At the corner of the first street, still a block from the docks and the marina where *Mollycoddle* was tied, a cluster of white civilians were crouched behind two overturned vegetable carts, looking up the street where the tank had stopped and where the shots were coming from. Most of the men had either a rifle or handgun.

Another explosion rocked the pavement, and Frank turned to see that the tank had turned around and its smoking cannon was now aimed down the street at them. Half the soldiers had disappeared, but the others were crouched down behind parked cars; two were firing at the whites.

"The bastards are firing at *us*!" someone shouted.

"Let's go!" another yelled, and two of them began running toward the docks, soon followed by the other four.

A piece of sidewalk popped up in front of Frank as he and Olly followed. It took him two strides to realize that it was a bullet.

They were all running now and within a minute's time had arrived at the dock area, where cars were being overturned as barricades while a few soldiers—here mostly white and looking bewildered—made halfhearted efforts to direct the flow of people. Along the three blocks of waterfront Frank could see only a single additional tank; it sat with its cannon aimed incongruously and ominously out to sea.

At the marina where *Mollycoddle* was moored were dozens of men, women, and children and mounds of luggage. Most were gathered near the small boat dock, trying to get out to the *Norway*, which was still at anchor a half-mile out in the harbor. There was no crowd around *Mollycoddle,* and as he approached Frank saw why: Macklin and Sheila were standing on the foredeck, each with an automatic rifle held at the hip and aimed at the dock. Although Sheila looked like she could probably handle her gun, Macklin looked like he *wanted* to use his, and his grim face alone would discourage most people.

The ground in the marina parking lot abruptly exploded less than fifty yards away, sending people running in all directions and leaving four or five men sprawled on the ground. When Frank turned back, he saw that rafted seaward to *Mollycoddle* was *Scorpio*, so low in the water compared to the Hatteras that he hadn't seen her at first. With a surge of joy he saw Jim and Lisa coming out of the main cabin with empty boxes for transferring *Mollycoddle*'s food to *Scorpio*. Jim waved and shouted, "We found her on *Scorpio*!"

"For Christ's sake don't stand there!" Macklin shouted. "Get aboard! We've got to get away!"

"Where's Jeanne and Neil?" Frank asked as he and Olly boarded *Mollycoddle*.

"They're not back!" Macklin shouted. "They'll never get back through this. Get us out of here."

Frank looked at Sheila, who looked back at him questioningly. Her face was pale. Glancing at his watch, Frank realized that Neil and Philip were already a half-hour overdue.

Oscar ran across from *Scorpio*.

"Pull us out of here," he said, his small eyes wider. "They'll sink us!"

"Tony!" Macklin shouted.

Ten feet away *Mollycoddle*'s main windshield shattered as three neat holes appeared in the glass; Macklin crouched down and Oscar threw himself to the deck. Frank, standing numbly, now realized there was gunfire all around them.

Tony sprang from *Scorpio* and in a crouching run joined Macklin and huddled behind *Mollycoddle*'s combing.

"Get us out of here!" Macklin shouted at him.

Tony crawled over to the controls and, glancing fearfully around him, finally stood up and turned on the engine.

"Get the dock lines!" Macklin shouted at Frank and Oscar.

Another explosion boomed behind them, and Frank turned to see the dock one berth away burst into fragments and a body go flying off into the water. Sheila clutched his arm.

"We can still wait," she said. "We can't desert them."

"Get the goddamn dock lines!" Macklin shrieked at Frank and Oscar.

Jim appeared beside Frank, slightly hunched over.

"We're not leaving yet, are we?" he asked. The smoke from the recent explosions, although it was blowing away from them, prevented them from seeing much of what was happening in the streets. Along the docks people were running, crouching, stampeding onto boats to get out to the *Norway,* occasionally shooting, seemingly at random, back into the smoke.

"No . . . no, we're not," Frank said in a low voice.

Macklin, wild-eyed, suddenly leapt up, knife in hand, ran forward along *Mollycoddle*'s side, and slashed the forward dock line. With the wind blowing the yacht against the dock, *Mollycoddle* remained where she was, but when the two aft lines were cut, Tony would be able to motor off. As Frank, Sheila, and Jim watched, Macklin ran aft and cut the two other dock lines.

"Go Tony!" he shouted.

But Frank and Jim both came alive at once and ran to the helm.

"Not yet," said Frank.

Tony stared back at him, his usually placid face filled with fear, then looked to Macklin for support.

"Get out of the way, Frank," Macklin said loudly but with his accustomed icy calm. "I'm saving our lives. Get us out of here, Tony." Macklin's automatic rifle was aimed directly at Frank and Jim. "If you're so hot to be with Neil and Jeanne and Philip, get off the boat. You too, Sheila."

Sheila, still holding her automatic rifle—aimed vaguely shoreward—looked at Frank, then at Macklin, and finally back at the scene on shore.

"Oh, my God," she said.

When Frank let his eyes follow hers, he saw Neil and Katya coming through the smoke in the parking lot, one pulling a garden cart, the other, a wheelbarrow.

Escaping from the estate had been a nightmare. Philip had been shot twice; one bullet had passed relatively harmlessly through the fleshy part of his side, but the second had buried itself in his back, just to the right of the fifth vertebra.

Jeanne had taken a bullet through her shoulder but, amazingly, after they had staunched the flow of blood, she could still use her other arm to help Katya (now fully dressed in shorts and T-shirt) transport food. When the car wouldn't start, Neil found in the garage a wheelbarrow and a large garden cart. He carried Philip outside and placed him in the two-wheeled cart. Jeanne and Katya brought out boxes, cartons, and plastic bags of food and packed them gently around the wounded Philip. They put the heavier foodstuffs into the wheelbarrow. With Neil towing the garden cart like a dray horse and Katya pushing the wheelbarrow, they fled. Jeanne, insisting that she was still strong enough, bicycled one-handed on ahead of them.

On the deserted road into town, an old black couple they passed looked enviously at the food and seemed to conclude that Philip was a rich man being pulled by a servant.

As they entered the outskirts of the city they began to hear gunfire, but the streets were still mostly empty; they saw only an occasional bicycle or motorcycle racing away from the violence. When they came to within a few hundred yards of the docks, the smoke from the explosions both masked and impeded their progress. Jeanne's wound finally had brought her near to collapse, and Neil carried her on his back the last hundred feet.

When he arrived coughing, sweat-soaked, exhausted, but unhurt by shell or shrapnel, he was disoriented, unaware of the conflict aboard *Mollycoddle*. Frank and Jim took Jeanne as she slid semiconscious from Neil's back, assuring her that Lisa had been found safe on *Scorpio*. Sheila and Tony carried Philip aboard; the others brought the food. Five minutes later they motored *Mollycoddle* away from the docks with *Scorpio* rafted to her side, then took her in tow with Olly, Jim, and Lisa aboard her to help Oscar.

Events were now out of control. *Mollycoddle* plunged and plowed against the wind and waves, which careered toward them as if pushed by white demons. Spray exploded aft against the windows, cutting off visibility. Philip and Jeanne were placed on the long settee in back of *Mollycoddle*'s lower steering controls and Macklin was trying to examine their wounds. Fifty yards away water burst high in the air, making Neil fear that waves were smashing against some wreck or uncharted rock—until he realized it was an explosion. A quarter-mile off to port the gigantic white *Norway* lay placidly at anchor, surrounded by a dozen small boats all scrambling to come alongside and unload passengers. The *Norway*'s wide boarding ladder was packed with people shoving their way upward. Waterspouts burst in the sea around her. When Neil looked back across a hundred yards of water to the dock, he saw an explosion rock the boat that had been moored behind them, sending its mast toppling over into the sea.

They motored out against the swells to the mouth of the harbor and there cut *Scorpio* loose to sail off to Anguilla, where they hoped to rendezvous the next day. Tony warned Neil that *Mollycoddle*'s fuel gauge registered empty, but this seemed trivial. As they continued on back to pick up *Vagabond,* the *Norway* gave four blasts of its horn and began hauling anchor. A fire was burning on the afterdeck, smoke streaming out horizontally shoreward on the fierce wind.

Vagabond, lying to two anchors veed out at about sixty degrees from her bow, tore and plunged like a maddened horse at her tether. When *Mollycoddle* came alongside Katya and Tony put fenders in place and got the mooring lines tight. Everyone began unloading the new food and transferring the wounded to *Vagabond,* and Neil had to force himself to consider the next steps. He felt weary, worried about Jeanne's wound, and burdened with the same nagging sense of foreboding that had been with him since the capture of the *Mollycoddle*. The seas were building too high; the civil war was too unpredictable. The sun would be gone in half an hour. Four more blasts from the *Norway*'s horn sent a chill through him.

"We can't get either of the anchors up," Frank reported to Neil between gasps.

"Cut one," said Neil. "Cut it now, and let's not waste time. If Tony can't pull the other out, cut it too if you have to."

Ten minutes later *Mollycoddle,* with *Vagabond* in tow, plunged toward the mouth of the harbor. Macklin had finished cleaning Jeanne's and Philip's bullet wounds. He couldn't tell how seriously Philip had been torn up inside, but with *Vagabond* bucking and rolling as she was, they agreed it was useless to poke around to see. Neil realized for the first time that leaving land might mean sentencing Philip to death, yet neither Philip nor Sheila had suggested they stay to look for a doctor. And now they were committed to the sea: ashore Michael and his men would be waiting for them.

When he stood up and peered forward into the wind and spray,

Neil felt frightened again. At any moment a towline might snap, an anchor drag, an engine fail, someone might fall overboard. As *Mollycoddle* crashed forward he watched the *Norway* moving seaward off their port beam; she was still hauling anchor, and smoke was still billowing out astern. Her decks were packed. When Macklin finished checking Jeanne, Neil carried her down to her cabin and lifted her up onto her berth. As he was tying Jeanne and Skip into the berth so they couldn't roll out, he felt a strange new motion and a new sound that at first he couldn't place. As he hurried back up on deck he suddenly knew: The engine had stopped. *Mollycoddle* had run out of fuel.

"Get aboard!" Neil shouted to Tony as *Mollycoddle* drifted rapidly back toward *Vagabond*. *"Frank, get ready to cut the towline!"*

He himself ran toward the mainmast, stumbling when *Mollycoddle* crashed into them, then getting up again to loose the halyard and begin hauling up the already triple-reefed mainsail. He was dimly concerned that no one had been assigned to *Vagabond*'s helm, but someone . . . The triple-reefed main, flogging loudly, went up, and he winched it up tight, tied it down, and began raising the storm jib. With a loud twang the towline flew past his leg, and *Vagabond* lurched away from *Mollycoddle*, which was drifting more slowly now. Neil quickly tied down the jib halyard and raced aft.

Sheila was at the helm, but as he approached she let go of the wheel to help Katya sheet in the storm jib, which was loose and flogging. They were drifting off on a starboard tack, and it seemed they were being pushed almost sideways downwind. *The dagger board was up*.

"Dagger board!" he shouted forward to Frank, pointing.

Frank nodded and staggered to the place just aft of the mast to begin forcing down the twelve-foot-long central dagger board, five feet of which should have been under the boat cutting down leeway. In the two minutes it took to get it down—Macklin had gone forward to lend his strength—*Vagabond* had plowed and plunged forward, sliding sideways, too, toward Smith Point on the left side of the harbor. Land was less than a quarter mile away. The docks behind them were about three-quarters of a mile off. With the dagger board finally down, the ship gained speed and began to point better up into the wind.

"Will she come about in this?" Sheila asked him.

"She'd better," Neil said, knowing their lives depended on it. "We'll make it," *"Prepare to come about!"* he added. Frank was already at the port jib sheet, Katya and Tony ready to release the jib in the opposite cockpit.

"Don't release the jib till I yell!" Neil shouted.

"You're backwinding the jib?" Sheila asked.

"Coming about!" he shouted and swung the wheel full to starboard. *Vagabond* labored slowly up into the wind, the five-foot seas smashing into her three hulls with loud cracks, spray flying aft.

Squinting forward through the holed and streaming Plexiglas windows of the wheelhouse, Neil could barely see the jib in the gathering dusk. *Vagabond* plunged, rocked, and shuddered dead into the wind, both sails snapping as they luffed. The jib, still held close-hauled for the starboard tack, was now beginning to be backwinded, pushing the bow further around onto the desired new tack. *Vagabond* swung around to starboard with increasing momentum; Katya released the jib the instant Neil gave the command, and Frank winched it in on the other side.

With two more tacks they were out of the harbor and heading east a half-mile from the south coast of St. Thomas.

The waves outside the harbor were immense; huge, gray, ugly, spume-covered swells barreling in at their starboard side, sending them sliding down into the trough, only to be hit broadside by the next crest with a sickening crash. Philip lay moaning now on the deck of the wheelhouse, where he had rolled off when the first angry swell had smacked them into a forty-five degree tilt. Frank had vomited onto the control panel shelf; Macklin had staggered below, useless with nausea. With Sheila tending to her husband, only Neil, Frank, Tony, and Katya remained in the central cockpit.

It was dark. During their last tack night had fallen with the swiftness of the tropics, and Neil had only his compass to steer by. The sky was totally overcast. There were no navigational aids along the south coast, only rocks. A breaking wave rolled into *Vagabond* with a shattering crash, which sounded as if a hand grenade had exploded against her right side.

"She can't take this," Frank said to Neil from beside him. Neil stared back at him uncomprehendingly.

"Vagabond can't take this beating!" Frank shouted.

Maybe she couldn't, but what the hell choice did they have? Neil thought. To run before the seas meant running onto the rocks of St. Thomas. Then he thought of the dagger board.

"Bring the dagger board halfway up!" Neil shouted to Tony. "We'll let her slide some," he explained to Frank, who nodded. Tony snapped on a safety harness and left to crawl forward. Even in the darkness Neil could get some sense of each wave as it approached, and he watched carefully as Tony snapped his safety line to a shroud and began crawling on his hands and knees across the main cabin roof to get to the dagger board. Once there, he began trying to winch the board up, but he needed someone to tail the line.

"Give him a hand!" Neil shouted instinctively, and Katya left to crawl up across the foredeck toward Tony. Even as she did Neil caught sight of an unusually large wave bearing down on them, breaking on top.

"Hold on!" he yelled and tried to turn *Vagabond* away to take the shock further aft, but it was too late. The wave struck *Vagabond* broadside with an explosive crack. A river of water two feet deep swirled across the main cabin top, burying Tony and Katya; water crashed into the starboard cockpit, and someone screamed. *Vagabond* was jolted to port by the blow, left wallowing, then sailed on.

Neil could feel water swirling around his feet, felt Frank's arms around him, saw Tony, saved by his safety line, clutching a shroud on the port side, then beginning to crawl back toward the dagger board, like some persistent insect momentarily pushed away by an intruding finger. Sheila came up beside him, she too clutching at him for balance.

"Where's Katya?" she shouted.

Neil searched the port side, hoping to see her clinging to a shroud, but she was gone. The next wave was big, but *Vagabond* appeared to slide away, letting it roll under her, and the wave only gave her a playful slap. As the trimaran surged forward Neil brought *Vagabond* up into the wind to stop her, but she turned sluggishly, unresponsive to the helm.

"No, Neil!" Frank shouted. "It's no use!"

Even as Neil had swung the wheel around his mind told him there was nothing he could do. It was dark, Katya did not have light, nor was *Vagabond* equipped with a marker buoy with a light or a transmitter—there was no point in trying to find her. Even if she could keep swimming until daylight, there was still no chance they could beat their way back and locate her with the wind and seas still running like this. He mechanically turned *Vagabond* back on course.

Tony had staggered back to him at the helm.

"Katya went over!" he shouted. "She's back there!" he added, pointing.

Shaken, Neil looked at him, nodded, and kept the helm steady.

"We can't help her," Frank said hoarsely from beside him.

"Aren't you coming about?" Tony asked them, still gasping for breath. "She's a good swimmer. We've got a searchlight."

"We can't do it, Tony," Neil said, staring ahead of him, aware now of the ache in his throat.

"We'd probably kill everyone if we stopped now," Frank added. "We've got to get past the point."

"But we've got to try!" Tony said fiercely.

"She's lost," Frank said, putting one of his huge, bony hands on Tony's shoulder. "Katya's gone, and there isn't a chance in a trillion we could find her. We've got to sail on."

Tony had finally realized how close he himself had come to being lost as well; he looked briefly at the huge seas rolling at them and then back astern, toward where Katya had disappeared, and emitted a low, harsh groan. He turned back and lowered his head.

"It was my fault," Neil said, shaking his head. "I should have gone forward myself. I should never have sent anyone without a safety harness."

"A stanchion broke off," Frank said, as if in defense of Neil.

"The sea will always break a stanchion if you give it a chance," Neil replied. "Never, never, never let her go . . ." he muttered.

For another minute they all stood in the darkness, staring forward.

"She's gone," Tony said softly, flatly.

"I'm sorry, Tony," said Neil, tears finally appearing on his cheeks. And then his grief was checked by sudden fear: *Vagabond*'s easier motion meant . . . that cracking noise when the wave hit . . .

"The dagger board's gone," Neil said harshly. Tony then informed them that he hadn't made any progress when the wave hit—

the twelve-foot dagger board must have broken off flush with the bottom of the boat.

"The ocean's way of correcting a captain's error," Neil added bitterly.

"Will we still clear the tip of the island?" Sheila asked.

A minor, casual, life-or-death question. And if we cleared St. Thomas, there was still St. John and Flanagan Island to clear.

"I doubt it," said Neil.

"Which anchor did you save?" Neil asked Frank.

"The CQR," Frank answered.

It would never hold. It didn't matter. Three anchors wouldn't hold in this. And he couldn't even see the coast of the islands he was trying to avoid, wouldn't see it even at the moment *Vagabond* first began smashing herself to pieces.

"We may not clear the tip of the island," he said, talking as much to himself as to the others, trying to clear his own mind. It was a no-win situation. If you tried sailing closer into the wind you'd lose speed and make three times as much leeway. If you continued on this reach, your course was so close to the tip of the island that the waves would still put you up on the rocks. And though they might clear the rest of St. Thomas, Dog Rocks stuck out even farther south. Dog Rocks: what a place to die.

"I'll shift the battery over so we can use the depthmeter," Frank said gently to Neil and went below.

"Can you reef the mizzen?" Sheila asked.

"Yes. Why?" asked Neil

"If we have to . . . to try to tack offshore, the mizzen could help us come about."

Come about? In this? With no dagger board! Neil felt like crying.

"I don't think I could even get *Vagabond* in irons, much less bring her about," he said quietly.

"Then it's in the hands of the gods," said Sheila softly.

"One of them's sure as hell got to be a better sailor than I am," Neil commented bitterly, thinking again of Katya.

And so they sailed on. Using the depthmeter and a local chart that Sheila had brought over to *Vagabond* with the gear from *Doubloon*, Neil guessed what the time was when they cleared the tip of St.

Thomas and what their course should be to clear Dog Rocks! He sent Tony forward to listen for the surf breaking ahead. Frank brought up the boat's twelve-volt spotlight to search ahead occasionally too. Neil turned the helm over to Sheila so that he could concentrate all his meager resources on determining *Vagabond*'s probable speed, leeway, and direction, plotting her progress on Sheila's chart, and ordering the minor course changes that might let them get a little bit farther over to windward.

And in the blackness of that night the sounds of waves crashing against rocks or reef less than a hundred yards away no less than three times terrified them into preparing for disaster, yet they somehow sailed through. At one point, when Sheila was wielding the spotlight, they saw surf shattering itself against a reef less than forty feet off to port. At another point *Vagabond* struck something—probably, since their depthmeter was registering eight feet of water, a little shaft of coral—but she sailed on.

By midnight the storm winds, as Philip and Neil had expected so long ago in their initial planning session, moved around to the southwest and the seas and wind began to fall. Free now of the last of the little cays and reefs, they were able to sail easily due east. It was just possible, thought Neil, as he came back up on deck after checking on Philip and Jeanne, that they might survive this night after all. They would live to suffer another day.

PART FIVE

SPIRIT

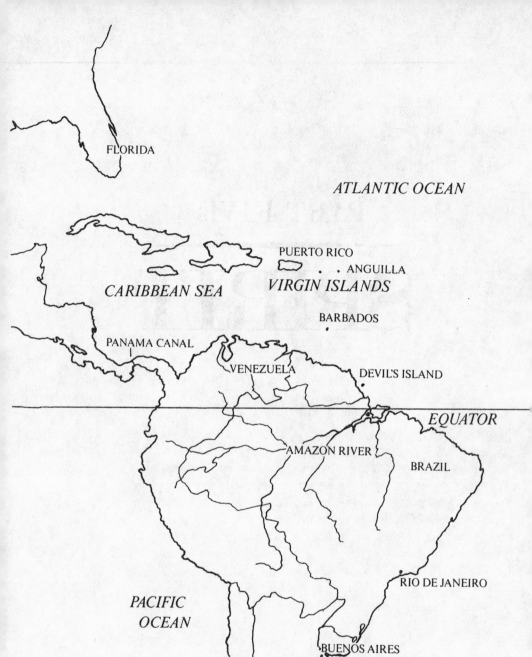

FLORIDA

ATLANTIC OCEAN

PUERTO RICO
. . ANGUILLA
CARIBBEAN SEA   VIRGIN ISLANDS

BARBADOS

PANAMA CANAL

VENEZUELA   DEVIL'S ISLAND

EQUATOR

AMAZON RIVER

BRAZIL

RIO DE JANEIRO

PACIFIC
OCEAN

BUENOS AIRES

ARGENTINA
MAR DEL PLATA

CHILE

SOUTH ATLANTIC

CABO DE LAS VIRGENES
PUNTA ARENAS   ∅∅ FALKLAND ISLANDS
STRAIT OF MAGELLAN

THE "War"—the holocaust, the war of missiles, bombers, submarines, lasers, satellites, and all the sophisticated technology of modern military science—this war between the United States with its Western and Oriental allies and the Soviet Union with her allies, was over. No more missiles were being fired; nuclear explosions had ceased. Although death still came out of the sky, it fell now gently, subtly, like a soft rain. Although people still died, they no longer disappeared in a flash of light or exploded into fragments like a smashed pumpkin, but died in more natural animal ways: of starvation, of typhoid, of cholera, of dysentery, of pneumonia, of weariness, and of grief. Although no victory had been declared, no defeat acknowledged, the big war was over. Another had begun.

The new war, in a tradition as old as humanity itself, found the former enemies fighting on the same side against new enemies. Those who had survived the first war, often finding themselves with radioactive food and undrinkable water, with diseases known and unknown afflicting them and medical care scarce or absent, fled to those places that they supposed to be safer. The southern nations were first appalled by the invasion, then frightened, and finally angered by it. If the white nations of the north had blown up the world, let them not try to escape the consequences by fleeing south. Thus the new war had begun.

It actually had been going on since the first week of the "War."

Venezuela's navy had forcibly prevented U.S. Navy ships from refueling in their ports. In the ensuing sea battle tactical nuclear bombs had been dropped. In miniature such battles had been repeated throughout the world ever since. American and Russian ships and planes, low on fuel, their home bases destroyed, sought refuge in neutral countries to the south. At first their ships or planes were impounded, their crews quarantined or interned. Later they were sunk or shot down, the survivors killed on the spot. As the warring nations slowly stopped being nations, so too did their armies, navies, and air forces slowly stop being armies, navies, and air forces. Individual units—a ship, a plane, a company of infantry, a tank squadron—began mini-invasions on their own. Soon *any* unidentified or foreign ship, plane, or person was considered an enemy to be eliminated. When the unknown epidemic that came to be called either "the plague" or "Nevada X" began to spread from the American West down through Mexico to Central America, and, in long, deadly bursts, to other countries around the world, foreigners, especially Americans, were feared, resented, and resisted all the more. To protect themselves the southern nations simply shut down all commercial air and sea traffic with the Northern Hemisphere. In effect they tried to build a wall and order the "War" and those who survived it not to enter.

Within the nations of the Southern Hemisphere other walls were also built. The rich retreated to their luxury homes and apartments and tried to keep the police and the military forces in line. In the West Indies and Central America the desperate and starving masses had already risen up and forcibly taken from those who still had something all that they had. Slow starvation and susceptibility to disease thus became universal. In South America, where food still was available and disease less rampant, the rich were able to hold on while the great masses of people, unemployed and barely fed, became weaker and weaker, more and more desperate.

And so, a third war was beginning: a war that was again as old as humanity, but was exacerbated by the gross overpopulation in the late twentieth century: the war between those who had enough to eat and those who did not. The governments of South America held out: shooting everyone who resisted, shooting all who tried to cross their borders, shooting everyone who questioned the siege mentality that they hoped would sustain them.

And thus throughout the world the war refugees were fighting a usually losing battle for survival. The "War" was over. The survivors didn't notice.

The "convoy" composed of *Vagabond* and *Scorpio* was reunited off the northern coast of Anguilla late in the afternoon of the day following their escape from St. Thomas. Olly and Jim had brought *Scorpio* through the wild, bone-jarring hundred-mile passage, but only after blowing out two sails, developing frightening leaks that had them pumping almost continuously, and having Gregg's arm broken.

With the wind and seas much diminished and their ships anchored off the lee shore of Anguilla, those on *Vagabond* and *Scorpio* transported supplies, adjusted ship's crews, established radio frequencies and hours of transmission, as well as signaling procedures and defense strategies in case of attack, and set their course and rendezvous points in case they unexpectedly lost sight of each other. But even as they took heart from their safe passage Lisa reported to Neil something that Katya had mentioned briefly as they were fleeing the pirate estate: Lisa and Katya had apparently smoked a joint with a plague victim aboard *Mollycoddle*. In Katya's brief, emotional account of her capture and imprisonment she had warned Neil tearfully that a black girl aboard *Mollycoddle* had been thrown overboard when Michael had realized how feverish she was. Katya had hysterically offered not to sail with them, but Neil had been obsessed with getting back to *Mollycoddle* and out to sea and had barely understood. And if he had, he still would have brought her along.

Neil passed this along to everyone and ordered them to always use the same personal cup for drinking and the same plate and utensils for eating. Oscar and his shipmates insisted that Jim and Lisa be transferred back to *Vagabond*. This was done, and neither one was to be involved with food preparation or galley cleanup. Jim joked that it was the best excuse for getting out of doing the dishes he'd ever had. Neil also suggested that mouth-to-mouth contact should be avoided. If the disease didn't appear in a week or ten days, they could assume they were safe and relax some of the stringency of this regime—"Perhaps permit the holding of hands." If there was no sign of the disease after ten days, they could "have an orgy." But despite Neil's efforts to make light of these new regulations, the effect was to make everyone realize that they might be carrying with them the very thing they had gone to sea to escape.

While they were anchored off Anguilla, Neil sent Jim and Sheila ashore to try to locate the nearest doctor. They returned ten hours later with the depressing information that there were no longer any doctors left on the whole island. They had all fled. Starvation was almost universal. Actually there was one old doctor they'd located in a small fishing village, but he was feeble and indicated he couldn't cope with a bullet wound in the stomach.

Philip had been placed on the dinette settee in the main cabin, where the pitching and rolling of *Vagabond* was least felt during their topsy-turvy passage through the storm; now he was running a fever. Macklin indicated that an infection had taken hold in the abdomen. He had started Philip on an antibiotic, was giving him codeine for the pain, and was feeding him only liquids. Philip was urinating normally but had not had a bowel movement since he had been shot. There was still no evidence of internal hemorrhaging. Most of the pain was in his back, where the bullet had shattered a rib. Jeanne's wound showed no signs of infection, and she insisted on being up and about with her left arm in a sling.

Since their proposed southeasterly course toward the eastern tip of Brazil and the mouth of the Amazon would leave them with never more than a day's sail downwind to land, Sheila advised Neil to go ahead and they would see if Philip improved. They both knew that medical skill on most of the islands was probably limited. The farther south they got, the more likely they'd be to find competent doctors.

Neil made no effort to hide how long and difficult a passage they would have simply to get south to the equator, much less to find a home someplace along the coast of Brazil or on the islands of Ascension or St. Helena if that was their decision. By their third day at sea Oscar and Tony were already complaining. It was a voyage of almost two thousand miles to the equator, largely against the prevailing winds and along an inhospitable coast. If the leaks in *Scorpio*'s hull couldn't be patched, they might not be able to continue as a fleet. Although the leaking was reduced from what it had been during the initial stormy passage from the Virgins, it still took five to ten minutes an hour of pumping to clear *Scorpio*'s bilge. Oscar and Tony maintained that Barbados might make a possible haven, but Neil, happy that the north-easterly wind was letting them head directly southeast toward the equator, refused. Their goal was to cross the equator to escape the fallout and "plague" of the Northern Hemisphere and to get to a country that had not been overwhelmed by the effects of the war. Neil also felt it was important to avoid land until the "plague" had run its course.

But from the beginning there was an atmosphere of heaviness and conflict aboard that was new. The death of Katya, the wounding of Philip and Jeanne, the knowledge that at any moment one or more of them might be stricken with a mortal illness, the awareness that for all the effort and the violence of their raid on the *Mollycoddle* pirates they were still living on short rations and still depending on the sea for their sustenance—all this created a depression in most of the crew that was deeper than ever before. Yet the effect on Neil was quite different and unexpected.

Something had broken inside him. Some coiled spring that had him tensely concentrating at every moment on the right strategies for sur- vival was no longer there. For him, even though he had acted with all his skill and energy, the worst had happened: a loved one killed, two others wounded. Some part of him gave up. Or rather, some major part of him now accepted his own fallibility, mortality, inabil- ity to deal with the forces attacking them. He still commanded, but without the vehemence that had driven him since the wars began. Instead of feeling his usual rage at the forces of destruction when he realized that Lisa might be infected with the plague, he felt strangely tranquil, even gentle. When Tony publicly attacked him for the death of Katya, Neil was not angry at Tony at all: he knew that he was at fault and that he was helpless to do otherwise, and he now ac- cepted both. He was helpless: somehow that new awareness liberated him.

Although he and Frank had had no formal reconciliation, Neil found himself feeling his old affection for him and turning most of the decisions about the sailing of *Vagabond* over to him. On *Scorpio* Olly was captain, with watch teams led by Tony, Oscar, and Arnie. On *Vagabond* Frank, Jim, and Sheila were the mates, Jeanne, Lisa, and Macklin crewing as necessary.

Neil no longer made any effort to disguise his feelings for Jeanne. He touched her, caressed her hair, tended to her wound, spoke to her lovingly. He made no effort to make love to her, both because of his concern for Frank and out of fear that he might be a carrier of the disease.

When Neil listened to the shortwave radio now and heard about the horrors others were facing throughout the world, he felt he was part of a larger family. On the second night out from Anguilla in particular he listened to two new ham operators, one in Florida, the other in Texas. At first he thought the anonymous voices had revived his Americanism, reminded him of his American roots and citizenship, but when he thought about it further, he realized that the larger family he felt connected to was that of the survivors.

He felt no connection with the President and his martial law and executive orders and his empty claims of victories. He felt no connection with the heroic pushers of buttons, the pilots of bombers, the submarine captains, the generals generaling from a half-mile down inside the earth somewhere. His people were the survivors, survivors all over the world, American, English, German, Russian, yes, Russian even, fleeing this incredible madness.

And, strangely, Neil found he could read again. From the first day of the holocaust until the evening that they dropped anchor off Anguilla he realized that he had been unable to read fiction or history or philosophy: everything had seemed so trivial or so irrelevant in the face of his quest for survival. Then suddenly that evening he spent two hours reading Tolstoy's *War and Peace,* one of two dozen classic novels he had aboard. The adolescent joys of Natasha and Sonya and young Count Rostov brought tears to his eyes: the joys that Lisa and Katya were missing—had missed. The battle of Austerlitz, although totally remote from their experiences of the previous month, seemed so real, so human, that his own life and the wounds of Philip and Jeanne seemed human, bearable. He knew that the joy he found in Tolstoy represented—paradoxically in the light of Katya's tragic death—his strangely recovered joy in life, and his acceptance of his powerlessness.

Jeanne seemed to have been affected by Katya's death, her own wound, and the fact that she had killed a man in a slightly different way. She appeared more pensive and puzzled. Neil could see that she too was less desperate than they both had been for most of the earlier time, but he could also see that as she watched for signs of illness in Lisa, she hadn't quite decided how she could take another such blow. Neil and Jeanne spent more time talking, not just about the day-to-day details of survival but also about the question of who was to blame for everything that had happened, large and small. Although Jeanne saw that her killing Larry had been an act of self-defense, she argued quietly that if they hadn't attacked the pirates' estate, her life might not have had to be defended. When Neil reminded her that the pirates had kidnaped Katya, she hadn't replied, and Neil felt remorse again: they had retrieved Katya only to sail her to her death.

As they talked away their third afternoon at sea *Scorpio* was visible two hundred yards off to starboard. Both boats were moving smoothly in the brisk tradewinds, sailing slightly to windward but not enough to cause heavy slamming. Neil was at the helm, Jeanne on the port seat of the newly open central cockpit. The sky was clear, the day already warm. Jeanne was dressed as she usually was in shorts and a bikini top, Neil in cutoff jeans. She noticed that the tendons in the backs of his legs were showing and realized that he had lost weight. His severe face was made even more severe by the deep lines that creased it. It saddened her to see him like this.

"We're failing," Jeanne said to him impulsively. "We're divided and failing. We're making all the same mistakes that led to the War in the first place." Like everyone else aboard, she referred to it as the "War," not the "Third World War" or anything else. To her, to them, it was the "War," all previous wars being insignificant skirmishes in comparison. It could not have a number because it had had no predecessor and couldn't conceivably have a sequel.

Neil turned to look at her but didn't reply.

"We're failing," she repeated.

"We're alive, Jeanne," he finally said. "We're not yet starving to death. We're sixteen people sailing away from danger. We've made mistakes, but we've avoided worse ones."

344 · LUKE RHINEHART

"But what's the sense?" said Jeanne. "To get food for a week or two, Philip and I get shot. To escape, Katya dies. We must be doing something wrong."

Neil winced. "I know it seems that way," he said. "But illness, violence, and death are the new norm. They can't be avoided."

"And there's Frank," Jeanne said, as if the name itself summarized an entire problem. She searched Neil's face to see if he had an answer for her, and nodding to her, he gestured with his free hand for her to come to him. She went to his side, and he took her hand.

"Frank hasn't asked us to stop loving each other," Neil went on, "although that's the only thing that would change things for him. He's only asked us not to make love. For the time being, with Frank as weak as he is, that's a sacrifice I'm willing to make for him."

"I know," said Jeanne. "But as you yourself said, it's really no solution. It doesn't stop him from resenting you . . . . us."

"No, it doesn't."

"That's what I can't stand," she said. "You and he were friends. He and I . . . now . . ."

When she looked up at him, he returned her gaze sternly and removed his hand from hers. He sighed.

"You expect too much of us, Jeanne," he said. "Good people hurt each other. It's built into the universe."

"There were only ten of us," Jeanne persisted. "Surely we're capable of creating a happy life for ten people."

"No, I don't think we are," Neil said. "Not when those ten are forced to live with each other whether they like it or not. Not when those ten are threatened with death every day. No, Jeanne, be thankful your children are with you, that I love you, that people like Olly and Philip and Sheila have come into our lives. For the rest, conflict and suffering and death will be in the air we breathe for a long time."

But if there was peace in Neil's heart, there was nothing but dissension in his fleet. In the late afternoon of the fifth day out from Anguilla Tony and Oscar, who had asked to come over to have a conference with Neil, arrived aboard *Vagabond*. Frank had visited *Scorpio* at midday while Neil was taking the noon sunshot, and he was to be in on the conference too. Although the main cabin would be hot and stuffy, Tony suggested they go below for privacy, forgetting that Philip was berthed there. Instead they sat in the back of the wheelhouse area. Actually the wheelhouse had ceased to exist; only the Plexiglas windows forward remained. Neil had ordered it torn down so that the six-by-ten plywood and Fiberglas roof could be sawed in two, glued together, and Fiberglassed over to make a new dagger board. The walls had come down too. *Vagabond* now had open cockpits running athwart the entire boat aft of the cabins in the three hulls. Two small sun awnings were rigged up over most of this area, but it was all open to wind and weather.

Oscar and Frank sat on the aft seat, Neil and Tony next to each other on the port seat. Gaunt, bearded, and unkempt, they reminded Neil of four derelicts gathering to share a bottle of cheap wine. Only there was no wine.

"Well, gentlemen," said Neil gaily. "This is quite a formal occasion. You apparently have something you want to discuss."

"That's right," said Tony, looking Neil firmly in the eye. "This beating to windward is going to break *Scorpio* apart. We're pumping half the time. It's time to change course."

"We've already discussed this," Neil replied quietly. "Jim, Olly, and I all agree our present course is best. Frank, Mac, and I have all been coming over to help with the pumping, and you won't take Jim."

"But everyone on my ship except the old guy is in favor of sailing to Barbados," said Oscar. "And since Frank agrees, we outvote you."

"Take *Scorpio* and go," said Neil quietly.

"No," said Oscar, "we don't want to split up if we can help it. We want to reestablish the normal order of things."

"Wouldn't that be nice?" said Neil.

"Tell him, Frank," said Tony. "First about the captain thing."

Frank cleared his throat and slowly raised his eyes to Neil. Great gray half-moons made deep hollows under both his eyes, and the skin around his neck was loose. Sitting hunched over, staring downward had become his characteristic posture.

"When you announced you were the captain of *Vagabond* in the Chesapeake," Frank began slowly, "I went along with it. I went along because back then there were twenty or so madmen aboard and your speech shaped them up." He paused.

"Nineteen madmen," Tony interjected. "Remember I was there then too."

Frank blinked once, cleared his throat again, and went on.

"Now there aren't," he said. "Now me, Tony, Jim, Olly . . . even Sheila I guess . . . any one of us could be captain of *Vagabond* and run the ship. Maybe not as well as you, but competently . . ."

Neil held his gaze steadily on Frank but didn't respond.

"In becoming your first mate I temporarily forfeited my ownership rights to *Vagabond*," Frank continued. "In those days, with an untrained crew, it was probably a good way to do things. Now . . . I'm reasserting my rights as owner."

"And I'm asserting my rights as owner of *Scorpio*," said Oscar.

"Oh?" said Neil, choosing to look at Oscar, whose long hair and bushy mustache were tangled and streaked with salt, making him look the least reputable of the derelicts. "And what does that mean?"

"It means I want Tony as captain and not the old man."

"And what's wrong with Captain Olly?"

"He never gives any orders except the ones you give him," Oscar replied. "Tony, Arnie, and I run the watches the way we want anyway."

Neil laughed. "I'd say he sounds like a perfect captain."

"I want Tony," Oscar repeated sullenly.

"And what does your reasserting ownership of *Vagabond* mean,

Frank?'' Neil asked. He saw that Frank's gaze could not entirely conceal the uncertainty, anxiety even, that Frank must have been feeling.

"It means that the captain serves at my pleasure," he replied slowly. "It means that I set the course, the captain only determines how to get there."

"And the same on my boat," said Oscar.

Neil was surprised that he felt no anger or resentment, but rather a strange kind of serenity that was only slightly tinged with sadness. Very slowly he shook his head.

"No, good friend," he said to Frank. "I didn't take the ownership of *Vagabond* away from you. The War did."

"The War's over, Neil," Frank replied. "You don't seem to accept it, but it's over."

"No, it's not, Frank," Neil said calmly. "At least not the war that deprived you of your ownership rights. And yours too, Oscar. No, I'm afraid none of us owns anything anymore."

"That's convenient for you to say," said Tony, "since you don't own a boat."

"Frank doesn't own *Vagabond,*" Neil went on. "And I don't own my captaincy or my other skills. You don't think I'm free to do what I want, do you? Your lives sometimes depend on my skills, so I'm not free to withdraw them, irrespective of likes or dislikes. Our lives depend on *Vagabond* and *Scorpio*. You two don't own *them* any more than the man who happens to 'own' all the water on a crowded desert island owns the water. By the nature of the situation everyone who needs it, owns it."

"Bullshit!" Tony exploded. "It's Frank's boat. All that intellectual crap doesn't change it!"

"You're right, Tony," Neil responded mildly. "My intellectual crap doesn't change it. The world changed it."

Frank was watching him, his uncertainty more evident now. Oscar looked sullen, Tony angry and defiant. Neil rose from his seat, stretched his arms, and yawned.

"If you think you own your boats, go ahead and think so," he said and then turned to look directly down at Frank. "But if you try to *act* as owner, then the world, your friends, your family, will collapse. You can't reinstate the old ways by decree." He watched Frank

349 · LUKE RHINEHART

for a moment—Frank was hunched over, looking at the floor—and then turned to Oscar and Tony.

"Olly is an excellent captain because he gives orders only to maintain order," he went on. "Tony here is an excellent sailor, stronger and quicker than Olly, and Tony would make an absolutely shitty captain. Tony would give orders not to maintain order but to demonstrate that he was captain, and that's the perfect formula for chaos."

"You conceited bastard!" said Tony.

"The War's over, Neil," Frank said in a husky voice. "You're still running, I believe you'll always be, but it's over."

"It's not over," Neil replied, "and I intend to keep running."

"Dragging us with you," Frank said.

"No. If enough people want to take a different course, then we'll split up," said Neil. "The cowards can come with me, and the brave ones return to the West Indies."

"And who determines which group takes which boat?" asked Frank.

"Not me, Frank. Not you. *Vagabond* should go to those who have to sail to windward. *Scorpio* to those who can use her best."

"And who decides that?" asked Frank.

"The goddamn owners decide, is who," snapped Tony.

"There are no easy solutions," Neil said softly to Frank. "Think about it, Frank. Would throwing me overboard really solve any of your problems?"

"We're not going to throw you overboard," Tony interjected. "Good as the idea may be."

"Think about it, Frank," said Neil, still without raising his voice. "Get away from these clowns and see the world as it is."

Tony's fist caught Neil just below his left ear and sent him stumbling across to the opposite seat, where he fell awkwardly, half on his knees.

"What the hell are you doing!?" Frank shouted, getting to his feet and holding out an arm to keep Tony from Neil.

Neil glanced up at Tony looming over him a few feet away and waited for his head to clear and the ringing to stop.

"This bastard can't keep calling me names and expect me to take it," Tony barked out in reply to Frank. "If he thinks he's captain, let him show it with his fists."

Neil's head was slowly clearing, and he stood up. He noticed that at the helm Sheila had half-turned toward them, watching.

"I'm sorry I called you names, Tony," he said quietly. "I don't blame you for being angry."

"You chickening out?"

"I made a mistake in insulting you," Neil went on. "I apologize."

"Jesus. What is this?"

"And if you ever pull something like that again I'll smash your nose out the back of your head," Neil concluded. He brushed past Tony and went down into the main cabin.

At the wheel Sheila held *Vagabond* steadily on course.

Over the next several days neither Oscar nor Frank renewed their request and both crews seemed to return to a contented routine. They were lucky with the wind: it blew steadily much more from the northeast than usual and let them sail more southeast than they had hoped. *Scorpio* began leaking less rapidly. Other events encouraged Neil.

Macklin had probed Philip's wound and removed the second bullet, and the infection seemed to be subsiding. Jeanne's wound was healing perfectly. No one had shown any symptoms of the plague. A squall had left them with a plentiful supply of fresh water.

The only continuing source of anxiety was their food situation. Neil and Frank had rationed the two boats for a three-week voyage, rations that assumed they would be catching at least one fish a day. They weren't. Both boats were trolling all the time and hooking nothing. The seas appeared to be empty. Macklin had machine-gunned a porpoise at dawn one day when he was alone on watch, but the creature had sunk before he could maneuver over to it. The bloodstained water had been somehow depressing to Neil and Frank, who had rushed up on deck at the sound of the gunshots.

Because they were sailing more southeast than expected, they were well away from the danger of pirates. Although *Vagabond* was about two knots faster than *Scorpio* in the tradewinds, Neil carried reduced sail and spent a day aboard *Scorpio* helping Olly get every last ounce of speed out of her. At night *Vagabond* would sometimes get a few miles ahead of Scorpio and then heave to in the early morning.

It was good to see Jim and Lisa looking so happy and well. They were sleeping together now in the forepeak; Jim said jokingly that he was determined to share everything with Lisa, even the plague. Macklin now roomed with Frank. Tony had taken up with the slender young woman named Mirabai, apparently stealing her from Gregg, the young man with the broken arm. Janice, Oscar's girl friend, was the only other woman aboard *Scorpio*, a third female crew member apparently having chosen to join the commune at Salt Point just before they left.

They met no other ships on their first six days out of Anguilla. They passed more than sixty miles east of Barbados and after a week were seventy miles northeast of Devil's Island off the coast of Guiana. The fear of the plague was receding. Jeanne was not only regaining her strength but her spirits, standing watch with Frank most of the time, playing more happily than usual with Skippy, even enjoying her food more.

Olly too seemed to have regained his high spirits. Frank sometimes spent a day aboard *Scorpio* as captain and, back aboard *Vagabond*, Olly entertained his friends with exaggerated praise for the "oldness" of Scorpio, claiming nothing was truly beautiful until it was "at least sixty."

"She's as bald and toothless as me," he said, "but she can still bite."

Olly was aboard *Vagabond* when they spotted their first vessel. Jim was alone at the helm in an overcast dawn, little different from each of the last several days. Neil was curled up on a wheelhouse cushion behind him. In the galley Jeanne had just begun to parcel out the small bits of dried fish and dried fruit that would be their morning meal. Visibility was only about a mile, and Jim was sleepy at the end of an uneventful watch. *Vagabond* was ghosting along at only three or four knots in a light wind, so he glanced mainly at the compass. There was nothing to see out on the water except the same gray slate they'd been staring at for so long.

And then, after exchanging a few idle words with Jeanne and yawning, Jim glanced ahead and saw, so large and clear and close that it was as if God had that very instant set it down in the sea in front of them, a long gray submarine. *Vagabond* was sailing forward, barely rocking, and there, ahead and a little to port, lay a submarine. With a red star. A Soviet submarine.

For several moments Jim stood staring in disbelief at this gray dawn's apparition. Then, almost incredulous, he turned to Neil.

"Neil!" he hissed in a loud whisper, as if his voice might reveal the fifty-foot trimaran's location to the enemy.

Neil sat up slowly rubbing his eyes. "Mmmhuh?"

"A submarine. Dead ahead."

Groggy, Neil stood up and peered forward.

"Living God," he murmured.

Jeanne, aware of suppressed sounds from above, came to the hatchway entrance and looked up.

"What'll I do?" Jim asked in a low voice.

"Hold your course." Neil knocked on the wheelhouse floor to awaken Olly, who was asleep below.

"All hands!" he called in a sharp but low voice.

"What's happening?" Jeanne asked from the hatchway, then climbed the three steps and looked out: ahead and off to port, now only two hundred yards away, was the submarine, fully surfaced, with a dozen men on the main deck and several in the conning tower. The boat was immense: almost two football fields long; it was like sailing past an island. Even as she watched, a gun—some sort of artillery—emerged from the forward deck. Several men clustered around it. She saw several officers in the conning tower looking at them through binoculars.

In his underwear Olly poked his head into the wheelhouse, hair disheveled, sleepy-eyed, the bones of his ribs showing prominently. He blinked at the gray monster. They were going to pass within a hundred feet of it. He could see two sailors pissing off the bow, and he could also see the eight-foot naval gun being swiveled into position to fire on *Vagabond*.

"Raise your arms!" Olly shouted to them. "Raise your arms! It'll help their morale."

Neil lifted his arms in surrender, as did Jeanne. Jim adjusted his position so that he could steer with his thighs and chest, and then he too raised his arms.

"Sheila, get on up here!" Olly shouted. "And bring Skip. Mac!" He himself, arms raised, clad only in his underdrawers, walked into the cockpit, closer to the enemy. When Sheila came on deck, she took in the scene in stunned silence and slowly raised her arms in surrender.

As quiet and softly as a feather drifting in a pond, *Vagabond* was now gliding past the Russian submarine, less than ninety feet away. On its deck stood almost twenty Soviet sailors, staring in disbelief. In *Vagabond*'s cockpit stood three men, two women, and a child, all with their arms raised in surrender, facing the barrel of a cannon aimed directly at them. From the conning tower three Soviet officers were conferring agitatedly. As *Vagabond* sailed gently by the gun crew turned a wheel and kept the cannon trained amidships. One of them was looking to the conning tower for instructions. The submarine crew had quite possibly discharged up to twelve missiles in the past two months and presumably killed hundreds of thousands, more likely millions, of people they had never seen. Now they had a puny cannon aimed at seven people they could see.

An officer on the conning tower shouted something at *Vagabond*; he sounded angry, and shouted again. *Vagabond* was now sailing serenely away from the submarine and was already a hundred and fifty feet off.

"Shouldn't we heave to?" Macklin asked in a whisper.

"Keep sailing!" Neil replied quietly, his arms still raised.

Again the Russian shouted, this time to his own men, and there was a flurry of activity in the conning tower. A sailor raced down the ladder to the deck. *Vagabond* sailed on. The cannon swiveled to follow her. A single shot would blow *Vagabond* to bits.

"We'd better heave to," Sheila said urgently to Neil.

But Neil and Olly were both grinning. "Keep sailing!" Olly shouted happily.

They sailed on. Slowly, softly, as if she were tiptoeing past a sleeping giant, *Vagabond* bore away from the great metal leviathan that threatened to destroy them. For a panicky moment Neil was convinced that the captain of the sub was going to wait until the range presented a challenge to his gun crew and then blast them out of the water. Then that moment passed. The Russian gun crew, or most of it, dispersed; now they seemed to be occupied with a different problem. The strange, otherworldly meeting of the great gray engine of destruction and the white sailing vessel was ended.

Still Neil and the others stood with their arms raised.

"Can't I put my arms down now?" Skippy complained.

"Yes," said Neil with strange seriousness. "You can lower your arms. We've beaten them."

As they all lowered their arms Jeanne stared at the distant smudge of gray on the horizon and then looked at Neil.

"Beaten them?" she asked.

"No, not beaten them," he said, correcting himself and still looking thoughtful. "But we won the only way we could have."

Olly slapped Macklin on the back and gave Sheila a hug and kiss.

"We showed 'em, didn't we?" he said, grinning wildly. "They didn't dare fire a shot. Totally bluffed 'em."

Vagabond ghosted on ahead.

All that day they celebrated their "victory" over the Russian submarine, rafting themselves to *Scorpio* for over an hour to make sure Olly had a chance to tell everyone the story. They broke out some of the last *Mollycoddle* rum and partied. They were less than seven hundred miles from the equator and began planning another celebration for that nautical event. They even caught a fifteen-pound fish, their first in four days.

It was nine days since they'd left St. Thomas, and with the fear of the plague disappearing, Jim and Lisa were even accepted as crew members back aboard *Scorpio,* Jim being a welcome fresh hand at the tedious task of pumping and Lisa happy to be back with some of the young people again.

Neil himself created his own celebration: that evening he again made love to Jeanne. With Frank seeming to have withdrawn from everybody, he went to her cabin openly, while Macklin and Sheila were on watch. The lovemaking with Jeanne was more tender than the first time, a long, quiet coming together that, strangely, left them both in tears. Afterward Jeanne talked in a long rush of her hopes for Lisa and Skip and of their finding a haven. For the first time Neil found himself sharing her hopes, even as he noticed with a start the boney knees and protruding ribs of Skip lying in the other berth. To bury his fears, to bury their fears, they made love again.

At eleven they went back topside. Macklin had gone below to sleep, and Sheila was steering. When Jeanne went below to check on Philip, Neil went aft to his cabin to radio Olly. There was something strange in Olly's voice when they made radio contact. After answering Neil's initial question about how badly *Scorpio* was leaking—it was taking fifteen minutes of manual pumping every hour to clear the bilges— Olly quietly lowered the boom: Lisa was sick. She had stomach cramps and a fever. She probably had "that disease thing we been worrying about."

So, thought Neil, after he'd given Olly instructions for isolating both Lisa and Jim in the forepeak, this was how it all ended. You could run, but you couldn't hide. You could do everything you could think of to flee south as fast as possible and still Death, in unhurried omnipotence, overtook you.

Sitting in his cabin in the darkness, he didn't feel like moving. He'd have to tell Jeanne, Sheila, the others. He'd have to deal with the panic, here and, probably worse, aboard *Scorpio*. He'd have to decide what to do.

What to do? He wondered how many thousand people, no, million people, in the last two months had looked up into the ash-gray sky, asked what to do, knowing all the time that there was nothing to do but die.

Had they reached that point? Was Jeanne doomed, even when he felt he'd barely met her? Was Jim, who had grown from a boy to a man in two months, now literally going to burn out at eighteen?

Lisa was sick, cramps and fever. There was an enemy to be fought. They had the advantage of an infinite supply of cool seawater to counteract the fever, and a good supply of aspirin from the *Morison*. Lisa, while thin, was still not weak or severely undernourished from their long weeks of short rations. She would begin her personal battle with youth on her side.

As for the disease spreading, Jim was probably infected, but whether others were or would be depended on luck and discipline.

The standing orders he'd given regarding food, sanitation, and personal contact had not been taken very seriously—until today.

And who was to care for the sick? Olly would do it. He didn't know about the others aboard *Scorpio*. Over here on *Vagabond* Jeanne would do it, would insist on doing it. Frank maybe; the old Frank would have. Sheila would volunteer. Himself? No. It wasn't his kind of suicide mission.

Well, time to go to it. He stood up, took a brush to his hair and beard, as if preparing for a formal call, and left his cabin. By the light of the kerosene lantern hanging down in the main cabin he could see Sheila at the helm. He could hear Jeanne's voice below in the main cabin. He came up to Sheila and impulsively put his arm around her.

"How are we doing?" he asked.

"Eight knots southeast," she said, glancing at him quickly, her small gray eyes looking at him slyly, like a cat, the lines of aging around them crinkling nicely.

"How's Philip?" he asked.

"The same. A hundred and two."

Neil frowned.

"Well, a hundred and two won't kill him," he said, "but it won't have him raising sails soon either."

"No, it won't."

"Olly thinks Lisa has the plague," Neil announced abruptly.

Sheila looked at him again and then half-leaned against him, taking her left hand from the wheel and letting it fall awkwardly against Neil's.

"Oh, Neil," she said, slipping her arm around his waist now. "What a bloody shame."

"You don't catch Death napping."

They stood beside each other, staring forward for another moment, then exchanged a warm look and a brief hug.

"I've got to tell . . . the others," he said, and went below. Jeanne was there with Frank, drinking tea and sitting up with Philip who, now that *Vagabond* was pounding to windward again, was propped up in position on his makeshift dinette berth. He was lying under a thin sheet, awake, staring at the ceiling. The paneled room had a warm glow from the kerosene lantern that hung from a hook right above his head. Frank was sitting on the edge of Philip's berth, Jeanne standing up. Both looked at him intently when he came in.

Neil had the same impulse to embrace each of them. He went up first to Frank, leaned down close to him, and put a hand gently on his shoulder. Frank stared back at him in surprise. Neil smiled.

"You're a wonderful man, Frank," he said.

Frank flushed. "You're stoned," he said. "You've raided *Mollycoddle*'s pot."

"You still alive, Phil?" Neil asked, then straightening up, leaving his hand on Frank's shoulder, gently kneading it. Philip smiled and turned his head slightly to look at Neil.

"I believe so," he said. "I just wet my pants again."

"Good sign," said Neil. "Corpses rarely piss."

When he turned next to Jeanne he saw that she was also staring at him in surprise. He went up to her and took her in his arms, caressing her lower back, careful of her left shoulder. Looking down at her, he asked, "How are you?"

"I'm fine. What's wrong? Has something happened?"

Neil, not smiling, nodded in reply. Then he released her, glanced at Frank, and paced over to the companionway steps before turning and facing them.

"Olly reports that Lisa has cramps and a fever," he said. "He assumes it's the disease we've been worying about."

All three of them looked at him without immediate response. He realized that this statement seemed so inconsistent with his earlier tone of humorous affection that they briefly wondered if this was a sick joke.

"We . . . I chose this risk," he went on, feeling embarrassed by the way he had acted earlier, though it had seemed so appropriate at the time. "Now we have to pay. I think there's a good chance we can pull her through. But we've got to take absolutely insane precautions to keep it from spreading further."

"I'll go take care of her," Jeanne said.

Neil felt his heart sink.

"I'm not letting you go," he said gently. "I've already assigned Jim to care for her. I don't think she can give him anything now she hasn't already given him."

"Is Jim all right?" Frank asked.

"Apparently. Olly said only Lisa is sick."

"I'm going over to her," said Jeanne.

So this is how it ends, thought Neil again. Modern technology finding ever new ways to kill brave people, and brave people rushing to get their share.

"No," said Neil. "Jim will take care of Lisa."

"I can see my own daughter, can't I?" Jeanne suddenly shouted at him.

"No, you can't," Neil replied quietly. "As you once said, we're one family now and you can't endanger the rest of us unnecessarily."

Jeanne turned away and began to cry. Both Neil and Frank went over to her and made comforting sounds and caressed her, and even as they did, Neil realized they were also trying to reassure themselves and each other as well. But of course there was no comfort or reassurance for any of them.

"Neil!" Sheila shouted from the helm.

Neil hurried up on deck. She was pointing off to starboard, where a bright red glow was visible off *Scorpio*'s stern.

"A red flare," she said. "Doesn't that mean an emergency radio transmission?"

"Yes," Neil said, hurrying past her. "I'll go take it."

In his cabin he groped for the flashlight and shone it on the VHF radio that he used for short-range ship-to-ship communication. It was already tuned to the correct frequency, and in less than half a minute he had established contact with *Scorpio*. The voice that came back at him was Tony's.

"Scorpio reads you, *Vagabond.* This is Tony. Lisa's got the plague. Those of us on *Scorpio* can't stay with her. Either she's got to go or we do. Over."

Neil at first wondered if he had heard correctly, but then he knew he had.

"What the hell do you mean?" he shot back nevertheless. "Over."

"I mean Lisa should be . . . buried at sea. Now. Before she fucking kills us all. Or . . . or . . . those that are willing to risk their lives for her come stay on *Scorpio* and we'll shift to *Vagabond.* . . . Over."

So that's what it's all about. "Let me speak to my captain over there," said Neil. "Over."

"You're speaking to him."

"I want Captain Olly."

When Neil shifted to Receive, he got nothing. He waited.

"Captain Olly can't make it," Tony finally said. "Over."

"I'll speak to Jim," Neil fired back.

"Jim's locked in with Lisa," Tony replied. "He can't talk to you either. Look—"

Neil snapped off the radio and stood up. What selfish cowards. Who were they? Tony, Oscar certainly, the two young women . . . Would they be so heartless or frightened? Probably. Gregg and Arnie? They were passive. He went back up on deck.

"I'm afraid Jeanne's gone to her cabin to get ready to go over to *Scorpio*," Sheila reported.

Neil looked at her and then nodded.

"There's been a mutiny on *Scorpio*," he announced. "Tony has deposed Olly and wants to abandon ship or toss Lisa overboard."

"Good Lord," said Sheila. "Poor stupid Tony . . ."

"Your poor stupid Tony is a . . ." Neil was about to vent his rage with a string of unimaginative obscenities but stopped himself.

"We should head for land, Neil," said Sheila suddenly. "There we can quarantine the sick and get the best treatment for them . . . and for Philip."

So this is how it ends, thought Neil a third time. The dying rushing to the dying for help. The well murdering the sick. What horrors stood next in line?

"We've no right to take our sickness to land," he said. "We fight our battle here, at sea. Some of us will live, some die, but we don't bring death to others."

"But you're forcing those people on *Scorpio* to take the biggest risk," Sheila pointed out.

"No," he answered wearily. "I'm ordering Lisa and Jim and Olly to return to *Vagabond*."

Neil informed *Scorpio* of his intention to take off Jim, Lisa, and Olly but said that they should wait until dawn, six hours hence, to make the transfer. In the interim Jim and Lisa should be kept isolated in their cabin. Oscar, who took the message, made no comment.

When Macklin came on duty at midnight, he was informed of the situation. Macklin grunted, asked Neil if there were anything special he wanted said to *Scorpio* at the regular two A.M. radio check, and took the helm. Jeanne was down in her cabin with Skippy, satisfied that Lisa would be returned to her. Sheila, off watch, was down with Philip. Neil took over the helm while Macklin had a cup of tea, compliments of *Mollycoddle*.

"So what's the use of staying at sea?" Frank asked from a seat behind Neil. "The worst has happened out here. There's nothing left to run from."

Neil was struck by how resigned Frank seemed to be. He still had expressed neither rage nor grief that his son might soon be in the grip of a fatal disease.

"We're still not welcome anywhere," Neil replied. "And now, carrying what we carry, people are justified in asking us to stay away."

"The whole world's dying, Neil," Frank said. 'You'll never find a place that isn't.

"No, I won't," Neil agreed.

"Then why stay out here?" Frank said with sudden vehemence. "You're sick. You're becoming some sort of crazy Flying Dutchman, cursing yourself and anyone stupid enough to follow you to spend eternity sailing around endlessly at sea."

"I don't see it that way, Frank," Neil replied. "I still see my best defense as being out here, the enemies still bunched up mostly on land."

Frank got up and came over to stand beside Neil. "So now you're ordering death brought directly on board," he said.

"He's your son," Neil countered.

"If it were Tony or Conrad who were sick, you'd throw him overboard," Frank insisted quietly.

Neil hesitated, then replied evenly, "If it had been them at Salt Point, I never would have let them back on board. You're right there."

"You'd throw them overboard," Frank repeated.

Neil didn't answer. He knew he wouldn't literally throw them overboard, but he recognized that his response would be quite different.

"And how would you handle things, Frank?"

"Put the sick ashore. Split up. Stop this fucking running."

Neil smiled bitterly. "I'll stop running when he stops chasing," he said sadly.

"You're mad."

"Let's just say we'd handle it differently," Neil commented, turning the wheel over to Macklin, who had just come up on deck. "Zero seventy-five degrees. Keep an eye on the number-two jib. It may be too much for her. Wake me up at three forty-five. Good night."

But Neil was not awakened at three forty-five. He was awakened at dawn by the sound of something rubbing against *Vagabond*'s port side. He sat up, instantly awake, listening for the sound again, and angry that daylight was there and he hadn't been called. The sound came again: a crunch and a squeal, something rubbing against her side. It even sounded like fenders rubbing against a dock, but *Vagabond* was hissing through the sea at a good speed. She was also sliding down a wave, sailing downwind. She had altered course and was running west.

He stood up, pulled on his cutoff jeans, and reached over to slide his hatch open. It didn't open. He banged on it several times, almost instantly regretting that he had when he realized that his orders had been disobeyed and he was probably locked in his cabin. He went to get his gun from beside his berth and saw it was gone. So.

He could hear voices now, Frank's and Tony's among them. The peculiar sounds he was hearing must be the two boats' hulls and fenders scraping against each other as *Scorpio* and *Vagabond* sailed downwind together. Neil banged on the hatch again and shouted loudly, calling Frank. He kept it up for a solid minute until finally he heard someone fiddling with a padlock.

The hatch slid open and Oscar, gun in hand, looked down at him warily. Neil climbed quickly up the steps and, even as Oscar began ordering him to stay put, brushed past him and made for the cockpit. On the port side *Scorpio* was rafted to *Vagabond*. Tony, Mirabai, and Janice were transferring food from *Scorpio* to the trimaran, the two women taking it down into *Vagabond*'s galley. Macklin, with his .45, stood guard. Sheila was at the wheel, Olly at *Scorpio*'s. The two boats, under reduced sail, were sailing downwind in a moderate tradewind. The sun was only a few degrees above the horizon in a clear sky. As Neil moved slowly toward the others Frank, who was standing next to Sheila, turned to face him.

"I asked to be awakened at three forty-five," Neil said to him, hearkening back instinctively to the first act of disobedience, as if being locked in his cabin and threatened with a gun were less noteworthy.

"It's over, Neil," Frank said wearily, looking strangely beaten and resigned. "I . . . I've taken, retaken command of *Vagabond*. We're splitting up."

Tony had waved off a cardboard carton of food that Mirabai was about to hand him and pulled out his gun. He now came cautiously toward the place where Neil was standing, just outside the old wheelhouse area on the starboard side. Macklin's gun was aimed at Neil now.

"And what's all this transfer business?" Neil asked Frank, ignoring Tony.

"Lisa and Jim are being left aboard *Scorpio*," Frank said. "Those who are still healthy are all coming aboard *Vagabond* . . ." Frank stopped, his eyes lifeless. He glanced at Tony.

"Jeanne's elected to stay with them," Tony said. "That's where she is now. So has Olly. We assume you will too."

"And you're taking *Vagabond* to Barbados?" Neil asked Tony.

"That's right," Tony replied, holding the gun at his side. "And since most of the people are coming with us, and you and Olly think you can feed yourselves from the sea, we're also taking most of the food. Besides, if things don't work out on Barbados, we'll have to

keep sailing downwind until we find some island or some place in
Colombia or Panama where we can make a go of it. I figure the weak
little countries in the West Indies or Central America are a lot safer
than places like Brazil. There are already a lot more Americans where
we're going too.''

"If you're going to land and I'm staying at sea," Neil said to
Frank, "then you should let me take *Vagabond*. You won't need
either her space of windward oceangoing ability.''

"It's settled," Macklin said sharply. "We're taking *Vagabond*."

"*Scorpio*'s not seaworthy enough for the voyage I recommend,"
Neil persisted, "but she's just as good for heading west. As soon as
she stops having to beat to windward, she'll stop leaking.''

"Mac said it's settled," Tony snapped back. "If you leave, you
have to take *Scorpio*.''

"*He* says it's settled," said Neil with a rush of anger. "I don't.''
There was another tense silence.

"Frank also says so, as the ship's owner," Macklin replied stonily. "And this gun says so too.''

"You're choosing to abandon Jim?" Neil asked Frank.

"He chose to go to Salt Point," Frank replied, looking dully at
Neil. "He chose Lisa. He chooses you. He has to take the consequences.''

"He's your *son*!" Neil said.

"He's dying," Frank said softly.

"Jim's already got the disease," Tony said. "His temperature's
already as high as Lisa's.''

The two boats, rubbing and rolling, suddenly spilled rapidly down
the face of a wave, and everyone staggered or stumbled to regain his
or her balance. Mirabai spilled a box of food onto the port cockpit
deck. As he regained his balance Neil felt a heaviness stealing into
him, the heaviness of giving up, the heaviness he'd experienced after
long days of battling a storm at sea when the body says "No more,"
"I'll do it later," "Sink the fucking ship." No matter how fast he
ran, the forces of dissolution ran faster. He couldn't believe that the
West Indies or Central America would offer anything but slow death;
he couldn't believe that any land could be as safe as remaining out
at sea for as long as possible. But with *Scorpio* he might no longer
have such a choice.

"Sheila and Philip?" he asked, almost to himself.

"Philip's too sedated right now to decide," Sheila answered. "I feel . . . his life may depend on getting him to a physician soon. *Scorpio* . . . given the alternatives Tony has given us . . . I feel that . . . *Vagabond* . . ."

"You're right, of course," Neil said, nodding.

Captain Olly had turned *Scorpio*'s helm over to Janice and came over to the rail.

"Jeanne says she needs more of *Vagabond*'s towels," he said loudly to all of them. Neil saw now that the left side of Olly's face was badly bruised, his eye almost swollen shut.

"What happened to you?" Frank asked, frowning, and apparently he too was seeing Olly up close for the first time.

"I ain't the ducker I used to be," he said, sniffing. "Sorry I let you down, cap," he added to Neil.

"Tell her to use old clothes," Tony responded. "We're not parting with any of *Vagabond*'s stuff."

"Get her some towels," Frank said to Mirabai, who brushed quickly past Tony and went below. Macklin was about to stop her, flushed with anger, then let her go and didn't comment. In a moment she reappeared with three rather ratty-looking towels from Jeanne's cabin and handed them across to Olly.

"You win, Frank," Neil said loudly. "I've decided I'm not going on that death ship either. I'm staying on *Vagabond*."

Mirabai, who was passing from the cockpit to the galley with *Scorpio*'s food supplies, carried on indifferently when he said this, but everyone else who had heard him stopped and looked at him, Tony and Macklin with suspicion, Sheila and Frank with surprise.

"It's a trick," said Macklin. "Don't trust him."

"It's quite simple," Neil went on. "The doomed are going on *Scorpio,* and the winners are taking *Vagabond*. Although I may not be captain, I'm still free to choose the winners."

"What about Jeanne?" Frank asked, looking at him with puzzled surprise.

"Yes, Frank," Neil replied, staring at him intently. *"What about Jeanne?"*

"I mean . . . she . . . ."

"She's doomed on *Scorpio*."

"Not if you're with her," Frank said.

"Let's cut this crap," Macklin broke in. "Neil's sailing on *Scorpio* no matter what he wants."

"No, Conrad, no," Neil replied quietly with a half-smile. "That would be mutiny and perhaps murder. *You*'re capable of that, but Frank isn't. Can I keep my same cabin, Frank?"

"I'm taking the aft cabin," Tony interjected.

"I'm addressing the owner," Neil said, continuing to look at Frank.

"You really want to stay?" Frank asked.

"As much as you do, Frank. As much as you."

"Me too," said Olly, who had been listening from the deck of *Scorpio*. Now he climbed aboard *Vagabond* with an exaggerated smile, rendered grotesque by his puffy face. "Gotten so I prefer three-wheelers," he added.

"Get back on board *Scorpio*," Macklin shouted, nervous and angry.

"Course the company ain't as nice here," Olly said, "but I'm used to the stink of rotting things so—"

Tony instinctively lashed out at Olly with his gunhand. When Olly parried the blow and knocked the gun away, Macklin swung his gun into Olly's chest, sending him back against the cockpit seat, groaning.

"Hey!" Frank yelled, rushing forward.

Macklin leveled his automatic and flicked off the safety.

"Hold it!" he snapped fiercely, backing into the corner of the cockpit and looking uneasily at Frank. Frank stopped only a few feet from where Tony was stooping to retrieve his gun.

"The charade's over," Macklin announced. "Tony and I are taking over."

"What's *that* mean?" Frank said, his fists clenched at his sides.

"It means Tony and I are taking *Vagabond,* and you can join your friends on *Scorpio*."

"You little bastard," Frank growled, "you couldn't handle *Vagabond* for a single second."

"Get off the boat," said Macklin.

"Jesus, you and Tony *are* clowns," said Frank, sneering. With a suddenness that surprised everyone he grabbed Tony's gun and tried to twist it free, using Tony's body as a shield. Crouching in the corner ten feet away, Mackin trained his gun first on Frank and then on Neil, who had taken three quick steps toward him; then he swung it back around and fired a single shot at the tangle of Frank and Tony.

For a moment that tangle seemed to continue its wrestling unaffected, but then Frank slumped to the cockpit floor. Tony, breathing heavily, straightened up and stared down fearfully at his fallen adversary.

Macklin, sweating, turned his gun back on Neil. Jeanne appeared in *Scorpio*'s cockpit next to Janice, at the helm.

"What happened?" she asked into the silence aboard *Vagabond*.

Macklin wheeled toward her with a scowl.

"Get back below or I'll kill you."

"Get below!" Sheila shouted to her. "He's shot Frank." A look of shock appeared on Jeanne's face, then she moved slowly past Janice to *Scorpio*'s starboard rail. She could now see Frank's bleeding body in *Vagabond*'s rear cockpit.

"Oh, my God," she said and climbed aboard.

Tony and Mirabai, still worried about infection, quickly left the cockpit area to avoid her. Mirabai returned to *Scorpio,* and Tony came into the wheelhouse. As Jeanne knelt beside Frank's fallen body, Macklin held his gun on Neil.

"Oscar," he said, "put the barrel of your gun in Loken's back and escort him over onto *Scorpio*."

As Neil felt Oscar's gun press into his back he began walking toward Macklin, who was still crouched back against the far corner of the cockpit, his eyes darting nervously. The two boats were sailing serenely forward at six knots, still lashed side to side, rubbing and crashing but held off by their fenders.

Neil glanced at Sheila as he passed her at the helm and hoped she might try to help. Mirabai came up on deck again aboard *Scorpio*.

"That's it," she said to Macklin. "I've brought over everything you asked me to."

Macklin glanced swiftly at her, then back at Neil, who was now only six feet away. *Vagabond* suddenly swung to port, her port bow crashing hard against *Scorpio* and throwing all of them off balance: Sheila had acted.

Neil wheeled and, grabbing Oscar's gun arm, hurled him across the wheelhouse. He crashed into the mizzenmast, his gun was ripped from his hand, and he slumped to the floor. As Neil turned back toward Macklin he saw Jeanne wrestling for possession of Macklin's gun. Neil leapt forward, throwing his weight against Macklin's left side and sending all three of them crashing against the combing. Jeanne screamed as her left arm struck, then sank slowly to the deck. Neil grabbed Macklin's gun arm and began banging it against the edge of the combing. Groaning, Macklin let go of the gun.

Grabbing Macklin by the belt and shirt front, Neil half-carried, half-dragged him past Frank and Jeanne to the rear of the cockpit, lifted him high up over his head, and hurled him into the sea. Macklin's head struck the side of *Vagabond*'s deck. He fell between the two boats, bobbed up briefly in the boats' wakes, then disappeared behind a swell.

Neil stood staring after him for a moment, then turned back to the cockpit. Jeanne had knelt down beside Frank again, rocking back and forth, almost as if she had forgotten the violence swirling around her. Neil crouched down beside them.

Frank's eyes were open and clear, but a thin line of blood trickled from his mouth. He was laboring for each breath, his chest rising, shuddering, and collapsing. Neil knew a lung must have been punctured. Jeanne had placed a towel beneath his ribcage, and Neil took it away, pushed up his shirt, and revealed what looked like an exit wound from the bullet. The sight of the copious bleeding gave Neil a sinking feeling.

He groaned, reaching out to touch Frank and letting a hand fall helplessly on his shoulder. Frank managed a grin that was mostly a grimace.

"Christ," he gasped out, "have I botched it."

"Can't we help him?" asked Jeanne.

"Yes," said Neil. "We've got to drain the blood from his lung. Somehow get new blood into him." He stood up. Tony was in a corner of the wheelhouse along with the still groggy Oscar. For Neil they had no more relevance than bothersome insects.

"We're taking *Vagabond*," he said to them, "and staying at sea for the time being. We'll redivide the food after we've tried to save Frank."

Tony stood with one arm holding the mizzenmast to steady himself, the other still clutching his pistol. He seemed to be groping for an appropriate course of action and not finding one.

"You'll have to tell me when you changed course during the night," Neil went on. "I'll plot your course for Barbados."

"You . . . you're letting us go?" Tony asked, as if it had been Neil who was holding a gun on him.

"Yes," said Neil, and went below to try to save what still could be saved.

Once again *Vagabond* sailed on alone. The two boats had parted. Tony, Oscar, and the four others had taken *Scorpio,* planning to sail it downwind back to Barbados. Neil had checked over the relative food supplies of the two ships, sent some back to *Scorpio,* and had given Tony one of the two automatic rifles and some ammunition. His last exchange with Tony was brief.

"Good luck," Neil said to him as they prepared to cast off the rafting lines.

Tony, who had been unusually subdued in the two hours since Frank had been shot, simply nodded.

"You too," he said, and as Neil released one line and was moving to untie the next, added quickly, "Sorry about . . ." but didn't finish.

Neil merely released the second line, signaled Olly on the port bow to release his, and the two boats, free of each other at last, angled out and away from each other. Since *Vagabond* was now altering course from west back to southeast, the two boats had to cross paths once more, *Vagabond* luffing her sails and then sailing across *Scorpio*'s wake. For a moment everyone on both boats acted as if the other boat weren't there, until Olly, still on *Vagabond*'s bow collecting the fenders, stood up and waved heartily.

"Go get 'em, Tony," he shouted. Tony gave a subdued wave in return, and then the two vessels were speeding away from each other, one to the west, one to the southeast, each to its own fate.

"Always give people encouragement when they're sailing off," Olly said to Neil after he'd returned aft. "Otherwise they might come back."

Philip and Sheila had remained with *Vagabond*. When Sheila had talked to her husband late that morning about joining *Scorpio*, Philip had shaken his head.

"I have to have something to live for," Philip told her. "With those people I wouldn't. Here . . . I do."

But his fever was now over a hundred and three degrees; Neil started a third antibiotic.

Frank, berthed in the dinette where Philip had been, was still alive. They had sedated him, drained the blood from the lung, and managed, with great difficulty and uncertainty, to draw almost a pint of blood from Sheila's arm and inject it into Frank. Neil knew that with the primitive syringe he was using there was danger of an embolism, but he had concluded that without a transfusion Frank wouldn't survive the first night. Lisa and Jim were quarantined in Frank's old cabin, Philip installed on a wheelhouse settee, with Sheila in the forepeak. Jeanne and Skippy remained in the port cabin, but Jeanne began to spend most of her time with Lisa and Jim, planning to sleep on their cabin floor. The disease would reach its climax in the first three or four days, so the battle might well be won or lost quickly. Knowing that the disease was not airborne and that cleanliness could have a decisive effect on whether it spread or not, Neil hoped that they could contain it.

Although he was less hopeful that they could save Jim and Lisa, it wouldn't be for lack of trying. All during that long first day Jeanne and Neil tended the two feverish patients. They lay on adjacent berths, only conscious occasionally, sometimes hallucinating, their temperatures over one hundred and five degrees. Jeanne worked tirelessly, putting on and taking off the seawater-soaked towels and shirts, carrying Lisa's bony, torrid body to immerse her in the side cockpit, which had been filled with six inches of seawater. She watched helplessly as the fever raged on unabated and Lisa's breath become faster and faster, shallower and shallower. Neil helped bring water and towels and moved Jim when necessary; Sheila often helped them, but most of the burden was Jeanne's.

Neil found it depressing to be down in the heat and stink of Frank's cabin to confront the sweating bodies, feverish eyes, and incoherent mutterings of Jim and Lisa. Jim kept trying to act as if he were only mildly sick, joking about it, always asking about Lisa, who was just out of sight around the partition that separated their two berths, and once even volunteering to help carry her to the seawater bath in the cockpit. When he found he couldn't even stand up, he lost some of his youthful cockiness.

With three of the ship's company close to death and those who were still healthy feeling almost powerless to help them, the gloom during the day was broken only once, when in late afternoon Olly unexpectedly announced that they should hold a short memorial service for Conrad Macklin, as they had ten days before for Katya.

"He was our shipmate," Olly explained. "And besides, burying him might put us in a better mood." So Olly, Neil, and Sheila had stood awkwardly in a side cockpit and Olly had spoken.

"Well, Lord, we want to pay our last respects to Conrad Macklin," Olly began in a serious voice and with bowed head. "Connie was probably beat on as a kid, and his mom probably weaned him too early and his dad must have kicked his butt, so he developed into something of a shit, Lord, pardon the expression, but he didn't work hard at it and was only that way when he felt like it. Still we figure You got the big picture, Lord, and will know exactly what to do with Connie. Us, we got the small picture. All we could think of doing with him was throw him to the sharks. . . . Amen, Lord. Over and out."

Neil and Sheila said nothing.

"Now we symbolically commit his body to the sea," said Olly and, when he slapped Neil on the back, Neil gathered the ceremony was over.

"Funny thing, death," Olly announced as they walked back into the wheelhouse area. Neil waited for him to come out with some sort of punchline but he didn't, as if his three words summarized his meager fund of wisdom on the subject.

Neil was doctoring Frank. When the wounded man spoke without bitterness of Tony and Macklin, his tranquility began to remind Neil of Sam Brumburger. Frank even joked about their triangular relationship with Jeanne, announcing that he was "retiring from the field." Feeling helpless in treating Frank, twelve hours after the mutiny Neil made the decision to head for land. Frank's chances were slim at best, and then only if they could find modern medical facilities on the coast of Brazil.

Neil was aware of the dangers involved: the Brazilian government was sinking unauthorized ships who tried to land. The day before an airplane had passed overhead, the first they'd seen since leaving the Virgin Islands, and a freighter had passed them heading south. These sightings had disturbed Neil at the time; he feared that *Vagabond*'s presence might be reported to the Brazilian military authorities. His hope lay in their lying off the northeastern coast of Brazil, relatively uninhabited, and in *Vagabond*'s approaching the coast at night and hopefully arriving at dawn. He consulted with each of the others, warned them of the terrible dangers of landing, but they all voted to risk it. Frank alone argued against it.

"I don't think I'm going to make it, no matter how many tubes they stick in me," he said painfully. "You ought to stay out to sea."

But they turned southwest, heading for one of the coastal towns to the north of the mouth of the Amazon. Neil didn't plan to sail into a harbor but to sneak in, find a sympathetic doctor, and only then to bring Frank ashore.

At dusk, after looking at his primitive large-scale map of the coast, he went to fetch their automatic rifle and to begin planning defensive strategies for their landfall. The rifle was missing. He asked Sheila if she had moved it, and she said no. Nor had Olly. Disturbed, he discovered the 9 mm automatic on his cabin shelf was missing too. He asked Olly to check for the two other weapons they kept in the main cabin, and he reported them missing too. He and Olly were leaving the main cabin feeling baffled when Jeanne met them coming from hers.

"I threw the guns overboard," she announced quietly, looking frightened of what Neil's reaction might be.

Neil stopped in front of her, stunned, staring at her, not wanting to believe her, but knowing that this was the only explanation. "All *four* of them?" he asked.

She nodded.

"My God," he commented, turning away from her and staring off astern.

"I know I seem crazy to you," she said quietly, "but I don't want to live in the kind of world they create." Neil still looked away, his lined, bearded face tense and puzzled. "I love you, Neil. I know you've saved us a dozen times, sometimes with guns, but never again. Now we live or die like the rest of God's creatures, by the strength of our bodies alone."

Neil still stared stiffly off to sea, Olly, behind him, stroking his wispy white beard and scowling.

"I can understand what you did, Jeanne," Sheila said from the helm. "The guns make us a part of the madness of the rest of the world. I'm glad they're gone."

Jeanne looked thankfully at Sheila and then back at Neil.

"Never trusted 'em myself either," said Olly. "Only thing I ever killed with a gun was a rabbit, and he died of a heart attack from my missing him so often."

Neil walked farther aft and stared out at *Vagabond*'s wake. At first he had felt enraged that Jeanne had acted behind his back like that, frightened by the unexpected loss of weapons he thought he needed to survive, but with the voices of Sheila and Olly echoing Jeanne's, he felt an unexpected sense of tranquility replace his anger. The guns were gone. They themselves were out at sea, only a half-day from land and the enemy. It was not possible that the kind of fighting they'd had to do was over, but even if it wasn't, the odds were heavily against their winning, even with guns. They'd have to fight the way they'd fought the submarine. We'd better, he thought, smiling ruefully to himself at the thought of their being armed now with Olly's gaff and the flare gun. He walked back to Jeanne and held her gently.

"You did what you had to do, Jeanne," he said, aware of the tension in her that these new horrors had caused. He could feel her yielding only slightly in his embrace. "We haven't had much luck holding off death with guns, so it can't be much worse without."

At dawn they were still twenty miles off the coast. An hour later land came into sight. Ten minutes after that a jet fighter-bomber, a

French Mirage, streaked out of the sky from the west and passed with a roar directly over them.

Neil had made contingency plans for both air and sea attacks, and, being unarmed, their plans involved either surrendering or playing possum. They were already flying the Brazilian flag—homemade from a piece of sheet—but it would be difficult to surrender to a jet plane they had no radio contact with. As the jet shrieked past and began to climb and turn he shouted at everyone to get down into Frank's cabin. He himself dashed below to prepare the flares. He didn't know whether the jet would return or whether it would attack them if it did, but as Olly and Sheila passed him carrying Philip they exchanged pained glances, the look of soldiers marching to a battle they didn't expect to win.

As he returned from the main cabin with the flares Neil had a chance to look back: the jet was making a long graceful sweep up the sky to the right, then around and back toward *Vagabond*. Neil was alone at the helm, making no effort to take evasive action, two smoke flares and two fire flares on the control panel shelf, a box of dry matches nearby. The plane grew rapidly larger, and Neil experienced the brief image of a man facing a firing squad. Then there was a brief flash from beneath the jet and almost simultaneously the rush and roar of the missile tearing past the trimaran. The jet shrieked past a second time.

His hands trembling, Neil lit one of the smoke flares and tossed it down into the main cabin. He lit the second and threw it down into the empty port cabin. Dark smoke billowed up out of both cabins within seconds as Neil returned to prepare to ignite one of the light flares. The missile had struck at least a half-mile ahead of *Vagabond*, but he doubted the pilot had been able to follow its trajectory. As the jet rose and swept to the right a second time the pilot would look back and see his target enveloped in dark smoke. Their hope lay in the pilot's being satisfied with a probable kill.

But the jet returned. As Neil lit his third flare it fired a second missile. So close did the second shot come to *Vagabond* that Neil thought it might have gone through the mainsail; it burst less than a hundred yards in front of them. The bright flash of the lit flare must have looked to the pilot—if he could see it, which was doubtful— like a direct hit. The jet roared over the smoke-enshrouded trimaran, and Neil, coughing and almost overcome by the smoke, rushed forward and dropped the jib and mainsail. Then he rushed back through the smoke and down into the starboard cabin with the others. Thick black smoke was pouring out of two of *Vagabond*'s cabins into the air.

Neil's hands were black, and one hand had been burned when he lit the third flare. Jeanne and the others looked at him, as if they were asking him to announce their fate. He didn't have to tell them they hadn't been hit, and only later did he realize that they didn't even know they'd been fired on.

The jet didn't return a fourth time. It returned to base apparently confident that it had prevailed in its battle with the trimaran.

After five minutes of waiting, with the smoke gradually getting worse even in the closed-off cabin, Neil and Olly went back up on deck. Both smoke flares were going out, but something was still burning in the galley. Neil had to go down and extinguish a smoldering rug. The whole interior of the main cabin was black with the smoke.

The others now climbed out of Jeanne's cabin to survey the damage, but there was no damage. The multimillion-dollar aircraft had fired two highly sophisticated missiles at the plywood and Fiberglas sailboat, but, as Neil explained, they had been metal- or heat-seeking missiles. *Vagabond*, engineless, gave off no heat and had so little metal in her aluminum spars that the missile couldn't find her. The pilot had been trained to fire in the general area of the target and let the missile do the fine tuning. *Vagabond* and her crew had been saved by modern technology.

Two hours later they raised sail again. After they had discussed their next course of action, they decided that they should get as far out of the area as possible: to run directly east for another sixty miles, which would put them fifty or sixty miles off the coast. They would have to do their best for Frank and Philip and Jim and Lisa without the help of the rest of the world. They were alone.

As they sailed on toward the equator the heat and humidity became stupefying; only the recurrent squalls, by refreshing their supply of water, kept them alive and sane.

All Neil felt he dared do for Frank was give him a second blood transfusion, but with the plague victims it was an hourly battle to try to cool off their bodies. The seawater was twenty degrees cooler than the air, and they used it continually. But over the next three days the fever raged on. Twice Lisa went into convulsions, twice she recovered. Jim jabbered on in some otherworldly hallucination about snow and cold and the bottom of the world, sometimes giggling hysterically.

On the third day, after Lisa had had her second bout of convulsions, Neil came down into the cabin and found Jeanne up on the berth with Lisa, her face buried on Lisa's bare chest and neck, sobbing. For a moment Neil thought that Lisa must have died; a wave of sadness immobilized him. Then he noticed her rapid, shallow breathing and realized that Jeanne, who had been driving herself beyond reason, was suddenly giving up. Pressing her face and mouth against Lisa's flesh was almost a kind of suicide.

He went up to the edge of the berth, gently pulled her back toward him and, as she wailed and struggled, less gently dragged her out of the cabin. With Olly and Sheila watching uncertainly, he took soap and seawater and scrubbed her face, neck, and arms. She struggled and cried like a child being punished. Neil even forced the soap rag inside her mouth before finally letting her go.

"Take her back to her own cabin," he said quietly to Sheila. "Keep her there. I'll take over responsibility for Jim and Lisa until Jeanne's rested."

Back belowdecks when he felt Lisa's forehead, he was horrified: he'd never felt a human body so hot. He dispensed with the side cockpit pool and the towels and instead began throwing buckets of seawater directly over Lisa and Jim and the towels and clothing that wrapped their naked bodies. For half an hour he lugged the buckets down and poured the cool seawater over them. Later he'd have to bail out the cabin's bilge.

Forty minutes later he went to see Jeanne in her cabin. She was alone and, after asking how she was and receiving a dull reply, he said to her, "I miss you, Jeanne."

"Miss me?" she said, looking puzzled. "Oh," she added, understanding.

"I know of no law saying I can't love you," he said. "Do you?"

"No," she replied, not looking at him.

"Nor a law prohibiting your loving me," he went on. "Is there?"

Her face still averted, she said, "Only a law of nature."

"What law is that?"

"When a mother is threatened with the loss of her child, she loses a part of herself."

"I see," said Neil. "That I can't help."

"Nor can I," said Jeanne.

"And I still miss you."

"I know," she whispered.

"There are no barriers between us now," Neil said gently, "except those we erect in our own hearts."

"I know," she whispered again, crying softly. "But I can't knock them down."

"But what *are* they?" Neil asked gently.

She looked up at him at last, warm tears in her eyes.

"Fear," she said.

"Fear?"

"We're all doomed," she said. "No matter how hard we try, one by one we're going to die. Our desperate acts are just dancing on a hot griddle before the end."

For a long moment he held her gaze, searching for words of reassurance, searching for the incantation that would smash the barrier. He could find none.

"Still," he finally managed. "Dancing is better than nothing."

"Until you get tired," she responded.

* * *

Although Frank felt better on the morning after the jet attack, some strangely detached part of himself knew he was going to die. It wasn't any rational conclusion based on medical or anatomical knowledge; it was some previously uncontacted part of himself informing him from some unknown world of reality, which, paradoxically, he didn't believe in. A mystic certainty had come to him, Frank, the most unmystical of men.

When the heavy sedation Neil had given him began to wear off and his mind began to clear, Frank was surprised at how he felt. His anger against Neil and his jealousy were totally gone. His earlier decision to abandon Jim, Jeanne, and his friends seemed totally senseless. He knew it had come out of his resentment and sadness at losing Jeanne, but to his new way of looking at things losing Jeanne seemed as trivial an event as losing an anchor. The thought of her, even now, made his heart ache, but the ache was somehow amusing, trivial, like hiccups.

Even his own death had a somewhat comic quality: wrestling with one big clown, being shot by a small one. Surviving megatons of destruction to succumb to a tiny piece of lead.

Jim's death, if Jim were going to die, was not comic. It was sad. It was the only thing that made him truly sad. It was the only thing that made him resent the war, resent the holocaust. Jim should live. Lisa should live. Children should live. It was he and Neil and Olly and Philip and their generation that had let things happen: they could die knowing they deserved it, but not their children. We are the one generation in human history to snuff out untold millions, no, billions, of lives of all creatures for untold centuries. We were the assholes that let it happen.

For even as he accepted his own fate with equanimity, he felt a quiet fury at the way he had led his life. He saw that his joyful playing with money, so dissociated from any human reality, was his personal contribution to the holocaust. He had been a part owner of General Electric and General Dynamics, both when he owned some of their stock and when he didn't. He never built a bomb or pushed a button, but he helped pay the men who did.

It made his life pathetic. All his successes and failures now seemed so trivial compared to the Big Failure; all his aspirations so selfish compared to those he might have had, but didn't. But could men have done anything to stop the flow of events to the ultimate madness? Although he had always thought they couldn't, though his reason even now argued they couldn't, that new voice from that strange detached world announced unreservedly that men could have stopped the flow of events as inefficiently, sporadically, and bumblingly as they had set that flow of events in motion. The creative capacity for building rockets that occasionally blew up on their pads was equally capable of tearing them all apart and burying them, and could have done it with the same margin of error.

Although it took a lot out of him to talk and though Neil reminded him that every ounce of energy was needed, Frank was thankful that first Jeanne and then Neil let him say a few things he wanted to say.

Jeanne was pale, puffy-eyed, and disheveled when he saw her, thirty hours after she'd begun taking care of Lisa and Jim. It seemed to Frank she was almost like a madwoman. When she came down into the main cabin and washed her hands and arms and then sat beside him for a moment, he smiled up at her.

"You look like *you're* the one who got shot," he said.

She looked startled and didn't smile.

"I'm sorry Lisa's sick, Jeannie," he went on, aware that his strange levity was out of place with her now.

"How are *you*, Frank?" she rejoined, finally centering her attention on him.

"Pretty good," he answered. "Even dying."

"You're not dying, Frank," she said urgently.

"It doesn't matter, dying's not what it's cracked up to be," Frank went on, vaguely thinking that he might be feverish. "And I'm sorry I butted in between you and Neil."

"That's not important now."

"I know it's not," Frank said, "but I still wanted to tell you."

"I'm sorry I can't love you the way you deserve."

"Hell, Jeanne," Frank said, smiling. "I'd want to be loved a lot more than that."

Again she looked at him questioningly as if she were uncertain he was in his right mind. Then she smiled.

"Thank you," she said, "for being the way you are."

He felt a wave of weariness pass through him and then responded. "It's simple to become wise," he said. "Just get shot."

The next day he and Neil talked.

"We're only a day's sail from the equator," Neil announced.

Frank, whose weariness was increasing and who now slept most of the time, opened his eyes to look at Neil. "You plan to bury me there?"

"I hope to save you."

Frank closed his eyes, nodded almost imperceptibly, then opened them again. "Too late, buddy."

"Maybe," said Neil. "But we'll try."

Frank struggled up into consciousness again. "I'm sorry I won't be rounding Cape Horn with you."

"Not very likely."

"The sailing was always great," he said softly. "It was . . . the human stuff that messed us up. . . ."

As Neil looked down, Frank thought he saw tears in his eyes.

"You, me, and the rest of the world," said Neil.

"Yeah," said Frank.

For another half-minute neither man spoke and a series of confused images raced through Frank's mind until Neil rose to leave.

"Last word," Frank mumbled, and Neil stopped. Frank opened his eyes and felt a strange giddy joy flowing through him. He smiled feverishly up at Neil. "Advice . . ." he announced to Neil. "I think . . . the market is . . . at a low. . . ." He felt like laughing. "Good time to buy."

Neil, like Jeanne, looked down at him uncertainly, then nodded, smiling slightly in return.

"Nowhere to go but up," Neil commented.

"Right . . ." said Frank, closing his eyes.

At dawn two days later Frank died.

Neil was surprised and unsettled by the grief he felt. He had known Frank was dying and thought he had hardened himself, but when Olly called him down and he saw Frank's limp body and open mouth, an emptiness and gloom descended upon him that left him immobilized. He realized how much unspoken companionship he and Frank had enjoyed, even during the estranged period of the last month. The two communicated in a shorthand about the way *Vagabond* sailed that

Neil couldn't share with anyone else. To realize that he had lost this friend, first to jealousy and now to death, grieved him.

Instead of giving Olly orders about what to do, he wandered back out of the cabin and walked aft to stare out at the sea. A distant part of him felt the burden of having to tell Jeanne. But he felt passive, weary. He felt a sad, self-pitying sense that everything was useless, that Death, like a cat playing with crippled mice, could take him and his loved ones at any time he wanted. A tickling on his cheeks and saltiness in a corner of his mouth made him realize that he was crying.

Jeanne came up to him. Seeing her eyes beaming with happiness, he realized that no one had told her about Frank's death. She didn't even notice his tears.

"Neil," she said softly, "the fever . . . the fever's down. I think . . . I think it's breaking."

Neil looked down at her, dazed, trying to absorb the meaning of her words. "Lisa?"

"Both of them," she answered, softly—as if she were afraid that if she announced it too loudly, the gods would change their minds. "Jim two hours ago, and now Lisa. Come see."

Mechanically Neil followed her down into Frank's old cabin. The floor was wet, the room sweltering in the heat of the equator. Lisa lay wanly on the first berth staring at him, a shy smile on her face, beads of perspiration or salt water all over her body. Jeanne adjusted a towel to hide Lisa's nakedness.

"I . . . I'm feeling better," Lisa said.

"I'm glad," said Neil simply, feeling tears for Frank and tears of joy for Lisa's recovery welling up in his eyes again.

"I'm . . . hungry," Lisa announced uncertainly, as if she had finally isolated the unique sensation she was feeling.

Neil nodded and reached out to put his hand briefly on hers. Then Jeanne, smiling, pulled him farther forward to see Jim, who was up on an elbow looking at him. Somehow Jim seemed to sense Neil's restrained mood.

"How . . . is dad?" he asked in a hoarse whisper.

Neil, aware of Jeanne beside him, still exhilarated by the survival of the two young people, couldn't answer.

"I'm glad you came through, Jim," he said.

But again Jim picked up Neil's unspoken feelings.

"Dad . . . isn't . . . isn't?" he asked Neil.

"Frank died," Neil said. "Just twenty minutes ago."

After a moment's hesitation, Jim began to nod slowly.

"He said good-bye to me," Jim whispered hoarsely. "He came to me an hour ago . . . his spirit, you know, and told me . . . to live . . . to take care of everybody."

Neil nodded as Jeanne leaned against him, absorbing the news of Frank's death. He put his arm around her.

"Frank probably saved us all back during the mutiny," Neil said. "Now we'll need you."

But Jim now had tears in his eyes. "But I wish . . ." he began again in a voice weak from three days of disuse. "I wish he could be with us when we . . . if we . . . finally . . ."

" . . . live." Jeanne finished softly.

After burying Frank at sea, they sailed on.

They kept *Vagabond* well off the Brazilian coast, hoping to reduce the chance of being attacked by another plane or a gunboat, their destination still uncertain. As long as food and water held out they would continue into the South Atlantic. Nothing they were hearing from around the world encouraged them to try to land. The plague was still spreading. Shortwave transmissions from all of Europe had ceased. Most U.S. broadcasters had shut down. An AM station in Uruguay reported that a series of food riots in Rio de Janeiro had been suppressed by the army and left over three thousand people dead, and the Brazilian air force had attacked and sunk a freighter crammed with refugees that had tried, after repeated warnings to turn back, to enter the harbor at Rio de Janeiro. Rio was staggering under the impact of her unemployed and starving millions, who were begging, stealing, rioting, and fleeing to and arriving from all over Brazil. Thousands had died in the last month from disease or starvation, many from the newly introduced plague.

But the alternatives to landing in Brazil were equally dismal. The few small islands in the South Atlantic were governed by Brazil or Argentina, and their friendliness to American refugees was as doubtful as that of the mainland.

Argentina, because it hadn't needed to import food, seemed slightly preferable. But the last Spanish-language broadcast that Sheila had been able to understand before their transistor radio batteries went dead had indicated that illegal immigrants were being quarantined and put in internment camps, a gloomy prospect unless and until they actually began to starve to death. In the meantime they would sail south, hope that the plague would run its course on land and would not reappear aboard *Vagabond,* hope that they could feed themselves from the sea, and wait.

In eleven days they reached the latitude of Rio, passing a hundred miles to the east. Their tentative destination was the coast below Mar del Plata, two hundred and fifty miles southeast of Buenos Aires in Argentina.

When their shortwave radio broke down, they were left without a functioning radio. They began sailing alone amidst a depressing silence from the rest of the world.

And the sea too seemed silent and empty. They saw no other ships. No seabirds accompanied them. Although they trolled all the time, usually with two rods and two lures, the fish, if they were there, usually spurned their offerings. As they grew weaker from their increasingly strict rationing they began to dip into their emergency food kit. They established a schedule of rationing that would permit them to reach southern Argentina with an empty larder.

But *Vagabond* sailed now in peace. Their harmony was not simply the result of the lassitude brought on by malnutrition, but rather of the trust and affection that had been forged out of their common experience of the horrors of the previous two and a half months. Neil and Jeanne were lovers, husband and wife; so too were Jim and Lisa, although Lisa still had not fully recovered from the disease and was barely able to walk. Sheila and Philip were their benevolent aunt and uncle; Olly the grandpa. Neil lived with Jeanne and Skippy in her port cabin; the Wellingtons had taken over his aft cabin.

Jim slowly recovered his strength. At first Neil and Jeanne had thought that his quiet dignity was only weakness, the aftereffects of the disease, but soon they realized that with death so near, Jim had found the same tranquility that Frank had come to during his last hours. He developed a new low-key sense of humor and was no longer in awe of Neil but able to poke fun at him.

Lisa, although the disease had left her pathetically weak, was childlike in the joy she showed in being alive and in love with Jim. Each morning he carried her from their starboard cabin to the open cockpit areas where she could be with the others. Neil urged books upon her, Skippy urged her to play games with him, Philip began to teach her navigation. She did a little of each. Although her weakness was sometimes heartrending—they had no idea how completely she might eventually recover—the joy she found in Jim, her happiness in living, made it impossible to be depressed in her presence.

But as they moved farther south they were also moving into the late winter of the Southern Hemisphere. They were pitifully unprepared for the cold, especially after having just suffered through two weeks at the equator. Their bodies were lacking in fat that could be burned off to warm them. There was little winter clothing aboard. With the propane supply exhausted and their kerosene almost gone, they had no fuel to warm the cabins, and the three women took the two wool blankets aboard and began to convert them into warm clothing. The only cold-weather gear they had was Neil's orange float suit, and they needed two or three additional winter garments so that at least three people could be out on deck at once if necessary. They cut and sewed one small woolen jumpsuit to fit Lisa and Sheila and another larger one to fit Jim, Neil, and Philip. From the remains of the blankets they managed to make a third jacket to fit Olly and Jeanne. Two pairs of sweatpants became winter underwear. Clothing was no longer individual but held in common by two or three similarly built individuals, and worn as the need arose. They were now without soap, so their clothing began to stink and their limited number of socks to disintegrate.

The strangeness of their clothing was only another symptom of their dissociation from their previous lives. Just as they were physically, electronically, and geographically isolated from most of the rest of the planet, so too they were now in some way detached from the incredible events that had transformed the earth. The fear and hatred that the inhabitants of the Southern Hemisphere felt for refugees like themselves seemed to be natural and as blameless as the squalls that had afflicted them north of the equator—something to reef for. The destruction of much of the world by nuclear war seemed like a natural tragedy, as if the earth had been hit by some errant comet.

The plague did not reappear. After two weeks they dared to assume that they were free of that danger. They were healthy. They were starving. Bringing in a single fish was cause for a major celebration. The loss of a hooked fish before they had boarded it left them limp, empty, afraid. When their emergency cache of food was mostly gone, when they were down to a few days' ration of dried fish, when all their previous stores of food were reduced to a few rotting potatoes and the last unopened, rusted can of Spam, they turned, filled with dread, again toward land.

Their lives, which for three weeks had taken on a peaceful, dreamlike quality brought about by their isolation and undernourishment, now, they feared, would once again take on the quality of a nightmare. They approached land feeling like aliens about to visit a foreign planet.

But the land came out to them. An Argentine frigate met them thirty miles off the coast and warned them through an electric bullhorn that no *Norteamericanos* were being allowed on the mainland of Argentina. If they came any closer to the coast their boat would be confiscated and they would be taken to the recently conquered Malvinas Islands with the other plague victims and illegal immigrants. They turned back out to sea.

Now sailing south seemed like an act of madness. They were sailing into winter, down toward the fiercest winds in the world, to the Straits of Magellan, to Cape Horn. They were sailing down to the very bottom of the civilized world, to a land so barren and infertile only the simplest and most impoverished Indian cultures had inhabited it until barely a century before. They were sailing away from man.

They had decided to try to sail through the Straits of Magellan to the Pacific. This proposal, which would have seemed so absurd, so impossible, two months before, seemed to all of them now to be inevitable and necessary. They had been driven south by forces beyond their control. Every time they had stopped running and tried to settle, they had been driven onward. Although the rest of the planet was silent now, all their radios silent, they sensed that where men were few and far from the holocaust, there peace might be found. To get to the islands of the South Pacific, they would have to round the tip of South America. So they would round it.

Strangely, even as they were turned away from land, the sea began again to feed them. They caught two large tuna, thirty pounds between them, at dusk of the very day they had been repulsed. They decided now to hold none of this blessing back, because they knew that all of them were near the end of their tethers. They decided to eat as if there were no tomorrow. "The Good Lord will provide," Olly pronounced. "Occasionally."

Watches had to be shortened to two hours, sometimes only one, because no one had the strength to stay at the helm any longer. Each person slept most of the time they weren't needed in sailing the boat. Carpets, life preservers, and unused sails were used as extra blankets. As they moved farther south the seas grew bigger, the winds fierce. Neil, fighting to bring down the mainsail in sudden forty-knot winds, wrenched his back, sending it into spasms and effectively incapacitating him.

As the cold became worse and the work even more demanding Olly too took to bed. After standing his watch one morning he staggered down into the main cabin and fainted. Later, revived, he announced he was "feeling poorly" and would prefer a vacation. With Neil already bedridden, Olly's dereliction made everyone realize how frail and bony he had become—a laughing skeleton, Philip had called him a few days earlier. He had a slight fever, complained of pains in his chest and belly, complained of a toothache, but what really ailed him couldn't be pinned down. His illness left Jim and the two women to sail *Vagabond* alone. Thus now Jeanne and Sheila each had to take two-hour shifts at the helm alone in thirty- to forty-knot winds. And *Vagabond,* scarred and jury-rigged, as tired in her bones as her sailors in theirs, slashed and pounded dutifully forward, her sails tearing more often, fittings coming loose, but still going forward.

When they finally arrived at Cabo Virgenes at the eastern end of the Straits, they arrived, as Philip had predicted, in a gale. It blew out their working jib; they lost a halyard up the mast; they were almost blown onto a rocky shore before they regained control and retreated back out of the Strait to anchor in the lee of a point.

They had to remain anchored there for four days, waiting for the gale to blow itself out. They mended sail, caught a half-dozen small tasty fish on the bottom, and rested. They sent a party ashore to search for food. The shore was barren, windswept, all in gray and brown. They felt immense relief that there were no humans in the area. The late winter–early spring season meant that there was no green vegetation except in the water. They plucked at the few dried berries they found as at the most luscious of strawberries; dried grasses were picked to be their lettuce. Seaweed and shellfish were gathered from the tidal pools. Thankful for these meager winter remnants, the party returned to *Vagabond* to rest, Olly joining the Wellingtons to conserve body warmth in the aft cabin.

Neil, although still bedridden and frustrated by being unable to share in the sailing, nevertheless found himself strangely content. Instead of feeling alone and isolated, he felt as if he were at home surrounded by a loving family. Jeanne had sawed a hole in the wall separating their cabin from the main cabin so he was able to talk to the others. He had once or twice tried shouting orders from his bunk, but even as he did he realized his contributions weren't needed. Philip and Sheila and Jim were all good sailors. Instead of making him feel unneeded, this awareness of his own superfluity was soothing. He could lie in his berth without the sense that unless he got himself up on deck in the bitter cold, *Vagabond* was doomed. The only thing that occasionally frightened him about his contentment was that it might be a sign that he was dying.

His own survival had given him hope for the group as well. He felt that down so far at the bottom of the world the disease called man might have escaped the fear and violence that was destroying the more civilized strains up north. Ultimately, he supposed, his feeling that they were going to make it was as absurd and groundless as his and Jeanne's earlier conviction that they were doomed. Deep down he knew that even now, after all they had been through, Death could squash them all effortlessly with one casual blow.

Yet, for now, they still lived, and despite the hardships, they found in the tiny haven of their cabin a quiet and confident happiness that had always eluded Neil.

Life was reduced to eating, keeping warm, and companionship. The violent conflicts that wracked the rest of mankind seemed distant and trivial. A conversation between Neil and Jeanne one afternoon when *Vagabond* was at anchor, riding out the snow squalls and forty-knot winds, showed how detached they had become from their previous world. They were lying under a pile of covers in their berth.

"You know," Neil said to Jeanne, "I've been thinking about how the war started." He paused as if he were still thinking about it and then went on. "I'm not sure that the Russians fired the first salvo of missiles."

Holding his hand as she lay beside him, Jeanne turned to look at him in the gray light of the late afternoon.

"You believed those Venezuelan broadcasts?" she asked, referring to programs they'd listened to more than a month earlier in which Venezuelan spokesmen had charged that the U.S. had started the war.

"No, not that," Neil replied. "The thing that's always bothered me is that the Russians attacked American cities and industries and military bases. We're told they attacked missile sites, too, but one station way back at the beginning said something that I've never forgotten: they suggested that people flee to North and South Dakota to escape the fallout."

Jeanne watched him as he paused, holding his gaze and waiting.

"I can't help concluding that if the Russians didn't hit South Dakota, it was because they knew there was nothing there to hit: all our missiles had already been fired."

"If the Russians had struck first," Jeanne prompted, "South Dakota would have been a primary target."

"Yes."

"So you think that the President gave the orders for a surprise attack?" she asked quietly.

"He wanted his nation to survive," Neil replied. "He thought it was sit and get clobbered or strike first. He ordered the first strike for the same reasons that a Russian premier would have done it: out of fear that the enemy was desperate enough to do it, so he'd better do it first."

Jeanne felt a distant sadness. She hadn't really questioned the assumption of all the American radio stations that the Russians had struck first. She realized that she felt it was only natural that they would do it; Americans had been fearing they would attack for years. Yet she understood that that very fear, so pervasive, so hopeless, might have led an American government to do what Neil was speculating it had done. She felt no anger, only the distant sadness.

"The missiles fired at South Dakota targets might have been intercepted," she suggested, "or might have missed on the first strike. And then after our Dakota-based missiles had been fired, the Russians left the area alone." Even as she spoke, most of her mind was accepting Neil's thesis.

"Yes, that's possible," agreed Neil. "I'd thought of that. But we know that the very *first* Soviet missiles hit American cities, targets that would always be vulnerable, whereas missile silos are worth hitting only on the very first strike, before they've launched their missiles."

Jeanne looked at him.

"How does it make you feel?" she asked.

"It doesn't make me feel much one way or another," he replied. "It doesn't change how hungry I am." He smiled. "The two sides had gotten each other into a position where, sooner or later, someone was going to hit first. The fact that our government may have been the first to give in to that fear doesn't really horrify me. The mistakes had already been made."

Jeanne stared out the cabin window at the almost horizontal line of snowflakes rushing past.

"No wonder we're outcasts."

And later that same afternoon their talk brought them to a subject that gave them new vitality. When Neil, still huddled under the covers with Jeanne, had first discussed Lisa's continuing weakness, he had expressed concern that Lisa might be pregnant, which, because the fetus's development might have been impaired by her high fever, would put an added strain on her health. Jeanne had responded that Lisa had had a regular period a few days before the plague struck her, and then, looking puzzled, suddenly looked with a flush of joy at Neil.

"What are you thinking?" Neil asked, aware of something special happening with her.

"I just realized that . . . that *I* may be pregnant," she said to him, looking half-joyful and half-awed.

Neil felt stunned. Their lovemaking had usually had an end-of-the-world desperation that was outside normal, everyday reality. Pregnancy belonged to the old world, not the ugly, tenuous one they now inhabited.

"My period's overdue," Jeanne went on, now looking uncertain. "I suppose it might just be . . . my wound . . . my worrying . . . diet . . ." She frowned as she considered these other explanations. But then she smiled again: she and Neil had made love without contraception during her most fertile time. In those days the possible consequences seemed irrelevant. Now they seemed divine. Even the shadow of the possible effects of her exposure to radiation didn't dim her joy.

"Lovemaking does tend to create babies, I suppose," Neil said to her, still somewhat dazed but with a grin on his face.

"Oh, Neil, I hope so, I hope so, I hope so," Jeanne said, hugging him.

Bright-eyed, he looked down at her and then off through the window at the snow swirling past. He had a boyishly happy, faraway expression.

"Now, we'll *have* to live," he said dreamily. "Just to see if it's a boy or a girl."

But an hour later, as he struggled up on deck for the first time in a week, he knew that his puny aspirations would have nothing to do with it. Their lives—even the new one growing within Jeanne—still hung by a thread.

When the gale lessened and the wind shifted they sailed on through the Straits. They were sailing mechanically now, without real hope that they would ever see the Pacific, but sailing because all other alternatives were worse. They made barely a hundred miles over the first three days, sailing only during the eight hours of daylight, anchoring at night. Neil at least was able to stand watch again.

The absence of any sign of life during their first days in the Straits made them suspect that there couldn't be a small bustling city only a little way off. As they neared the place in the Straits where their map showed Punta Arenas to be and they still had seen no boats, no smoke, no planes, they decided that there couldn't be much of a military presence and thus humans in Punta Arenas might not be a threat, might, in fact, be helpful and sympathetic. So they proceeded to try it by day.

Uncertain of their exact location, they had almost sailed past the town when Philip spotted it through the binoculars three miles to the north—the charred wreckage of buildings and a few small houses on the hillsides. Nervously they altered course to sail over. Although the temperatures were in the forties the scene that drew toward them was bleak. All the buildings on the waterfront were blackened shells or had burned to the ground. The hulks of a large freighter and several smaller ships lay half-sunk along the waterfront. As they anchored off a burned-out wharf a few stray dogs scurried like overgrown rats among the blackened timbers of the wreckage. The hills above the town were brown and gray with only occasional patches of white from the recent snow. Nowhere was there any sign of human life. So fearful of man had those aboard *Vagabond* become that the emptiness of the city was as much a relief as a source of sadness. Neil, who had joined the others on deck, felt the same sense of being an alien on another planet that he had felt at each of their last landfalls.

They had lowered their dinghy into the water, and Jim, Neil, and Sheila were preparing to go ashore when two, three, and then half a dozen people appeared along one small section of unburned bulkhead fifty feet away. There were four men, a woman, and a child. Two of the men were carrying rifles. All were dressed in woolen ponchos and several wore the distinctive bowler hats of the Andes. The Chileans stared at the trimaran and its occupants, who stared back. Then one of the men with a rifle shouted something. Jeanne, frowning, shouted back in Spanish a request that he say it again. The man shouted the same thing a second time. Jeanne frowned a moment and consulted with Sheila.

"What's he saying?" Neil asked.

"As near as we can tell," said Jeanne with a puzzled smile on her face, "he's saying—roughly translated— 'Hi, where the hell did you get that weird boat?' "

In the next two days, after making friends with the few Chileans who were still living in Punta Arenas, they gradually learned that the city had been destroyed in a brief war between Chile and Argentina ten weeks earlier. No one was certain why the war had started, although the two countries had long disputed over parts of Tierra del Fuego. It wasn't even certain who had won the war, but Argentinian jets had destroyed the city and sunk most of the Chilean ships during the four days of fighting. With the city mostly destroyed, the Chilean government had ordered it evacuated, perhaps because they were obliged to under the peace treaty, perhaps because they were unwilling to spend money supplying it with food and fuel during the winter. Thousands of people had sailed off in freighters and navy ships for Santiago, leaving less than a hundred people who either chose to stay or got left behind out of ignorance. There was no phone, radio, road, or air contact between this part of Chile and the more civilized parts farther north. A single Chilean navy ship had turned up a month ago, looked around, and disappeared.

They also learned that *Vagabond* was not the only ship to have arrived since the town's destruction. Six weeks before, an English sailboat had arrived, made some repairs, reprovisioned as best they could, and then sailed on. A damaged Dutch sloop had arrived three weeks earlier and was beached a mile to the east. A Rumanian sailboat had arrived only three days before *Vagabond*. The small, wiry Chilean man in his thirties who had become their unofficial guide joked that Punta Arenas was becoming the "new French Riviera."

They met the crews of both ships, and for Neil and the others, friendly people were unreal. The absence of threat was vaguely unnerving. The chance to live on land, perhaps in the shell of a house, seemed too good to be true. Food there was very scarce. Spring, although it officially began on September 21, the day they arrived, was still almost a month away. The friendly Chileans had no provisions to spare, but they did show the sailors where they could hunt small game—mostly rodents and wild dogs—and where they could gather shellfish.

It was unreal, too, to meet the three Dutchmen and one woman and her eight-year-old child who were making a winter home a mile east of Punta Arenas while they tried to repair their holed thirty-eight-foot Fiberglas sloop. Two of the Dutch spoke good English, as did one of the Rumanians. They, along with six others, two of them women, had sailed a forty-eight-foot Fiberglas ketch all the way from the Black Sea. It was also anchored east of the wrecked town. Each of the crews was wary and suspicious of the other for a day or two. It wasn't until they had shared the stories of their long voyages of survival that they all began not only to trust one another but to feel a bond of brotherhood. The Rumanians, like those aboard *Vagabond*, were still in shock after being greeted with friendliness by fellow human beings.

The Dutch had fled Amsterdam on the first morning of the war, landing briefly in Portugal and again in the Canary Islands for supplies. They hadn't encountered the resentment and violence that fleeing Americans had experienced; no one blamed the Dutch for the War. But conditions were harsh in the Canaries, the islands crowded with European refugees and food so scarce that aristocrats with millions of dollars in gold found it almost useless. The Dutch decided to sail across to Argentina, which, they thought, had plenty of food and would welcome them. When they landed in a small Argentinian fishing village, they learned they would lose their boat and be interned. They opted to try for the South Pacific.

The Rumanians' story was more harrowing. Vacationing on the Black Sea when the War began, they had all, including the three

Communist Party members aboard, decided that the war was a meaningless disaster and chosen to run. By the time they got to the Bosphorus, a nuclear explosion had blocked the straits to all commercial and military traffic but they were able to sail through. They touched on North Africa only once, losing two of their shipmates in an attack by brigands, then escaped out through the Mediterranean to the Atlantic. They stopped in Cape Verde to reprovision but found food so scarce they could obtain almost nothing. Sailing on, they'd been dismasted in a storm off Brazil, spent three weeks in a jungle south of the Amazon fitting another mast, and then sailed on. They too had been attacked by a jet, an Argentine jet, but it had fired just once, missed literally by a mile, and then flown off.

Both the Dutch and the Rumanians seemed surrealistically skinny and bony at first, until Neil realized that he must look even worse.

It took Neil and Jeanne and the others only two days to decide that their plan to sail on soon to the South Pacific was madness born of their desperation. They had no food and little prospect of getting much until the summer offered a chance to plant and harvest crops. Jeanne was pregnant, Lisa and Olly still very weak, although both were out of bed now. Sheila and Jeanne had pulled two of Olly's rotting teeth a week earlier, and his debilitating low-grade fever was disappearing. He had recovered sufficiently to pinch Sheila's behind and begin entertaining himself and others again with monologues.

On their third day they moved *Vagabond* east to beach her closer to the other sailboats. The terrain was desolate: the few trees were twisted like grotesque cripples by the fierce westerly winds. Aboard *Vagabond* as Philip and Sheila and Lisa began preparing to cook a wild dog Jim had caught and killed, Olly suggested a barbecue. Philip said that of course that was the easiest way to cook, the only way, but Olly shook his head.

"I mean a real barbecue," he said. "With people, talk, laughter. You know, like they do on Smith Island."

"You mean . . . invite other people?" asked Jeanne.

"Sure," said Olly. "Shit, this poor critter's so thin and bony, none of us gonna get fat anyhow, but we got to give him his self-respect, make him feel he's worthy of dying for us."

They all stared at him. *Share* their first meat in a month?

"Who'll we invite?" asked Jeanne.

"Well, those fellas with the funny round hats for one," said Olly.

"Everyone," said Neil.

"What?" said Philip.

"We'll invite everyone," Neil repeated almost dreamily. "We'll invite everyone. . . ."

"By God, that's a bloody good idea, Neil," Philip said, grinning. "To share with friends again, even if it leaves us back with dried grasses and barnacles."

"Don't criticize barnacles, dear," said Sheila. "Lisa and I are concocting a marvelous barnacle salad."

"Save it for the barbecue," said Neil. "Save everything good. Tomorrow we'll share every bit of food we have so we can start from scratch."

"Bit mad, I suppose," said Philip, still smiling. "Still, it beats hoarding. . . ."

Jim was the official messenger, and he spoke first to their little Chilean guide, who nodded and looked pleased and hurried away to tell his friends.

But the Dutch were confused and wary.

"You want to share your food with us?" the oldest Dutchman asked, frowning.

"Yes," said Jim. "But . . . but we only have the dog. We . . . don't have much else to eat or drink. It's—"

"It's what you call 'potluck', no?" the Dutchman said, smiling.

"And 'Bring your own bottle,' " added another, also smiling.

"Yeah, I guess so," said Jim. "But you don't have to bring anything. . . ."

"Well, we'll come," said the oldest Dutchman. "We'll come with much thanks."

The Rumanians were even more dumbfounded. Jim could sense that they suspected some kind of trap. They had greeted him with their rifles at port arms. They whispered together in Rumanian, glancing at him nervously.

"Why you do this?" the Rumanian captain asked after he had finally understood Jim's invitation. "You have much food?"

"No," said Jim. "But . . . we want . . . we decided . . . to share what we have. . . ."

"You want us share our food too, no?"

Jim frowned. "We want to share our food with you," he finally said. "It seems . . . right to us. That's all."

"We bring our guns?"

"I guess so," Jim replied. "We don't have any guns."

"Ah . . . no guns . . ."

"We'd . . . be honored if you'd come eat with us," Jim repeated.

"Honored, yes," echoed the Rumanian, looking puzzled. "Well, maybe we come. We see."

"Two o'clock," said Jim.

"Two o'clock, yes. Well . . . And meat, you say? Well . . . And honor . . . yes . . . Maybe we come."

And so at two o'clock the next afternoon the five Dutch and seven Rumanians and twelve Chileans came. The Dutch and Rumanians approached as warily as if they were threading their way through a minefield. The Chileans, having already accepted the weirdness of their latest visitors, came fearlessly. The Dutch brought their last flask of wine and a specially baked loaf of bread—their first in a week. The Rumanians brought a tiny tin—their last—of caviar, and a freshly caught and baked fish. The Chileans brought a basket of corn and some of their homemade wine. No one brought guns.

And they ate. And though each was limited to a small cup of wine, a single cob of corn, and a few bites of tough stringy dogmeat, they ate happily. And slowly, very slowly, it began to dawn on each of *Vagabond*'s crew members that they might live. For Neil it was the friendliness of the Chileans and the Dutch and the Rumanians, expressed primarily in exaggerated gestures of delight at the feast and continual smiles, that made him realize that some deep part of him had begun to feel that he would be running and on the edge of death forever. Now the act of sharing the treasured bit of wine with Jacob and his friends, and a pipeful of tobacco with one of the Rumanians, altered his view of things entirely. The running, at long last, was over. The Rumanians and Dutch had decided, as they had, to remain in the Straits at least through the summer. Although everyone left in the destroyed city was on starvation rations—*Vagabond* was now in fact totally out of food—fishing in the Straits was good, there were small animals to be hunted, and spring was now only a few weeks away.

To the north the wars they had fled were presumably continuing. Here, at the bottom of the world, a few survivors had gathered. They still were struggling to survive, but now with each other rather than against. It was a small first step on the long voyage back.

It was Olly who summed up the new feeling. He came up to Neil and Jeanne after an hour of feasting and mingling and unfolding his monologues with the two dozen strangers, few of whom understood him. There were tears in his eyes.

"I been feeling funny," he said to them, "and I think I fnally figured out what it is . . ." He looked up at them, a laughing skeleton. "I may have to get used to living again . . ."